STUDIES in the AGRICULTURAL and FOOD SCIENCES

A series of high-level monographs which review recent research in various areas of agriculture and food science

Consultant Editors:

D.J.A. Cole	University of Nottingham
W. Haresign	University of Nottingham
W. Henrichsmeyer	Director, Institut für Agrärpolitik, University of Bonn
J.P. Hudson	formerly Director, Long Ashton Research Station, University of Bristol
G. Kimber	Professor of Agronomy, University of Missouri-Columbia
J.L. Krider	Professor of Animal Sciences, Purdue University
D.E. Tribe	Director, Australian Universities' International Development Program, Canberra
V.R. Young	Professor of Nutritional Biochemistry, Massachusetts Institute of Technology

STUDIES IN THE AGRICULTURAL
AND FOOD SCIENCES

Recent Advances in Animal Nutrition—1985

W. Haresign, PhD
D.J.A. Cole, PhD
University of Nottingham School of Agriculture

BUTTERWORTHS
London Boston Durban Singapore Sydney Toronto Wellington

First published 1985

© Chapter 1, UKASTA, ADAS, COSAC, 1985
   The several authors listed in the contents list, 1985

British Library Cataloguing in Publication Data

Recent advances in animal nutrition.—1985
   —(Studies in the agricultural and food sciences)
   1. Animal nutrition
   I. Haresign, William   II. Cole, D.J.A.   III. Series
   636.08′52   SF95

   ISBN 0–407–01161–7

Typeset by Scribe Design, Gillingham, Kent.
Printed in England by Robert Hartnoll Ltd, Bodmin, Cornwall

PREFACE

This, the proceedings of the Nineteenth Annual Nutrition Conference for Feed Manufacturers, contains chapters on a range of topics related to the nutrition of farm livestock.

The first chapter considers the accuracy of predicting the energy value of pig, poultry and ruminant feedstuffs from chemical measurements, a factor of paramount importance if the declaration of energy values is made compulsory within the EEC.

Following a chapter describing the various definitions of fibre in animal feedstuffs, a series of further chapters consider the importance of fibre in feeds for the different classes of farm livestock. The first of these discusses the influence of fibre on the digestibility of poultry feeds, the second discusses the role of fibre in pig feeds and the final one of the group discusses the effect of fibre level in compound feedstuffs on the performance of dairy cattle.

Three chapters relate to aspects of pig nutrition and production. The first of these attempts to model the relationship between feed inputs and outputs in the breeding animals, with the ultimate objective of assessing the effects of different strategies for sow nutrition on animal performance. Two further chapters relate to meat quality in pigs, the first providing information on how to achieve grading standards by genetic and nutritional means and the second highlighting the consequences of changes in carcass composition on meat quality.

There are two chapters within the general area of poultry nutrition. The first describes recent developments in the use of coccidiostats in broiler diets, highlighting the various types of materials available, the development of resistance to them and how to prevent resistance occurring by alternating the compounds used. A major factor influencing returns from laying poultry is downgrading of eggs because of poor shell quality. One chapter describes the changes in quality that can occur and discusses both the physiological and nutritional reasons for them.

The final group of chapters relate to ruminant nutrition. The first of these describes the extent of natural variation in appetite with season, which occurs independently of diet quality, and the possible mechanisms underlying such changes. One aspect of season which can be readily and cheaply manipulated is daylength, and one chapter describes the beneficial effects that increasing daylength in winter can have on growth rate and milk production in dairy cattle. Since many ruminant production systems revolve around silage as the basal part of the ration, it was particularly opportune to have a further chapter discuss recent developments in our understanding of the factors affecting the nutritive value of silages. The ruminant chapters are completed by a consideration of the amino acid requirement of ruminants and how one might be able to influence amino acid supply to the hind-gut by dietary manipulation.

Each chapter is written in a clear and informative manner, and should be useful to research workers, advisers and students alike.

The organizers and the University of Nottingham are grateful to BP Nutrition (UK) Ltd, for the support they gave in the organization of this conference.

W. Haresign
D.J.A. Cole

CONTENTS

I

General Nutrition

1

PREDICTION OF THE ENERGY VALUE OF COMPOUND FEEDS

G. ALDERMAN
ADAS, London, UK

Introduction

Both in the UK and in other member states of the European Community, farmers' organizations have been expressing their concern over the lack of information about the nutritive value of compound feeds conveyed to them as purchasers of the major input into most animal production systems. This concern has intensified as the traditional cereals and protein sources in animal feeds have been replaced by less traditional plant materials and by-products of human food production. Allied to these changes farmers feel that with the general introduction of computer formulation, the feeds they are purchasing are of a more variable ingredient make-up than they used to be. This has resulted in pressure for the full declaration of ingredients.

For its part, the feed industry has pointed out that the increased use of by-products has kept down the price of compound feeds and that it has carried out research and implemented technical developments for the benefit of its customers as well as their companies. They are not willing to make available the results of their researches to their trade rivals, which is what ingredient declaration would mean in their view. A major gap in the information concerned the energy content of compound feeds.

In the UK, the megajoule (MJ) is the agreed metric unit for energy, metabolizable energy (ME) is used for ruminant feeds, apparent metabolizable energy (AME) is used for poultry feeds and digestible energy (DE) for pig feeds. For ruminants the values are expressed per kg dry matter (DM) and for pigs and poultry they are expressed on an as-fed basis. The prediction of such values, for example from chemical analysis, has been of interest to the farmer, adviser, feed compounder and research worker for some time. This chapter gives the approach taken by a joint working party of the United Kingdom Agricultural Supply Trade Association (UKASTA), the Agricultural Development and Advisory Service (ADAS) and the Council of Scottish Agricultural Colleges (COSAC) whose full report is published elsewhere (UKASTA/ADAS/COSAC, 1985). It is based on collaborative research programmes at the Rowett Research Institute (ruminants), the East of Scotland College of Agriculture (pigs) and the Poultry Research Centre. The accuracy of prediction is examined for voluntary use by the member organizations, for possible incorporation into legislation on energy declaration for compound feeds and for reference purposes.

The following is a glossary of the terms and abbreviations used throughout this chapter.

Glossary of terms used and abbreviations

CHEMICAL ANALYSES

Acid detergent fibre	ADF	Goering and Van Soest (1970)
Acid detergent lignin	ADL	Goering and Van Soest (1970)
Available carbohydrate	AV.CHO	Bolton (1962)
Cellulase digestibility	NCD	Dowman and Collins (1977, 1982) (see Appendix II)
Crude fibre	CF	The Feedingstuffs (Sampling and Analysis) Regulations (1982)
Christian lignin	CL	Christian (1971)
Crude protein	CP	The Feedingstuffs (Sampling and Analysis) Regulations (1982)
Dry matter	DM	ADAS RB 427
Ether extract (see also OIL(PT))	EE	The Feedingstuffs (Sampling and Analysis) Regulations (1982)
In vitro digestibility	IVD	Tilley and Terry (1963)
In vitro organic matter digestibility	IVOMD	Tilley and Terry (1963)
Modified acid detergent fibre	MADF	Clancy and Wilson (1966)
Neutral detergent fibre	NDF	Wainman, Dewey and Boyne (1981)
Nitrogen free extractives as %	NFE	$100 - (CP + EE + CF + TA)$
Oil (acid hydrolysis)	OIL(AH)	B.S. Method No. 4401
Oil (petroleum ether) (see also EE)	OIL(PT)	The Feedingstuffs (Sampling and Analysis) Regulations (1982)
Organic matter	OM	DM—TA
Starch	STA	EC Regulation 72/119/EEC
Sugar	SUG	AOAC 10th Edition (1965) Methods 29.039 and 43.012
Total ash	TA	The Feedingstuffs (Sampling and Analysis) Regulations (1982)
Ratio unsaturated:saturated fatty acids	USR	

DIGESTIBILITY TERMS

Digestible crude fibre	DCF
Digestible crude protein	DCP
Digestible ether extract	DEE
Digestible N free extractives	DNFE
Digestible organic matter in DM	DOMD
Organic matter digestibility	OMD

ENERGY TERMS

Apparent metabolizable energy   AME
Digestible energy   DE
Gross energy   GE
Megajoule, unit of energy   MJ
Metabolizable energy   ME
True metabolizable energy   TME   Sibbald (1976)

STATISTICAL TERMS

Analytical tolerance   A
Coefficient of variation, (%)   CV
Repeatability   r
Reproducibility   R
Residual mean square   RMS
Residual standard deviation   S
Prediction error (S modified by R)   S''
Standard deviation   SD
Technical tolerance   T
Reproducibility variance   V
  covariance matrix

Existing methods for the prediction of ME or DE from chemical composition

Numerous prediction equations have been published for pig and poultry feeds, and have been reviewed recently (Morgan and Whittemore, 1982; Fisher, 1982). A well-known example for poultry feeds is equation (1), from Bolton (1962):

$$\text{ME (kcal/kg)} = 40.8\,[0.87\,\text{CP\%} + 0.87 \times 2.25\,\text{EE\%} + \text{AV.CHO\%} + 4.9] \quad (1)$$

For pigs, the work of Morgan, Cole and Lewis (1975) gave equation (2)

$$\text{DE (MJ/kg DM)} = 0.479\,\text{CP\%} + 0.472\,\text{EE\%} + 0.375\,\text{NFE\%} - 21.2 \quad (2)$$

Crude fibre has been found to be less effective as a predictor of DE for pigs than other fibre fractions such as modified acid-detergent fibre (MADF) or acid detergent lignin (ADL). In the main, the published equations were derived for raw materials such as cereals and not for compound feeds.

For ruminants, no suitable equations were available in 1976, when ME was introduced as a practical system in UK, so use was made of an equation (equation (3)) published by workers at the Oskar Kellner Institute in East Germany (DLVB, 1971)

$$\text{ME (MJ/kg)} = 0.0152\,\text{DCP} + 0.0342\,\text{DEE} + 0.0128\,\text{DCF} + 0.0159\,\text{DNFE}$$
$$\text{(all as g/kg)} \quad (3)$$

This equation was used to convert existing tables of feed composition from digestibility and starch equivalent to ME. In the case of compound feeds, although digestibility varies depending on the quality of the raw materials used, it was decided to use average digestibility coefficients for each parameter, CP digestibility = 0.8; EE digestibility = 0.9; CF digestibility = 0.4; NFE digestibility = 0.9.

This resulted in equation (4) (Equation (**75**) of Technical Bulletin 33, MAFF, 1976) in which CP, EE, etc. are as g/kg dry matter and NFE = 1000 − (CP + EE + CF + TA)

$$ME \text{ (MJ/kg DM)} = 0.012\,CP + 0.031\,EE + 0.005\,CF + 0.014\,NFE \tag{4}$$

At the time of its publication, this equation could not be used with the declared analyses, since the presence of the term NFE required the total ash content to be known. Since February, 1983, this deficiency has been remedied in the UK by the coming into force of the Feeding Stuffs (Sampling and Analysis) Regulations 1982.

Ruminant compound feeds

PROCEDURE

A series of 24 compound formulations, based on raw materials used in the UK feed industry for cattle and sheep feeds, was made to meet a number of criteria. Each raw material was limited to inclusion in only a proportion of the feeds, usually six out of 24, except for the cereals, two cereal by-products and rape seed meal which occurred in the majority. The range of chemical composition was specified for ether extract (either 2–3.9 % or 5–7 % in DM), crude protein (either 12–14.9 %, 15–17.9 % or 18–20.9 % in DM), and crude fibre (either 4–6 % or 8–12 % in DM). ME values covered the range 9–14 MJ/kg DM, with a good spread over the range.

Each compound was fed to two wether sheep at maintenance in combination with hay or silage in three ratios 25:75, 50:50 and 75:25. All feeds were comprehensively analysed at five collaborating laboratories from ARC, ADAS and UKASTA. The work was carried out at the Rowett Research Institute Feed Evaluation Unit (RRI/FEU) and reported by Wainman, Dewey and Boyne, 1981.

STATISTICAL ANALYSIS

Detailed statistical analysis of the results and regression of the measured ME values on the chemical analyses, resulted in the listing of 73 equations with a residual standard deviation (S) of less than 0.5 MJ of ME/kg DM. The statistical analysis also considered the important question of interlaboratory variation for the methods used. With the exception of GE measurements made with adiabatic bomb calorimeters, significant differences were obtained between all laboratory mean values at the 1 per cent level of probability for EE and ADL, and at the 0.1 per cent level for all other analyses.

A technique was devised to take interlaboratory error into account when ranking prediction equations for application in a multi-laboratory situation. Details of the calculation of S′ are given in the RRI/FEU Report (Wainman, Dewey and Boyne, 1981).

COMPARISON WITH OTHER ESTIMATES OF ME VALUE

The measured ME values of the test feeds were compared with calculated values, using the MAFF Tables of Feed Composition in *Technical Bulletin 33* (MAFF, 1976) (Estimate A), and an agreed set of values from UKASTA (Estimate B), which were typical of those in use to formulate ruminant compound feeds. Estimate A overestimated ME on average by 0.49 MJ/kg DM, and Estimate B by 0.25 MJ/kg DM. It is interesting to note that the residual standard deviations, S, about the means were 0.65 and 0.71 MJ/kg DM for Estimates A and B respectively, greater than the S values for chemical prediction techniques. This indicates a discrepancy between the measured ME using wether sheep at maintenance and the values in the databases used for feed formulation.

ADAS Nutrition Chemists had adopted a prediction equation, based on the use of *in vitro* digestibility (IVD) and equation (3), which uses digestible proximate values. A common digestibility was applied to all the coefficients to give equation (5) where CP, EE, CF and NFE are % in dry matter.

$$
\text{ME (MJ/kg DM)} = \frac{\text{IVD}\,[0.152\,CP\% + 0.342\,EE\% + 0.128\,CF\% + 0.159\,NFE\%]}{[100 - TA\%]} \tag{5}
$$

This theoretically derived equation was found from the data of Wainman, Dewey and Boyne (1981) to underestimate ME on average by 0.12 MJ/kg DM, and to have an S of 0.48 MJ/kg DM.

Equation **75** of *Technical Bulletin 33* (MAFF, 1976) was similarly examined, and shown seriously to overestimate ME values by 0.73 MJ/kg DM on average, the bias increasing at the lower values. The use of equation **75** has now been discontinued by MAFF.

An alternative approach has been suggested by Morgan and Piggot (1978), which combines an *in vitro* estimate of organic matter digestibility (IVOMD) with an estimate of the GE of the feed, to calculate DE. This was then converted to an estimated ME value by multiplication by a factor of 0.81 to correct for average urine and methane losses, as shown in equation (6). This equation was found to underestimate *in vivo* ME values on average by 0.23 MJ/kg DM, and to have an S of 0.42 MJ/kg DM.

$$
\text{ME} = \frac{GE \times 0.81\,\text{IVOMD}}{100} \tag{6}
$$

Subsequently, Belgian workers at the Institute of Animal Nutrition, Melle, have presented results which confirm those of the RRI/FEU study, although they used a much narrower range of ME values, ingredients and chemical composition.

Poultry compound feeds

PROCEDURE

From a list of 29 raw materials used in the feed industry to manufacture poultry compound feeds, a series of 32 formulations were made to meet a number of criteria. Each raw material was limited in the number of formulations in which it could be included. The range of chemical composition was specified for ether extract (2, 4, 8 or 16% in air-dry feed) and crude protein (either 12 or 25% in air-dry feed). The AME values were 9, 11, 13 or 15 MJ/kg air-dry feed.

This gave 32 possible formulations, but some combinations such as 2% EE and 15 MJ/kg of AME were technically impossible with the ingredients available. The number of diets was reduced to 28, which were to be tested both as meal and as pellets, to give a total of 56 diets in the programme.

The True Metabolizable Energy (TME), of each feed was measured by a modification of the technique of Sibbald (1976), using six mature cockerels for each feed. Feed intakes were fixed at 30 g, and the Apparent Metabolizable Energy (AME), calculated from the TME value. The completed programme was published by Fisher (1982).

STATISTICAL ANALYSIS

Analysis of variance was used to estimate the main effects of the test feeds (formulation × form) and of different laboratories. The feed × laboratory interaction was used as an estimate of error. Regression equations for the AME value on chemical composition were calculated and evaluated both in the conventional way, using laboratory mean values, and also taking into account interlaboratory variation to derive the term S''. For all analyses there were significant differences between laboratories, but none large enough for data to be rejected.

The AME values calculated from TME assays had a standard deviation of 0.372 MJ/kg, and the standard error of the mean of six determinations was 0.152 MJ/kg or 1.15% of the mean, indicating the high precision of this biological assay. The mean values for meals and pellets were 13.185 and 13.155 MJ/kg, a mean difference of −0.03, with a range of +0.465 to −0.996 MJ/kg due to pelleting. The highest negative effects occurred at high fat levels, and a significant correlation ($r = 0.712$), between EE and this difference was found. This suggests that during pelleting there is some loss of the more volatile components of added fat.

A number of two, three and four factor equations were derived, and those with residual standard deviations, S, of less than 0.5 MJ/kg were listed. No two factor equations met this requirement, although of 364 possible three-factor equations, 41 did. A total of 1001 four-factor equations was possible. Of these 329 had S values of less than 0.5 MJ/kg, and 30 were more accurate than the best three-factor equation.

A four-factor equation proposed by Hartel (1979) was also examined. This features CP, EE, STA and SUG, but no measure of fibre in the feed. It is represented by equation (7) and has been recalculated to MJ/kg from kcal/kg. The residual standard deviation, S, takes no account of interlaboratory variation. The bias, however, was large at −1.18 MJ/kg.

$$AME\ (MJ/kg) = 0.322\ EE\% + 0.151\ CP\% + 0.170\ STA\% + 0.109\ SUG\%$$
$$S = 0.31\ MJ \tag{7}$$

An equation of the same type (equation (8)) was derived from the PRC set of data. However, the best equation found (equation (9)) included a term for the ratio of unsaturated fat to saturated fat, (USR), as determined by gas chromatography of the anhydrous methyl esters of the EE fraction. Since this equation accounted for 98.5% of the total variation in AME values, it was concluded that 'it seems improbable that the addition of further analytical variables could be more effective, though they might replace those used or be more cost effective' (Fisher, 1982).

$$\text{AME (MJ/kg)} = 0.343\,\text{EE\%} + 0.167\,\text{CP\%} + 0.179\,\text{STA\%} + 0.185\,\text{SUG\%}$$
$$S = 0.31 \text{ MJ/kg} \tag{77) (8}$$

$$\text{AME (MJ/kg)} = 7.42 + 0.262\,\text{EE\%} + 0.079\,\text{CP\%} + 0.098\,\text{STA\%}$$
$$- 0.093\,\text{NDF\%} + 0.069\,\text{USR}$$
$$S = 0.25 \text{ MJ/kg} \tag{74) (9}$$

Equation numbers in bold type relate to the original reports.

COMPARISON WITH OTHER ESTIMATES OF AME VALUE

The report compared the measured AME values of the test feeds with calculated values, using Tables of Feed Composition given by Bolton and Blair (1974) in MAFF *Bulletin 174*, 'Poultry Nutrition', and with tabulated American, German and Dutch values. As assessed by overall means, all the predictions were below the observed values, although highly correlated with them. The MAFF values were 0.57 MJ/kg and the Dutch 0.22 MJ/kg below. Residual standard deviations about the means were 0.42 and 0.50 MJ/kg respectively.

A number of published prediction equations were also tested on the data, including those of Bolton (1962), and Carpenter and Clegg (1956). Both equations were a good fit to the data, but were for AME values uncorrected for nitrogen retention, whereas all the values in the PRC study were corrected to zero N balance. The agreement is therefore partly fortuitous.

SUBSEQUENT ACTIVITY IN UK AND EEC

It became clear that there was a good deal of additional poultry data available from Germany, Denmark, France and Holland. Dr Fisher was asked to pool the data if possible and to produce an equation of the Hartel type, which used only official EEC analytical methods. The resulting equation (10) was accepted by a European Working Group of poultry nutritionists. The residual standard deviation, S, for this equation is 0.315 MJ/kg, but it is the result of fitting parallel lines to the different data sets, with intercepts ranging from −0.268 to +0.106 MJ/kg.

$$\text{AME (MJ/kg)} = 0.342\,\text{EE\%} + 0.155\,\text{CP\%} + 0.167\,\text{STA\%}$$
$$+ 0.130\,\text{SUG\%} \tag{EEC) (10}$$

Laboratory variability has been reported by Fisher (1983). Large interlaboratory differences were found, but there was high repeatability within laboratories, all nominally using EEC official methods. The equation predicted relative AME values with an S value of 0.51 MJ/kg. The important implication of this work is that it requires declaration of starch (STA) and sugar (SUG) analyses in the UK to be compulsory instead of optional as at present.

Pig compound feeds

PROCEDURE

From 33 raw materials used by the feed industry to manufacture pig compound feeds, a series of 36 diets were formulated to specifications for ether extract (2, 4 or

8% in air-dry feed), crude protein (either 14 or 20% in air-dry feed), crude fibre (2.5, 5 or 10% in air-dry feed), and starch content (either <35 or >40% in air-dry feed).

All raw materials were check analysed before delivery and incorporation in the experimental diets. These were also analysed to check for conformity to the diet specification. Each diet was evaluated with four pigs (45–60 kg live weight), one balance period taking 28 days. One seven-day collection period for faeces and urine were used to measure energy and nitrogen balance. The collaborative analytical programme between laboratories was increased by the addition of ether extract following acid hydrolysis, OIL(AH), SAC (1973). The completed work has been reported by Morgan, Whittemore, Phillips and Crooks (1984b).

STATISTICAL ANALYSIS

Laboratories were consistent in their estimation of all constituents. No significant differences between laboratories were found for EE, STA and SUG. All other analyses showed between laboratory differences, but none were large enough to warrant the exclusion of data from any centre. Regression analyses were carried out, and linear equations for determined DE values against all combinations of two, three or four analytical components were again calculated.

If three factors are included, 20 equations were found with S values of less than 0.44 MJ/kg. The most accurate was equation (11). Omitting GE, the following equations (12) and (13) had an S value below the required limit. The best four-factor equation (equation (14)) only used chemical analyses. If only the statutory declaration analyses were used, the errors of prediction increased considerably.

$$DE\ (MJ/kg) = 5.01 - 0.136\,TA\% - 0.173\,NDF\% + 0.738\,GE$$
$$S = 0.36\,MJ/kg \qquad\qquad (3d)\ \ (11)$$

$$DE\ (MJ/kg) = 18.04 + 0.156\,EE\% - 0.158\,TA\% - 0.166\,NDF\%$$
$$S = 0.41\,MJ/kg \qquad\qquad (12d)\ \ (12)$$

$$DE\ (MJ/kg) = 5.98 + 0.188\,EE\% + 0.181\,CP\% + 0.115\,STA\%$$
$$S = 0.43\,MJ/kg \qquad\qquad (16d)\ \ (13)$$

$$DE = 17.49 + 0.157\,EE\% + 0.078\,CP\% - 0.325\,TA\% - 0.149\,NDF\%$$
$$S = 0.32\,MJ/kg \qquad\qquad (1d)\ \ (14)$$

COMPARISON WITH OTHER ESTIMATES OF DE VALUE

The expected DE of the diets calculated by summing the values for raw materials from the data banks of UKASTA members gave good overall agreement with measured *in vivo* DE values. These calculated values underestimated the observed DE by an average of 0.22 MJ/kg, with S = 0.46 MJ/g.

Equation (2) from Morgan, Cole and Lewis (1975), consistently underpredicted DE by −1.35 MJ/kg, with S = 0.55 MJ/kg. Equation (15), derived by Morgan and Whittemore (1982), gave a good prediction of DE on average, but overpredicted at low DE values by (on average) 0.08 MJ/kg. Wiseman and Cole (1983), also derived equation (16) using only CP, EE, CF and TA and based on 99 compound feeds. This has a tendency to overpredict DE by 0.46 MJ/kg on average, rising to over 1 MJ/kg for low DE feeds.

$$DE = 16.7 + 0.15\,EE\% - 0.4\,CF\% \tag{15}$$
$$S = 0.67\,MJ/kg$$

$$DE = 16.56 + 0.014\,CP\% + 0.23\,EE\% - 0.308\,CF\% - 0.101\,TA\% \tag{16}$$
$$S = 0.46\,MJ/kg$$

Analytical studies

During the experimental work on the evaluation of energy values for ruminant feeds, an analytical protocol was agreed and this was maintained in subsequent studies. For each study a total of five laboratories participated, consisting of the Research Station carrying out the study, three UKASTA member laboratories and an ADAS laboratory. In some instances different ADAS laboratories were used for different determinations within the same study. The Laboratory of the Government Chemist (LGC) carried out starch determinations during the poultry feed study, using the EEC polarimetric method.

All determinations were carried out in duplicate and all analyses were carried out on fresh material, as is normal for compound feeds. A separate sample of each diet was dried in each laboratory using agreed procedures and results were corrected to this and reported on a dry-matter basis (100°C).

ESTABLISHMENT OF AGREED DETERMINATIONS

Before the beginning of the feeding trials it was agreed that the samples would be analysed for Total Ash (TA), Crude Protein (CP), Ether Extract/Oil (EE), Crude Fibre (CF), Sugar (SUG), Starch (STA), Acid Detergent Fibre (ADF), Modified Acid Detergent Fibre (MADF), Christian Lignin (CL), *in-vitro* Digestible Organic Matter (IVD) and Gross Energy (GE). For the ruminant trials, the basal feeds of hay and silage also were analysed by the collaborating laboratories. It was agreed that a minimum of three laboratories would undertake each determination in order to assess the within and between laboratory variability. Starch determination was carried out in the ruminant and poultry feeds studies by two colorimetric techniques involving enzymic breakdown of starch, in addition to the EEC official polarimetric method. Samples in the pig feed study were analysed for starch by the polarimetric method only. An additional method for oil involving acid hydrolysis, OIL(AH), to release 'bound' fat was included for the pig feeds.

Following the analysis of the first six ruminant compound feeds it was found that there were discrepancies in the results between laboratories for SUG, STA and NDF. Discussion between the analysts showed that there were differences in the reagents and procedures used. Procedures were agreed, including sources of reagents. These procedures were followed during the analysis of poultry and pig feeds. References to all the methods are contained in Wainman, Dewey and Boyne (1981), Fisher (1982; 1983), Morgan *et al.* (1984b) and Appendix 1.

COLLABORATIVE STUDIES

ADAS and UKASTA laboratories

The report of Wainman, Dewey and Boyne (1981) refers to the possibility that the S values quoted were for laboratories operating under very closely monitored conditions, and possibly atypical. Therefore a collaborative study was carried out involving 12 compound feeds, each analysed in 16 laboratories. The results were statistically analysed in order to compare the within and between laboratory variability. The results of the statistical analysis are given in *Table 1.1*. The results for CF, CP, TA and EE were considered satisfactory but the wide range of results for CL (not quoted) indicated that a ruggedness test was necessary if this determination were to be considered for prediction purposes.

Table 1.1   VARIABILITY IN STATUTORY ANALYSES

	Crude fibre (CF)	Crude protein (CP)	Ash (TA)	Oil (EE)
Mean (%)	9.05	16.94	9.28	4.14
Repeatability, r	0.44	0.49	0.30	0.31
CV (%)	1.72	1.02	1.14	2.65
Reproducibility, R	1.45	1.41	0.74	0.65
CV (%)	5.67	2.94	2.82	5.55

Table 1.2   ADAS COLLABORATIVE STUDY OF THE NEUTRAL DETERGENT CELLULASE DIGESTIBILITY (NCD) PROCEDURE

Mean digestibility (%)	76.57
Range	65.10–82.46
Repeatability, r	1.52
CV (%)	0.70
Reproducibility, R	3.19
CV (%)	1.47

The Neutral Detergent Cellulase (NCD) digestibility procedure (Dowman and Collins, 1977; 1982) has been developed with a view to replacing the *in-vitro* digestibility (IVD) technique which depends upon a consistent supply of rumen liquor. It is applicable to both forage and compound feed samples. In 1980, when the ruminant feed study was undertaken, the cellulase technique was still being developed by ADAS as a research method. Subsequently the procedure (see Appendix II) has become a routine method in ADAS laboratories, and a collaborative study of the technique, which uses a pre-digestion of starch with amylase, was carried out in 11 ADAS laboratories using 21 of the RRI/FEU feeds. The results have been used to determine whether improvements in the procedure have led to significant changes in the prediction equations using this parameter. Results and prediction equations are shown in *Tables 1.2* and *1.3*.

Other data are available on the reproducibility of statutory analyses by both ADAS and UKASTA laboratories. Since 1974, ADAS laboratories have run an Analytical Monitor Scheme, with samples circulated every week for standard

Table 1.3 REVISED RRI/FEU EQUATIONS WITH CELLULASE DIGESTIBILITY, NCD, INCLUDED, RANKED BY S''

Rank	Equation number[a]	S	Original S''	Recalculated S''	Increase in variance
1	**U2**	0.232	0.311	0.317	0.165
2	**5**	0.260	0.374	0.360	0.198
3	**6**	0.256	0.383	0.369	0.215
4	**21**	0.319	0.385	0.372	0.166
5	**28**	0.290	0.411	0.377	0.204
6	**11**	0.290	0.393	0.383	0.214
7	**41**	0.337	0.417	0.396	0.187
8	**40**	0.368	0.452	0.426	0.199
9	**23**	0.233	0.462	0.437	0.332
10	**60**	0.410	0.466	0.447	0.176
11	**39**	0.350	0.487	0.483	0.308
12	**42**	0.376	0.487	0.487	0.294

Equation number[a]	Equation
U2	$ME = 0.03\,EE\% \times NCD\% - 2.375\,EE\% + 0.030\,EE\%^2 - 0.034\,TA\% + 11.56$
5	$0.101\,NCD\% + 0.615\,GE - 0.185\,CL\% - 6.56$
6	$0.109\,NCD\% + 0.618\,GE - 0.203\,ADL\% - 7.24$
21	$0.152\,NCD\% + 0.208\,EE\% - 0.95$
28	$0.171\,NCD\% + 0.127\,CP\% + 0.129\,SUG\% - 4.59$
11	$0.149\,NCD\% + 0.575\,GE - 10.27$
41	$0.168\,NCD\% + 0.135\,CP\% - 3.58$
40	$0.169\,NCD\% + 0.142\,SUG\% - 2.39$
23	$0.272\,NCD\% - 0.080\,STA\% - 6.75$
60	$0.166\,NCD\% - 1.12$
39	$0.237\,NCD\% + 0.179\,MADF\% - 0.264\,CL\% - 7.65$
42	$0.257\,NCD\% + 0.081\,NDF\% - 9.96$

[a]Equation numbers correspond to those of UKASTA/ADAS/COSAC (1985)

Table 1.4 WEEKLY VARIATION IN STATUTORY ANALYSES IN ADAS LABORATORIES IN FOUR QUARTERLY PERIODS

	Reproducibility coefficient of variation (%)			
	July–Sept 1983	Oct–Dec 1983	Jan–Mar 1984	Apr–June 1984
Crude fibre	2.3	3.8	4.4	3.7
Crude protein	1.4	1.3	1.1	0.9
Ash	1.0	0.9	1.0	0.8
Ether extract	1.3	1.6	1.7	1.8

analyses, which were reported centrally, statistically analysed and the national mean values reported back to the analysts in charge at each centre. Each quarter, the accumulated data are used to compute reproducibility, R. Recent results are shown in *Table 1.4*.

Since 1979, UKASTA laboratories have joined this Monitor Scheme at least once a year, to ensure that results of analyses on the same feed would be comparable, a situation that does arise in practice quite commonly, with particular batches of compound feed. The coefficients of variation of reproducibility obtained

Table 1.5 VARIATION IN STATUTORY ANALYSES IN ADAS AND UKASTA LABORATORIES, 1979–84

	Reproducibility coefficient of variation (%)					
	1979	*1980*	*1981*	*1982*	*1983*	*1984*
Crude fibre	7.5	6.0	14.6	7.7	7.7	4.2
Crude protein	1.9	1.4	2.0	1.4	1.4	1.6
Ash	—	4.3	3.9	2.1	1.9	2.1
Ether extract	5.9	3.0	4.0	6.0	7.1	4.9

since 1979 are given in *Table 1.5*. Notable is the low value for CP, and the increase in accuracy of TA determination since its declaration became mandatory in 1983. The value for CF has also improved considerably since 1981.

The study by Morgan *et al.* (1984b) on pig compound feeds found that NDF had the highest correlation with DE and was therefore the best single predictor. Because some laboratories have reported problems when measuring NDF in high starch feeds, a collaborative study was undertaken by ten laboratories using eight of the feeds, selected to cover the range. Problems were encountered when filtering the suspension which resulted from treatment of the diet with neutral detergent-amylase. Further work is in hand to develop a satisfactory procedure to overcome these difficulties.

European laboratories

The Poultry Research Centre organized a collaborative study on behalf of the CEC Committee of Experts on Straight and Compound Feedingstuffs. This study involved 21 laboratories which analysed four feeds for EE, CP, STA and SUG by official EEC methods. In general, the intralaboratory errors associated with the analytical determinations were low with CVs of the order of 2 per cent. By contrast, interlaboratory differences in this work were large and this has been discussed by Fisher (1983). It should be noted that the method used in this study for sugar determination (Luff/Schoorl) was different from that used in the three major studies in the UK, and that problems have been experienced with this EEC official method in some of the participating laboratories.

Technical and analytical variation in the chemical composition of compound feeds; practical aspects

Compound feeds are routinely reformulated for each mill, usually at monthly intervals, taking into account the latest information on the chemical composition, prices and availability of raw materials. Each compound is formulated within closely defined nutrient specification limits, so that large changes in nutrient content between successive formulae do not occur.

Even when a single formula is used, some variation in the chemical composition of the finished feed is inevitable as a result of variations in ingredients, weighing and mixing, sampling and in the laboratory analysis of the feed.

Legislation with which feed compounders in the UK must comply (EEC Directive 80/509 and the Feedingstuffs Regulations, 1982), acknowledges that variation in the chemical analysis of compounds will occur, and incorporates specified tolerance limits for each declaration. Provided a check analysis of a feed sample lies within the tolerance limits, then no fraudulent declaration on the part of the compounder is presumed.

The sources and extent of variation in the chemical composition of compounds produced in feed mills under normal commercial conditions was considered by the Working Party.

SOURCES OF VARIATION IN THE PRODUCTION OF A COMPOUND

There are few published data on the variation in the chemical composition of compound feeds but the factors affecting their production were reviewed by Burdett and Laws (1979). The sources of variation considered were ingredients, manufacturing, and sampling and analysis.

In the modern feed mill, the turnover of raw materials is usually so rapid that it is not possible to analyse each consignment of an ingredient and to use its chemical analysis for formulating batches in which it is included. By the time the full chemical analysis of the consignment of raw material is available it could be mixed and fed. However, the chemical analysis and nutritive value of raw materials are constantly updated in the computer database, so that formulations reflect the average analysis of the raw materials being used as closely as possible. The effects of ingredient variation on chemical composition of the finished compound can be minimized by classifying data on individual raw materials by source of supply, and by restricting the use of more variable raw materials to low rates of inclusion.

Each of the manufacturing operations of conveying, grinding, weighing, mixing and packing is common to all feed mills and is a potential source of cross contamination or mixing error, so that the nutrient content of a batch of finished feed differs from that specified. The size and complexity of feed mills ranges from simple weighing, mixing and packing units with an annual throughput of below 500 tonnes per annum to complex computer controlled mills with sophisticated blending, mixing and packing systems and an annual output in excess of 100 000 tonnes per annum. Burdett and Laws (1979), showed that the variation in composition of a finished layers' feed was greater in older mills and that about 45 per cent of the total variation in the crude protein content was contributed by the manufacturing process. A further 25 per cent of the variation arose from ingredients, and the remainder from sampling and analysis.

A code of practice has been adopted by UKASTA to minimize cross contamination in feed mills, and covers subjects like training of mill personnel, scheduling of mixes to maximize long runs of a single product, control of discard material, and correct cleaning of equipment. Its adoption reduces the variation in finished feeds arising from manufacturing processes, within the physical constraints imposed by the age and design of the mill.

VARIATION IN CHEMICAL COMPOSITION OF COMPOUND OF FEEDS IN COMMERCIAL PRACTICE

UKASTA provided data to demonstrate the variation in oil, crude protein, crude fibre and ash contents of dairy compound feeds produced under normal conditions of mill operation. The analytical data included samples which were found to be out

Table 1.6 EFFECTS OF DIFFERENT FORMULAE ON THE CHEMICAL ANALYSIS OF A SINGLE PRODUCT AT A NUMBER OF PRODUCTION POINTS

Mill	Formula version	No. of batches sampled per formula	Oil (%)			Laboratory analysis Crude protein (%)			Ash (%)		
			Mean	SD	CV	Mean	SD	CV	Mean	SD	CV
1	A	19	4.01	0.34	4.04	16.29	0.88	5.41	8.55	0.66	7.71
	B	15	4.37	0.36	3.03	16.97	0.48	8.23	8.20	0.70	8.50
	C	11	4.33	0.23	3.10	16.08	0.46	2.88	8.14	0.53	6.59
2	D	7	4.38	0.36	2.59	16.35	0.28	1.71	—	—	—
	E	14	4.70	0.26	3.20	16.45	0.30	1.80	—	—	—
	F	5	4.75	0.19	3.29	16.59	0.16	0.95	9.52	0.21	2.19
	G	11	4.69	0.19	2.15	16.18	0.61	3.78	9.69	1.19	12.26
3	H	9	4.20	0.36	6.41	17.39	0.46	2.67	7.64	1.18	15.52
	I	9	4.17	0.34	4.02	17.14	0.61	3.59	8.12	0.55	6.81
	J	8	4.42	0.41	2.74	17.34	0.32	1.85	8.03	0.82	10.22
	K	7	4.63	0.24	4.86	16.44	0.84	5.09	8.66	0.42	4.80
4	L	9	4.94	0.51	3.63	16.77	0.38	2.27	7.77	0.32	4.07
	M	9	5.13	0.58	4.87	16.36	0.93	5.68	7.97	0.73	9.16
	N	17	5.03	0.48	8.68	16.44	0.78	4.74	8.48	0.79	9.32
	O	7	4.85	0.51	7.22	17.01	0.67	3.94	7.47	0.26	3.48
5	P	7	4.67	0.24	6.23	15.47	0.64	4.14	9.80	0.60	6.09
	Q	3	4.90	0.69	3.32	16.50	0.26	1.60	8.35	0.64	7.62
	R	8	5.16	0.59	3.95	16.27	0.76	4.66	8.80	0.51	5.76
	S	5	4.58	0.22	2.04	17.10	0.33	1.94	8.96	0.43	4.84
	T	3	4.77	0.40	10.29	16.13	0.65	4.03	8.20	1.21	14.78
6	U	3	5.17	0.06	4.13	17.17	0.32	1.87	9.40	0.20	2.13
	V	3	4.37	0.23	5.29	16.27	0.32	1.97	9.63	0.40	4.19
	W	4	4.32	0.60	4.44	17.03	0.67	3.94	9.80	0.50	5.06
Weighted means			4.59			16.57			8.51		
Pooled estimate of within-mill/formula SD, ±				0.390	8.50		0.616	3.71		0.704	8.27
Pooled estimate between-mill/formula SD, ±				0.295	6.43		0.411	2.48		0.698	8.20
Overall SD, ±				0.477	10.37		0.720	4.35		0.981	11.53

of specification, and batches of feed which were re-processed, since it was not possible to include only samples from batches that were delivered on farm.

The variation in oil, crude protein, and ash contents of a dairy compound manufactured at six different locations, differing in output from 20000 to more than 100000 tonnes per annum is shown in *Table 1.6*. The nutrient specifications for the product were the same at each location, and for different formulae. Each covered a period of manufacture of about four weeks. The numbers of samples analysed differed between mills and between formulae and tended to reflect the volume of that product being produced in the mill. The variation in EE, CF and TA under commercial conditions were greater than observed in the collaborative study (*Table 1.1*). However, the UKASTA survey was carried out before TA declaration was compulsory, and when fat addition equipment was less sophisticated.

A pooled estimate of variance indicated that between-mill variance was lower for oil and protein than within-mill variance, whereas for ash, the two sources of variance contributed a similar amount to the total.

Table 1.7 EFFECTS OF DIFFERENT FORMULAE ON THE CRUDE FIBRE CONTENT OF A SINGLE PRODUCT AT A NUMBER OF PRODUCTION POINTS

| Mill | No. of samples | | Crude fibre (%) | |
		Mean	SD	CV
1	29	6.6	1.2	17.4
2	44	5.9	1.1	17.9
3	41	5.7	0.9	15.9
Weighted mean		6.1	—	—
Pooled estimate of within-mill SD			1.060	17.38
Pooled estimate of between-mill SD			0.438	7.18
Pooled estimate of overall SD			1.125	18.44

Fewer data are available on variation in crude fibre content of compound feeds during manufacture. Samples were analysed from three mills and from a number of different formulations for a single compound feed with the same nutrient specifications at each mill. The results are presented in *Table 1.7*, and show higher variation within mill than between mills. The general level of variation is higher than those for CP, EE and TA shown in *Table 1.6*.

VARIATION IN CHEMICAL COMPOSITION OF COMPOUND FEEDS COMPARED WITH DECLARED ANALYSES

A survey of 905 samples of compound feeds taken by local authorities was made in 1979 (MAFF, unpublished), and the manufacturers' statutory declarations of oil, crude protein and crude fibre were compared with the Public Analysts' certified results. Highly significant ($P<0.001$) differences were found between the declared oil, crude protein and crude fibre levels and those obtained by analysis. The mean oil and crude protein declarations underestimated the actual contents by 0.10 and 0.16 per cent respectively, while the declared crude fibre content was 0.65 per cent greater than the level found by analysis. As the differences between mean declared oil, crude protein and crude fibre contents of the compound feed samples and those obtained by analysis were all in favour of the customer, these data did not support the view that compounders systematically take advantage of statutory tolerance limits in formulating their feeds.

Calculation of variation in the energy value of compound feedingstuffs predicted from check analyses or analytical declarations

INTRODUCTION

The CEC Committee of Experts on Straight and Compound Feedingstuffs is concerned to establish a set of prediction equations of adequate precision, capable of predicting the metabolizable energy or digestible energy content of manufactured animal compound feedingstuffs using declarations (existing or proposed) of chemical composition required under EEC Directive 80/509. Specified tolerances are assigned to the compulsory declarations for each parameter. The check analysis may not fall outside these limits without a presumption of fraudulent declaration being raised. It is a matter of some complexity to establish the likely variation in an energy value which is predicted from parameters, which themselves are liable to variation within specified limits. This section attempts to calculate limits to the variability of energy values, as a guide to the degree of reliance which may be placed upon these values.

DEFINITION OF TOLERANCE

By convention and existing usage, tolerances are calculated as twice the standard deviation of the measurements under consideration. The variation in the determined level of a particular chemical constituent, e.g. crude protein, derived from a single analytical determination upon a sample of manufactured compound feed, has four components

(1) raw material variation;
(2) weighing and mixing variations;
(3) sampling variations (influenced by (1) and (2));
(4) analytical variation.

Components (1), (2) and (3) are difficult to measure separately and are often combined and referred to as 'technical' variation. Data on (4) are readily available from laboratory ring tests, particularly where ISO or EEC standard methods are in use.

TECHNICAL VARIATION

If analytical variation was eliminated by taking and analysing a large number of samples of the same batch of compound feed, then in this hypothetical situation, the batch would comply with legislation if its actual content, V, were in the range $(D - T_\mathrm{L}, D + T_U)$.

where D = declared level,
T_L = lower technical tolerance, and
T_U = upper technical tolerance.

The critical actual contents are thus $(D - T_L)$ and $(D + T_U)$. In practice, analysis and sampling are not sufficiently extensive for the true content to be estimated without error. It is generally agreed that before one can reasonably argue that the content differs from V the estimated content should be outside the range ($V - A$, $V + A$) where A is the analytical tolerance.

Thus before reasonable doubt is cast on the true value being less than its lower allowed limit ($D - T_L$), the estimated content would need to be less than $D - T_L - A$. Similarly the estimated content would need to exceed $D + T_U + A$ before reasonable doubt is cast on its true content exceeding $D + T_U$.

The combination of tolerances takes this simple linear addition form because in any dispute it is a particular batch of compound that is under consideration, and it is allowed to have a content at the technical tolerance limits.

VARIATION IN PREDICTED ENERGY VALUE

An ME or DE value calculated using a prediction equation may be expected to vary over a range which depends upon the variability of the parameters in the equation. If these are the subject of a statutory declaration, the maximum allowable tolerances are legally defined and include analytical and technical components. The effects of the two types of variation upon the calculation are different. It is therefore proposed that variation in predicted DE or ME (ME_t), due to technical variation within the declared analyses, should correspond to the extremes of the predictive equation for all acceptable *true* values, V, for the declared analyses, i.e. analytical variation should be deducted from the total tolerance allowed.

CALCULATION OF VARIATION IN PREDICTED ENERGY VALUE DUE TO TECHNICAL VARIATION

It follows from the arguments above, that these variations in predicted energy value can be calculated by substituting the relevant technical variation limits directly into the chosen prediction equation, as shown in equation (17).

$$ME_t = aX1 + bX2 + cX3 + dX4 \tag{17}$$

where a, b, c, d are the coefficients from linear prediction equations. The lower (ME_{tl}) and upper (ME_{tu}) technical tolerances are thus described by equations (18) and (19), respectively

Technical Tolerance

$$ME_{tl} = aT1_L + bT2_L + cT3_L + dT4_L \tag{18}$$

$$\text{or } ME_{tu} = aT1_U + bT2_U + cT3_U + dT4_U \tag{19}$$

It should be noted that the correct sign of the coefficients a, b, c and d should be used, that is negative coefficients result in interchange of T_L and T_U.

CALCULATION OF VARIATION IN PREDICTED ENERGY VALUE DUE TO ANALYTICAL VARIATION

The legal tolerances for analytical variation should be calculated as twice the reproducibility standard deviation which applies to the results of *single* analyses in

Table 1.8 TOLERANCES FOR DECLARATIONS OF PROTEIN, OIL, FIBRE, ASH, SUGAR AND STARCH

Set out below are the minimum tolerances permitted by Directive 80/509 which amended the Compounds Directive. Where the tolerances differ from those in the Feedingstuffs Regulations 1982, they appear in the right hand column.

EEC Directive	UK Regulations (1982)

(1) *Crude protein*
 If present in excess:
     4 for declarations of 20% or more.
     20% of the amount stated for declarations of 10% or more but less than 20%.
     2 for declarations less than 10%.
 In case of deficiency:
     2 for declarations of 20% or more 10% of the amount stated for declarations of 10% or more but less than 20%.
     1 for declarations of less than 10%.
	
	 Three for declaration of 30% or more.

(2) *Oil*
 If present in excess:
     3 for declarations of 15% or more.
     20% of the amount for declarations of 8% or more but less than 15%.
     1.6 for declarations less than 8%.
 In case of deficiency:
     1.5 for declarations of 15% or more.
     10% of the amount stated for declarations of 8% or more but less than 15%.
     0.8 for declarations less than 8%.	

(3) *Crude fibre*
 If present in excess:
     1.8 for declarations of 12% or more.
     15% of the amount stated for declarations of 6% or more but less than 12%.
     0.9 for declarations less than 6%.
 In case of deficiency:
     5.4 for declarations of 12% or more.
     45% of the amount stated for declarations of 6% or more but less than 12%.
     2.7 for declarations less than 6%.
	
	 1.8 for all declarations.
	
	 45% of the amount stated.

(4) *Ash*
 If present in excess:
     1 for declarations of 10% or more.
     10% of the amount stated for declarations of 5% or more but less than 10%.
 	
     0.5 for declarations less than 5%.
 In case of deficiency:
     3 for declarations of 10% or more.
     30% of the amount stated for declarations of 5% or more but less than 10%.
     1.5 for declarations less than 5%.
	
	 2 for declarations of 10% or more.
	 20% of the amount stated for declarations of 5% or more but less than 10%.
	 1 for declarations less than 5%.

(5) *Sugar*
 If present in excess:
     4 for declarations of 20% or more.
     20% of the amount stated for declarations of 10% or more but less than 20%.
     2 for declarations less than 10%.
 In case of deficiency:
     2 for declarations of 20% or more.
     10% of the amount stated for declarations of 10% or more but less than 20%.
     1 for declarations less than 10%.
	Required only for molassed feeds. Optional for compounds.

Table 1.8 CONTINUED

EEC Directive	*UK Regulations (1982)*
(6) *Starch*	
If present in excess:	
5 for declarations of 25% or more.	Optional for compounds.
20% of amount stated for declarations of 10% or more but less than 25%.	
2 for declarations less than 10%.	
In case of deficiency:	
2.5 for declarations of 25% or more. 10% of the amount stated for declarations of 10% or more but less than 25%.	
1 for declarations less than 10%.	

Table 1.9 EEC TOLERANCES FOR A TYPICAL COMPOUND FEED

Analytical component	*Declared analysis (% as-fed)*	*Tolerances (units %)*	
		Deficiency	*Excess*
Crude protein	18	1.8	3.6
Ether extract	6	0.8	1.6
Crude fibre	6	2.7	0.9
Total ash	10	3.0	1.0

different laboratories. Results from both EEC and UK ring tests suggest that the magnitudes of the tolerances thus calculated, are usually of the order of one half of the smaller permitted legal tolerance for the particular parameter.

Pooled residual standard deviations are calculated by the use of equation (20)

$$S = [(aS1)^2 + (bS2)^2 + (cS3)^2 + (dS4)^2]^{1/2} \tag{20}$$

where S1, etc, are the residual standard deviations for the analytical parameter concerned. Since tolerances have been defined as twice the residual standard deviation, the expected tolerance in the predicted DE or ME value, ME_a, attributable to analytical variation, A, can be calculated from equation (21)

$$ME_a = [(aA1)^2 + (bA2)^2 + (cA3)^2 + (dA4)^2]^{1/2} \tag{21}$$

Because of the negative effect of crude fibre and total ash upon predicted ME value, the lowest predicted values are obtained when these two parameters are at the upper (or excess) permitted tolerances, whereas crude protein and ether extract are at their lower (or deficiency) tolerance limits. The converse will be true for the maximum predicted energy value obtainable by any combination of the legal tolerances outlined above. Calculations of the upper and lower predicted energy values must take these factors into account.

TOLERANCES IN EEC AND UK REGULATIONS

Details of EEC and UK tolerances are shown in *Table 1.8*. For a typical compound feed with the analysis shown, the relevant EEC tolerances are as shown in *Table 1.9*.

PARTITIONING OF TOLERANCES

An example may clarify the calculation of the various tolerances, T_L, T_U, and A. For a compound feed having a declared crude protein content of 18 per cent, the tolerances are 1.8 units per cent when in deficit and 3.6 units per cent when in excess, a range of 16.2–21.6 per cent within which the determined value must lie. The analytical tolerances, A, would be 1.8/2 = 0.9 units per cent and the lower technical tolerance, T_L, when the determined value is in deficit is 1.8–0.9 = 0.9 per cent. When the protein content is above the declared value, the upper technical tolerance, T_U, would be 3.6–0.9 = 2.7 per cent.

The relevant values for the example chosen are given in *Table 1.10*.

Table 1.10   PARTITIONING OF TOLERANCES OF AN EXAMPLE COMPOUND PIG FEED

Analytical component	Coefficients	EEC tolerances (units %)		
		Analytical (A)	Lower technical (T_L)	Upper technical (T_U)
Crude protein	(a)	0.9	0.9	2.7
Ether extract	(b)	0.4	0.4	1.2
Crude fibre	(c)	0.45	2.25	0.45
Total ash	(d)	0.5	2.5	0.5

Application to pig compound feed

The equation which uses the statutory declaration is equation (22)

$$DE\ (MJ/kg) = 17.38 + 0.105\ CP\% + 0.114\ EE\% - 0.317\ CF\%$$
$$- 0.402\ TA\% \qquad \text{(CF) (22)}$$

Using the declared analyses and apportioned tolerances from *Tables 1.9* and *1.10*, and inserting these values into equations (18), (19) and (21), the variation due to analytical tolerance $DE_a = 0.268\ MJ/kg$, that due to lower technical tolerance $DE_{tl} = 0.484\ MJ/kg$ and that due to upper technical tolerance $DE_{tu} = 2.139\ MJ/kg$. Thus the total lower variation is 0.268 + 0.484 = 0.752 MJ/kg, and the total upper variation is 0.268 + 2.139 = 2.407 MJ/kg. The estimated DE of the pig compound feed, using the data in *Table 1.9*, is 14.03 MJ/kg, and therefore the range within which the predicted DE can be expected to lie with at least 95 per cent probability is 13.28 to 16.44 MJ/kg. If only a 66 per cent probability is accepted, the range in predicted DE will be half of that calculated, i.e. 13.65 to 15.23 MJ/kg. This does not imply that the true *in vivo* DE of the compound feed lies within this range, but that, assuming that the compound feed conforms to the statutory declaration and that the designated equation was used, then the predicted value should do so.

Application to poultry compound feed

Equation (23) has been proposed as the relevant one for poultry compound feeds.

$$AME\ (MJ/kg) = 0.165\ CP\% + 0.345\ EE\% + 0.172\ STA\%$$
$$+ 0.158\ SUG\% \qquad \text{(77R) (23)}$$

The additional tolerance limits required for this equation are:

Starch: deficiency 2.5 units above 25 per cent starch
    excess   5.0 units above 25 per cent starch
Sugar: deficiency 1.0 units if less than 10 per cent sugar
    excess   2.0 units if less than 10 per cent sugar

This results in the partitioning of tolerances given in *Table 1.11*. After insertion of these values and their associated tolerances in *Table 1.11* into equations (18), (19) and (21) the variation due to analytical tolerance, $ME_a = 0.306$ MJ/kg, that due to lower technical tolerance, $ME_{tl} = 0.580$ MJ/kg, and that due to upper technical tolerance, $ME_{tu} = 1.742$ MJ/kg. The total lower variation is thus $0.306 + 0.580 = 0.886$ MJ/kg, and the total upper variation is $0.306 + 1.742 = 2.048$ MJ/kg.

Table 1.11 PARTITIONING OF TOLERANCES OF A COMPOUND POULTRY FEED

Analytical component	Coefficients	EEC tolerances (units %)		
		Analytical (A)	Lower technical (T_L)	Upper technical T_U)
Crude protein	(a)	0.9	0.9	2.7
Ether extract	(b)	0.4	0.4	1.2
Starch	(c)	1.25	1.25	3.75
Sugar	(d)	0.50	0.50	1.5

The high calculated variability in the examples, when upper tolerance units are used in the calculations should be noted, since a higher ME value than predicted from declared analyses, is not necessarily to the users' advantage. The chief reason for the legislation, and the concerns expressed by farmers are with compound feed where energy value is *below* expectation.

EXPECTED ACCURACY OF PREDICTED DE OR ME VALUES

A distinction needs to be drawn between the 'value to be predicted'—*in vivo* ME or DE—and the value given by the prediction equation. Variation in the latter can be 'technical', corresponding to deviations of declared from actual content, and/or 'analytical', corresponding to variation in analysis—depending on the origin of the parameter values substituted in the prediction equation. This is discussed in the preceding section, which describes the calculation of tolerances for ME analogous to present legal tolerances for individual declared analyses. If legal tolerances for ME or DE were required they would need to be calculated as described since checks would be based on analyses rather than *in-vivo* assessment of ME or DE. However, it is important to know the accuracy with which *in-vivo* values are predicted.

To assess the accuracy of predictions, account needs to be taken of the goodness-of-fit of the prediction equation to the *in-vivo* data. If predictions of ME are on an as-fed basis, and based on analyses on an as-fed basis by a single laboratory, then a suitable measure of accuracy is $0.87\,S''$, assuming an average DM content of 87 per cent.

Alternatively, if predictions are based on declarations on an as-fed basis, a different measure of accuracy (equation (24)) is appropriate. The term $b\,V\,b'$ is subtracted from S'', since this corresponds to the variation associated with the single laboratory's analyses (see Appendix I). Instead the technical tolerance is introduced, but is brought in as a simple linear addition, on the grounds that technical deviations are not entirely random—as argued in the preceding section. The square-root expression corresponds to the accuracy of predictions, given actual values for analyses, which should be within the technical tolerance range. If a better estimate than V of reproducibility variance/covariances becomes available, W say, then S''^2 should be replaced by $S''^2 - b\,V\,b' + b\,W\,b'$ but equation (24) stands.

$$2 \times 0.87\,(S''^2 - b\,V\,b)^{1/2} \pm \text{technical tolerance} \qquad (24)$$

The following section illustrates appropriate calculations of accuracy for analysis based and declaration based equations.

Pig compound feed/equation (22) (CF)—declaration based

$S'' = 0.594\,\text{MJ/kg}$
$(b\,V\,b')^{1/2} = 0.20\,\text{MJ/kg}$

Technical tolerance limits are -0.48, $+2.14\,\text{MJ/kg}$ (see preceding section).
Thus accuracy limits are

$$\pm\,2 \times 0.87\,(S''^2 - b\,V\,b')^{1/2} \pm \text{technical tolerance}$$
$$= \pm\,1.74\,(0.594^2 - 0.20^2)^{1/2} + (-0.48, +2.14)\,\text{MJ/kg}$$
$$= -1.45, +3.11\,\text{MJ/kg}$$

Pig compound feed/equation (22) (CF)—analysis based

S'' could be used directly. However, it may be considered that an alternative estimate of reproducibility variance to that derived from the laboratories in the original exercise should be used. For example, using equation (21), analytical variance may be approximated as 0.08^2 on an as-fed basis. Using this estimate gives tolerance limits of

$$\pm\,2[0.87^2\,(S''^2 - b\,V\,b') + \text{analytical variance}]^{1/2}$$
$$= \pm\,2[0.76\,(0.594^2 - 0.20^{1/2}) + 0.08^2]^{1/2}\,\text{MJ/kg}$$
$$= \pm\,0.99\,\text{MJ/kg}$$

APPLICATION TO NON-LINEAR EQUATIONS

Any measure of predictive precision (e.g. S''), is liable to be optimistic if it is used as the sole basis for selecting an equation, and the wider the class of equations considered, the greater is the potential bias. Such meaures are most appropriate to assess equations determined from independent considerations, but failing that it is advisable that selection is guided by nutritional principles. It is generally the case that when equations are entirely empirical, extrapolation is more reliable for linear equations than non-linear equations.

ME can be considered at least approximately additive (corresponding to linear regressors) since there was little evidence for non-linearity of compound/roughage mixtures in RRI/FEU Report 3 (Wainman, Dewey and Boyne, 1981). On the other hand it has been established that increasing fibre levels reduces digestibility, and it is also the case that higher ME compounds tend to have a greater proportion of added oil. For the latter reasons, equations which effectively allow regressor coefficients in notionally linear regressor equations to depend on fibre, and also on oil were considered. This explains the candidacy of some equations which apparently reduced the underestimation of the high oil compound tested, which was a feature of all linear regressor equations, coupled with the observation that it brought predictions of current commercial compounds into closer agreement with previous ADAS estimates.

It should be emphasized, especially for non-linear regressor equations, that use of the prediction equations should be confined to the ranges of composition covered by the original test compounds used in their derivation. A preliminary exercise (Morgan, Whittemore and Cockburn, 1984a), set up specifically for the purpose of assessing additivity, did not disprove the additivity of DE for pigs, thus weighting selection towards linear equations. In the case of AME for poultry, arguments for non-linear equations have been given by Fisher (1982).

Tolerances

The same arguments apply as for linear equations, but four new issues are introduced:

(1) The regression coefficients on an 'as-fed' basis differ from those on a 'dry matter' basis.
(2) Correlations between regressors arising from analytical variation may be non-zero.
(3) Technical variation extremes for the predictive equation may not correspond to extremes for the regressors.
(4) Regressor variances depend on level.

Example (and general formulae)

Consider equation (25) (**U1**) for ruminants in which components are included on a dry matter basis.

$$ME (MJ/kg\,DM) = 11.78 + 0.0654\,CP\% + 0.0665\,EE\%^2$$
$$- 0.0414\,EE\% \times CF\% - 0.118\,TA\% \qquad (\textbf{U1})\ (25)$$
$$(S = 0.320,\ S'' = 0.356\,MJ/kg\,DM)$$

Table 1.12   TECHNICAL TOLERANCES AND FIRST DERIVATIVES OF COEFFICIENTS FOR A COMPOUND FEED

Component	Declaration	Technical tolerance		First derivative of coefficients
		Lower	Upper	
CP	18	0.9	2.7	0.0654
EE	6	0.4	1.2	$2 \times EE \times 0.0764$ $- 0.0476 \times CF$
CF	6	2.25	0.45	$- 0.0476 \times EE$
TA	10	2.5	0.5	$- 0.118$

Table 1.13   UPPER AND LOWER EXTREMES OF COMPONENT ANALYSIS USING EQUATION 26, COMPARED TO THE DECLARED ANALYSIS OF A COMPOUND FEED

Component	Declaration	Extremes	
		Lower	Upper
CP (%)	18	17.1	20.7
EE (%)	6	5.6	7.2
CF (%)	6	6.45	3.75
TA (%)	10	10.5	7.5
ME (MJ/kg)	11.28	10.81	13.39

Assuming 87 per cent dry matter, equation (25) becomes equation (26) when components are considered on an as-fed basis.

$$ME \text{ (MJ/kg as-fed)} = 10.25 + 0.0654\,CP\% + 0.0764\,EE\%^2$$
$$- 0.0476\,EE \times CF\% - 0.118\,TA\% \tag{26}$$
$$(S = 0.278, S'' = 0.310\,MJ/kg)$$

In general, the coefficients of linear terms are unaltered and those for quadratic terms are divided by 0.87. Both S and S'' are multiplied by 0.87.

Table 1.12 presents the calculated technical tolerances and derivatives of coefficients for the declaration given in *Table 1.9*. It can be seen that the protein derivative is positive, and both the fibre and ash derivatives are negative. The oil derivative is positive provided (EE > 0.31 CF), which applies over the whole technical tolerance region. Thus the predictive maximum corresponds to high oil and protein, and low fibre and ash, and vice versa for the predictive minimum. The upper and lower extremes for the various components when using equation (26) are presented in *Table 1.13*. This results in a Lower Technical Tolerance of $-0.47\,MJ/kg$ and an Upper Technical Tolerance of $+2.11\,MJ/kg$.

When considering analytical tolerance the following general approximations are used:

Variance–Co-variance Matrix

	X^2		X.Y	X	X.Z
X^2	$[(2X)^2$	Var (X)		Symmetric	
X.Y	$[(2X.Y)$	Var (X)	$(X)^2Var(Y)$ $+ (Y^2)Var(X)$		
X	$[(2X)$	Var (X)	$(Y)Var(X)$	Var(X)	
X.Z	$[(2X.Z)$	Var (X)	$(Y.Z)Var(X)$	$(Z)Var(X)$	$(Z^2)VarX$ $+ (X)^2Var Z$

For equation (26) the formula for analytical variance is

$$0.0654^2 \text{ Var (CP)} + 0.0764^2 \text{ Var (EE}^2) + 0.0476^2 \text{ Var (EE} \times \text{CF)}$$
$$+ 0.118^2 \text{ Var (TA)} - 2 \times 0.0764 \times 0.0476 \text{ Cov. (EE}^2, \text{EE} \times \text{CF)} \qquad (27)$$

Evaluating this at the upper and lower technical tolerance limits gives an Upper analytical tolerance of $+0.408$ MJ/kg and a Lower analytical tolerance of -0.264 MJ/kg.

The *Total Tolerances* for check analyses are the sum of the technical and analytical tolerances listed above, namely a lower tolerance of -0.73 MJ/kg and an upper value of $+2.52$ MJ/kg.

Accuracy of predictions

As indicated previously, $2S''$ suffices to measure the accuracy of predictions based on analysis on a scale analogous to tolerances. For the example based on equation (26) above, $\pm 2S'' = \pm 0.62$ MJ/kg. This measure is an average over 24 points corresponding to the test compounds, and provides valid comparison with linear equations. However, the non-linearity implies a greater variation in accuracy over the test region.

A figure for the accuracy of predictions based on declarations was previously quoted (p. 24) for equation (22) and was derived from S''. This referred to an average over the 36 test compounds.

With non-linear equations it is preferable to consider a specific declaration, in view of the substantial variation in accuracy over the test region. The formula given in Appendix I for variance (ME) can be generalized to predictions from the average of L laboratories' analyses using equations that possibly do not include an intercept, and becomes equation (28).

$$\text{var (ME)} = \text{RMS} + y\text{W}y' + b\text{V}b' (1/L + 1/p) \qquad (28)$$

where y is the row vector of observed values of the constituents, W is the variance-covariance matrix of the regressor coefficients and L is the number of laboratories.

For predictions using actual values for the constituents—equivalently large L—this simplifies to equation (29) and needs to be evaluated at the points corresponding to the predictive equation tolerance limits.

$$\text{var (ME)} = \text{RMS} + y\text{W}y' + b\text{V}b'/p \qquad (29)$$

Using the upper and lower extremes of component analysis presented in *Table 1.13*, this produces the following estimates.

	Lower	*Upper*
ME	10.81	13.39
$b\text{V}b'$	0.0174	0.0416
$y\text{W}y'$	0.0111	0.0631
var (ME)	0.0919	0.1487
Analytical tolerance, $2 \text{ (var (ME))}^{1/2}$	0.606	0.771

Combining these analytical tolerances with the technical tolerances presented on p. 26 gives Total tolerances of 1.08, + 2.88 MJ/kg.

Criteria for choice of recommended equations

Early in the discussions of the working party, it was agreed that since any equations, which were recommended, would be used by a number of UKASTA, ADAS, COSAC and Public Analysts' laboratories, interlaboratory variation for the different analytical methods for determining the various parameters would have to be taken into account. A statistical technique to do this was now available (see Appendix 1), and the various research reports gave data on interlaboratory variation for the methods used therein. Additional data on some methods were asked for by the working party, and special collaborative studies involving ADAS and UKASTA laboratories were set up to provide the data requested.

This enabled the relevant statistical parameter, S'', to be calculated for all equations for all three classes of compound feeds. Equations were then selected primarily on the basis of those with the lowest S'' value. Goodness of fit and possible bias at the extremes were also considered. The number of additional parameters required above those already being determined, were to be minimized. Both speed and cost were considered differently for the three classes of intended use.

Equations recommended for prospective legal purposes were limited to those parameters required by the current UK Feedingstuffs Regulations 1982, namely crude protein, crude fibre, ether extract and total ash, but with the addition of EEC official methods for starch and sugar. These are optional under the UK Regulations, and both ADAS and UKASTA laboratories now have some experience of their use.

In the case of a possible voluntary scheme for energy declaration, a slightly wider choice of parameters was thought possible, provided that the methods were rugged, reasonably rapid and cheap to carry out. Examples are neutral detergent fibre for pig feeds and cellulase digestibility (NCD) for ruminant feeds. A possible changeover to a legal system and subsequent changes of parameters are arguments against this approach.

For reference purposes, precision was the major determinant in choosing equations, irrespective of cost and speed.

The working party's agreed recommendations of equations for predicting the energy value of ruminant, pig and poultry compound feeds are given below. The numbers in bold in parentheses are those assigned in the relevant research report (ruminants, Wainman, Dewey and Boyne, 1981; pigs, Morgan *et al.*, 1984b; poultry, Fisher, 1982), with the exception of those prefixed U, which were derived by the UKASTA members from the original RRI/FEU database.

Recommended prediction equations

RUMINANTS

(a) *For voluntary use:* Equations (25) (**U1**) or (29) (**U3**).

$$ME\ (MJ/kg\ DM) = 11.78 + 0.0654\,CP\% + 0.0665\,EE\%^2$$
$$- 0.0414\,EE\% \times CF\% - 0.118\,TA\%$$
$$S'' = 0.36\,MJ/kg\ DM$$

(U1) (25)

$$ME\ (MJ/kg\ DM) = 13.83 - 0.488\,EE\% + 0.0394\,EE\% \times CP\%$$
$$- 0.0085\,MADF\% \times CP\% - 0.138\,TA\%$$
$$S'' = 0.35\,MJ/kg\ DM$$

(U3) (29)

A simple linear equation which uses only those parameters already declared on the feed label is equation **F** in the RRI/FEU Report (Wainman, Dewey and Boyne, 1981). This equation showed under prediction at very high ME values, and over prediction for low ME values, particularly with compounds 25 and 26, which contained 15 per cent barley straw and over 10 per cent of oat feed. However, two other feeds containing oat feed were quite well predicted. The working party studied the effects of removing these feeds from the calculation of the line of best fit in equation **F** and others under consideration. The results are shown in *Table 1.14*

Table 1.14   EFFECT OF OMITTING SOME RUMINANT DIETS ON REGRESSION EQUATION RESIDUAL STANDARD DEVIATION, S

Equation number[a]	Equation number[b]	All 24 diets	Excluding diets 25 and 26	Excluding diets 2, 18, 25 and 26
25	**F**	0.384	0.314	0.299
	U1	0.320	0.316	0.293
	5	0.300	0.281	0.271
	81	0.368	0.259	0.259
29	**U3**	0.264	0.210	0.235
30	**U2**	0.207	0.207	0.207

[a]Number used in this chapter.
[b]Relates to the numbers given in the report of Wainman, Dewey and Boyne (1981), or as derived by UKASTA (prefix U) from this original report.

in the form of the residual standard deviation, S, of the recalculated equations when these feeds were omitted in sequence. The S values for equation (25) (**F**) showed a marked reduction when feeds 2, 18, 25 and 26 were omitted, but other equations were much more stable in their S values, particularly equation (3) (**U2**). It was concluded that since equation (25) (**U1**) uses the same parameters as **F**, the latter should not be recommended for use, nor was there good reason to exclude feeds 2, 18, 25 and 26 from the population of feeds used to fit equations to predict ME value of ruminant feeds. These findings show that over a wide range of fibre level, equations using CF do not fit observed ME values as well as those using MADF and NCD, (29, 30) (**U3, U2**).

Equation (25) (**U1**) has a square term for EE, which improves the fit with high energy, (high fat) feeds. This agrees with what is known about the metabolism of fat, but implies non-linearity of the ME of fat when added to diets. The equation also has a negative product term, EE × CF, implying a depressing effect of fat on fibre digestibility. Its goodness of fit for the 24 test diets is illustrated in *Figure 1.1*.

Equation (29) (**U3**) is very similar to (25) (**U1**), but uses MADF instead of CF as a measure of fibre. MADF is a single stage procedure, which has a low

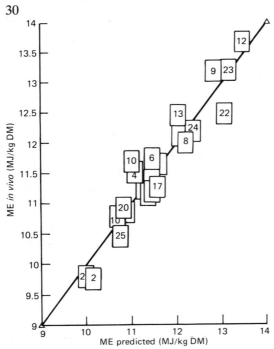

Figure 1.1 Relationship between predicted (from equation 25) and the *in vivo* measured ME content of 24 ruminant compound feeds ($\triangle$—$\triangle$, y = x)

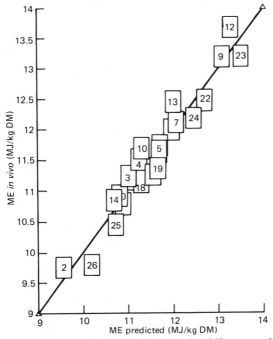

Figure 1.2 Relationship between predicted (from equation 29) and the *in vivo* measured ME content of 24 ruminant compound feeds ($\triangle$—$\triangle$, y = x)

interlaboratory variation, and this is reflected in its lower S'' value. The goodness of fit is shown in *Figure 1.2*.
(b) *For legislation:* Equation (25) (**U1**) as above.
(c) *For reference purposes:* Equation (30) (**U2**).

$$ME \text{ (MJ/kg DM)} = 11.56 - 2.375\,EE\% + 0.030\,EE\%^2 + 0.030\,EE\% \times NCD\%$$
$$- 0.034\,TA\%$$
$$S'' = 0.32\,\text{MJ/kg DM} \tag{30} \text{ (U2)}$$

Equation (30) (**U2**) relies on cellulase digestibility, NCD, a modern enzyme procedure, which measures organic matter digestibility. The product term with EE, implies a positive effect of fat on the energy content of the digested organic matter. The goodness of fit is shown in *Figure 1.3*.

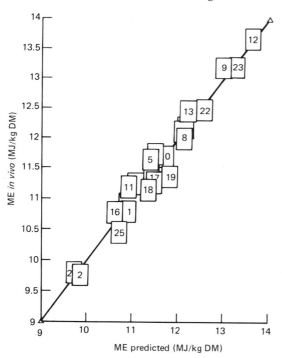

Figure 1.3 Relationship between predicted (from equation 30) and the *in vivo* measured ME content of 24 ruminant compound feeds ($\triangle - \triangle$, y = x)

PIGS

(a) *For voluntary use:* Equations (14) (**1d**) or (31) (**22d**).

$$DE \text{ (MJ/kg)} = 17.49 + 0.157\,EE\% + 0.078\,CP\% - 0.325\,TA\% - 0.149\,NDF\%$$
$$S'' = 0.44\,\text{MJ/kg} \tag{14} \text{ (1d)}$$

$$DE \text{ (MJ/kg)} = 17.95 + 0.01\,EE\%^2 + 0.069\,CP\% - 0.305\,TA\% - 0.151\,NDF\%$$
$$S'' = 0.43\,\text{MJ/kg} \tag{31} \text{ (22d)}$$

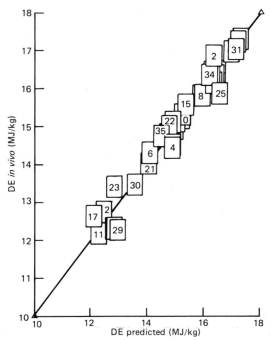

Figure 1.4   Relationship between predicted (from equation 14) and the *in vivo* measured DE content of 36 pig compound feeds (△–△ , y = x)

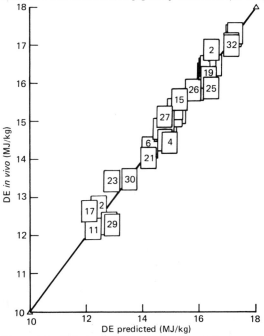

Figure 1.5   Relationship between predicted (from equation 31) and the *in vivo* measured DE content of 36 pig compound feeds (△–△ , y = x)

Both of the equations listed above feature neutral detergent fibre, NDF, which is a measure of the cell wall constituents in the feed, and includes hemicellulose, as well as the cellulose and lignin fraction, which MADF and ADF measure. All these fractions are not well digested by the pig, being subject mainly to fermentation in the lower gut. Substantial increases in precision are obtained by using NDF instead of CF, as may be seen by comparing equation (14) (**1d**) in *Figure 1.4* with equation (22) (**CF**) in *Figure 1.7*, as well as by its higher S'' value given below. The coefficient on the NDF term in equation (14) (**1d**), implies that NDF contributes little DE to the pig. The inclusion of a square term for EE in equation (31) (**22d**) gives only a small increase in precision, but the non-linear effect of fat as seen again, as in ruminant feeds (see *Figure 1.5*).

(b) *For legislation:* Equations (13) (**16d**) or (22) (**CF**).

$$DE \ (MJ/kg) = 5.98 + 0.181 \ CP\% + 0.188 \ EE\% + 0.115 \ STA\%$$
$$S'' = 0.49 \ MJ/kg$$
$$\text{(13) (\textbf{16d})}$$

or

$$DE \ (MJ/kg) = 17.38 + 0.105 \ CP\% + 0.114 \ EE\% - 0.317 \ CF\% - 0.402 \ TA\%$$
$$S'' = 0.59 \ MJ/kg$$
$$\text{(22) (\textbf{CF})}$$

Equation (13) (**16d**) is a biologically realistic equation, since it only contains parameters describing nutrients known to be well digested by the pig. It is appreciably less accurate than equation (14) (**1d**), and its goodness of fit is shown in *Figure 1.6*. Equation (22) (**CF**) is an unnumbered equation involving CP, EE, CF

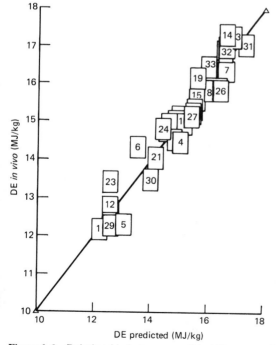

Figure 1.6 Relationship between predicted (from equation 13) and the *in vivo* measured DE content of 36 pig compound feeds ($\triangle-\triangle$, y = x)

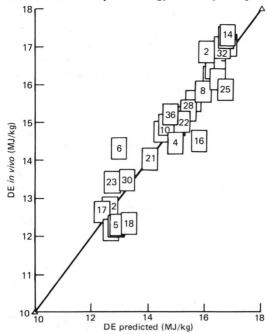

Figure 1.7 Relationship between predicted (from equation 22) and the *in vivo* measured DE content of 36 pig compound feeds ($\triangle$–$\triangle$, y = x)

and TA, which appears in Tables 12 and 29 of Morgan *et al.* (1984b). Whilst it can be used with statutory declarations, its precision is poor, as can be seen in *Figure 1.7*.

(c) *For reference purposes:* Equations (14) (**1d**), or (31) (**22d**) as above.

(a) *For voluntary use:* Equations (32) (**32R**), (33) (**74R**) or (34) (**77R**).

$$\text{AME (MJ/kg)} = 5.39 + 0.113\,\text{CP\%} + 0.281\,\text{EE\%} + 0.113\,\text{STA\%}$$
$$- 0.136\,\text{CF\%}$$
$$\text{S}'' = 0.36\,\text{MJ/kg} \tag{32} \text{(32R)}$$

or

$$\text{AME (MJ/kg)} = 5.39 + 0.103\,\text{CP\%} + 0.282\,\text{EE\%} + 0.114\,\text{STA\%}$$
$$- 0.062\,\text{NDF\%} + 0.095\,\text{USR}$$
$$\text{S}'' = 0.34\,\text{MJ/kg} \tag{33} \text{(74R)}$$

$$\text{AME (MJ/kg)} = 0.345\,\text{EE\%} + 0.165\,\text{CP\%} + 0.172\,\text{STA\%} + 0.158\,\text{SUG\%}$$
$$\text{S}'' = 0.43\,\text{MJ/kg} \tag{34} \text{(77R)}$$

A minor transcription error in the AME data of the original study (Fisher, 1982), meant that all equations had to be recalculated. The original equation numbers from that report have been retained, but the suffix '**R**' indicates it is a revised equation.

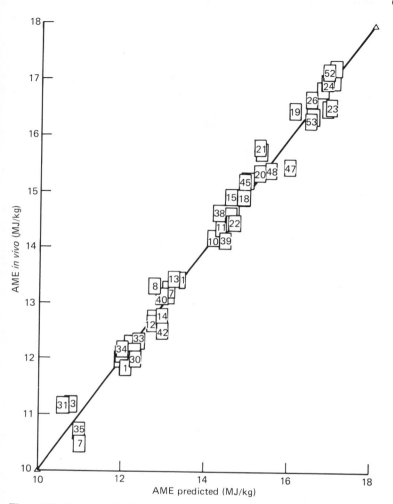

Figure 1.8 Relationship between predicted (from equation 32) and the *in vivo* measured AME content of 29 poultry compound feeds ($\triangle-\triangle$, y = x)

Equation (32) (**32R**) is of high precision, combining CP, EE, and STA with CF as a measure of indigestibility. Its goodness of fit is shown in *Figure 1.8*.

A predictor of AME of similar accuracy was equation (33) (**74R**), which brings in NDF, also used in the pig equations, and the parameter, USR, a measure of the unsaturation of the fat in the feed. Its goodness of fit is shown in *Figure 1.9*.

Equation (34) (**77R**) is a biologically realistic equation, of a form favoured by European workers. It contains only parameters describing nutrients of value to poultry. Despite its theoretical soundness, it is not as accurate as equation (32) (**32R**), as *Figure 1.10* shows.

(b) *For legislation:* Equations (32) (**32R**) or (34) (**77R**).
(c) *For reference purposes:* Equations (32) (**32R**), (33) (**74R**) or (34) (**77R**).

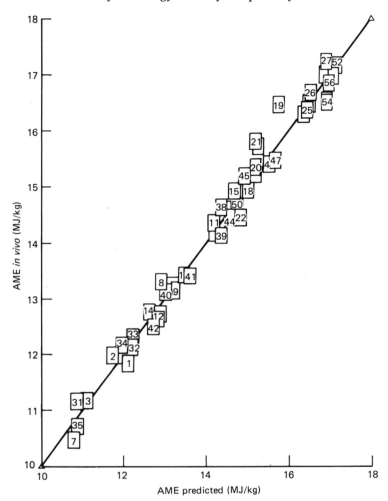

Figure 1.9   Relationship between predicted (from equation 33) and the *in vivo* measured AME content of 29 poultry compound feeds ($\triangle$–$\triangle$, y = x)

Remaining problems

Despite the substantial amount of research undertaken in this specialist field in the UK since 1979, the working party found that some problems in predicting energy values for feeds from chemical analysis, still remained. These included

(1) the underestimation of the ME values of high fat ruminant feeds;
(2) discrepancies between measured ME values of ruminant feeds, and those calculated from databases;
(3) determination of oil and fat in animal feeds;
(4) interference of starch with NDF determinations;

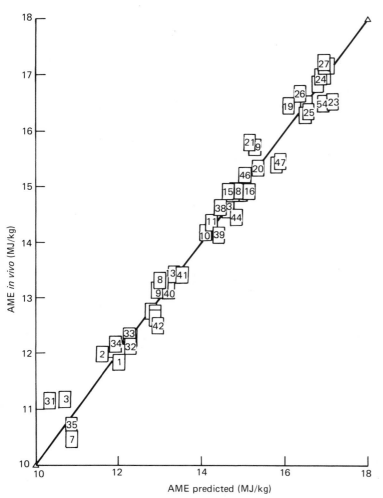

Figure 1.10 Relationship between predicted (from equation 34) and the *in vivo* measured AME content of 29 poultry compound feeds ($\triangle$–$\triangle$, y = x)

(5) conversion of predicted energy values to an 'as-fed' basis;
(6) effect of permitted tolerances on precision of predicted energy value.

HIGH FAT RUMINANT FEEDS

In the Rowett study, the ruminant compound, number D12, with the highest ME content (13.66 MJ/kg DM) was seriously underestimated by the simple linear equation F, which uses the components of the statutory declaration, CP, EE, CF and TA. The range of fat levels used in this study, when it was set up in 1979, represented that then in use by the industry for ruminant feeds. Compound D12 contained 7 per cent of fat in the dry matter, 6 per cent as-fed, the highest level in the 24 diets studied. Since then however, there has been a significant move to higher levels of fat inclusion, partly because the high cost of cereals has made energy from fat a cheaper option, as well as being advantageous in dairy feeds in maintaining high butterfat levels in milk. The present situation is that about 25 per cent of dairy compound feeds contain more than 6 per cent fat as-fed, of which only 3 per cent are above 7 per cent as-fed. A further 40 per cent are in the range 5–6 per cent fat as-fed, or 6–7 per cent on a dry matter basis.

The working party considered research findings on this topic, both with sheep (Wainman, Dewey and Smith, 1982), and with dairy cows (Van der Honing, 1980). Neither study produced evidence that the inclusion of fat resulted in a significant disturbance of the usual additivity of the ME of the components of a feed, although methane production was reduced in both studies with 5 per cent inclusions of tallow or soya bean oil. Nevertheless, the inclusion of a square term for EE, as well as a product term for EE × CF, in equation (25) (**U1**), significantly improved the fit of predicted values at the higher ME levels. Additional studies are required on dairy compound feeds at the higher levels of fat now commonly in use. This might also contribute to resolving the other problem with ruminant feeds.

INGREDIENT VALUES IN DATABASES

The process of diet formulation by computer relies upon a set of values for the chemical composition and nutritive value, in this case DE or ME, for all raw materials offered for inclusion in the diet. Additivity is assumed for both the chemical composition and the DE or ME values of these raw materials. The consequences of summing the raw material ME or DE values was examined in all three studies, and in the case of pig and poultry feeds, no discrepancies or significant bias between calculated and measured DE or AME values were found. For ruminant feeds, however, both the MAFF and UKASTA sets of values were found to overestimate the ME values (determined by the accepted standard procedure using wether sheep fed at the maintenance plane of nutrition) by on average 0.49 and 0.25 MJ/kg DM, with residual standard deviations of 0.71 and 0.65 MJ/kg DM respectively (see Figure 1.4, estimates A and B of Wainman, Dewey and Boyne, 1981). The difference also changed with the estimated value, overestimation being less at low values.

Since 1979, the average (or typical) ME values of a number of the major raw materials have been measured, either at the RRI/FEU or at the ADAS Feed Evaluation Unit. These values have now been approved for publication in standard MAFF/ADAS publications, and the new and old MAFF values are given in *Table 1.15*. A revised set of average ME values for raw materials, in use by UKASTA

Table 1.15   RECENTLY DETERMINED METABOLIZABLE ENERGY VALUES FOR RAW MATERIALS USED IN RUMINANT FEEDS

Name of feed		New ME value (MJ/kg DM)	Old ME value (MJ/kg DM)
Maize		13.8	14.2
Barley		12.9	13.7
Wheat		13.5	14.0
Oats		12.0	11.5
Cassava		12.8	12.6
Maize gluten feed		12.5	13.5
Dried sugar beet pulp		12.5	12.3
	Mean value	12.9	13.1

member companies, was also made available to the working party, and revealed a small downward shift in some of the values. However, for the main cereals, maize gluten feed and sugar beet pulp, the mean values still averaged 0.5 MJ ME/kg DM above the new values listed in *Table 1.15*.

A computer study was undertaken using the current UKASTA and ADAS databases. The latter uses the ME values in *Table 1.15*, extended by incorporation of UKASTA mean ME values for unusual raw materials, such as cocoa byproduct and grape follicle, which were used in the ruminant study.

The data are plotted in *Figures 1.11* (UKASTA) and *1.12* (ADAS) against the Y = X line. The lines of best fit, (not plotted), are given by equations (35) and (36).

$$\text{UKASTA} \quad Y = 0.58\,X + 4.85 \tag{35}$$
$$S = 0.51\,\text{MJ}$$
$$\text{ADAS(1)} \quad Y = 0.60\,X + 4.53 \tag{36}$$
$$S = 0.52\,\text{MJ}$$

This study also revealed the anomalous position of the low ME feeds (2, 18, 25 and 26 containing oat feed) which were underestimated by both sets of calculations. Removing these feeds from the ADAS database calculations resulted in the line of best fit indicated in equation (37).

$$\text{ADAS(2)} \quad Y = 0.92\,X + 1.03 \tag{37}$$
$$S = 0.33\,\text{MJ}$$

The ADAS database was also used to examine the relationship between the ME predicted from calculated chemical composition of the feeds using equation (25) (U1), and their ME values measured *in vivo*. The results are shown in *Figure 1.13*, and the line of best fit is shown in equation (38).

$$\text{ADAS(3)} \quad Y = 0.65\,X + 4.05 \tag{38}$$
$$S = 0.46\,\text{MJ}$$

The results of the ring test organized by the working party, demonstrated the ability of laboratories to predict the ME values of the original set of compound feeds with satisfactory precision and small bias. There is general agreement that the chemical composition of a diet can be accurately calculated. Without challenging the whole Rowett FEU study, it must be accepted that the ME values of the diets were as reported.

It has been argued that metabolizable energy values based on trials with wether sheep fed at the maintenance energy level, are not valid for use with dairy cows. The UK ME system is based on measurements with sheep, as are all the European energy systems for ruminants. It is accepted that ME values measured with cows decline by about 2 per cent for each multiple above maintenance, of the ration fed. Dairy cows are commonly fed at three times maintenance, so that a depression of ME of the ration of about 5 per cent can be expected. Adjustments can be made for the effects of level of feeding within the system, by adjusting the ME requirements accordingly. However, this effect is in the opposite direction to the discrepancies between calculated and measured ME values being discussed. Further studies are being planned, particularly with high fat compound feeds.

The working party concluded that the discrepancies between database values and measured ME values were a cause for concern. Urgent examination of the ME

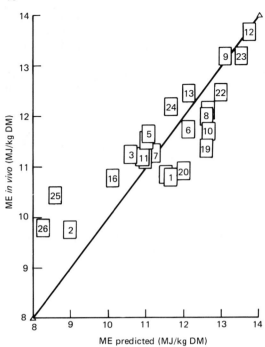

Figure 1.11 Relationship between predicted and the *in vivo* measured ME content of 24 ruminant compound feeds. The predicted values were determined using summation of UKASTA database values for the ME content of the individual ingredients used ($\triangle$–$\triangle$, y = x)

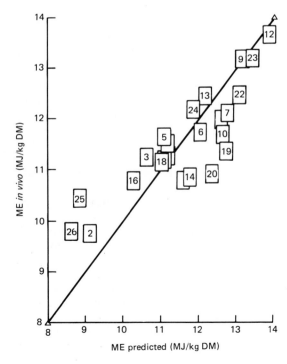

Figure 1.12 Relationship between predicted and the *in vivo* measured ME content of 24 ruminant compound feeds. The predicted values were determined using summation of ADAS database values for the ME contents of the individual ingredients used ($\triangle$–$\triangle$, y = x)

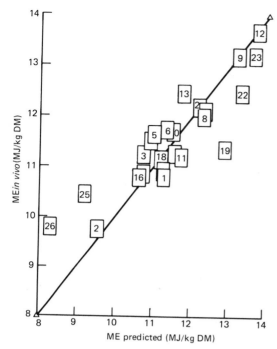

Figure 1.13 Relationship between predicted and the *in vivo* measured ME content of 24 ruminant compound feeds. The predicted values were calculated using the chemical composition of the individual ingredients from the ADAS database fitted into equation (25) ($\triangle$–$\triangle$, y = x)

values in databases should be carried out, and recently determined values for raw materials should be used wherever possible. However, the appearance of square and product terms in the more precise prediction equations, indicates that the assumption of linearity when summing raw material ME values needs further study.

DETERMINATION OF OIL AND FAT IN ANIMAL FEEDS

Some of the types of fat supplements used in ruminant compound feeds are protected against microbial attack in the rumen by various types of coating. This also has the effect that the existing official method for the determination of oil and fat in such feeds, OIL(PT), which uses petroleum ether solvent alone, tends to underestimate the level of oil and fat in the feed. An alternative method, OIL(AH), uses a preliminary hydrolysis with hydrochloric acid, before the extraction with petroleum ether. This dissolves the coating of protected fats, to give a better recovery of oil and fat. It also gives a higher value for animal feeds generally, an increase of about 0.7 per cent being observed.

A change to OIL(AH) as the official EEC method is under consideration and will be implemented in UK legislation in due course. Since all the recommended equations use OIL(PT), the change will require some adjustment or recalculation. However, the work on pig compound feeds did use both techniques. The data of Morgan *et al.* (1984a) showed no advantage of OIL(AH) over OIL(PT) as a predictor of DE. The relationship between the two methods was studied, using the data from Morgan *et al.* (1984b), with the results shown in equation (39). The accuracy of the relationship is sufficient to enable conversion of an OIL(AH) value to an OIL(PT) value for insertion in any of the equations recommended in this report for pigs and poultry only.

$$\text{OIL(PT)}\% = 1.0036 \times \text{OIL(AH)}\% - 0.4753 \tag{39}$$
$$S = 0.254.$$

STARCH INTERFERENCE IN NDF DETERMINATIONS

The laboratories participating in the original analysis of pig feeds using the NDF method did not experience difficulties with feeds containing high levels of starch. Filtration problems were encountered, however, when additional laboratories took part in a collaborative study, which was organized when the importance of using NDF in equations to predict the DE of pig compound feeds was noted. These filtration problems were also met by workers who had not previously encountered them. The problem may arise from differing batches of amylase used as a pretreatment before boiling the sample with neutral detergent solution. Preliminary work has not succeeded in overcoming these filtration difficulties, but the problem continues to be studied by the working group originally responsible for the analytical work on pig compound feeds.

CONVERSION OF PREDICTED ENERGY VALUES TO AN 'AS-FED' BASIS

All the equations listed in the three research reports studied by the working party are based on the composition of the animal feed on a dry matter basis, thus eliminating variability due to moisture content. Nevertheless, currently in the pig and poultry sector, values for DE and AME on the as-fed basis are used, usually allowing for 12–14 per cent moisture in the animal feed. Ruminant feed ME values are reported on a dry matter basis, but the declared composition is on the as-fed basis. The relevant EEC Directive requires all declarations on chemical composition and energy to be on the as-fed basis. Therefore, the conversion of equations from a dry matter basis to the as-fed basis requires some comment.

Equations without constant terms in them, such as (34) (**77R**) for poultry, do not change when converted from the dry matter basis to as-fed. If values for CP, EE, STA, and SUG are inserted on an as-fed basis, the predicted AME obtained will be on an as-fed basis also. However, equations with constant terms in them, which form the majority of these recommended, are affected by the change from dry matter to as-fed, depending on the level of moisture content.

Thus for example, for a moisture content of 13 per cent, (or 87 per cent dry matter), equation (22) (**CF**) becomes equation 40 when EE, CP etc. are on a dry matter basis and equation (41) when they are on an as-fed basis at 13 per cent moisture.

$$\text{DE} = 0.87\,(17.38 + 0.105\,\text{CP}\% + 0.114\,\text{EE}\% - 0.317\,\text{CF}\% - 0.402\,\text{TA}\%) \tag{40}$$

$$\text{DE} = 15.12 + 0.105\,\text{CP}\% + 0.114\,\text{EE}\% - 0.317\,\text{CF}\% - 0.402\,\text{TA}\% \tag{41}$$

Equations with square and product terms, such as (25) (**U1**) require different treatment. The coefficients for unmultiplied parameters remain unchanged by the conversion as above, whereas any constant term is multiplied by the appropriate conversion factor (0.87), etc., depending on moisture content. The coefficients for square and product terms however require to be divided by the conversion factor, in order to maintain equality when the values of CP, EE, etc. are changed from dry matter to the as-fed basis. Thus equation (25) (**U1**) becomes equation (42), which then converts to equation (43), in which CP, EE, CF and TA are on an as-fed basis at 13 per cent moisture.

$$ME = 11.78 \times 0.87 + 0.065\,CP\% + \frac{0.0665\,EE\%^2}{0.87} - \frac{0.0414\,EE\% \times CF\%}{0.87}$$
$$- 0.118\,TA\% \tag{42}$$
$$ME = 10.25 + 0.065\,CP\% + 0.0764\,EE\%^2 - 0.0476\,EE\% \times CF\%$$
$$- 0.118\,TA\% \tag{43}$$

It follows that agreement on a standard assumed moisture content of compound feeds will be required to operate any scheme of energy declaration. The figure of 13 per cent is recommended for use on compound feeds of all types. This implies multiplication through of all the recommended equations by 0.87 according to the rules laid down above.

EFFECT OF PERMITTED TOLERANCES ON PRECISION OF PREDICTED ENERGY VALUE

The tolerances permitted by EEC and UK legislation on declared chemical composition parameters are not symmetrical about their declared values. This is because of the presumption that deficiencies of CP and EE are to the detriment of the purchaser of the compound feed, while excess of CP and EE are a benefit, and thus unlikely to be the cause of litigation. With CF and TA, excesses are regarded as detrimental to the nutritive value of the feed, and deficits beneficial. The signs attached to the coefficients in the recommended equations bear this out very well. Tolerances on the side favouring the purchaser are usually twice those which are to his detriment.

The consequences of this asymmetry upon predicted DE or ME value are considerable. They need to be studied in the context of any scheme for energy declaration which may be considered. The earlier section on the 'Calculation of the variation in the predicted energy value of compound feeds' showed how the total variation in DE or ME could be calculated. This is done by combining the chosen equation coefficients with the relevant tolerances in the UK Regulations. About two-thirds of the total variation calculated comes from the larger tolerances in favour of the purchaser.

The needs of the purchaser, however, need to be redefined when considering the utility of a declared energy value. The purchaser will require some assurance that the value stated is meaningful in relation to his livestock enterprise. A higher energy feed than a farmer asks for is not necessarily advantageous to him. Excessive energy intake by bacon pigs results in overfatness and loss of premium payments for carcass quality. The daily feed intake would have to be reduced to achieve the desired DE intake, thus reducing feed costs and allowing premium payments to be maintained. It is therefore recommended that consideration be given to making the tolerances permitted on declared chemical composition of compound feeds symmetrical about the declared value. This would improve the usefulness to the purchaser, of the energy value predicted from declared chemical composition of the feed.

Appendix I

INTERLABORATORY VARIATION FOR SPECIFIC ANALYTICAL METHODS, AND ITS EFFECTS UPON THE RANKING OF PREDICTION EQUATIONS FOR GENERAL USE

The entry under S in the various reports is the residual standard deviation in ME or DE after eliminating variability accounted for by the regression equation. The measurements made at the collaborating laboratories were carried out under very closely monitored conditions. It is probable that this has led to lower values of S and V than would have been attained under less closely controlled measurements of the laboratory data. The equations are based, in general, on the means from five laboratories and the indicator of precision, S, in the tables refers to predictions made on the same basis. It is most likely, however, that any equation will be used with analytical measures made at a single laboratory.

To obtain an indication of the effect which this has on precision it is necessary to assume that the laboratories involved are a random sample of all possible laboratories. These assumptions allow the estimation of the variance of an observation made at a laboratory chosen at random, and from this, the variance of the difference between such an observation and the mean of the observations made at five laboratories. If the variance of such a difference is V, and if the value of the regression coefficient is b, then the variance of an estimate of ME is increased by b^2V. This describes the situation where regression is on a single variable.

If there is more than one independent variable, V becomes the variance-covariance matrix and b is replaced by b, the vector of regression coefficients, and the increase in the variance of the estimate of ME becomes bVb'. The revised variance of an estimate then becomes $S'^2 = 1.042 \, S^2 + bVb'$ as indicated above ($1.042 = 1 + 1/$No. of diets(24)). As these measurements were made under very closely monitored conditions, in addition to yielding a low S, it might be expected that laboratory differences themselves would be underestimated. Consequently all the error figures quoted in the reports may be smaller than might be expected in practice.

CALCULATION OF S′ AND S″

The residual standard deviation gives an acceptable estimate of the precision of an estimated DE or ME value if the only contributor to the deviations from the regression equation is random error in the measurement of constituent levels. In this exercise, in addition to this random error, there is the variation between the estimates of constituents of the diets from the several laboratories and also the variation within diets of the *in vivo* determinations of ME or DE.

DERIVATION OF THE FORMULA FOR S′

If laboratory variation is included in the predictive error, an estimate of the variation is given by

$$\text{var DE} = \text{RMS} + \text{RMS} (1/n + xCx') + bVb' (1 + 1/p)$$

where RMS is the residual mean square after fitting the regression equation

n is the number of diets
b is the row vector of regression coefficients
p is the number of laboratories
V is the variance-covariance matrix of a single analysis for each constituent in the equation
x is the row vector of differences between observed values of the constituent, and
C is the inverse of the between diet matrix of corrected sums of squares and products for the constituents in the regression equation.

The covariance terms of V are assumed to be zero except where interactions between constituents are present in the regression equation. The *j*th diagonal term of V is an estimate of the variance of determination of a constituent about its true mean by one laboratory and is obtained from the analysis of variance for the constituent as

$$\sigma^2_{\text{lab.diet}} + \sigma^2_{\text{lab}} \tag{A1}$$

assuming that 'lab' and the 'lab diet' interaction are random effects. This variance is sometimes called the 'reproducibility' but we prefer to use the longer term, the 'reproducibility variance'. The estimates are given as standard deviations, in *Table 1.16*.

The number of laboratories is not the same for all constituents so the third term of the expression is replaced by

$$bV(I + P^{-1})b' \tag{A2}$$

where
P^{-1} is a diagonal matrix with *j*th diagonal element $= p_j^{-1}$, p being the number of laboratories determining the *j*th constituent in the regression equation, and
I is the unit matrix.

Table 1.16 ESTIMATES OF REPRODUCIBILITY STANDARD DEVIATION USED TO CALCULATE S''

Constituent (%)	Reproducibility SD (No. of laboratories) Pigs	Ruminants and poultry
OIL(PT)/EE	0.228 (3)	0.184 (5)
CP	0.379 (5)	0.413 (5)
CF	0.458 (5)	0.532 (5)
ASH	0.328 (5)	0.331 (5)
OIL(AH)	0.368 (3)	NA
STA	1.360 (3)	1.468 (4)
SUG	0.377 (3)	0.600 (5)
ADF	0.703 (4)	0.665 (5)
NDF	1.134 (4)	1.336 (5)
CL	0.507 (4)	0.332 (5)
IVD	NA	2.871 (5)
MADF	NA	0.863 (5)
ADL	NA	0.461 (5)
NCD	NA	1.128 (11)
GE,MJ/kg	0.150 (4)	0.252 (4)
USR	NA	0.198 (3)

The matrix V is not diagonal when a regression equation includes interaction terms. The third term is then

$$b(I + P^{-\frac{1}{2}}) V (I + P^{-\frac{1}{2}})b' \tag{A3}$$

where $P^{-\frac{1}{2}}$ is diagonal with jth element $- P_j^{-\frac{1}{2}}$.

The values of the vector x are different for each diet but zero if a diet has the mean amount of each of the constituents in the equation. For such a diet, the estimate of variation is lowest. The standard deviation of prediction, S', estimated by the square root of

$$\text{var DE} = \text{RMS}(1 + 1/n) + bV(1 + P^{-1})b' \tag{A4}$$

is therefore applicable only for a diet with composition equivalent to the mean, over the 36 diets, of the constituents represented in the equation.

DERIVATION OF THE FORMULA FOR S''

An assumption made in the formula for S' is that every regression model is able to give unbiased predictions of ME or DE if the correct regression coefficients can be estimated. Denote by σ^2 the variance of *in vivo* DE for the number of diets tested. (There is no unbiased estimate of σ^2 available, but the minimum value it can take is the variance of *in vivo* ME values within classes of feeds, which are identical as regards all analytical parameters.)

The RMS is the estimate of $\sigma^2 + (B_i^2)/(n - m)$ (A5)

where RMS is the residual mean square after fitting the regression equation
       m is the number of regressors including the intercept in the equation
       B_i is the bias for the ith diet ($i = 1,2,3 \ldots\ldots, n$)

and the estimate of the contribution to the variance by diet i is

$$\text{var DE} = \sigma^2 + B_i^2 + \sigma^2 (1/n + x_i C x_i') + b V(I + P^{-1}) b' \tag{A6}$$

Now an average value for the square of bias is obtainable from (A5) and

$$\text{mean } (x_i C x_i') = (m - 1)/n \tag{A7}$$

so with a suitable value for σ^2, an average standard deviation for all diets, S'', is given by the square root of

$$\text{var DE} = \sigma^2 (2m/n) + \text{RMS}(1 - m/n) + b V(I + P^{-1}) b' \tag{A8}$$

This estimate of predictive variance is applicable to the whole range of diets as well as taking into account the variability of the *in vivo* determinations.

THE USE OF NEUTRAL DETERGENT AND ENZYMES TO PREDICT THE DIGESTIBILITY OF FEEDINGSTUFFS

PRINCIPLE

The oil and fat free feeding stuff is treated with neutral detergent to extract the cell contents. During this digestion the starch is removed by conversion to soluble sugars by the action of α-amylase. The resultant neutral detergent fibre (NDF) is thoroughly washed with hot water and digested with buffered cellulase. Finally the indigestible material is collected and the organic matter determined; in addition, the total ash of the sample is determined. The percentage of organic matter digested by the neutral detergent and cellulase is then calculated (NCD).

DETERMINATION

Apparatus

(a) Refluxing equipment for $150 \, cm^3$ flat bottomed round Quickfit flasks.
(b) $150 \, cm^3$, flat bottomed Quickfit flasks.
(c) Dispensers for dispensing $50 \, cm^3$, $30 \, cm^3$, $2 \, cm^3$ and $0.5 \, cm^3$ of solution.
(d) Desiccators containing an efficient desiccant. If silica gel is used it must be dehydrated at least once a week.
(e) Sintered glass pyrex filter tubes, porosity 1 with No. 70 suba-seal and plastic cap, available from Soham Scientific, Unit 6, Mereside, Soham, Ely, Cambs. CB7 5EE.

Reagents

(a) Cellulase–Derived from Trichoderma viride (Available from BDH Chemicals Ltd, Poole, Dorset) (See note on p. 51). The activity of the cellulase will be checked by ADAS, Reading.
(b) Acetate Buffer pH 4.8.

49

Dissolve 1.36 g of sodium acetate ($CH_3COONa.3H_2O$) in 500 cm^3 of distilled water, add 0.6 cm^3 of glacial acetic acid and dilute the solution to 1 litre. If necessary, adjust the pH to 4.8 by the addition of sodium hydroxide. The pH should be checked each day before use.

(c) Cellulase–buffer solution.

Weigh 20 g cellulase plus 0.1 g of chloramphenicol into a 2 litre flask and add 1 litre of buffer solution, shake and incubate at 40 °C for at least 1 hour in order to dissolve completely. Transfer solution to Zippette container.

(d) Neutral detergent solution.

Dissolve 93 g disodium ethylene diamine tetra-acetate dihydrate (EDTA) and 34 g sodium borate ($Na_2B_4O_7,10H_2O$) in distilled water by gently heating; to this solution add 150 g sodium lauryl sulphate and 50 cm^3 of 2-ethoxy ethanol (ethylene glycol mono-ethyl ether). Dissolve 22.8 g disodium hydrogen phosphate (anhydrous) in distilled water separately. Mix the two solutions and dilute to 5 litres. Adjust the pH if necessary to lie within the range 6.9–7.1.

(e) Silicone anti-foaming agent, available from BDH Chemicals Ltd. (An aqueous emulsion containing 30% w/w silicone.) Shake 2.5 cm of this solution with 250 cm^3 of distilled water.

(f) Chloramphenicol available from Sigma Chemical Co., London.

(g) α-amylase (Ex *Bacillus subtilis* type XI-A) available from Sigma Chemical Co. Ltd, Cat No A1278. Dissolve 2 g α-amylase in 90 cm^3 distilled water. Filter, and to the filtrate add 10 cm^3 2-ethoxy ethanol; store at 5 °C.

Procedure

(1) Remove the oil from 0.5 g of sample, ground to pass 1 mm sieve, either by Soxhlet extraction or by stirring, settling and decanting three times with petroleum ether.

(2) Transfer the air-dried fat-free sample into a 150 cm^3 flask, add 25 cm^3 of neutral detergent and 0.5 cm^3 of the diluted antifoam solution. Connect to the refluxing apparatus, bring to the boil and digest the sample for half an hour. During this period ensure the sample and solution are well mixed to avoid overheating.

(3) Turn off the heat, add 25 cm^3 of cold neutral detergent to each digest plus 2 cm^3 of α-amylase. Heat to boiling and maintain for a further 30 minutes. Swirl the flasks occasionally and keep the samples boiling steadily and well mixed during the digestions.

(4) Filter immediately into a sintered glass pyrex tube, wash thoroughly at least three times with 20 cm^3 of hot distilled water. (Removal of the NDF reagent by thorough washing is essential.)

(5) When filtration is complete, dampen a suba-seal, and carefully push it onto the bottom surface of the sinter. Add 25 cm^3 hot water (80 °C) and 2 cm^3 α-amylase. Mix with sample and allow to stand for 15 minutes.

(6) Remove the suba-seal and filter off the solution. Replace the suba-seal and Zippette 30 cm^3 of buffered cellulase into the tube, cap the tube and shake so that the fibre is mixed with the cellulase solution.

(7) Incubate at 40 ± 2 °C for 24 hours. During this period shake the solution morning and evening.

(8) Remove the cap and suba-seal, wash any fibre back into the filter tube,

remove the cellulase solution by suction with a vacuum pump and wash the indigestible fibre with very hot distilled water. Finally wash it twice with $20\,cm^3$ of acetone.

(9) Dry the residue in an oven overnight (16 hours), at $100 \pm 2\,°C$. Cool in a desiccator and weigh.

(10) Ignite at 550°C for 4h. Cool and re-weigh. Calculate the percentage of indigestible organic matter.

(11) Independently determine the percentage of total ash.

Calculation of results

The percentage of indigestible organic matter and percentage of total ash are calculated on 100% DM basis.

NCD = 100 − (% indigestible organic matter + total ash).

NOTES ON CELLULASE ENZYME

Cellulase storage

Store in a col dry atmosphere in a refrigerator. Instructions are normally written on the container.

Precautions when using cellulase

Cellulase is a very fine powder and care should be taken when using this type of enzyme. It is advisable that disposable gloves and a face mask are worn when there is contact with the enzyme solution.

Certain people are very sensitive to cellulase (compare with enzyme washing washing powders).

Cellulase buffer solution

This solution is made up daily as required.

Reference: Dowman, M.G. and Collins, F.C. (1982).

References

AOAC 10TH EDITION (1965). Methods 29.039 and 43.012

BOLTON, W. (1962). *Proceedings XIIth World's Poultry Congress*, **2**, 38

BOLTON, W. and BLAIR, R. (1974). *Poultry Nutrition*. Bulletin 174. Ministry of Agriculture, Fisheries and Food. HMSO; London

BURDETT, B.M. and LAWS, B.M. (1979). *Food intake regulation in poultry*, p. 405. Ed. Boorman and Freeman, British Poultry Sciences, Edinburgh

CARPENTER, K.J. and CLEGG, K.M. (1956). *Journal of Science of Food and Agriculture,* **7**, 45

CHRISTIAN, K.R. (1971). *Field Station Record Div. Pl. Ind. CSIRO (Aust.),* **10**, 29

CLANCY, M.L. and WILSON, R.K. (1966). *Proceedings Xth International Grassland Congress, Helsinki,* p. 445

DLVB (1971). *Energetische Futterbewertung und Energienormen,* VIB Deutscher Landwirtschafts verlag; Berlin

DOWMAN, M.G. and COLLINS, F.C. (1977). *Journal of the Science of Food and Agriculture,* **28**, 1071

DOWMAN, M.G. and COLLINS, F.C. (1982). *Journal of the Science of Food and Agriculture,* **33**, 689

EC REGULATION 72/199/EEC (1982). *OJ L123/6,* 25th September, 1972

FISHER, C. (1982). *Energy values of poultry compound feeds. Occ. Pub. No. 2,* Poultry Research Centre; Roslin, Midlothian

FISHER, C. (1983). *Report on a Ring Test to evaluate the proposed EEC Equation for the declaration of ME values, poultry. Occ. Pub. No. 3,* Poultry Research Centre; Roslin, Midlothian

GOERING, H.H. and VAN SOEST, P.J. (1970). *Forage fiber analysis. Agricultural Handbook No. 379,* USDA; Washington

HARTEL, H. (1979). *Proceedings 2nd European Symposium on Poultry Nutrition,* p. 6

MAFF (1976). *Energy Allowances and Feeding Systems for Ruminants, Technical Bulletin 33.* HMSO; London

MORGAN, C.A. and WHITTEMORE, C.T. (1982). *Animal Feed Science and Technology,* **7**, 387

MORGAN, C.A., WHITTEMORE, C.T. and COCKBURN, J.H.S. (1984a). *Animal Feed Science and Technology,* **11**, 11

MORGAN, C.A., WHITTEMORE, C.T., PHILLIPS, P. and CROOKS, P. (1984b). *The Energy Value of Compound Foods for Pigs.* Edinburgh Sch. Agric.

MORGAN, D.E. and PIGOTT, A. (1978). *Report to ADAS Nutrition Chemists Investigations Committee.* MAFF; London

MORGAN, D.J., COLE, D.J.A. and LEWIS, D. (1975). *Journal of Agricultural Science,* **84**, 7

SIBBALD, I.R. (1976). *Poultry Science,* **55**, 303

SAC (1973). *Official, Standardised and Recommended Methods of Analysis, Society of Analytical Chemists,* 2nd Ed., p. 160

THE FEEDINGSTUFFS (SAMPLING AND ANALYSIS) REGULATIONS (1982). HMSO; London

TILLEY, J.M.A. and TERRY, R.A. (1963). *Journal of the British Grassland Society,* **18**, 104

UKASTA/ADAS/COSAC (1985). *Prediction of energy values of compound feed.* The report of an UKASTA/ADAS/COSAC Working Party. MAFF; London

VAN DER HONING, Y. (1980). *Proceedings 8th Symposium on Energy Metabolism of Farm Animals,* p. 315–318. Ed. L.E. Mount. EAAP Pub. No. 26; Butterworths; London

WAINMAN, F.W., DEWEY, P.J.S. and BOYNE, A.W. (1981). *Feedingstuffs Evaluation Unit, Rowett Research Institute, Third Report 1981.* Department of Agriculture and Fisheries for Scotland; Edinburgh

WAINMAN, F.W., DEWEY, P.J.S. and SMITH, J.S. (1982). *Proceedings 9th Symposium on Energy Metabolism of Farm Animals,* p. 116–119. Ed. Ekern and Sundstol. EAAP Pub. No. 29, Agricultural University of Norway; Norway

WISEMAN, J. and COLE, D.J.A. (1983). In *Recent Advances in Animal Nutrition— 1983,* p. 65. Ed. W. Haresign. Butterworths; London

II

Fibre in Animal Feeds

2

DEFINITION OF FIBRE IN ANIMAL FEEDS

P.J. VAN SOEST
Cornell University, Ithaca, NY, USA

The concepts regarding the role of fibre in animal and human foods have undergone a considerable revolution in the past ten years. The concern over the lack of dietary fibre in the human diet and the relation to disease (Burkitt, 1973) has elicited much research on the composition and effect of fibre in human and animal diets. This development had the effect of bringing fibre back into the main stream of nutritional research and out of the province of ruminant nutrition where it has resided so long. As a result the definitions, methods and standards for fibre have had to be modified, and they may yet evolve more.

Historically crude fibre has been the standard for more than a century, since the time of Wolff (1856) and Henneberg and Stohmann (1860). However, other procedures were current in the UK at the Cirencester Agricultural College (Voelcker, 1852; 1861) that trace back to the original cell wall maceration procedures of Einhof (1806). These values correspond closely to modern neutral detergent fibre (NDF) values (*Table 2.1*).

The relevance of this history is to appreciate the logic and definition that promoted the crude fibre standard for so long. Nineteenth century chemical science discovered the constant composition of pure chemical substances: for fibre the standard was cellulose or pure carbohydrate. Crude fibre (which is largely cellulose) therefore prevailed over the macerated fibre of Einhof which had a variable and mixed composition. Early chemists carefully corrected crude fibre for

Table 2.1 COMPARISON OF THE ESTIMATES OF FIBRE CONTENT OF FEEDSTUFFS BY THE EINHOF (1806) MACERATION TECHNIQUE WITH THAT FOR NEUTRAL DETERGENT FIBRE (NDF) AND CRUDE FIBRE

Feed	Einhof maceration (g/kg)	NDF (g/kg)	Crude fibre (g/kg)
Barley	213	190	57
Oats	328	320	108
Potatoes	56	47	24
Rye	220	220	22
Wheat	138	140	26
Hay[a]	430	400–550	250–300

(Van Soest, Fadel and Sniffen, 1979; Van Soest, 1982)
[a]Mixed clover and grasses

55

protein and ash, and checked its composition for pure carbohydrate (Horsford, 1846).

There was, however, another concept derived from early studies (Tyler, 1975), namely that fibre represented the indigestible matter of plant foods. Since acidic and alkaline digestion occurs in the digestive tract, why not mimic this in the chemical isolation of fibre? Hence, the sequential extraction by acid and alkali of the crude fibre method is in a sense a nineteenth century version of an *in vitro* procedure. It should be remembered that at the time no concept of enzymology existed.

The defects of the concepts and methodology of crude fibre became apparent through Henneberg's (1860–1864) research. Crude fibre estimations did not recover all of the indigestible matter. Lignin and what later came to be called hemicellulose were largely dissolved. Furthermore, ruminants and other large animals (horses) could digest much of the cellulosic matter, though it was not understood how they did it. In the case of human and monogastric nutrition, the original assumptions remained until recently, despite minor attacks (Williams and Olmsted, 1936). Generally, fibre was regarded as inert and non-nutritive, and exerting little more effect than dilution of the diet.

However, it was in ruminant nutrition that most of the newer concepts and developments in methodologies arose. Methods for lignin and cellulose in forages appeared (Armitage, Ashworth and Ferguson, 1948; Crampton and Maynard, 1938); the normal acid fibre (NAF) developed out of the work of Norman (1935), the hemicellulose and pectin fractions, as well as total cell wall, from work by Paloheimo and Paloheimo (1949), Harwood (1954) and Gaillard (1958). The difficulty with most of these methodologies was their length and tediousness, and the high nitrogen contents that often contaminated them. The NAF offered rapidity of laboratory determination but suffered particularly from protein contamination. These problems were considerably reduced with the advent of detergent methods of isolation (Van Soest, 1963).

Most of these represented attempts at the isolation and determination of plant cell wall which was regarded as fibre, a concept that seemed to satisfy a definition appropriate to ruminants. However, in the case of pectin an anomaly arose. Pectin is a part of the cell wall, but ruminants digest it rapidly and completely. Since most of it is not covalently linked to the rest of the plant cell wall, it dissolves in neutral chelating systems, including neutral detergent, and also gels in the digestive tract. The result is that plant cell wall is not synonymous with dietary fibre for ruminants, which is currently regarded as an insoluble matrix that has important physical effects in the rumen and upon rumen fermentation (Balch, 1971).

Some (see for example, Fonnesbeck and Harris, 1979) have regarded pectin as a part of the nutritional fibre even though it is potentially soluble. This is parallel to the development in human nutrition that generally regards soluble non-starch polysaccharides (gum) as dietary fibre.

Current definitions of fibre

The agreement among human nutritionists to recognize as dietary fibre those polysaccharides and related substances that are resistant to mammalian digestive enzymes, has brought most of the gums, that are hardly fibrous in a physical sense, under the definition (Trowell, 1977). This concept is currently accepted in the field.

This definition follows the concept of Southgate (1969) that so-called fibrous carbohydrates are not digested by mammalian enzymes and do not yield sugar as a metabolite, and are thus called *unavailable*. This does not mean that unavailable carbohydrates do not yield energy to the monogastric animal, since volatile fatty acids are the major fermentation products and are well absorbed by man and other animals (McNeil *et al.*, 1978; Argenzio and Southworth, 1974). In this sense virtually all carbohydrates are unavailable to ruminants that require massive gluconeogenesis.

Thus, the practical definition of nutritional fibre diverges between ruminants and non-ruminants. The soluble polysaccharides, pectin, galactans, beta glucans, etc., share a fate in the rumen that is not easily distinguished from that of starch or sucrose. They differ in their fate if they can escape ruminal digestion. On the other hand, all unavailable carbohydrate is passed to the lower tract in non-ruminants. If starch escapes the upper tract of non-ruminants it will be fermented in the caecum and colon like the other unavailable carbohydrates. However, this fermentation will tend to produce more lactic and propionic acids (Argenzio and Southworth, 1974; Hintz *et al.*, 1971; Kern *et al.*, 1973; 1974) as it does in the rumen of high-grain fed ruminants. Lactose intolerance in humans is a parallel phenomenon.

The higher acidity and rapid fermentation associated with starch has placed an emphasis on the physical qualities of insoluble fibre, which include particle size and buffering capacity. For these reasons the practical definition of nutritional fibre for the ruminant is limited to insoluble substances from the plant cell wall which is essentially neutral detergent fibre (NDF).

Differences in animal species

For non-ruminants, the soluble substances resistant to mammalian digestive enzymes have significance because they can feed the microbial fermentations in the caecum and colon just as well if not better than the insoluble fibre. This occurs because most of those soluble carbohydrates ferment faster than cellulose or hemicellulose. A further factor here is that the soluble and insoluble components differ in their overall physiological effects and are worth distinguishing as independent dietary entities. Physical effects of coarse insoluble fibre are probably important in the non-ruminant for some of the same reasons as they are for the ruminant.

For example, in human digestion balances at Cornell (Heller *et al.*, 1980) finely ground bran fed at the same level as coarse bran failed to alleviate constipation, caused an increase in faecal dry matter and failed to significantly influence retention times in contrast to coarse bran. Grinding produced an increase in density and a reduction in water-holding capacity of the faeces (*Table 2.2*).

The effect of grinding upon passage is opposite to that observed in ruminants. However, man and other non-ruminants do not have the filtering mechanisms by which coarse fibre is retained. Fine grinding increases effective density of the feed and increases the capacity of the gut to contain fine fibre. Thus passage is apparently slowed. On the other hand, in the human study fine grinding decreased microbial yield (Van Soest, 1981b). Not all non-ruminant animals are equal in their capacity to consume, digest, or accomodate dietary fibre. Anatomically, they can be subdivided into those in which the primary fermentation site is the caecum (rodents) and those that are colonic fermenters (most large mammals). There are

Table 2.2 FAECAL COMPOSITION AND PASSAGE CRITERIA IN HUMANS

Component	Coarse bran	Fine bran	Solka floc	Cabbage	Control
Particulate marker (Cr):					
First appearance (h)	33	41	31	44	40
Peak time (h)	46[a]	61	54	65	69
Mean retention (h)	52[d]	68	60[b]	74	74
Large bowel retention (h)	18	22	22	28	25
Liquid marker (PEG)					
First appearance (h)	32	32	30[a]	39	40
Peak time (h)	45[c]	59	53	68	63
Mean retention (h)	39[d]	64	57[b]	71	69
Large bowel retention (h)	18[c]	27	25	25	31
Stool characteristics					
Wet weight (g/week)	1097[d]	893	957	772	718
Total water (g/week)	846[d]	665[b]	772[d]	599	545
Water content (g/kg)	773[d]	736[d]	743	768[c]	747
No. stools/week	7.7[d]	7.1[d]	6.9[d]	6.0[a]	5.2
Increase in metabolic N (g/kg fibre)	57	37	24	42	—

(After Heller *et al.*, 1980).
Values with superscript letters are significantly different from controls as follows:
a, $P<0.05$; b, $P<0.01$; c, $P<0.001$; d, $P<0.0001$

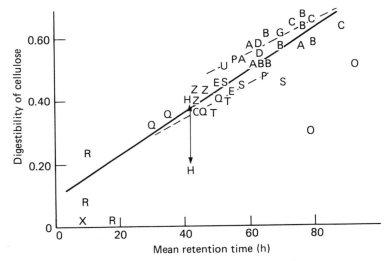

Figure 2.1 The relationship between cellulose digestion and mean retention in 46 species of herbivorous mammals fed grass-type fibre. Most herbivores have sacculated colons (or sacculation in other parts of the digestive tract), which presumes that fibre is a normal constituent of their diet (Van Soest *et al.*, 1983). The capacity of ruminants (A, B, C, D, G, S) to digest fibre is somewhat greater than non-ruminants, but in both cases smaller species are at a disadvantage (Van Soest, 1982). The range of values for man (H) are shown in the figure by the vertical arrows (Van Soest *et al.*, 1978), and are somewhat less than the figure for pigs (U) (Ehle *et al.*, 1982) but more than that for rodents (R). Some large animals (Hippo O, Rhino P) may approach the capacity of ruminants, but Elephants (E), Equids (Q, Z) and Tapirs (T) are less efficient. The overall correlation between retention and digestion is 0.86; the individual correlation for ruminants is 0.69 and that for non-ruminants is 0.78

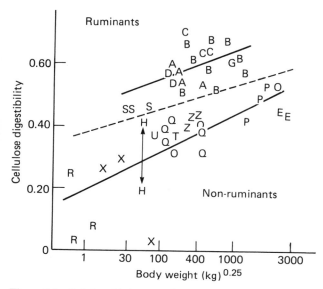

Figure 2.2 Relationship between body weight and cellulose digestibility in various animal species fed grass-based diets. A range of values on high fibre graminaceous cereal diets observed in man (H) is designated by arrows. For a description of the symbols see *Figure 2.1*. The broken line separates ruminants from non-ruminant species. The regression equation for ruminants denoted by upper solid line is Y = 42.0 + 4.0 X (r = 0.56; 21 degrees of freedom) and that for non-ruminants (lower solid line) is Y = 14.5 + 5.4 X (r = 0.74; 24 degrees of freedom)

some pregastric fermenters (colobine monkeys, hippopotamus, vole, hamster) that have some ruminant-like features (Demment and Van Soest, 1983).

The major factors affecting digestive capacity for fibrous carbohydrate are gastrointestinal retention and body size (*Figures 2.1* and *2.2*). Body size, to a degree, determines retention because metabolic requirements, and therefore intake, are a function of (body weight)$^{0.75}$. Thus smaller animals must consume a daily intake at a larger proportion of their body weight than larger ones (Van Soest, 1982). Gastrointestinal size is directly proportional to body weight (Parra, 1978). This leads to the predicted association between digestive capacity for fibre and body size (*Figure 2.2*).

Some smaller animals may not digest any fibrous carbohydrate at all. This may occur if passage rate exceeds the potential growth rate of fibre-digesting bacteria. The survival of micro-organisms in a chemostat requires their reproduction (Tempest, 1970), and therefore if passage is faster than their growth rate, bacteria will be eliminated from the system. Growth rate of cellulolytic bacteria is set by the physicochemical characteristics of the substrate that determines its potential degradability, and slower-degrading substrates place more stringent time limitations upon their survivability in a system. For example in the Cornell human study cellulolytic organisms were eliminated in certain individuals by feeding crystalline cellulose of very low fermentation rate. Also people with inherently fast transits do not harbour bacteria capable of digesting crystalline cellulose and probably also methanogens (Van Soest, 1981b; 1983).

Variation in fibre

Many factors influence the composition and quality of plant fibre. Species of plant determines the fundamental proportions of pectin, hemicellulose and lignin in the plant cell wall. The most important division is between monocotyledonous and dicotyledonous plants, largely represented in our agriculture by grasses and legumes, respectively. Some of the contrasting characteristics are listed in *Table 2.3*. Legume fibre is comparatively low in hemicellulose and high in pectin, while

Table 2.3   COMPOSITION OF FRESH FORAGES (g/kg DM) AND DIGESTION COEFFICIENTS OF CELL WALL COMPONENTS

	Grass		*Lucerne*		*Red clover*	
	DM[a]	*D*[b]	*DM*	*D*	*DM*	*D*
Hemicellulosic components						
Soluble in 0.5% ammonium oxalate: (pectin)						
Anhydrous galacturonic acid	26	0.95	50	0.95	50	0.97
Anhydrous arabinose	18	0.99	6	0.97	5	0.97
Soluble in 5% and 24% KOH:						
Anhydrous galactose	13	0.85	5	0.82	6	0.78
Anhydrous glucose	19	0.88	9	0.91	8	0.96
Anhydrous arabinose	35	0.86	8	0.85	6	0.95
Anhydrous xylose	85	0.72	58	0.33	36	0.28
Cellulose residue:						
Anhydrous arabinose	3	0.60	4	0.79	4	0.60
Anhydrous xylose	6	0.38	3	0.29	1	0.00
Pure cellulose	211	0.79	222	0.41	182	0.60
Aldobiuronic acid of xylan	73	0.79	73	0.52	71	0.64
Lignin	62	0.002	91	0.004	70	0.01
Organic matter	900	0.72	894	0.59	888	0.71

(Gaillard, 1962).
[a]DM, Content of individual components expressed as g/kg DM original forage organic matter
[b]D, Digestibility of individual component

pectin in grasses is so low as to be practically unimportant. At the same overall forage digestibility or stage of growth, legume cell walls contain roughly twice the lignin content with a corresponding lower digestibility of fibre, which is compensated for in the whole plant by a lower cell wall content relative to grasses. The relatively low lignification of grass cell wall implies a high digestibility, realized only in ruminants and some other large herbivores. Many non-ruminants may digest legume fibre better than that of grain because of the faster rate of fermentation of the legume (Keys, Van Soest and Young, 1969).

The amount of fibre and its composition may vary between different plant parts. Generally leaves are lower in fibre than stems, but this relative contrast is generally much greater in legumes than in grasses since the leaves of the latter contain considerable lignin in the ribbing which affords structural support. Differences in the physical effects of milling are also apparent. The less lignified grasses fracture into thin long sections, while the more woody stems of legumes fracture into shorter and fatter pieces. The same phenomenon is also apparent in chewing and rumination.

PLANT MATURITY AND ENVIRONMENT

The maturation of most annual or herbaceous plants is associated with an increase in the lignification of the plant cell wall. This increase is associated with an increase in toughness and rigidity, and a decrease in digestibility. Lignification is a primary variable of quality in forages that are harvested at varying degrees of immaturity, but is less variable in the fibre of plants grown to seed stage (full maturity). Thus the brans and fibrous by-products derived from cereals represent comparatively mature sources of fibre.

Lignification is also profoundly influenced by conditions of plant growth. High environmental temperatures and lack of plant stress factors allow maturity to develop faster, thereby leading to a greater rate and final extent of lignification. This is the primary reason why tropical forages are more lignified and less digestible than temperate ones. Environmental temperature tends to override other factors affecting lignification (Deinum, Van Es and Van Soest, 1968), so that in lower temperate latitudes lignification may actually decrease with age during late summer and autumn (Van Soest, Mertens and Deinum, 1978). At higher latitudes of northern Europe, daylength and light become important and temperature is less variable. This probably leads to a decline in nutritive value in the autumn due to lack of photosynthesis. However, the overall level of lignification remains low compared with some other regions of the world (Van Soest, 1982). This factor is probably why forage is capable of a greater level of animal production in northwestern Europe than it is in regions less maritime and of more southerly latitude.

LIGNIN

Crude lignin represents the collective aggregation of non-carbohydrate components of the cell wall that are insoluble in 12 M sulphuric acid. True lignin is polyphenolic but cutin (partly lipid) is a conspicuous component of the acid insoluble matter. It is a small component of the crude lignin in leaf and stem, but may be substantial in seed hulls and other specialized plant parts (Van Soest, 1982). Maillard products formed upon heat damage, and tannin–protein complexes are also isolated along with the crude lignin.

Lignin is the primary factor causing a decline in digestibility of plant cell walls with maturity. It reduces the digestibility of the cell wall carbohydrates (principally hemicellulose and cellulose) with which it is cobonded, but has no effect on the true digestibilities of cell wall components like pectin that are not co-bonded with it. Pectin and the non-cell wall polysaccharides have very high to nearly complete digestibilities (Gaillard, 1962; Bailey, 1973). Despite the differences in lignin content between legumes and grasses, the quantitative effects upon digestibility are similar. Lignin protects about 2.4–3.0 times its weight of plant cell wall from ultimate degradation (Mertens, 1973; Chandler *et al.*, 1980).

Lignin is the primary factor setting the potential extent of digestion, but it is less well correlated with rate of digestion. Most such associations are found within a species in respect to maturity, while no consistent relationships occur between species or of the same species grown in different environments which promote different degrees of lignification. For these reasons correlations between lignin content and apparent digestion of fibre are greatest with ruminants at low levels of intake since this causes digestion to approach the limits set by lignification. Increasing intake or feeding forage to non-ruminants where much available cellulosic carbohydrate is lost to digestion usually reduces the correlation of lignin with digestibility. With non-ruminants the relationship is usually insignificant.

Forage plants in general differ from woody plants (trees) in that their lignin contains significant nitrogen that does not appear to be digestible (Van Soest, 1982). This may involve peptides covalently linked to lignin, and is perhaps characteristic of vegetative plants (Lamport and Mort, 1984). The nature of forage lignins has been less investigated but they are probably more variable and differ from wood lignins (Hartley, 1978). The application of concepts from the wood and timber field must therefore be treated with caution.

The grasses, and probably all of the monocotyledonous plants as well, appear to have lignin acids (*p*-coumaric and ferulic acids) esterified to hemicellulose of the arabinoxylan type (Hartley, 1972). Cross-linking though oxidative polymerization probably occurs as the lignin matures. Alkali-cleavable lignin appears to account for the indigestibility of the cell wall in grasses (Lau and Van Soest, 1981; Hartley, 1983). These lignins are comparatively soluble and easily cleaved by cold alkali into their phenolic and carbohydrate components. This is in contrast to leguminous straws that are comparatively resistant to such treatment (Van Soest, 1981a).

Increases in digestible matter from alkali treatment of legume fibre results from the cleavage of substituent hemicellulose from the lignocellulosic complex. Cleavage of β-1-3 glycosidic linkages is important. Bonds of carbohydrate to lignin are not broken unless very high temperatures are employed and the digestibility of the insoluble lignified core tends to remain unaltered. In contrast, the attack by cold alkali is principally upon the lignin–carbohydrate linkages in graminaceous straws.

Grasses (and straws) also tend to accumulate silica as a secondary protective factor for plant cell wall, while legumes and many other dicotyledonous plants tend to calcify. The siliceous factor is also quite susceptible to alkaline treatments (Jackson, 1977).

Chemical structure and uniformity of fibre

CELLULOSES

Historically the classification of cellulose was based on chemical uniformity, being polyglucan with β-1-4 linkage. This structure is associated with high insolubility and refractoriness to many reagents that will dissolve most other polysaccharides. However, the isolation of cellulose is always based on delignification and refluxing with normal acid. The product always includes some pentosan that cannot be completely removed without destruction of the cellulose. The insolubility of cellulose has not necessarily indicated low digestibility, since cellulose can be more digestible than the more soluble hemicellulosic fractions (*Table 2.3*).

While cellulose may have chemical uniformity as β-glucan, nutritionally it is quite variable, principally because as forage ages the lignin-to-cellulose ratio rises and digestibility declines. This factor plus the interspecific variation in physical properties leads to nutritional non-uniformity. Rates of digestion also vary and probably reflect modifications at the macromolecular level that are not entirely understood. Native celluloses vary widely in fermentation rates, which may be limited by crystallinity or some kind of cross-linking. Most forage or vegetable celluloses are apparently uncrystalline, as they exist in the plant cell wall but may become crystallized when the branched hemicelluloses and three-dimensional lignin components are removed by chemical treatment. This allows cellulose chains to come together. Drying may be an important part of the process to elicit such crystallization (Van Soest, 1973). Thus it is possible through delignification to obtain a cellulose that is both more potentially digestible, but which ferments at a slower rate than the available part of the original native carbohydrate.

HEMICELLULOSE

This polysaccharide fraction is neither chemically nor nutritionally uniform. Containing a variety of sugars and linkages (Bailey, 1973) it also is co-associated with lignin; in fact, all demonstrated linkages between lignin and carbohydrate are between lignin and arabinoxylan. Hemicellulose has been classed as a water-insoluble polysaccharide that is released with acid or alkali. However, delignification results in a soluble gum-like material (Sullivan, Phillips and Routley, 1960) that has similar properties to pectin. Since both hemicellulose and pectin have some common sugars and linkages, that is probably why Southgate (1969) combined them together as acid soluble polysaccharides.

While this combination may be satisfactory for unlignified vegetables, the distinction for lignified plants depends whether these pentose and uronic acid-containing polymers are lignified. Such lignification renders them insoluble and partially indigestible, whereas the soluble unlignified fraction is completely digestible. This distinction is also relevant to alkali-treated grasses and straws where freed hemicellulose becomes pectin-like in its physical and digestive behaviour.

The digestibility and rate of digestion of hemicellulose is, in part at least, greater than that of cellulose, sufficiently so that fewer differences exist between ruminants and non-ruminants in their abilities to ferment it (Keys, Van Soest and Young, 1969). While this is true, hemicellulose (or a fraction of it) is the most likely polysaccharide to escape ruminal digestion. The hemicellulose also contains some of the least degradable carbohydrates of forage. These reside in the micellular pentosans that are so difficult to remove in the preparation of cellulose (Lyford, Smart and Matrone, 1963) and acid-detergent fibre. Comparison of the digestibilities of the sugar components show that the arabinose and xylose 'contamination' of cellulose are less digestible than the cellulosic glucose or the pentosans in the more soluble portion of the hemicellulose (*Table 2.3*). Further, arabinose is always more digestible than xylose within any fraction even though they are probably a part of the same arabinoxylan polymer.

The micellular pentosans may be more linear and exist in a crystalline state in the cellulose matrix, while the arabinose (furanosidic) links are more easily broken by chemical or digestive action than the pyranosidic linkages of glucosan and xylan. The more soluble pentosans are probably more branched, which renders them less crystalline and more susceptible to mild acid extraction (Gaillard, 1965; Dekker, 1976). These are some possibilities that might account for the non-uniform behaviour of hemicellulosic subfractions.

Physical properties and physiological effects

The macromolecular association and large scale physical structure are major factors determining some of the nutritional properties of fibre. These factors are more evident in the less digested fibres when the insoluble fibrous matrix persists in the digestive tract. In this instance, chemical composition may have little to do with quality of fibre.

If fibre is fermented extensively, intrinsic factors (crystallinity, hydration, etc.) influencing fermentation rate become important and lignification becomes a dominant factor limiting extent of degradation. Since some of the hemicellulose is generally more rapidly fermented than cellulose, this ratio also becomes important. Indigestible matter increases the rate of passage, so that highly fermented sources such as vegetables, pectin, etc., have little effect on transit time (Wrick *et al.*, 1983).

On the other hand, gellable and any very bulky fibre sources have major effects in the upper digestive tract for non-ruminants. These effects include delay of gastric emptying, in contrast to speeding up of the rate of passage in the lower gut by bulky indigestible fibres. Gums and other gellable sources like pectin rank above insoluble fibres for passage in the upper tract, but have less effect upon the colon and caecum. The effect of insoluble fibres to increase rate of passage and turnover in the lower tract is usually larger than the delay in the upper tract caused by delay in gastric emptying. Thus the overall effect of fibre to increase passage masks more complex procedures in particular segments of the digestive tract. Recent human digestion studies have disclosed that hydrated gellable fibre promotes more complete absorption of vitamins (Roe *et al.*, 1978) and possibly minerals (Van Soest, unpublished) while the spike of glucose absorption is oblated, with a lower insulin response (Heaton *et al.*, 1978; Jenkins *et al.*, 1983). This effect is sufficient to allow the treatment of diabetics with dietary fibre (Anderson, 1983).

This insulin-sparing effect may not be entirely accounted for by physical effects in the upper tract, since most soluble fibres (particularly pectin and β-glucan gums) are fermented in the human colon, giving rise to volatile fatty acids that are largely absorbed (McNeil, Cummings and James, 1978). Propionate and probably isoacids are antiketogenic, supply gluconeogenesis and spare insulin. The VFA absorption supplies a replacement for carbohydrate calories that may modify metabolism.

The feeding of fibre to pigs results in a leaner carcass (Kass *et al.*, 1980), and up to a point increases efficiency (Kornegay, 1981) because of the moderating effects of fibre in the digestive tract. The pigs fed low fibre diets had heavier caecal and colonic mucosa. The VFA (probably butyrate) may stimulate colonic growth (Stevens, 1978), in much the same way as they stimulate rumen development of calves (Warner and Flatt, 1965).

Fibre may have positive effects in non-ruminant diets. Discussions of a requirement for fibre have even been made in human nutrition. The positive effects may include maintenance of normal gastrointestinal microflora and the buffering effect of fibre through cation exchange (McBurney, Van Soest and Chase, 1983; Van Soest, McBurney and Russell, 1984).

The feeding of fibre at increasing levels elicits diminishing returns in animal response, at least in those animals with some capacity for herbivory. The postulated effect for humans (Spiller, 1983) and other non-ruminants (Foose, 1982) are shown in *Figure 2.3*. There is some evidence of optimal fibre levels for humans, pigs and ruminants.

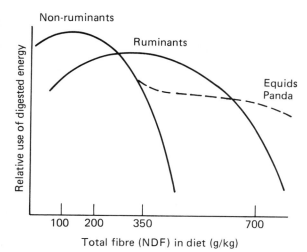

Figure 2.3 The effect of dietary fibre level on the relative efficiency of ruminants and non-ruminants (Van Soest, 1982). The optimum fibre level for non-ruminants is less than that for ruminants because microbial protein is lost in the faeces of non-ruminants, and the digestive capacity for fibrous carbohydrates is less than in the ruminant. The maximum efficiency of ruminants is less than non-ruminants because potentially digestible sugars and starches are prefermented in the rumen with consequent energy loss. A few non-ruminants such as the panda (Dierenfeld *et al.*, 1982) tolerate very high fibre diets by being able to ingest very high intakes to achieve their requirements from non-fibre components. This results in fast passages and low fibre digestibilities. Ruminants fail on low quality very high fibre diets because of the cost of rumination and other digestive work required to eliminate lignified fibre from their complex gut

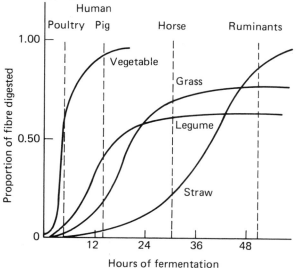

Figure 2.4 The relationship between typical fermentation curves for various sources of fibre and the average retention of residues in the respective fermentative compartments of some animals. Short retentions leading to potential digestion of carbohydrate of <0.20 tend to lead to loss of fermentive capacity if the generation time of the respective digestive micro-organisms exceeds the gut turnover time

EFFICIENCY, PASSAGE AND RATE OF FERMENTATION

Overfeeding of fibre leads to colonic dilution and inefficiency. Ruminants lose energy through rumination and gastrointestinal work (Webster, 1978), that associates heat increment with level of fibre in the diet. Since insoluble, undigested fibre increases rate of passage in all animals, faecal caloric loss becomes associated with passage (*Figure 2.1*). Passage also turns the microbial fermentation over more rapidly leading to increased microbial efficiency and in turn to increased loss of faecal nitrogen in the form of microbial matter (Mason, 1979; Van Soest, 1981b).

The competition between passage and the rate of fermentation sets the limits of fermentive digestion, the extent of which is determined by the retention time in the fermentive compartment (Mertens, 1973). This model can provide a basis for classifying herbivorous animals relative to their digestive capacities, if their average retention time is considered (*Figure 2.4*).

Very rapidly fermentable sources like gums and pectin may not be fermentive in some animals with sufficiently fast passage, and this is probably the case for poultry. Animals with somewhat longer retention (humans, pigs) can ferment pectin and vegetable celluloses very well but are quite limited on more lignified sources of fibre. Generally, leguminous sources of fibre are utilized by non-ruminants better than those of grasses because of more rapid fermentability in the time range up to 24 h.

EXCHANGE AND HYDRATION

Factors affecting fermentation rate include the hydratability and exchange of plant fibres, probably through the attraction and attachment by microflora (Stotsky, 1980; Marshall, 1980; Van Soest, McBurney and Russell, 1984). Hydration is associated with physical structure. Larger particle size, with more pore spaces but also with hydrophilic ionizable groups on the surface of the plant fibre, lead to cation exchange and binding of minerals. Exchange probably promotes wetability of fibre surfaces and is correlated with hydration capacity (Van Soest and Robertson, 1976).

Fibre sources that are high in pectin (with many uronic acid groups) have more water holding capacity and exchange. These include beet pulp and citrus pulp, which are also rapidly fermentable (*Table 2.4*). Beet pulp, brewers' and distillers' grains have undergone considerable heat treatments creating Maillard products in the form of artefact lignin and this reduces their protein availability. An extreme case is coffee grounds that are so badly heat damaged that there is no remaining available nitrogen. All nitrogen in coffee grounds is recovered in acid detergent fibre and lignin, and the entire fibre fraction is indigestible (Van Soest *et al.*, 1984b).

Soya bean hulls represent a case of no real lignification. Apparent lignin content is largely due to cutin. As a result soya bean hulls tend to fragment into a mush when they ferment, and in ruminants this leads to ruminal loss and escape (D.R. Mertens, unpublished). Thus soya bean hulls show a high depression in digestibility with level of intake (Van Soest, Fadel and Sniffen, 1979). Distillers' and brewers' grains encounter rumen escape, a factor which has promoted their use as a means of protein 'by-pass' for ruminants. However, this feature, together with their fineness of particle size, leads to loss of potential digestible fibre from the rumen.

Table 2.4 COMPOSITION AND PROPERTIES OF SOME SOURCES OF DIETARY FIBRE (VAN SOEST *ET AL.*, 1984; VAN SOEST AND ROBERTSON, 1976)

	NDF (g/kg)	ADF (g/kg)	Lignin[a] (g/kg)	Cation exchange (mEq/100 g NDF)	Proportion N unavailable	Proportional fermentation rate/h
Beet pulp	510	330	20	70	0.11	0.15
Citrus pulp	230	220	30	249	0.11	0.20
Soya bean hulls	670	500	20	37	0.02	0.15
Brewers' grains	460	240	60	29	0.13	0.10
Distillers' grains	500	170	50	35	0.20	0.10
Coffee grounds[b]	740	650	200	—	0.99	0.00
White clover	300	250	40	249	0.05	0.20
Lucerne	400	310	70	90	0.10	0.12
Cocksfoot	630	370	40	28	0.01	0.08

[a]Inclusive of heat-damaged artefacts.
[b]Coffee grounds analyse about 12% crude protein, none of which is available. Cellulose and hemicellulose are similarly totally indigestible in this material.

A similar problem exists with alkali-treated straws where the removal of lignin as a cross-linking factor also leads to particulate disintegration and ruminal loss so that *in vitro* fibre digestibilities do not match those obtained by *in vivo* balance (Berger, Klopfenstein and Britton, 1979). The incorporation of adequate coarse fibre of some lignification would probably reduce the escape of potential digestible cellulose from the rumen. The ruminant animal has evolved on partially lignified (cross-linked) fibrous foods (Foose, 1982). Retention in the rumen is regulated by rumination that is required to comminute lignified fibrous particles.

Conclusions

The definition of dietary fibre will vary according to the digestive anatomy of the respective animal species. A definition that will suffice for many non-ruminants is: the polymers of plant origin that are resistant to their digestive enzymes. However, the response of non-ruminants to fibre will vary according to their capacity to handle it.

The soluble gum-like substances (pectin, β-glucans, etc.) are of significance for non-ruminants and influence gastric emptying and absorption, but may also ferment in the colon and caecum.

Ruminants depend on insoluble fibre and its physical properties to promote rumination and rumen function. Lignification is important since it determines physical character, but also reduces the availability of fibrous carbohydrates associated with it.

Physical properties of hydration, particle size and exchange are important for both ruminants and non-ruminants, and can be easily altered by processing and chemical treatments.

It is not possible to account for all of the nutritional effects of fibre through chemical analysis of carbohydrate components because of the importance of physical properties that are determined by association at the macromolecular level.

The negative influence of lignification upon the biodegradability and solubility of hemicellulose and cellulose is a primary reason for the nutritive non-uniformity of these polysaccharides.

References

ANDERSON, J.W. (1983). In *Fibre in Human and Animal Nutrition*, p. 183. Ed. G. Wallace and L. Bell. The Royal Society of New Zealand, Bulletin 20; Wellington, New Zealand

ARMITAGE, E.R., ASHWORTH, R. DE B. and FERGUSON, W.S. (1948). *Journal of Science of the Chemical Industry*, **67**, 241

ARGENZIO, R.A. and SOUTHWORTH, M. (1974). *American Journal of Physiology*, **228**, 454

BAILEY, R.W. (1973). In *Chemistry and Biochemistry of Herbage*, **1**, 157. Ed. G.W. Butler and R.W. Bailey. Academic Press; London

BALCH, C.C. (1971). *British Journal of Nutrition*, **26**, 383

BERGER, L., KLOPFENSTEIN, T. and BRITTON, R. (1979). *Journal of Animal Science*, **49**, 1317

BURKITT, D. (1973). *British Medical Journal*, **1**, 274

CHANDLER, J.A., JEWELL, W.J., GOSSETT, J.M., VAN SOEST, P.J. and ROBERTSON, J.B. (1980). *Journal of Biotechnology and Bioengineering*, **10**, 93

CRAMPTON, E.W. and MAYNARD, L.A. (1938). *Journal of Nutrition*, **15**, 383

DEINUM, B.A., VAN ES, J.H. and VAN SOEST, P.J. (1968). *Netherlands Journal of Agricultural Science*, **16**, 217

DEINUM, B. (1976). In *Carbohydrate Research in Plants and Animals*, p. 29. Wageningen, The Netherlands

DEMMENT, M. and VAN SOEST, P.J. (1983). *Body Size, Digestive Capacity, and Feeding Strategies of Herbivores*, pp. 1–66. Winrock International; Morrilton, AR

DEKKER, R.F.H. (1976). In *Carbohydrate Research in Plants and Animals*, p. 43. Wageningen, The Netherlands

DIERENFELD, E.S., HINTZ, H.F., ROBERTSON, J.B., VAN SOEST, P.J. and OFTEDAL, O.T. (1982). *Journal of Nutrition*, **112**, 636

EHLE, F.R., JERACI, J.L., ROBERTSON, J.B. and VAN SOEST, P.J. (1982). *Journal of Animal Science*, **55**, 1071

EINHOF, H. (1806). *Annales Ackerbaues*, **4**, 627

FONNESBECK, P.V. and HARRIS, L.E. (1970). *Proceedings of W. Sect. American Society of Animal Science*, **21**, 153

FOOSE, T. (1982). Thesis, University of Chicago, Chicago, IL.

GAILLARD, B.D.E. (1958). *Journal of the Science of Food and Agriculture*, **9**, 170

GAILLARD, B.D.E. (1962). *Journal of Agricultural Science (Cambridge)*, **59**, 369

GAILLARD, B.D.E. (1965). *Phytochemistry*, **4**, 631

HARTLEY, R.D. (1972). *Journal of the Science of Food and Agriculture*, **23**, 1374

HARTLEY, R.D. (1978). *American Journal of Clinical Nutrition*, (Suppl.), **31**, S590

HARTLEY, R.D. (1983). *Journal of the Science of Food and Agriculture*, **34**, 29

HARWOOD, V.D. (1954). *Journal of the Science of Food and Agriculture*, **5**, 270

HEATON, K., HABER, G.B., BURROUGHS, L. and MURPHY, D. (1978). *American Journal of Clinical Nutrition*, (Suppl.) **31**, S280

HELLER, S.N., HACKLER, L.R., RIVERS, J.M., VAN SOEST, P.J., ROE, D.A., LEWIS, B.M. and ROBERTSON, J.B. (1980). *American Journal of Clinical Nutrition*, **33**, 1734

HENNEBERG, W. and STOHMANN, F. (1860–64). *Begrundung einer rationellen Futterung der Wiederkauer*, Vols 1 and 2. Schwetschke und Sohne; Braunschweig

HINTZ, H.F., ARGENZIO, R.A. and SCHRYVER, H.F. (1971). *Journal of Animal Science*, **33**, 992

HORSEFORD, E. (1846). *Philosophical Magazine Series 3*, **79**, 365

JENKINS, D.J.A., LEEDS, A.R., GASSULL, M.A., COCHET, B. and ALBERTI, K.G. (1977). *Annals of Internal Medicine*, **86**, 20

JENKINS, D.J.A. (1983). *Diabetes Case*, **6**, 155

KASS, M.L., VAN SOEST, P.J., POND, W.G., LEWIS, B. and MCDOWELL, R.E. (1980). *Journal of Animal Science*, **50**, 175

KERN, D.L., SLYTER, L.L., WEAVER, J.M., LEFFEL, E.C. and SAMUELSON, G. (1973). *Journal of Animal Science*, **37**, 463

KERN, D.L., SLYTER, L.L., WEAVER, J.M. and OLTJEN, R.R. (1974). *Journal of Animal Science*, **38**, 559

KEYS, J.E., VAN SOEST, P.J. and YOUNG, E.P. (1969). *Journal of Animal Science*, **29**, 11

KORNEGAY, E.T. (1981). *Journal of Animal Science*, **53**, 138

JACKSON, M.A. (1977). *Animal Feed Science and Technology*, **2**, 105

LAMPORT, D.T.A. and MORT, J.A. (1984). *Advances in Carbohydrate Chemistry and Biochemistry* (in press)

LAU, M.M. and VAN SOEST, P.J. (1981). *Animal Feed Science and Technology*, **6**, 123

LYFORD, S.J. JR., SMART, W.W.G. JR. and FLATRONE, G. (1963). *Journal of Nutrition*, **79**, 105

MARSHALL, K.C. (1980). In *Microbial Adhesion to Surfaces*, Chapter 9, p. 187. Society of Chemists in Industry; London

MASON, V.C. (1979). *Zeitschrift für Tierphysiologie, Tierernährung und Futtermittelkunde*, **41**, 131

MCBURNEY, M.I., VAN SOEST, P.J. and CHASE, L.E. (1983). *Journal of the Science of Food and Agriculture*, **34**, 910

MCNEIL, N.I., CUMMINGS, J.H. and JAMES, W.P.T. (1978). *Gut*, **19**, 819

MCQUEEN, R.E. and NICHOLSON, J.W.G. (1979). *Journal of the Association of Official Agricultural Chemists*, **62**, 676

MERTENS, D.R. (1973). PhD Thesis. Cornell University, Ithaca, NY

MERTENS, D.R. (1977). *Federation Proceedings*, **36**, 187

NORMAN, A.G. (1935). *Journal of Agricultural Sciences*, **25**, 529

PALOHEIMO, L. and PALOHEIMO, I. (1949). *Maataloustieteellinen Aikakauskirja*, **21**, 1

PARRA, R. (1978). In *The Ecology of Arboreal Folivores*, p. 205. Ed. G.G. Montgomery. Smithsonian Institution Press; Washington, DC

ROE, D.A., WRICK, K., MCLAIN, D. and SOEST, P.J. VAN (1978). *Federation Proceedings*, **37**, 756

SOEST, P.J. VAN (1963). *Journal of the Association of Official Agricultural Chemists*, **46**, 825

SOEST, P.J. VAN (1973). *Federation Proceedings*, **32**, 1804

SOEST, P.J. VAN (1981a). *Agriculture and Environment*, **6**, 135

SOEST, P.J. VAN (1981b). In *Banbury Report 7: Gastrointestinal Cancer: Endogenous Factors*, p. 61. Cold Spring Harbor Laboratory

SOEST, P.J. VAN (1982). *Nutritional Ecology of the Ruminant*. O&B Book Inc.; Corvallis, OR

SOEST, P.J. VAN, FADEL, J.G. and SNIFFEN, C.J. (1979). *Proceedings of Cornell Nutrition Conference*, p. 63. Syracuse; NY

SOEST, P.J. VAN, FOX, D.G., MERTENS, D.R. and SNIFFEN, C.J. (1984). *Proceedings of Cornell Nutrition Conference*, p. 121. Syracuse; NY

SOEST, P.J. VAN, MCBURNEY, M.I. and RUSSELL, J. (1984). *Proceedings of California Animal Nutrition Conference*, p. 53. Pomona; CA

SOEST, P.J. VAN, JERACI, J.L., FOOSE, T., WRICK, K. and EHLE, F. (1983). In *Fibre in*

Human and Animal Nutrition, p. 75. Ed. G. Wallace and L. Bell. The Royal Society of New Zealand, Bulletin 20; Wellington, NZ

SOEST, P.J. VAN, MERTENS, D.R. and DEINUM, B. (1978). *Journal of Animal Science*, **47**, 712

SOEST, P.J. VAN and ROBERTSON, J.B. (1976). *Proceedings of the Miles Symposium of the Nutrition Society, Canada*, p. 13. Halifax; Nova Scotia

SOUTHGATE, D.A.T. (1969). *Journal of the Science of Food and Agriculture*, **20**, 331

SOUTHGATE, D.A.T. (1976). *Determination of Food Carbohydrates*. Applied Science Publishers Ltd; London

SPILLER, G. (1983). In *Fibre in Human and Animal Nutrition*, p. 9. Eds. G. Wallace and L. Bell. The Royal Society of New Zealand, Bulletin 20; Wellington, NZ

STEVENS, C.E. (1978). *American Journal of Clinical Nutrition*, (Suppl.), **31**, S161

STOTZKY, G. (1980). In *Microbial Adhesion to Surfaces*, p. 231. Society of Chemists in Industry; London

SULLIVAN, J.T., PHILLIPS, T.G. and ROUTLEY, D.G. (1960). *Journal of Agriculture and Food Chemistry*, **8**, 152

TEMPEST, D.W. (1970). In *Methods in Microbiology*, **2**, 259. Eds. J.R. Norris and D.W. Ribbons. Academic Press; London

TROWELL, H. (1977). *Nutrition Reviews*, **35**, 6

TYLER, C. (1975). *Nutrition Abstracts and Reviews*, **45**, 1

VOELCKER, A. VON (1852). *Journal of the Royal Agricultural Society of England*, **13**, 385

VOELCKER, A. VON (1861). *Journal of the Royal Agricultural Society of England*, **22**, 382

WARNER, R.G. and FLATT, W.P. (1965). In *Physiology of Digestion in the Ruminant*, p. 24. Ed. R.W. Dougherty *et al.* Butterworth, Washington

WEBSTER, A.J.F. (1978). *World Review of Nutrition and Dietetics*, **30**, 189

WILLIAMS, R.S. and OLMSTEAD, W.H. (1936). *Journal of Nutrition*, **11**, 433

WRICK, K.L., ROBERTSON, J.B., SOEST, P.J. VAN, LEWIS, B.A., RIVERS, J.M., ROE, D.A. and HACKLER, L.R. (1983). *Journal of Nutrition*, **113**, 1464

WOLFF, E. (1856). *Die naturgesetzlichen Grundlagen des Ackerbaues*, p. 953. 3rd ed., Otto Weigand; Leipzig

3

INFLUENCE OF FIBRE ON DIGESTIBILITY OF POULTRY FEEDS

W.M.M.A. JANSSEN
Spelderholt Centre for Poultry Research and Extension, Beekbergen, The Netherlands
and
B. CARRÉ
Station de Recherches Avicoles, INRA, Nouzilly, France

Characteristics of fibre in feedstuffs

Two sorts of fibre can be distinguished: water-insoluble fibre and water-soluble fibre.

Water-soluble fibre corresponds chemically with the non-starchy water-soluble polysaccharides. These polysaccharides can be extracted by cold or hot water and precipitated by ethanol or acetone. Water-soluble fibre includes β-$(1\rightarrow3)$ glucan from barley, arabinoxylan from rye, highly methylated pectin from fruits, galactomannan from leguminosae such as guar gum, polysaccharides from algae such as alginate (linear chains of mannuronic acid and guluronic acid) or carrageenan (linear chain of sulphated galactose).

Water-insoluble fibre consists of insoluble cell wall material and is composed of cellulose, hemicellulose, pectic substances, protein and lignin. The proportions of these components vary widely, depending on the origin of the plant material.

Plant cell walls can originate from 'primary' cells or from secondary cells; the 'primary' cells being little differentiated and the 'secondary' cells highly differentiated. This differentiation of cells leads to the deposition of additional cell wall components such as cellulose, hemicelluloses and lignin. The 'primary' cells are encountered, for example, in the starchy endosperm of cereal grains or in the parenchyma of roots and cotyledons. The 'primary' cell walls of the starchy cereal endosperm are characterized by a very low cellulose and lignin content and by the weakness of their ultrastructure.

The bulk of hemicelluloses of cereal 'primary' cell walls, which are mainly arabinoxylan, are readily soluble in water or dilute alkali (Mares and Stone, 1973). The 'primary' cell walls of dicotyledonous plants, such as cell walls located in cotyledon seeds of leguminosae, are characterized by the presence of pectic substances, which can represent up to 70 per cent of the cell wall material (Brillouet and Carré, 1983; Carré, Brillouet and Thibault, 1985). The pectic substances are made of a rhamnogalacturonan backbone bearing branched side chains mainly composed of arabinose and galactose (Aspinall, 1980). Pectic substances can sometimes be extracted by hot water, but, very often, the use of chelating agents such as ethylenediamine tetracetic acid (EDTA) or ammonium oxalate diluted in hot water, is needed to extract them (Aspinall *et al.*, 1967).

The hemicellulose compounds of dicotyledonous 'primary' cell walls can be xyloglucan or type II arabinogalactan (Albersheim, 1976). The cellulose content of dicotyledonous 'primary' cell walls varies generally from 5 per cent (Carré, Brillouet and Thibault, 1985) to 30 per cent (O'Neill and Selvendran, 1980); their lignin content is normally very low (Brillouet and Carré, 1983).

The secondary plant cells are, for instance, the xylem vascular bundles, the pericarp cells of cereal grains, the palisade cells and the spool-shaped cells located in hulls of leguminosae seeds. The ultrastructure of secondary cell walls is generally more resistant than the ultrastructure of 'primary' cell walls. Cellulose, a major component of secondary cell walls, exhibits a high crystallinity in these types of cell walls. The major hemicellulose polymers of secondary walls are generally xylan-related polysaccharides such as arabinoglucuronoxylan of wheat bran (Brillouet *et al.*, 1982) or glucuronoxylan of soya bean hull (Aspinall, Hunt and Morrison, 1966). Pectic substances are generally very minor components in secondary cell walls. Lignin, which is a characteristic component of secondary cell walls, rarely exceeds 20 per cent of the cell wall material. The importance of lignin arises from the possibility of connections between lignin and polysaccharides through ether or ester linkages (Neilson and Richards, 1982; Chesson, Gordon and Lomax, 1983; Scalbert *et al.*, 1984). These linkages probably explain the resistance of cell wall to bacterial degradation (Morrison, 1972).

METHODS OF ANALYSIS OF FIBRE

Crude fibre

This is the commonest method of determination of fibre and is defined as the residue after successively boiling of the material in 0.26 N sulphuric acid and 0.23 N potassium hydroxide. The major component of crude fibre is cellulose, together with residual hemicelluloses (5–40 per cent of crude fibre), residual protein (2–10 per cent of crude fibre) and lignin (10–50 per cent of crude fibre; 50–100 per cent of the original lignin) (Rinaudo and Chambat, 1976).

Acid detergent fibre

Acid detergent fibre content (ADF) (Van Soest, 1963) is in general similar to crude fibre content (Baker, 1977; Nyman *et al.*, 1984). Like crude fibre, ADF may be contaminated by non-cellulosic polysaccharides (2–50 per cent of ADF) and by residual protein (1–25 per cent of ADF) (Bailey and Ulyatt, 1970; Rinaudo and Chambat, 1976; Theander and Aman, 1980). Both ADF and crude fibre may also be contaminated by condensed tannins (Theander *et al.*, 1977); probably the highest residual protein contents in ADF and crude fibre correspond to the presence of highly insoluble protein–tannin complexes. ADF and lignin contents in sorghums are positively correlated with tannin content (ITCF, 1982).

Cellulose

Cellulose can be determined more accurately by the measurement of glucose, specifically liberated by hydrolysis with concentrated sulphuric acid according to the method of Saeman *et al.* (1954).

Table 3.1 CRUDE PROTEIN, CRUDE FIBRE, NDF[a] AND ER[b] CONTENTS OF SOME IMPORTANT FEEDINGSTUFFS (% OF DRY MATTER)

	Maize	Wheat	Barley	Cassava root	Wheat bran	Lucerne	Sunflower meal	Rapeseed meal	Soya bean meal	Pea	Field bean	White lupin (Lutop)
Crude protein	10.4	13.7	11.0	3.1	15.9	16.9	35.5	37.7	54.0	25.6	29.1	45.0
Crude fibre	2.3	2.6	4.6	4.5	11.0	28.2	25.2	15.4	4.1	5.5	8.2	12.6
NDF	10.5	12.7	17.7	11.2	47.3	46.1	42.5	26.1	8.5	8.7	13.9	18.3
ER	10.3	11.8	16.7	12.7	44.7	45.0	40.2	32.0	17.1	13.1	17.4	30.9

[a]Neutral detergent fibre, obtained after destarching with a gelatinization step at 95°C (10 min) followed by α-amylase (from *Bacillus subtilis*; 3 × crystallized; Boehringer Mannheim) treatment (1 h; 50°C in water). Residues are recovered and rinsed by centrifugation (40000 g) and not corrected for ash.
[b]Enzymatic residue measured as the residue of pronase and α-amylase treatments (Brillouet and Carré, 1983), recovered and rinsed by centrifugation (40000 g). Not corrected for ash.

Water-insoluble fibre

The total water-insoluble fibre can be estimated either by neutral detergent fibre (NDF) determination (Van Soest and Wine, 1967) or by isolation of the water-insoluble residue after enzymatic removal of protein and starch (Hellendoorn, Noordhoff and Slagman, 1975; Asp *et al.*, 1983; Brillouet and Carré, 1983). NDF and enzymatic methods generally lead to similar results, except with legumes, where the values for enzymatic residue (ER) are considerably higher than for NDF (*Table 3.1*). The cell wall pectic substances present in leguminosae are responsible for this difference as these substances are dissolved by EDTA present in the solution of Van Soest's method (Bailey and Ulyatt, 1970; Schweizer and Würsch, 1979; Carré, Brillouet and Thibault, 1985).

Prediction of feeding value of feeds and feedstuffs

In the past, several methods have been developed to predict the metabolizable energy (ME) value of feeds and feedstuffs for poultry.

METHODS BASED ON DIGESTIBLE NUTRIENTS

If complete information on chemical composition and on digestibility of the nutrients is available, ME can be estimated very accurately with formulae of the following basic form (Janssen, 1976):

$$\text{ME} = a \times \text{digestible CP} + b \times \text{digestible F} + c \times \text{digestible NFE} + d \times \text{digestible CF}$$

where CP, F, NFE and CF represent respectively 1 g or 1 per cent of digestible crude protein, fat, nitrogen-free extract and crude fibre. A great variety of energy equivalents are found in the literature (Janssen, 1976). For many years in the USA and Japan, nutritive value was based on total digestible nutrients (TDN) which is defined as follows:

$$\text{TDN} = \text{digestible CP} + \text{digestible (NFE} + \text{CF)} + 2.25 \text{ digestible F}$$

According to Carpenter (1962), Fraps and Carlyle found the following relation between 'effective digestible nutrients' (EDN) and ME:

$$\text{ME (MJ)} = 17.6 \text{ EDN}$$

The only difference between TDN and EDN is that EDN does not take crude fibre into account. Fraps and Carlyle considered the direct contribution of crude fibre to the nutritive value of a feed or feedstuffs as negligible. Nowadays, ME is used as a measure of feeding value for poultry all over the world.

METHODS BASED ON CHEMICAL ANALYSIS

Many attempts have been made to find (simple) relations between ME and one or more chemical or physical characteristics of a feedstuff, a group of feedstuffs or even all feedstuffs. In this connection, Carpenter (1961) pointed out '... In general it is true that the higher the fibre content the lower the metabolizable energy, and for a range of materials, such as wheat offals from a generally similar process, there is a high negative correlation between fibre content and metabolizable energy so that analysis for this alone in a sample can allow a more accurate assessment of its energy value'.

Table 3.2 THE RELATIONSHIP BETWEEN DIGESTIBILITY (%) OF THE ORGANIC MATTER (Y) AND CRUDE FIBRE (X) CONTENT (% IN DRY MATTER)

Cattle	: Y = 90.1 − 0.879 X
Rabbit	: Y = 96.48 − 1.551 X ($r = -0.899$)
Poultry	: Y = 86.06 − 1.995 X ($r = -0.746$)

Mitchell (1942) found a good correlation between crude fibre and the digestibility of organic matter of feedstuffs (*Table 3.2*). This table shows that the negative influence of crude fibre on digestibility increases from cattle to rabbits and from rabbits to poultry. Mitchell (1942) calculated the following equation based on 60 experiments of Fraps:

$$Y = 86.90 - 3.624 \ X$$
Y = metabolizability (%) of the gross energy and
X = % crude fibre in dry matter

At Spelderholt Institute the following equations having an important relationship with fibre were found (Janssen *et al.*, 1979):

	ME (MJ/kg DM) =
(1) Wheat products	16.539 − 0.769 CF%
(2) Barley and barley products	12.88 − 0.378 CF% + 0.038 starch%
(3) Oats and oat products	12.43 − 0.25 CF% + 0.489 F%
(4) Maize products	17.74 − 0.144 CP% + 0.057 F% − 0.668 CF%
(5) Rice products	19.91 − 0.371 CP% − 0.534 CF% + 0.218 F%
(6) Soya beans (in meal feeds)	11.59 − 0.247 CF% + 0.257 F%
(7) Soya beans (in pelleted feeds)	11.03 − 0.233 CF% + 0.345 F%
(8) Tapioca root meal	16.96 − 0.182 ash% − 0.431 CF%
(9) Groundnut products	12.85 − 0.164 ash% − 0.199 CF% + 0.267 F%
(10) Sunflower seed products	16.73 − 0.791 ash% − 0.245 CF% + 0.249 F%
(11) Cotton seed products	9.01 − 0.133 CF% + 0.182 F%

Carpenter (1961) derived the following equation from digestion data of 17 feedstuffs and compound feeds:

$$\text{ME(MJ/kg 90\% dry matter)} = 0.945 \times \text{gross energy } (1 - \frac{\text{CF\%}}{21})$$

The residual standard deviation was 1.339 MJ/kg. Substituting the average gross energy of the wheat products (17.25 MJ/kg) used in the experiments by Carpenter and Clegg (1956) the following equation was derived:

$$\text{ME(MJ/kg dry matter)} = 18.113 - 0.862 \text{ CF\%}$$

This shows a good agreement with Spelderholt's equation for wheat products. The difference in intercept can be explained by the fact that Carpenter and Clegg (1956) determined the 'classical' ME and Janssen *et al.* (1979) determined the ME value corrected for nitrogen retention.

Thomke (1960) found the following relationships for oats:

$$\text{ME(MJ/kg dry matter)} \quad = 16.694 - 0.481 \text{ CF\% (for laying hens)}$$
$$\text{or} = 16.234 - 0.498 \text{ CF\% (for young chicks)}$$

Hill, Carew and Renner (1957) studied the feeding value of five maize by-products of different quality. The variability in ME could be explained by the variability in fat and fibre content. An increase in 1 per cent fat (ether extract) and crude fibre resulted in an increase in ME of 0.368 MJ/kg and a decrease of 1.059 MJ/kg respectively. For cottonseed meals Watts and Davenport (1971) found:

$$\text{ME(MJ/kg)} = 3.552 + 0.097 \text{ CP\%} + 1.254 \text{ F\%} - 0.20 \text{CF\%}$$

Comparing this with the Spelderholt equation, the calculated ME values differ considerably. This is because of the very large value for fat in the equation of Watts and Davenport (1971).

The majority of these relationships clearly demonstrate the important influence of crude fibre on the feeding value of the products concerned, but also the large differences in regression-coefficients sometimes found for the same groups of products.

In order to improve the predictive value of fibres, several methods of fibre measurement have been tested (Carré, Prévotel and Leclercq, 1984): 48 mixed diets of different composition were analysed and their ME value determined. From this study it appears that the enzymatic residue (ER) content was the most efficient fibre indicator for predicting ME value. Crude fibre, acid detergent fibre (ADF) and neutral detergent fibre (NDF) exhibited similar efficiency. Lignin content had the poorest predictive value. The best equation was as follows:

$$\text{ME(MJ/kg air-dry matter)} = 0.914 \text{ GE (MJ/kg)} - 0.061 \text{ \% CP}$$
$$- 0.041 \text{ \% ER}^{1.5}$$
$$(n = 48; \text{r.s.d.} = 0.20)$$

Analytical ranges of the 48 diets were on air-dry matter basis:

ME (MJ/kg)   : 9.43 − 14.66
Crude protein (%)   : 7.4 − 27.3
Fat (%)   : 1.6 − 11.0
Crude fibre (%)   : 1.5 − 8.4
ER (%)   : 7.6 − 22.2

The equation was in good agreement with a theoretical equation which was established on the principle that the water-insoluble fibres act as diluter of available nutrients.

THE RELATIONSHIP OF CRUDE FIBRE WITH THE DIGESTIBILITY OF THE NUTRIENTS IN SPELDERHOLT EXPERIMENTS

Due to the indirect nature of this relationship many regression coefficients are incomprehensible from a physiological point of view. In the Spelderholt experiments digestibility of the nutrients was also determined in order to gather more information on the basis of these relationships.

In these experiments mature Araucana × White Leghorn cocks were used. Every day a moderately restricted amount of food was given to each bird. The experimental feeds consisted of a basal diet and mixtures of the basal diet + the feedstuff under study. The method was based on quantitative faeces collection. A detailed description has been given by Terpstra and Janssen (1976).

The results give data on by-products of wheat, barley, rice, tapioca and cottonseed. In *Tables 3.3* to *3.7* the percentages of crude fibre, crude protein, fat, nitrogen free extract (NFE) and starch of the products concerned are shown. Also metabolizable energy (MJ/kg DM) and the digestibility of crude fibre, crude protein, fat and NFE are presented. The digestibility of starch was not determined. For the wheat, rice and cottonseed products, some experimental diets were given both in meal and in pellet form in order to study the effect of pelleting. These results are also included.

Wheat by-products

The products studied varied widely in composition as the ranges of crude fibre (1.0–13.9 per cent), of NFE (57.3–75.8 per cent) and of starch (9.7–66.1 per cent) demonstrate (*Table 3.3*).

The positive contribution of crude fibre to the feeding value is small since its digestibility is generally very low. The negative influence is substantial as there is a strong negative relationship with the digestibility of protein, fat and NFE. The last relationship is probably due to the high negative correlation between crude fibre and starch as with increasing fibre content, the percentage of starch in NFE diminishes (87 to 17 per cent for products 1 and 10 respectively).

There is a large pelleting effect on the digestibility of fat, a moderate effect on the digestibility of protein and only a minor effect on the digestibility of NFE. It is worth noting that the effects of pelleting are larger at the higher crude fibre contents.

Table 3.3   WHEAT BY-PRODUCTS

Product			Composition (% in dry matter)			
		Crude fibre	Crude protein	Fat	NFE	Starch
1		1.0	17.8	3.5	75.8	66.1
2		1.8	24.6	5.5	65.1	50.6
3		3.3	20.9	5.3	67.4	45.8
4		3.6	20.9	7.5	64.3	ND
5		3.9	20.2	7.9	63.7	37.8
6		8.6	20.1	6.2	60.0	25.0
7		9.4	18.9	4.5	60.5	ND
8		11.1	18.6	5.2	58.8	16.9
9		13.3	18.0	4.0	57.5	ND
10		13.9	16.5	5.0	57.3	9.7

Product	Pellet/meal	ME content (MJ/kg DM)	Digestibility (%)				
1	P	16.07	8.4	87.1	89.0	93.1	ND
2	P	15.04	13.2	81.7	87.7	86.6	
3	P	13.78	10.0	81.9	86.7	77.4	
4	P	13.46	2.6	81.2	82.4	73.4	
5	P	13.41	5.7	79.4	88.8	72.2	
6	P	10.19	8.4	77.6	76.2	51.3	
7	P	9.00	5.8	74.1	63.4	49.5	
8	P	7.93	10.3	71.7	65.8	37.1	
9	P	6.44	10.4	69.7	31.3	32.2	
10	P	5.84	14.0	70.6	54.5	22.5	
4	M	13.24	−14.2	80.8	80.2	73.4	
7	M	8.59	4.0	68.2	38.2	50.5	
9	M	5.41	10.6	57.6	7.8	28.9	
	$\bar{P}^a$	9.70	6.3	75.0	59.0	51.7	
	$\bar{M}^a$	9.08	0.3	68.8	42.1	50.9	

	Relationship with crude fibre		
		r	r.s.d.
Metabolizable energy (MJ/kg DM)	$= 16.43 - 0.76\,CF(\%)$	0.998	0.25
Protein digestibility (%)	$= 85.6 \; - 1.15\,CF(\%)$	0.97	1.58
Fat digestibility (%)	$= 97.2 \; - 3.53\,CF(\%)$	0.90	8.76
NFE digestibility (%)	$= 94.5 \; - 5.00\,CF(\%)$	0.99	2.82
Starch (%)	$= 60.0 \; - 3.86\,CF(\%)$	0.96	5.88

[a]Based on samples 4, 7 and 9.
ND, not determined

Barley by-products

The barley products showed considerable variation in composition (crude fibre NFE and starch) (*Table 3.4*). The positive contribution of crude fibre to feeding value is negligible in these products. The high digestibility of crude fibre of produc 1 is probably an artefact and due to the very low crude fibre level. At this level it i practically impossible to determine digestibility accurately. In this series o products no clear relationship was found between crude fibre and digestibility of fa and protein. There was a high negative correlation between crude fibre and th NFE digestibility, due to the negative correlation between the starch content i

Table 3.4 BARLEY BY-PRODUCTS (PELLETED)

Product	Composition (% in dry matter)				
	Crude fibre	*Crude protein*	*Fat*	*NFE*	*Starch*
1	0.7	8.2	1.4	88.7	79.7
2	3.1	15.1	4.7	74.0	55.4
3	4.6	11.1	2.2	79.6	59.7
4	5.1	21.9	7.6	60.6	32.6
5	8.4	11.9	3.1	71.5	48.2
6	12.0	12.9	4.3	64.8	32.3
7	15.9	11.9	3.9	61.8	25.8
8	19.4	11.7	4.3	56.0	16.5

Product	*ME content (MJ/kg DM)*	Digestibility (%)				
1	15.69	24.6	67.4	73.1	92.6	ND
2	13.77	7.4	71.4	85.9	79.9	
3	13.39	6.0	69.5	60.1	82.0	
4	12.25	−6.0	73.9	85.9	64.7	
5	11.64	−2.8	71.3	76.0	73.6	
6	9.49	−4.6	69.3	81.0	58.6	
7	7.97	−0.5	69.2	76.2	49.5	
8	6.10	−1.1	65.7	71.4	36.5	

	Relationship with crude fibre		
		r	*r.s.d.*
Metabolizable energy (MJ/kg DM)	= 15.48 − 0.48 CF(%)	0.99	0.42
NFE digestibility (%)	= 90.4 − 2.69 CF(%)	0.95	6.07
Starch (%)	= 67.7 − 2.77 CF(%)	0.88	10.80

ND, not determined

NFE and crude fibre. The starch content decreased from 90 per cent in the product with the lowest crude fibre content to 29 per cent in the product with 19.4 per cent crude fibre. As a consequence there is a strong negative correlation between crude fibre and ME ($r = 0.99$).

Rice by-products

In this series the positive contribution of fibre seems to be larger than in the other series. The first three products had particularly high crude fibre digestibilities (*Table 3.5*). However, in absolute terms the fibre contribution is of only minor importance, as the levels in these three products were very low and subject to the inaccuracies already mentioned. The other products with considerably higher crude fibre content showed slightly positive to slightly negative digestibilities of fibre.

The relationship between crude fibre and feeding value is worse than that for wheat and barley. An explanation for this may be that the large variability in fat content is not related to fibre content. The negative correlation between crude fibre and ME seems to be due to the rather strong relationship between crude fibre and the digestibility of NFE and to the relationship between crude fibre and the starch content of NFE.

Table 3.5 RICE BY-PRODUCTS

Product			Crude fibre	Composition (% in dry matter) Crude protein	Fat	NFE	Starch
1			0.5	8.1	0.7	90.2	88.6
2			0.9	11.4	6.4	77.7	71.0
3			1.1	8.4	2.3	87.0	82.5
4			2.9	13.5	12.7	65.2	53.9
5			6.8	14.9	14.0	56.4	37.0
6			9.1	16.0	20.3	45.8	22.2
7			11.2	13.3	14.6	48.7	27.1
8			14.1	19.9	1.7	44.8	15.9
9			15.0	16.4	1.3	49.2	24.3

Product	Pellet/ meal	ME content (MJ/kg DM)	Digestibility (%)				
1	P	16.84	77.6	83.8	88.0	98.5	ND
2	P	16.61	32.1	79.1	90.0	94.3	
3	P	16.72	23.9	79.6	81.3	97.8	
4	P	16.15	6.3	73.9	90.2	88.2	
5	P	13.64	−8.1	65.8	85.7	75.8	
6	P	13.60	1.7	62.0	87.2	62.8	
7	P	11.94	2.4	67.9	86.7	62.1	
8	P	5.36	−7.0	52.5	15.8	35.1	
9	P	6.74	7.9	62.7	25.9	54.0	
7	M	11.90	6.4	60.5	87.1	63.6	
9	M	6.42	4.2	61.2	21.3	52.3	
	P̄[a]	9.34	5.2	65.3	56.3	58.0	
	M̄[a]	9.16	5.3	60.8	54.2	58.0	

	Relationship with crude fibre			r		r.s.d.
Metabolizable energy (MJ/kg DM)	= 17.92 − 0.71 CF(%)			0.94		1.55
Protein digestibility (%)	= 80.6 − 1.59 CF(%)			0.91		4.59
NFE digestibility (%)	= 99.7 − 3.71 CF(%)			0.96		6.41
Starch (%)	= 77.4 − 4.45 CF(%)			0.92		11.37
Starch (%)	= 88.2 − 10.85 CF(%) + 0.43 CF (%)^2			0.98		6.48

[a]Based on samples 7 and 9.
ND, not determined

Tapioca by-products

There is a very high negative correlation between crude fibre and ME, mainly due to the relationship between crude fibre and digestibility of NFE and the relationship between crude fibre and starch in NFE (*Table 3.6*).

This experiment once again clearly shows the problems of determining the digestibility of the nutrients present at a very low level.

Cottonseed by-products

Roughly one can distinguish two groups of products (*Table 3.7*): the first group with a low fibre and high protein content (products 1–5) and the second one containing

Table 3.6 TAPIOCA BY-PRODUCTS (PELLETED)

Product	Composition (% in dry matter)				
	Crude fibre	Crude protein	Fat	NFE	Starch
1	0.1	0.5	0.1	99.2	99.3
2	4.4	3.0	0.6	86.6	75.7
3	4.6	3.2	0.6	86.5	76.2
4	5.0	3.0	0.8	85.4	74.1
5	6.3	4.1	0.9	80.5	67.2

Product	ME content (MJ/kg DM)	Digestibility (%)				
1	17.23	−1205.5	−42.2	419.1	101.7	ND
2	14.23	5.2	50.6	27.5	94.4	
3	14.00	−0.7	42.3	17.1	93.4	
4	14.05	1.6	50.3	27.7	91.9	
5	12.97	−5.0	56.6	1.6	88.6	

Relationship with crude fibre		r	r.s.d.
Metabolizable energy (MJ/kg DM)	$= 17.28 - 0.68\,CF(\%)$	0.997	0.14
NFE digestibility (%)	$= 102.3 - 2.04\,CF(\%)$	0.99	0.88
Starch (%)	$= 99.7 - 5.19\,CF(\%)$	0.999	0.75

ND, not determined.

high levels of fibre and low levels of protein (products 6–9). The digestibility of crude protein was higher in the first group with a low level of crude fibre than in the other group. The digestibility of fat is mainly regulated by the fat content. At high levels the fat was well digested, at low levels the digestibility was quite variable. No clear pelleting effects could be demonstrated.

Discussion

The influence of fibre may be based on the following effects:
1 Positive effects —digestibility of fibre and thus direct contribution to the feeding value
2 Negative effects—increasing effects on the production of endogenous material
      —diluting effect on other nutrients
      —barrier to the penetration of digestive enzymes

POSITIVE EFFECTS

Digestibility of fibre

Most data in the literature tend to demonstrate that the cellulose complex from plant feedstuffs is not digested by poultry (Bolton, 1955a; Almquist and Halloran, 1971; Vogt and Stute, 1971). The results of the experiments presented in *Tables 3.3* to *3.7* confirm these data. Recently Duke *et al.* (1984) found that adult turkeys

Table 3.7 COTTONSEED BY-PRODUCTS

Product	Composition (% in dry matter)			
	Crude fibre	Crude protein	Fat	NFE
1	12.0	41.3	6.3	33.6
2	14.3	44.3	0.8	33.1
3	16.6	44.7	1.6	30.0
4	17.1	40.8	1.6	34.1
5	18.4	44.1	1.3	30.0
6	24.6	26.2	7.6	36.3
7	25.2	27.6	7.3	34.3
8	25.9	27.0	7.1	35.0
9	26.2	26.3	6.5	35.8

Product	Pellet/ meal	ME content (MJ/kg DM)	Digestibility (%)		
1	P	8.59	−6.2	62.0	83.9	41.0
2	P	7.31	−5.3	66.7	−2.5	34.8
3	P	6.91	−11.3	70.7	54.2	30.6
4	P	7.07	−7.1	70.8	18.3	37.2
5	P	6.77	−7.2	69.9	46.4	30.1
6	P	7.24	−11.9	59.6	87.0	35.0
7	P	6.84	−11.9	59.9	88.7	34.1
8	P	6.86	−4.1	59.4	87.7	26.6
9	P	7.11	−2.0	55.9	83.9	33.3
3	M	7.17	−8.4	70.6	47.6	33.8
8	M	6.77	−8.9	58.9	89.6	31.0
$\bar{P}^a$		6.88	−7.7	65.0	71.0	28.6
$\bar{M}^a$		6.91	−8.6	64.8	68.6	32.4

	Relationship with crude fibre	r	r.s.d.
Metabolizable energy (MJ/kg DM)	= 11.53 − 0.27 CF(%)	0.93	0.32
NFE digestibility (%)	= 56.7 − 1.40 CF(%)	0.78	3.33

[a]Based on samples 3 and 8

utilized about 10 per cent of a ^{14}C labelled purified cellulose. However, the cellulose preparation used was able to form a gel (Duke *et al.*, 1984); therefore this cellulose preparation was quite different from naturally occurring cellulose which normally exhibits a high crystallinity and water insolubility.

Hemicellulosic compounds measured as 'whole pentosan' are not digested by young birds (Bolton, 1955a; Antonion, Marquardt and Cansfield, 1981). However, it has often been reported that adult birds are able to digest a substantial amount of 'whole pentosans'; but in the procedure for determining pentosans no fractionation was made to distinguish water-soluble and water-insoluble polysaccharides (Bolton, 1955a; Vogt and Stute, 1974). Carré (1983) demonstrated that the water-insoluble xylosyl polymers of white lupin cotyledon were not digested by adult cocks. So the digestible fraction of the pentosans would correspond with the water-soluble pentosans. This is supported by the observation that the highest digestibility of pentosans was found in the cereal grain with the largest proportion of endosperm (wheat) (Bolton, 1955b) in which, according to Mares and Stone (1973), the water-soluble pentosans are concentrated. Carré (1983) found that the digestibility of the water-insoluble pectic substances for adult birds was very low.

NEGATIVE EFFECTS

Added fibre

Numerous experiments have been conducted to study the influence of added fibre on the digestibility of protein and lipids. Thus, they investigated the effects due to the physicochemical properties of fibre such as water-binding capacity, cation-exchange capacity and bile acid adsorption capacity. Mostly it has been found that the addition of water-insoluble fibre has little or no effect on digestibility of protein and lipids (Kibe, Tasaki and Saito, 1964; Sibbald, 1980; Akiba and Matsumoto, 1980; Parsons, Potter and Brown, 1982; Carré, 1983).

The decrease of apparent protein digestibility sometimes observed with added fibre, might be due to an increase of endogenous losses, thus decreasing apparent digestibility (Farrell, 1981; Raharjo and Farrell, 1984).

Fibre occurring naturally in feedstuffs

Water-insoluble fibre (WIF), being undigestible, may act as a diluter of the nutrients. Carré, Prévotel and Leclerq (1984) determined several estimates of fibre (NDF, ADF, crude fibre, etc.). For 13 cereal-based diets, an average of 22 per cent of the cell wall fraction (CW) determined by the enzymatic residue method was crude fibre.

When crude fibre was substituted in the Spelderholt equation for wheat by-products by 0.22 CW, it gave the equation:

$$\text{ME (MJ/kg DM)} = 16.539 - 0.169 \text{ CW}$$

This equation indicates a slight negative ME value for cell wall material (-0.36 MJ/kg), although it is statistically not valid to extrapolate to 100 per cent CW.

Substituting crude fibre by 0.22 CW in the equation of Carpenter and Clegg (1956) the following equation, for material standardized to 90 per cent dry matter, is derived

$$\text{ME (MJ/kg 90\% DM)} = 0.945 \times \text{GE} \times \left(1 - \frac{\text{CF(\%)}}{21}\right)$$

This also gives an estimated value for cell wall content which is slightly negative but close to zero. It can be concluded that the cell wall fraction does not have any positive contribution to the energy value. An objection to this approach may be that the crude fibre content in the cell wall is based on mixed feeds used by Carré, Prévotel and Leclerq (1984). For further evidence, determination of crude fibre as well as of cell wall needs to be done in ME studies.

The plant cell walls may act as a barrier to the attack of intracellular compounds by enzymes of the gastrointestinal tract. The fibre content in wheat by-products was indicative of its origin; from the inside to the outside of the grain, fibre content increases. The higher the fibre content, the stronger the barrier effect. This latest point can explain the negative relationship between fibre and digestibility of crude protein and fat.

These effects have also been described by Saunders, Walker and Kohler (1969) using microscopic examination of plant tissues in diets and excreta.

Fibre also seems to be an indicator of the available nutrient content. For example, a highly significant negative relationship existed between crude fibre and starch level in the nitrogen free extractives of the grain by-products studied. The starch content increased from the outside part to the inside part of the grain.

Sometimes, the effect of crude fibre seems to be very complicated as described by Scheele (1983). He found an increase in digestibility of added fat when increasing the fibre content originating from sunflower seed meal or alfalfa meal in the diet, but a decrease in digestibility of the fat when the increased fibre content of the basal ration was based on wheat bran. Thus the fibre of wheat bran seems to have a negative effect on the digestibility of added fat while the fibre of sunflower seed meal and alfalfa meal seem to have a positive effect.

Conclusions

The positive contribution of fibre to the feeding value of feedstuffs for poultry seems to be of negligible importance as the cell wall fraction is undigestible.

It is strongly suggested that in several kinds of feedstuffs, fibre may be a good predictor of the feeding value. This is due to a diluting effect of the cell wall fraction and to the strong negative correlation between crude fibre content and the digestibility of crude protein and fat.

In the grain by-products studied, there also appeared to be a strong negative correlation between crude fibre and the starch content in the nitrogen free extract, probably causing the decreasing digestibility of this fraction with increasing crude fibre content.

References

AKIBA, Y. and MATSUMOTO, T. (1980). *Journal of Nutrition,* **110**, 1112

ALBERSHEIM, P. (1976). In *Plant Biochemistry*, p. 225. Ed. J. Bonner and J.E. Varner. Academic Press; New York

ALMQUIST, H.J. and HALLORAN, H.R. (1971). *Poultry Science,* **50**, 1233

ANTONION, T.C., MARQUARDT, R.R. and CANSFIELD, P.E. (1981). *Journal of Agricultural and Food Chemistry,* **29**, 1240

ASP, N.G., JOHANSSON, C.G., HALLMER, H. and SILJESTRÖM, M. (1983). *Journal of Agricultural and Food Chemistry,* **31**, 476

ASPINALL, G.O. (1980). In *The Biochemistry of Plants,* **12**, 473. Ed. J. Preiss. Academic Press; New York, London, Toronto, Sydney, San Francisco

ASPINALL, G.O., HUNT, K. and MORRISON, I.M. (1966). *Journal of the Chemical Society,* Part C, 1945

ASPINALL, G.O., BEGBIE, R., HAMILTON, A. and WHYTE, J.N.C. (1967). *Journal of the Chemical Society*, Part C, 1065

BAILEY, R.W. and ULYATT, M.J. (1970). *New Zealand Journal of Agricultural Research,* **13**, 591

BAKER, D. (1977). *Cereal Chemistry,* **54**, 360

BOLTON, W. (1955a). *Journal of Agricultural Science,* **46**, 420

BOLTON, W. (1955b). *Journal of Agricultural Science,* **46**, 119

BRILLOUET, J.M. and CARRÉ, B. (1983). *Phytochemistry,* **22**, 841

BRILLOUET, J.M., JOSELEAU, J.P., UTILLE, J.P. and LELIÈVRE, D. (1982). *Journal of Agricultural and Food Chemistry,* **30**, 488

CARPENTER, K.J. (1961). In *Nutrition of Pigs and Poultry,* p. 29. Ed. J.T. Morgan and D. Lewis. Butterworths; London

CARPENTER, K.J. and CLEGG, K.M. (1956). *Journal of the Science of Food and Agriculture,* **7**, 45

CARRÉ, B. (1983). *Thèse de 3ᵉ cycle.* Université Pierre et Marie Curie, Paris

CARRÉ, B., BRILLOUET, J.M. and THIBAULT, J.F. (1985). *Journal of Agricultural and Food Chemistry,* **33**, 285

CARRÉ, B., PRÉVOTEL, B. and LECLERCQ, B. (1984). *British Poultry Science,* **25**, 561

CHESSON, A., GORDON, A.H. and LOMAX, J.A. (1983). *Journal of the Science of Food and Agriculture,* **34**, 1330

DUKE, G.E., ECCLESTON, E., KIRKWOOD, S., LOUIS, C.F. and BEDBURY, H.P. (1984). *Journal of Nutrition,* **114**, 95

FARRELL, D.J. (1981). *World's Poultry Science Journal,* **37**, 72

HELLENDOORN, E.W., NOORDHOFF, M.G. and SLAGMAN, J. (1975). *Journal of the Science of Food and Agriculture,* **26**, 1461

HILL, F.W., CAREW JR., L.B. and RENNER, R. (1957). *Feedstuffs,* **29** (37), 84

ITCF (1982). *Le Sorgho grain. Composition Chimique et Valeur Alimentaire. Résultats récolte 1980.* Institut Technique des Céréales et des Fourrages; Paris

JANSSEN, W.M.M.A. (1976). In *Proceedings International Symposium on Computer Use in Feed Formulation.* National Renderers Association; Brussels

JANSSEN, W.M.M.A., TERPSTRA, K., BEEKING, F.F.E. and BISALSKY, A.J.N. (1979). *Feeding values for poultry,* 2nd edn. Mededeling 303. Spelderholt Institute for Poultry Research, Beekbergen; The Netherlands

KIBE, K., TASAKI, I. and SAITO, M. (1964). *Japanese Journal of Zootechnical Science,* **35**, 159

MARES, D.J. and STONE, B.A. (1973). *Australian Journal of Biological Sciences,* **26**, 793

MITCHELL, H.H. (1942). *Journal of Animal Science,* **1**, 159

MORRISON, I.M. (1972). *Journal of the Science of Food and Agriculture,* **23**, 455

NEILSON, M.J. and RICHARDS, G.N. (1982). *Carbohydrate Research,* **104**, 121

NYMAN, M., SILJESTRÖM, M., PEDERSEN, B., BACHKNUDSEN, K.E., ASP, N.G., JOHANSSON, C.G. and EGGUM, B.O. (1984). *Cereal Chemistry,* **61**, 14

O'NEILL, M.A. and SELVENDRAN, R.R. (1980). *Carbohydrate Research,* **79**, 115

PARSONS, C.M., POTTER, L.M. and BROWN, R.D. (1982). *Poultry Science,* **61**, 939

RAHARJO, Y. and FARRELL, D.J. (1984). *Animal Feed Science and Technology,* **12**, 29

RINAUDO, M. and CHAMBAT, G. (1976). *Revue française des corps gras,* **23**, 605

SAEMAN, J.F., MOORE, W.E., MITCHELL, R.L. and MILLETT, M.A. (1954). *Tappi,* **37**, 336

SAUNDERS, R.M., WALKER JR., H.G. and KOHLER, G.O. (1969). *Poultry Science,* **48**, 1497

SCALBERT, A., BRILLOUET, J.M., ROLANDO, C. and MONTIES, B. (1984). In *International Workshop on Plant Polysaccharides, Structure and Function,* Nantes, p. 164. Institut National de la Recherche Agronomique, Centre National de la Recherche Scientifique; Paris

SCHEELE, C.W. (1983). In *Proceedings of the 4th European Symposium on Poultry Nutrition, Tours.* Ed. M. Larbier. INRA; Nouzilly, France

SCHWEIZER, T.F. and WÜRSCH, P. (1979). *Journal of the Science of Food and Agriculture,* **30**, 613

SIBBALD, I.R. (1980). *Poultry Science,* **59**, 836

SOEST, P.J. VAN (1963). *Journal of the Association of Official Agricultural Chemists,* **46**, 829

SOEST, P.J. VAN and WINE, R.H. (1967). *Journal of the Association of Official Agricultural Chemists,* **50**, 50

TERPSTRA, K. and JANSSEN, W.M.M.A. (1976). *Report 101.75*, Spelderholt Institute for Poultry Research, Beekbergen; The Netherlands

THEANDER, O. and AMAN, P. (1980). *Journal of the Science of Food and Agriculture,* **31**, 31

THEANDER, O., AMAN, P., MIKSCHE, G.E. and YASUDA, S. (1977). *Journal of Agricultural and Food Chemistry,* **25**, 270

THOMKE, S. (1960). *Archiv für Geflügelkunde,* **24**, 557

VOGT, H. and STUTE, K. (1971). *Archiv für Geflügelkunde,* **35**, 29

VOGT, H. and STUTE, K. (1974). *Archiv für Geflügelkunde,* **38**, 117

WATTS, A.B. and DAVENPORT, R.F. (1971). *Poultry Science,* **50**, 1643

4

ROLE OF DIETARY FIBRE IN PIG DIETS

A.G. LOW*
*Current address: The Animal and Grassland Research Institute, Shinfield, Reading, Berks RG2 9AQ, UK.

Introduction

Contemporary pig production in western countries is heavily dependent upon diets based on grain and high-quality protein supplements, which can also be used directly to provide a nutritious diet for man. At a time when the world population is increasing, while more than half of the human race is inadequately fed, it is clear that the future of feeding pigs on high quality feedstuffs will be increasingly questioned. Attention is therefore being given to the ability of pigs to consume and use feedstuffs which are unacceptable to man. Many of these have a high content of plant cell walls and are rich in dietary fibre. The aim of this review is to consider our present knowledge about the effects that dietary fibre may have upon intake, digestion, absorption, metabolism and growth of pigs.

Definitions of dietary fibre

Many attempts have been made to define dietary fibre, but each definition is lacking in some way or other because of the variety and complexity of the chemical components of plant cell walls, their physical composition, and their metabolic effects. A widely accepted definition is 'the sum of lignin and the polysaccharides that are not digested by the endogenous secretions of the digestive tract' (Trowell *et al.*, 1976). This broad conceptual definition combines both chemical and physiological aspects of dietary fibre and does not apply directly to an entity that can be easily measured. Thus, it is important to have a practical definition which describes attributes of dietary fibre which can be analysed by existing methods. For this purpose dietary fibre may be defined as 'non-starch polysaccharides and lignin'. The importance of describing dietary fibre in as much chemical and physical detail as possible needs to be emphasized. The lack of such detailed information makes comparison of most published studies on the effects of dietary fibre very difficult. Much of the problem arises because different components of dietary fibre

*Current address: The Animal and Grassland Research Institute, Shinfield, Reading, Berks RG2 9AQ, UK.

are measured by different analytical methods. A further difficulty is that the same method used by different laboratories on samples of the same ingredient can lead to a surprisingly wide scatter of estimates.

Some properties of dietary fibre

The primary cell wall of plants contains (mg/g fresh weight) water 600, hemicellulose 50–150, cellulose 100–150, pectic substances 20–80, lipid 5–30, protein 10–20. The cellulose is a highly ordered fibrillar component while the rest is less ordered and may contain lignin. As the cell matures the cellulose and lignin content increase while the other components decrease; the botanical composition of cell walls in different parts of the plant varies greatly. The outer coat or husk of mature grain is made up in part of compressed cellulose and cuticle. The husk (about 130 g/kg of the grain) also includes the pericarp (about 40 g/kg of the grain); the outer epidermis and cell layers (containing about 320 g/kg cellulose and 350 g/kg hemicellulose) and the aleurone layer (60–70 g/kg of the grain) and containing about 560 g/kg hemicellulose, 290 g/kg cellulose and lignin.

Dietary fibre swells to a variable extent in water: for example, isolated pectin swells greatly, but when contained within a mesh of less hydrophilic substances it swells much less. The water-holding capacity is determined by the physicochemical structure of the molecule, and also by the pH and electrolyte concentration of the surrounding fluid; thus during passage through the gut, dietary fibre may swell to a very variable extent. There are several different methods of measuring the water-holding capacity of dietary fibre (centrifugation, dialysis bags, filtration) each leading to different results. Furthermore, the particle size and method of preparation of samples are important determinants of water-holding capacity, as measured in the laboratory.

The acidic sugars of polysaccharides confer ion exchange properties; several cations are known to bind to dietary fibre, but so far no anion exchange properties have been found. Adsorption of bile acids to dietary fibre, especially in the colon, is well established as a pH-dependent process, the degree of adsorption varying between types of dietary fibre.

Analytical methods

CRUDE FIBRE

This method was developed over 150 years ago as a means of measuring the indigestible fraction of feedstuffs. The sample is treated sequentially with petroleum ether, hot sulphuric acid, boiling water and alkali. It is now clear that the resultant insoluble residue contains mainly cellulose and lignin but the recovery is not always complete (Van Soest and McQueen, 1973). In spite of these shortcomings this is still an official method of measuring dietary fibre in animal feedstuffs in many countries.

NEUTRAL DETERGENT FIBRE

During this method developed by Van Soest (1963a), the sample is digested by boiling in a neutral detergent solution, filtered, dried and weighed. Although lignin and cellulose are completely recovered, there may be some loss of hemicelluloses while water soluble carbohydrates are normally completely lost during the procedure.

ACID DETERGENT FIBRE

This method, also developed by Van Soest (1963b) involves digestion by boiling in an acid detergent solution, followed by filtration, drying and weighing. This method is usually considered to provide a reasonably reliable estimate of the sum of cellulose and lignin; thus almost all other components of fibre are excluded.

NON-STARCH POLYSACCHARIDES

Following starch removal (by enzymic hydrolysis) the residue in the sample is separated into cellulose, non-cellulosic polysaccharides and lignin, followed by acid hydrolysis and colorimetric measurement of the component sugars (Southgate, 1969). A modified version of this procedure in which alditol acetate derivatives of the sugars are measured by gas-liquid chromatography has recently been developed by Englyst, Wiggins and Cummings (1982).

ENZYMIC ASSAY OF INSOLUBLE AND SOLUBLE DIETARY FIBRE

A rapid gravimetric method of enzymic hydrolysis of the sample has been described by Asp *et al.* (1983). Initial gelatinization by boiling is followed by incubation with pepsin and then pancreatin. Insoluble dietary fibre is separated by filtration and the components are then analysed in as much detail as required.

Table 4.1 TYPICAL CRUDE FIBRE AND POLYSACCHARIDE CONTENTS OF FEEDSTUFFS (AS % OF DRY MATTER)

		Crude fibre			
Alfalfa	28	Cowpea	6	White rice	0.4
Barley hay	26	Fishmeal	1	Rye straw	48
Barley grain	5	Swill (restaurant)	3	Rye grain	2
Barley screenings	9	Millet	9	Rye grass	22
Kidney bean	5	Oat hulls	29	Sorghum grain	2
Sugar beet	20	Oat grain	12	Sorghum fodder	27
Bermuda grass	30	Oat meal	4	Soyabean meal	7
Buckwheat	20	Orchard grass hay	34	Sunflower meal	14
Milk (bovine)	<0.1	Pea	10	Timothy grass	33
Citrus pulp	15	Peanut meal	14	Wheat straw	42
Clover	30	Peanut shells	65	Wheat bran	11
Maize	2	Potato (cooked)	3	Wheat grain	3
Cottonseed	18	Rapeseed	15	Yeast	3
		Rice bran	12		

	Polysaccharides content of some feedstuffs[a]			
	Starch	*Cellulose*	*Non-cellulosic polysaccharides*	*Total non-starch polysaccharides*
			Soluble *Insoluble*	
Barley grain	72.1	1.44	3.89 6.50	11.83
Oat meal	64.0	0.40	3.93 2.96	7.29
Rye grain	66.7	1.52	4.47 7.24	13.23
Wheat bran	16.4	8.17	4.25 28.60	41.06
Wheat grain	64.6	1.52	2.57 5.48	9.58

[a]Data from Englyst, Anderson and Cummings (1983).

A critical review of the many methods of dietary fibre analysis now available has been edited by James and Theander (1981).

Some examples of the crude fibre and non-starch polysaccharide content of feedstuffs are shown in *Table 4.1*. The large differences that can be seen serve to emphasize the need for an agreed standard method of chemical analysis. Reliable methods of characterizing the physical properties of dietary fibre are not well developed and are urgently needed. There are signs that the present lack of agreement on standard analytical methods may be resolved before long in clinical circles, and it is to be hoped that agricultural science will follow suit.

Fibre and the digestive processes

STOMACH

The possibility that dietary fibre may prevent the development of oesophagastric ulcers was examined by Henry (1970) who found a decreased incidence of lesions when wood cellulose was added to the diet of growing-finishing pigs. The effect was greater with coarsely-ground than finely-ground cellulose. However, the addition of unground or ground bran to barley based diets did not significantly reduce the incidence of oesophagogastric ulceration in growing pigs (Potkins, Lawrence and Thomlinson, 1984). It is probable that several factors contribute to the development of oesophagogastric ulcerations and no firm conclusions about the role of dietary fibre in this process can be drawn at present.

DIGESTIVE SECRETIONS

The effects of dietary fibre on gastric, biliary and pancreatic secretion appear to be considerable. For example, Zebrowska *et al.* (1983) and Sambrook (1981) found significantly higher outputs of all three secretions in pigs fed a barley-based diet (A) containing a wide variety of types of dietary fibre, than in the same pigs when they received a semi-purified diet containing cellulose as the only dietary fibre source (B). Although crude fibre intakes were similar in both cases, neutral detergent fibre intakes were 180 (diet A) and 50 g per day (diet B), which emphasizes the large contribution of non-cellulosic components of dietary fibre in diet A. Some of the main results of these studies are shown in *Table 4.2*.

Table 4.2   EFFECT OF DIETARY FIBRE ON GASTRIC AND PANCREATIC FUNCTION IN 40 kg PIGS DURING 24 h PERIODS

	Diet A High fibre (barley–soya)	Diet B Low fibre (starch–casein–cellulose)
Gastric juice (1)	8.0	4.0
Pepsin (units $\times$ 10^{-6})	1.47	0.76
Pancreatic juice (1)	2.18	1.20
Ash (g)	17.3	9.5
Trypsin (units $\times$ 10^{-3})	114	138
Chymotrypsin (units $\times$ 10^{-3})	84	84
Amylase (units $\times$ 10^{-3})	981	1061
Bile (1)[a]	1.72	1.17

Data from Zebrowska, Low and Żebrowska (1983) and [a]Sambrook (1981).

Certain types of soluble dietary fibre such as guar gum, pectin and sodium carboxymethyl cellulose increase the viscosity of solutions in which they are dissolved. Our recent studies on the effect of these gums on gastric emptying in growing pigs showed that while they did not affect the rate of emptying of dry matter (Rainbird, Low and Sambrook, 1983; Rainbird and Low, 1983) they did delay the rate of digesta emptying. In other words these materials reduced the rate of water passage into the duodenum, partly because of their large water holding capacity.

Further secretory responses to dietary fibre have been found by Low and Rainbird (1984) in isolated loops of jejunum in conscious growing pigs. Addition of guar gum to glucose solutions perfused through such loops increased nitrogen secretion from 35 to 67 mg/m/h (equivalent to a calculated increase in the whole small intestine from 15 to 27 g per day). The nature of the secreted nitrogen has not yet been fully elucidated but it is included in proteins and DNA. It has been estimated that 20–25 per cent of total body protein synthesis in growing pigs occurs in the gut (for example Reeds *et al.*, 1980; Simon *et al.*, 1978), and much of this is secreted into the gut lumen. These endogenous secretions are a major component of those amino acids which are not absorbed by the end of the small intestine (after which they have no further nutritional value to the pig), and have been estimated to amount to half of the amino acids in the terminal ileal digesta (Zebrowska *et al.*, 1982). Studies in other species of animals have shown that dietary fibre can increase the rate of synthesis and migration of epithelial cells along intestinal villi. Sauer, Stothers and Parker (1977) and Taverner, Hume and Farrell (1981) observed increases in the ileal digesta content of nitrogen and amino acids when graded levels of cellulose were added to protein-free diets for pigs indicating that insoluble dietary fibre can also markedly influence gut secretion. Similar studies by Behm (1954) showed that graded cellulose addition increased faecal N output. Whiting and Bezeau (1957) again found a similar effect of cellulose on faecal N; oat hulls had less effect and methylcelluloses only led to small increases. It is thus possible that dietary fibre in both soluble and insoluble forms may be an important determinant of apparent protein digestibility, and thus may also influence the efficiency of conversion of dietary protein into carcass protein. However, the mechanisms by which such effects of dietary fibre may be mediated are not yet understood.

Several types of dietary fibre increase the water content of both the small and large intestines and of faeces: Cooper and Tyler (1959) found this to be so for bran and fibrous cellulose but not for finely powdered cellulose. Partridge (1978) similarly found much larger volumes of digesta in the ileum of pigs given additional wood cellulose. Whether this effect is one of increased water secretion into the gut, reduced water absorption or a combination of both effects, in some way mediated by dietary fibre, is not understood.

EFFECT OF DIETARY FIBRE ON ABSORPTION FROM THE SMALL INTESTINE

Recent studies by Rainbird, Low and Zebrowska (1984) have shown that the addition of guar gum to a glucose solution perfused through isolated loops of pig jejunum halved the rate of glucose absorption: the mechanism by which this occurs is not fully understood but it is thought to be associated with reduced diffusion from the intestinal lumen to the epithelial cells or inhibition of the absorption process.

The appearance of glucose and α-NH$_2$ nitrogen in blood plasma is delayed and peak concentrations are lower, following meals containing guar gum (Sambrook, Rainbird and Low, 1982) indicating that this source of dietary fibre has an effect on both carbohydrate and protein digestion and absorption. The more rapid rate of absorption of glucose and amino acids following wheat meals than barley meals, found by Rerat, Vaissade and Vaugelade (1979), may have been due in part to the higher dietary fibre content (especially soluble components; see *Table 4.1*) of barley than of wheat. Guar gum is an interesting 'model' of soluble dietary fibre because it can be obtained in a purified form and because its physiological effects are probably very similar to the various soluble types of dietary fibre found in substantial amounts in most feedstuffs for pigs, and especially cereal grains.

EFFECT OF DIETARY FIBRE ON NUTRIENT ABSORPTION MEASURED AT THE END OF THE SMALL INTESTINE

The effects of cellulose (100 g/kg), the gel-forming methyl cellulose (60 g/kg) and pectin (60 g/kg) on the apparent digestibility of nitrogen in the terminal ileum of 50–100 kg pigs given a barley–soya–starch diet were measured by Murray, Fuller and Pirie (1977). Cellulose had no effect, but methyl cellulose reduced the value from 76 (control) to 48 per cent, and increased the rate of passage. Pectin had an intermediate effect. The authors suggested that impaired protein digestion and absorption were due to inhibition of protein hydrolysis when the gel-forming polysaccharides were given, because they did not affect the absorption of free lysine given in the diet.

The apparent digestibility of dry matter, organic matter, nitrogen, gross energy, crude fibre and amino acids was measured in the terminal ileum of growing pigs

Table 4.3   EFFECT OF SOYA BEAN MEAL, MALT CULMS, DARK GRAINS AND WEATINGS ON DRY MATTER (DM), ORGANIC MATTER (OM), NITROGEN (N), GROSS ENERGY (GE), CRUDE FIBRE (CF) AND APPARENT DIGESTIBILITY (%) IN THE TERMINAL ILEUM AND OVERALL OF GROWING PIGS

	Diet			
	Barley + soya	*Barley + malt culms*	*Barley + dark grains*	*Barley + weatings*
DM				
ileum	72	68	64	59
overall	80	76	70	66
OM				
ileum	74	70	66	62
overall	82	78	73	68
N				
ileum	75	66	63	67
overall	76	68	66	62
GE				
ileum	74	68	65	61
overall	79	74	70	65
CF				
ileum	17	38	38	26
overall	30	19	9	–2
(CF content of diet, g/kg)	3.88	5.04	5.65	5.85)

(Data from Zoiopoulos, Topps and English, 1983b)

Table 4.4 APPARENT DIGESTIBILITY (%) OF NUTRIENTS IN THE TERMINAL ILEUM AND OVERALL OF GROWING PIGS GIVEN DIETS CONTAINING 33-161 g CRUDE FIBRE/kg

	Diet					
	1	*2*	*3*	*4*	*5*	*6*
Nitrogen diet (g/kg)	35.7	35.8	36.0	35.0	35.4	35.7
ileum	78	84	82	78	76	75
faeces	93	91	87	84	81	77
Stoldt fat diet (g/kg)	72	72	72	72	77	78
ileum	75	81	81	79	81	79
faeces	85	83	80	76	80	78
Crude fibre diet (g/kg)	33	57	84	109	137	161
ileum	0	0	0	0	0	0
faeces	55	60	68	63	51	59
Gross energy diet (MJ/kg)	19.36	19.19	19.25	19.09	19.27	19.2
ileum	75	72	69	65	56	52
faeces	92	90	87	84	79	78
Lysine diet			(not shown in paper)			
ileum	0.92	0.93	0.91	0.90	0.87	0.86
faeces	0.95	0.93	0.90	0.87	0.84	0.80
% of that digested disappearing in large intestine						
Nitrogen	16	8	6	7	6	2
Stoldt fat	12	2	−1	−4	−1	−1
Crude fibre	100	100	100	100	100	100
Gross energy	18	20	21	23	29	33
Lysine	3	0	−1	−3	−4	17

(data from Just, Fernandez and Jørgensen, 1983)

fitted with a 'T' cannula and given a barley-based diet supplemented with soya bean meal, malt culms, dark grains or weatings by Zoiopoulos, Topps and English (1983). The results are summarized in *Table 4.3*. In general the higher the crude fibre content of the diet, the lower was the apparent digestibility of each component. A similar conclusion was reached by Just, Fernandez and Jorgenson (1983) who gave pigs a series of six diets containing 33 to 161 g crude fibre/kg (96–285 g neutral detergent fibre), and based on combinations of casein, soya bean meal, meat and bone meal, oats, barley, maize starch, potato starch cellulose, soya oil, sugar beet molasses, minerals and vitamins. The apparent digestibility of a variety of dietary components is shown in *Table 4.4*. Kass *et al.* (1980) investigated the digestion of diets containing 0, 200, 400 or 600 g/kg alfalfa meal in pigs after slaughter at 48 or 89 kg. Increasing depression of digestibility of dry matter, nitrogen and cell wall components was found in the small intestine (measured in a single sample from the whole organ) and in the caecum, colon and faeces, was found as the level of alfalfa in the diet rose.

The disappearance of dietary fibre components from diets containing 300 g/kg of cell wall material from alfalfa, grain sorghum, Texas Kleingrass and Coastal Bermuda Grass was examined in four 82–90 kg pigs with 'T' cannulas in the terminal ileum by Keys and Debarthe (1974). Faeces were also collected. The results are summarized in *Table 4.5*.

The effect of supplementary cellulose in a semi-purified diet on mineral absorption of pigs measured in the terminal ileum and overall was studied by Partridge (1978) and is summarized in *Table 4.6*. The supplementary cellulose significantly increased the amounts of digesta, faeces and organic matter.

Table 4.5 APPARENT DIGESTIBILITY (%) IN THE ILEUM AND OVERALL OF DRY MATTER, CELL WALLS, CELLULOSE AND HEMICELLULOSE IN PIGS GIVEN DIETS CONTAINING ALFALFA, GRAIN SORGHUM, TEXAS KLEINGRASS AND COASTAL BERMUDA GRASS

	Diet			
	Alfalfa	*Grain sorghum*	*Texas Kleingrass*	*Coastal Bermuda grass*
Dry matter				
intake (g/kg)	912.5	928.6	926.6	928.9
ileum	39	41	38	47
faeces	68	70	66	75
Cell walls				
intake (g/kg)	275.9	281.3	305.6	328.7
ileum	−5	−3	−6	39
faeces	32	31	22	50
Cellulose				
intake (g/kg)	174.6	143.5	148.9	144.9
ileum	−9	−8	−7	33
faeces	38	33	21	48
Hemicellulose				
intake (g/kg)	64.5	119.9	127.9	161.9
ileum	10	4	5	47
faeces	33	32	25	54

(Data from Keys and Debarthe, 1974)

Table 4.6 EFFECT OF CELLULOSE ON APPARENT DIGESTIBILITY (%) OF ORGANIC MATTER, WATER AND MINERALS IN THE TERMINAL ILEUM AND OVERALL IN GROWING PIGS

	Cellulose (g/kg)			
	30		*90*	
	Ileum	*Faeces*	*Ileum*	*Faeces*
Digesta/faeces	84	99	76	97
Organic matter	94	99	90	95
Water	81	99	72	98
Sodium	46	99	15	98
Potassium	90	97	88	86
Calcium	43	74	44	63
Phosphorus	64	81	69	74
Magnesium	−1	73	3	62
Zinc	10	60	24	37

(Data from Partridge, 1978)

The effects of supplementary cellulose, pectin and dried sugar beet pulp in semi-purified diets on dry matter, nitrogen and amino acid digestibility in the ileum and faeces of growing pigs and on nitrogen retention were studied by Dierick *et al.* (1983). As the level of fibre in the diet increased, so the nutrient digestibility in the ileum fell, to a much greater extent with pectin and dried sugar beet pulp than with cellulose. However, although a similar pattern of effects of dietary fibre could be seen in the faeces, the differences between treatments were much less than in ileal digesta. The principal results are shown in *Table 4.7.*

Table 4.7 THE EFFECTS OF CELLULOSE, PECTIN AND SUGAR BEET PULP ON THE APPARENT DIGESTIBILITY (%) OF DRY MATTER (DM), NITROGEN (N), ESSENTIAL (EAA) AND NON-ESSENTIAL (NEAA) AMINO ACIDS IN GROWING PIGS, MEASURED IN THE ILEUM AND OVERALL

Diet	Ileal digesta				Faeces			
	DM	*N*	*EAA*	*NEAA*	*DM*	*N*	*EAA*	*NEAA*
Experiment 1								
Fibre-free	91	88	90	89	95	94	93	93
Cellulose (75 g/kg)	84	86	90	88	84	90	91	92
Pectin (50 g/kg)	80	76	81	75	93	92	91	92
Experiment 2								
Fibre-free	92	89	94	93	95	95	96	96
Cellulose (50 g/kg)	85	89	93	92	93	95	96	96
Cellulose (100 g/kg)	79	88	93	92	89	93	95	96
Cellulose (150 g/kg)	74	84	94	93	84	91	93	93
Dried sugar								
Beet pulp (50 g/kg)	87	90	96	95	94	95	96	96
Beet pulp (100 g/kg)	81	86	92	89	93	94	94	94
Beet pulp (150 g/kg)	72	81	90	88	92	92	94	94

(Data from Dierick *et al.*, 1983)

The present level of knowledge makes it very difficult to make predictions about the effects of specific types of dietary fibre on nutrient absorption in the small intestine of pigs, though it is evident that some important changes may occur. At present nothing is known about the effects of dietary fibre on vitamin absorption and little is known of the effects on carbohydrate and lipid absorption. However, enough is known from studies in man and rat to indicate that inclusion of supplementary dietary fibre tends to reduce the rate or the amount of apparent absorption of all nutrient types, to a degree that is determined in part by the source and level used. Such effects may vary with the age of the pig and the level of feeding applied. Clearly some of the effects may be considerable and current views on the nutrient requirements or responses of pigs may need modification when more detailed information is available. This may be especially so for amino acids because any amino acids which are not absorbed by the end of the small intestine appear to play no further role in the nutrition of the animal (Zebrowska, 1973).

Large intestine

Striking as the effects of dietary fibre may be on the function of the small intestine, it is in the large intestine that it becomes an identifiable nutrient source, rather than a medium eliciting diverse physiological responses. The transit time of digesta is much longer through the large intestine (generally 20–40 h) than through the stomach and small intestine (generally in the range 2–16 h). These conditions allow considerable net absorption of water: for example mean values for 40 kg pigs of 3152 g for a cereal-based diet and 986 g for a semi-purified (low dietary fibre) diet were found during 24 h periods by Low, Partridge and Sambrook (1978). Addition of cellulose to the diet caused a major increase in the volume of water passing into and out of the large intestine (Partridge, 1978).

A major consequence of the slow passage of digesta through the large intestine is that it encourages prolific bacterial growth: up to 10^{11} bacteria of both obligate anaerobic and aerobic species have been found per gram of fresh digesta. Although the population is generally thought to be stable, antibiotic treatment may cause big disturbances in the microbial balance. A detailed review of microbial fermentation in the pig alimentary tract was published by Cranwell (1968), but relatively few bacteriological studies have been published since, the main interest in the pig now being focused on the products of the bacterial activity and their potential nutritive value.

It has been recognized for many years that the weight and volume of the gut of pigs tends to increase when diets of a high dietary fibre content are used (for example Coey and Robinson, 1954). Kass *et al.* (1980) found in growing pigs that increasing the dietary fibre content of the diet by means of alfalfa meal reduced the stomach weight, as a proportion of the weight of the whole gut, while the weights of the small intestine, caecum and colon increased, as a proportion of body weight (*Table 4.8*) (all expressed on an empty gut weight basis). The percentage dry matter content of the digesta decreased significantly in all regions of the gut except the caecum as the amount of alfalfa meal in the diet increased. The effect of a high dietary fibre diet on 120–130 kg pigs was to increase the volume of the gut, and in particular that of the stomach and caecum (Horszczaruk, 1962).

Table 4.8   THE EFFECT OF ALFALFA MEAL ON EMPTY GUT WEIGHT IN GROWING PIGS (EXPRESSED AS % OF BODY WEIGHT)

Level of dietary alfalfa meal (%)	Stomach	Small intestine	Caecum	Colon
0	0.75	1.98	0.18	1.40
20	0.79	2.09	0.17	1.60
40	0.76	2.33	0.20	1.79
60	0.77	2.57	0.22	2.02

(Data from Kass *et al.*, 1980)

The decomposition of dietary fibre in the caecum and colon of pigs was measured using the nylon bag technique by Horszczaruk and Sljivovacki (1971). Four 18-month-old pigs fitted with caecal and colonic cannulas were used. Nylon bags containing ground raw cellulose or lucerne meal were placed on short threads through the cannulas for two or four days. Cellulose was digested faster than lucerne meal: 70 and 30 per cent in two days and 95 and 35 per cent in four days respectively. It was noted that these latter values compared with values of 0 and 17 per cent in young growing pigs.

The rate of flow of digesta through different regions of the large intestine is generally accelerated by the addition of dietary fibre to the diet (Horszczaruk, 1962; Kass *et al.*, 1980). Recent studies at Shinfield indicate that the water phase of digesta moves more rapidly through the caecum and ascending colon than the dry matter, irrespective of the source of dietary fibre (supplementary bran, lactulose and pectin were used) but the effect is much less for pectin which has the greatest water-binding capacity of the sources tested. However the time of arrival of the liquid and solid phases in the faeces did not differ between types of dietary fibre.

The role of the caecum in pigs has been investigated by comparing the digestibility of diets with low or high dietary fibre content in intact and caecectomized pigs by Lloyd, Dale and Crampton (1958) and Gargallo and Zimmerman (1981). In neither case did caecectomy significantly affect the performance of the pigs or the digestibility of crude fibre.

Volatile fatty acids (VFA)

Large concentrations (150–250 mM of VFA are found throughout the large intestine: smaller amounts (5–40 mM) are found in the stomach and small intestine, as shown by Argenzio and Southworth (1975) and Clemens, Stevens and Southworth (1975). The VFA derived by microbial activity from dietary fibre are predominantly found in the large intestine where cellulolytic bacteria are abundant: although such bacteria may be found in the ileum their importance in this part of the gut is comparatively minor. VFA can be produced from all the components of dietary fibre, as well as undigested starch, lipid and proteins which may enter the large intestine. Acetic acid tends to predominate in the digesta, with smaller amounts of propionic acid and butyric acid, the proportions varying with the type of dietary fibre fed and the particular site. In general as the dietary fibre content of the diet increases, so the proportion of acetate to the other VFA rises, as shown for alfalfa by Kass *et al* (1980) and for sunflower hulls by Gargallo and Zimmerman (1981b). Volatile fatty acids are readily absorbed and their concentrations in blood of pigs were first measured by Barcroft, McAnally and Phillipson (1944).

The rates of VFA production have been measured by a variety of methods in order to calculate the degree to which VFA may contribute to the energy supply of the pig. Among the earliest studies was a comparison of portal-venous VFA concentration differences in 30 kg pigs by Friend, Nicholson and Cunningham (1964) who calculated that 15–28 per cent of the maintenance energy requirements might be met by VFA. However, these values do not allow for hepatic production of VFA, which was demonstrated by Imoto and Namioka (1978a), and are thus open to doubt. A more recent attempt to calculate the amounts of VFA which may be formed in the large intestine of pigs fed diets containing 0, 200, 400 and 600 g alfalfa meal was made by Kass *et al.* (1980) by use of regression equations for each acid after measurement in the caecum and colon 2, 4, 8 or 12 h after feeding. Based on gross caloric values of 3.40, 4.96 and 5.95 kcal/g for acetic, propionic and butyric acids, respectively, the energy values of VFA disappearing from the caecum and colon (assuming complete absorption) were calculated to be 79, 147, 227 and 155 kcal/day for 48 kg pigs and 47, 231, 285 and 245 kcal/day for 89 kg pigs, the values corresponding to diets containing 0, 200, 400 or 600 g alfalfa meal/kg, respectively. The net maintenance requirement of the 48 and 89 kg pigs was calculated to be 1296 and 2028 kcal/kg $W^{0.75}$, so VFA could provide 6.9, 11.3, 12.5 and 12.0 per cent of the energy needed for maintenance in 48 kg pigs and 4.8, 11.4, 14.0 and 12.9 per cent in 89 kg pigs given the diets containing 0, 200, 400 or 600 g alfalfa meal/kg, respectively. These figures are based on the difference between VFA production and absorption and are underestimates of the actual production and absorption rates, to an unknown degree.

Kennelly, Aherne and Sauer (1981) measured VFA production in the caecum by continuous isotope infusion. In the case of a barley–soya diet, net VFA production rates indicated that caecal fermentation could provide 19.7 per cent maintenance energy requirements of growing pigs fed hourly. When alfalfa supplements were provided and the pigs were fed three times daily, it was calculated that VFA from the caecum could provide 10.1, 15.5 or 11.1 per cent of maintenance energy requirements when the diet contained 0, 27.3 or 52.0 per cent alfalfa. The problem with this method is that although accurate values may be obtained, if corrected for VFA interconversions, the isotope is not contained within the caecum and thus a pool of unknown size is obtained and sampled from.

Imoto and Namioka (1978a) attempted to measure VFA production in pigs by examining VFA in blood entering and leaving both the liver and gut. Extensive hepatic production of acetate was seen and this was the major component of circulating acetate. Furthermore extensive metabolism of absorbed VFA was found to occur in the large intestinal wall.

When short-term (30 or 60 min) incubation of caecal contents of pigs was employed by Farrell and Johnson (1972) to measure VFA production, it was concluded that VFA from the caecum provided 2.7 or 1.9 per cent of the apparently digestible energy of pigs given diets with 80 or 260 g cellulose/kg (equivalent to 5.5 or 3.9 per cent of maintenance energy requirements). In a similar way (but using caecal and colonic contents), Imoto and Namioka (1978b) calculated that VFA production from the whole of the large intestine could provide 9.6–11.6 per cent of maintenance energy requirements of growing pigs. Gargallo and Zimmerman (1981b) also used the latter approach and calculated that VFA could provide 6.2, 5.6 and 5.0 per cent of the maintenance energy requirements of 95 kg pigs given diets with 20, 100 and 200 g sunflower hulls/kg, respectively. More recently Argenzio (1982) suggested that VFA could provide 19–25 per cent of daily maintenance energy requirements, using *in vitro* incubation data. Measurements of fermentation by *in vitro* methods rely on steady state assumptions, and must be related to the entire pool of caecal or colonic contents, neither of which can be measured accurately.

There are thus problems of such magnitude that presently available estimates of the contribution of VFA from the large intestine to meeting the energy requirements of the pig must be viewed with a great deal of caution. The different techniques, diets and assumptions used in the experiments reported above make a comparative view almost meaningless. Nevertheless the results available do indicate that further research to quantitate the contribution of VFA to metabolism is warranted.

VOLATILE FATTY ACID METABOLISM IN PIGS

Although it is believed that a large proportion of absorbed volatile fatty acids may be metabolized in the gut wall, substantial amounts do enter the blood as indicated earlier. Acetate introduced orally (in the form of 1-^{14}C-acetate) into newborn piglets was metabolized very rapidly to $^{14}CO_2$ (within minutes of dosing) and 89–92 per cent was recovered within 12 h in this form, while less than 3 per cent appeared in urine and faeces (Mohme, Molnar and Lenkheit, 1970). Small amounts of radioactivity were found in most tissues. More recently Latymer and Woodley (1984) found that ^{14}C from U-^{14}C-acetate injected at physiological levels into the caecum of 22–28 kg pigs was also rapidly absorbed and peak blood concentrations were already observed 30 min later. From this time until 5 h after the injection ^{14}C was found in all the major lipid classes (including free cholesterol and cholesteryl esters), plasma proteins and other water-soluble compounds. In a second study in two of the same pigs (when they weighed 70 and 78 kg) Latymer and Low (1984) infused U-^{14}C acetate into the caecum and collected all urine and faeces for 96 h. The pigs were then killed and the mean distribution of radioactivity found throughout the body is shown in *Table 4.9*. It can be seen that a substantial portion of the dose was retained in the carcass (mainly in the subcutaneous fat). This contrasts with the situation in the newborn piglet which has minimal energy

Table 4.9 MEAN PERCENTAGE OF U ^{14}C FROM U ^{14}C ACETATE INJECTED INTO THE CAECUM OF TWO PIGS RECOVERED AFTER 96 h

Small intestine wall and contents	0.8
Large intestine contents	0.1
Large intestine wall	1.5
Liver	0.6
Kidney	0.1
Blood	0.1
Carcass	23.6
Urine	2.7
Faeces	5.2
Total	34.7

Losses, assumed to be as $^{14}CO_2$, by difference 65.3
(Data from Latymer and Low, 1984)

reserves and thus used oral acetate as an immediate energy source (Mohme, Molnar and Lenkheit, 1970). During studies *in vitro* using tissue slices from various parts of growing pigs Huang and Kummerow (1976) demonstrated the incorporation of 1-^{14}C acetate or U-^{14}C acetate into fatty acids and cholesterol; the rate of incorporation was highest in adipose tissue.

The nutritive value of acetate was estimated to be 59 per cent in terms of the percentage use of metabolizable energy, in growing pigs by Jentsch, Schiemann and Hoffman (1968): these authors observed that 2100 calories were deposited per gram of supplementary dietary acetate. This value corresponds well with the values of 56–59 per cent for growing pigs obtained by Imoto and Namioko (1983a), who gave acetate orally as triacetin. In another part of the same studies, Imoto and Namioka (1983b) observed a reciprocal relationship between the metabolism of acetate and glucose, depending on the time of day; 12 h after feeding glucose was the dominant blood energy source, replacing acetate which was present at higher concentrations following feeding.

These results indicate that the principal product of fibre digestion is not only absorbed but is metabolized, to an efficiency which is approximately three-quarters of that of glucose, when measured under conditions of growth. Energetic efficiency is generally higher for maintenance than for growth (in other species) but so far no data on the efficiency of acetate use in pigs under the former conditions are available. Furthermore, data on the metabolism of propionic and butyric acids in pigs do not appear to exist, either in growing or maintenance conditions.

The apparently digested energy from fermentation of dietary fibre in the large intestine, in terms of its potential value to the animal, is less than that obtained from the enzymic digestion of starch because some of the apparently absorbed energy is lost, not as volatile fatty acids, but as heat of bacterial fermentation and a further amount is lost as methane. The latter has been calculated to be 14–17 per cent of the apparently digested energy arising from fermentation (Agricultural Research Council, 1981).

Influence of dietary fibre on nutrient absorption in the large intestine

Although quite a large number of comparisons between ileal and faecal apparent digestibility of nutrients have been made in pigs, the effects of dietary fibre have generally been made using diets differing in both its source and amount. Increasing the fibre content of the diet has been shown to reduce both the ileal and faecal digestibility of nitrogen and organic matter, as shown in the examples in *Tables 4.3, 4.4* and *4.7*. In other reports, similar effects of rye straw meal (Zebrowska, 1982), whole vs. dehulled barley (Just *et al.*, 1980), ground barley straw (Just, 1982a) and wheat and oat brain (Just, 1982b) have been shown. The results are characterized by an increasing proportion of the energy digested in the large intestine as the dietary fibre content is increased, with corresponding reductions in nitrogen and Stoldt fat absorption, as exemplified in *Table 4.4*. In addition, net synthesis of certain amino acids between the ileum and faeces was seen as the barley straw content of the diet was increased (Just, 1982a). The amounts of dietary fibre (measured as crude fibre) which disappeared in the large intestine were not significantly altered when barley straw meal was added to diets (Just, 1982a) or wheat and oat bran (Just, 1982b). *Tables 4.5* and *4.6* show the disappearance of dietary fibre and of minerals respectively during digesta passage through the large intestine. Detailed results on the effects of cereal fibre on the apparent disappearance of fatty acids in the large intestine shows that this generally corresponds with that of crude fat (Just, Andersen and Jorgensen, 1980). Varying the level of feeding of growing pigs between 70 and 100 per cent of the current Danish standard had no effect on the apparent digestibility of the main nutrients either measured in the ileum or faeces (Just, Jorgensen and Fernandez, 1983).

Influence of dietary fibre on nutrient digestibility measured overall

Although a considerable literature exists on this theme, some of which has already been cited, it is difficult to draw firm conclusions because of the great variety of diets, pigs, sources of dietary fibre, feeding levels and levels of dietary fibre inclusion used. The following examples have been chosen to demonstrate typical effects.

NITROGEN

Although ground wood cellulose supplements have tended to reduce nitrogen digestibility (Horszczaruk, 1962; Kirchgessner, Roth-Maier and Roth, 1975; Partridge, Keal and Mitchell, 1982), oat feed, by contrast, had no such effect in the studies of Potkins, Lawrence and Tomlinson (1984) although it did depress dry matter and energy digestibility. The soluble galactomannan guar gum did not significantly alter the digestibility or retention of nitrogen in growing pigs (though nitrogen digestibility and retention tended to rise) (Low and Keal, 1981). Alkali-treated straw, which contains a considerable quantity of soluble carbohydrates, tends to reduce nitrogen digestibility as in the work of Farrell (1973) and Bergner, Simon and Bergner (1980). While corn cobs (150 g/kg diet) had little effect on nitrogen digestibility, they depressed energy and dietary fibre digestibility: however the weights of neutral detergent fibre, acid detergent fibre and hemicellulose digested increased by 55, 15 and 90 per cent respectively (Frank, Aherne and Jensen, 1983). Oat hulls (Kennelly and Aherne, 1980) and barley hulls (Bell, Shires and Keith, 1983) had little effect on nitrogen digestibility, but energy and dietary fibre digestibility fell. Pectin reduced nitrogen digestibility in the experiments of Albers and Henkel (1979) and Mosenthin and Henkel (1983), but nitrogen balance was unaffected because nitrogen losses in urine fell.

ENERGY

The effect of rapeseed hulls was to depress energy and dietary fibre digestibility in trials by Bell and Shires (1982). Similar effects of supplementary lucerne leaf meal were observed by Kuan, Stanogias and Dunkin (1983); although nitrogen digestibility fell, daily nitrogen retention increased. Increases in the length and weight of various sections of the gut were also found as the level of dietary lucerne leaf meal increased, in the same studies. Kass *et al.* (1980) measured the effects of alfalfa on energy and dietary fibre digestibility (*Table 4.10*). The apparent

Table 4.10 EFFECT OF LEVEL OF DIETARY ALFALFA MEAL ON OVERALL APPARENT DIGESTIBILITY (%) OF DRY MATTER, CELL WALL, ACID DETERGENT FIBRE, HEMICELLULOSE, CELLULOSE AND NITROGEN IN PIGS

	% alfalfa meal in diet			
	0	20	40	60
Dry matter	77	61	52	28
Cell wall	62	34	27	8
Acid detergent fibre	56	10	11	1
Hemicellulose	67	54	49	22
Cellulose	58	20	9	7
Nitrogen	70	52	41	41

(Data from Kass *et al.*, 1980)

digestibility of wood cellulose has often been found to be between 20 and 30 per cent, but wide variation has been noted by several authors. Some explanation for this comes from the work of Cunningham, Friend and Nicholson (1962) who found that the digestibility was 29.1 per cent when pigs were fed at a maintenance level. The same pigs had previously been fed at a growing pig level and only digested 5.0 per cent of the cellulose. In a later growing phase the digestibility was 18.3 per cent. This indicates that age and physiological state may be important determinants of the digestibility of dietary fibre. Straw cellulose is highly digestible (80–95 per cent) after lignin removal (Woodman and Evans, 1947; Forbes and Hamilton, 1952). The reduction in energy digestibility resulting from feeding diets with six levels of wood cellulose was found to be linear, up to a level of 175 g crude fibre/kg diet by Tullis and Whittemore (1981). The digestibility of the dietary fibre in various types of forages was found to be remarkably high by Yoshimoto and Matsubara (1983): some of their results are summarized in *Table 4.11*. Morgan, Whittemore and

Table 4.11 APPARENT DIGESTIBILITY (%) OF FORAGES MEASURED OVERALL IN PIGS

	Organic matter	Nitrogen	Neutral detergent fibre	Cellulose	Hemicellulose
Shimofusa turnip	70	80	66	71	79
Cabbage leaf	74	69	86	85	94
Alfalfa	42	58	38	44	57
Ladino clover	59	67	57	61	70
Tall fescue grass	28	43	32	29	50
Italian rye grass	42	63	44	42	50

Each forage source formed 50% of the diet by weight, except turnip and cabbage (40%). Values are corrected for contributions by the basal diets.
(Data from Yoshimoto and Matsubara, 1983)

Cockburn (1984) examined the effects of straw, oatfeed, rice bran and beet pulp on the energy value of compound pig feeds and concluded that prediction of the digestible energy content of diets was best when based on their neutral detergent fibre content.

MINERALS

Although the retention of phosphorus and calcium was unaffected by oat hulls in the studies of Moser *et al.* (1982a) the apparent digestibility of phosphorus fell. In contrast, wood cellulose increased phosphorus retention and bone breaking strength (Moser *et al.*, 1982b); no explanation for this effect is immediately apparent. Supplementary wheat bran has been shown to decrease zinc absorption in pig diets by Newton, Hale and Plank (1983).

Influence of dietary fibre on overall transit time

The results of recently published studies on the effect of dietary fibre on transit time are summarized in *Table 4.12*. It is evident that when graded levels of a single type of dietary fibre, or different types of fibre were added to semi-purified or milk-based diets (i.e. free of dietary fibre), variable and often large effects were seen. When bran was added to a cereal-based diet, no effect was seen (Canguilhem and Labie, 1977); this has also been found in recent studies in which supplements of bran, pectin and lactulose were given to growing pigs by Latymer (unpublished). This lack of effect of supplementary dietary fibre in reducing transit time of cereal-based diets (which have a high dietary fibre content) may imply that there is

Table 4.12   EFFECTS OF DIETARY FIBRE ON OVERALL MEAN TRANSIT TIME IN PIGS

Source and level in diet	(g/kg)	Diet type	Initial pig weight (kg)	Time (h)	Reference
Lucerne leaf meal	50	Semi-purified	44	43.7	1
Lucerne leaf meal	100	Semi-purified	44	41.6	
Lucerne leaf meal	150	Semi-purified	44	29.7	
Lucerne leaf meal	200	Semi-purified	44	28.4	
Coarse bran	312	Semi-purified	70	51.6	2
Fine bran	472	Semi-purified	70	49.7	
Lucerne meal	308	Semi-purified	70	36.0	
Solka floc	150	Semi-purified	70	71.0	
Bran	170	Milk powder	50	66.0	3
No dietary fibre		Milk powder	50	120.0	
Bran (100 g/day)		Milk	90	64.3	4
No dietary fibre		Milk	90	98.6	
Bran (100 g or 200 g/day)		Cereal	30	52.0	5
No extra dietary fibre		Cereal	30	49.0	
Bran (100 g/day)		Milk replacer	30	79.0	
No extra dietary fibre		Milk replacer	30	107.0	

Data from 1. Kuan, Stanogias and Dunkin (1983)
       2. Ehle *et al.* (1982)
       3. Fioramonti and Bueno (1980)
       4. Bardon and Fioramonti (1983)
       5. Canguilhem and Labie (1977)

Table 4.13   EFFECT OF BRAN SUPPLEMENTATION OF A WEANER DIET FOR PIGLETS OF 9.5 kg INITIAL WEIGHT AT WEANING ON MEAN TRANSIT TIME (80% RECOVERY OF MARKER)

% crude fibre (as bran)	Mean transit time (h) Weeks post weaning			
	1	*2*	*3*	*4*
0	192	361	215	141
2.1	155	113	111	103
3.1	133	118	118	92
5.5	117	98	63	78

(Data from Schnabel, Bolduan and Guldenpenning, 1983)

a minimum transit time in growing pigs irrespective of the dietary fibre content of the diet.

Very little information exists on the effects of dietary fibre on transit time in weaner pigs. Schnabel, Bolduan and Guldenpenning (1983) demonstrated that bran supplements accelerated transit through the gut and also that transit time decreased over four weeks after weaning (*Table 4.13*). A crude fibre content of 50–60 g/kg diet was recommended for piglet starter diets by these authors.

Effects of dietary fibre on the whole animal

VOLUNTARY FEED INTAKE

It is well known that additional dietary fibre tends to increase voluntary feed intake of pigs. This topic was reviewed in detail by the Agricultural Research Council (1967), which concluded that every 1 per cent increase in the dietary fibre content of the diet is accompanied by an increase of approximately 3 per cent in feed intake. At the same time it was observed that additional dietary fibre reduced the growth rate despite the increased intake, which did not appear to compensate fully for the lower digestible energy content of the diet. The data available did not allow an estimate to be made of the plateau of intake imposed by dietary fibre. A feature of the data reviewed was the great variability, which was probably related to such factors as the age of the pig, the particular botanical type of dietary fibre used and the way in which it had been processed.

Since that time a number of studies have provided additional insight into the role that fibre can play in voluntary feed intake. For example, Owen and Ridgman (1967) found that intakes of high dietary-fibre diets (barley-based, with sawdust and oat feed) were consistently higher than those of low dietary-fibre content only when the pigs were in the finishing phase of growth. The time spent eating corresponded with the weights of feed eaten. In the early phases of growth (27–50 kg) reduced digestible energy intakes were found but these were compensated by higher intakes, when diets of high dietary fibre content were given in the 50–118 kg finishing phase. In a second report Owen and Ridgman (1968) pointed out that the adaptive response to diets of higher dietary fibre content takes a long time to occur, especially in young pigs. The quality of the carcasses was not significantly improved by feeding the high dietary fibre diet.

In experiments with growing-finishing pigs, Baker *et al.* (1968) fed diets with 0, 100, 200 or 400 g/kg added cellulose on an *ad libitum* basis; corresponding feed intakes of 2.63, 2.42, 2.00 and 1.50 kg/day and daily gains of 0.76, 0.68, 0.48 and 0.25 kg/day respectively were obtained. Contrasting daily voluntary feed intakes of lactating sows given oat husks (400 g/kg diet) or straw (300 g/kg diet) of 7.79 and 5.80 kg dry matter (85.0 and 6.04 MJ digestible energy) were found by Zoiopoulos, English and Topps (1982). Another interesting example of the complexity of voluntary feed intake mechanisms is provided by Taverner, Campbell and Biden (1984) who found intakes of growing pigs fell from 2.18 to 1.92 kg/day as the digestible energy content rose from 11.8 to 14.4 MJ/kg diet; all diets contained 120 g acid detergent fibre/kg and supplementary fat provided the increases in energy density. Although there was a 7 per cent increase in digestible energy intake (as the fat content of the diets was increased) the maximum daily digestible energy intake was 27 MJ; intakes of 34 MJ had been found by the same group when similar but low fibre diets had been given (Campbell, Taverner and Curic, 1983).

A recent study by Zoiopoulos, English and Topps (1983) showed that pigs growing between 55 and 87 kg ate different amounts of dry matter per day, when fed a semi-*ad libitum* basis (as much as could be eaten during 1 h in the morning and 1 h in the evening); malt culms and dark grains depressed intake to 1.81 and 1.94 kg/day respectively compared with a control intake of 2.30 kg/day and a high weatings intake of 2.05 kg/day.

The bacterial population of the large intestine hydrolyses undigested proteins to a wide range of products, including tyramine and tryptamine, amine derivatives of tyrosine and tryptophan respectively. These can saturate the hypothalamus and reduce feed intake. Inhibition of the formation of these compounds can be achieved by lowering the pH of the caecal and colonic contents below the high pH requirements of amine-producing bacteria. Such an effect may be caused by volatile fatty acids, produced by degradation of dietary fibre. This mechanism may explain how dietary fibre could influence voluntary feed intake (Bergner, 1981).

It is thus apparent that different types of dietary fibre influence voluntary feed intake in different ways and it is also evident that pigs do not eat to maintain a strictly controlled energy intake. It seems that further studies on the interactions between fibre source, other energy sources and voluntary feed intake are merited.

EFFECTS OF DIETARY FIBRE ON GROWTH AND FEED:GAIN

The Agricultural Research Council (1967) concluded after a thorough review of the literature that increasing the percentage of crude fibre in the diet depressed the growth of pigs: for every 1 per cent additional crude fibre in the diet, a 2 per cent decrease in growth could be expected. However, the data were very variable. Crude fibre addition to the diet similarly worsened feed:gain ratios; for every 1 per cent increase in crude fibre, a 3 per cent increase in feed required per kg gain was shown. Again, the results were very variable. Although many new publications describing responses to dietary fibre have followed since publication by the Agricultural Research Council (1967) it is doubtful whether these conclusions can be modified or improved, largely because the types of fibre used in experiments have not been well characterized.

The effect of purified cellulose on growth and body composition of growing pigs fed on an *ad libitum* basis by Cunningham, Friend and Nicholson (1961) was to

Table 4.14   EFFECTS OF CELLULOSE ADDITION TO AN ENERGY-DEFICIENT
BASAL DIET FOR GROWING PIGS. ALL VALUES ARE RATIOS OF INTAKE
(12 PIGS/TREATMENT)

	Basal regime	Basal + cellulose	
35 kg liveweight:			
Energy digestibility	0.81	0.69	***
Energy retention	0.79	0.67	***
N digestibility	0.82	0.76	***
N retention	0.48	0.46	NS
ADF digestibility	0.41	0.35	NS
NDF digestibility	0.53	0.46	NS
65 kg liveweight:			
Energy digestibility	0.83	0.71	***
Energy retention	0.80	0.69	***
N digestibility	0.85	0.78	***
N retention	0.51	0.48	NS
ADF digestibility	0.39	0.35	NS
NDF digestibility	0.56	0.47	**

Significance of differences: NS, $P < 0.05$; **, $P < 0.01$; ***, $P < 0.001$.
(Data from Partridge, Keal and Mitchell, 1982)

decrease the dressing percentage (and increase the iodine number of the fat). No net gain was obtained from energy derived from cellulose, a conclusion which was also drawn by De Goey and Ewan (1975). Kupke and Henkel (1977) compared straw and wood cellulose and found the former led to fatter carcasses, while wood cellulose reduced nitrogen digestibility; usually nitrogen output in the urine fell so nitrogen balance was not affected. Partridge, Keal and Mitchell (1982) measured the energy value of cellulose (150 g/kg diet) added to barley–soya diets, fed at a restricted and energy-limiting level to growing pigs. The results are shown in *Table 4.14*. Growth rates and nitrogen retention were unaffected by cellulose addition, while dressing percentage fell. The amount of energy digested and absorbed (MJ/day) was the same for both diets (16.59 and 16.60 at 35 kg and 29.81 and 29.91 at 65 kg for control and cellulose-supplemented diets respectively). The results indicate that either the energy from cellulose was not absorbed (i.e. it was used in bacterial metabolism or lost as methane), or it was used in the gut wall, or the energy absorbed from dietary fibre was offset by reduced energy absorption from other sources. In a balance study, including respiration measurements, in sows, Muller and Kirchgessner (1983) measured the energy value of cellulose by subtraction, using data from control and cellulose-supplemented diets. Under these conditions, 29 per cent of the cellulose was digested; 95 and 68 per cent of the absorbed cellulose energy was metabolizable and retained respectively. Nitrogen balance was improved, urinary nitrogen output falling while faecal nitrogen output increased. Thus sows appeared to make better use of supplementary cellulose than growing pigs.

Recently it has been shown that, for every 1 per cent increase in the crude fibre content of the diet by barley straw (Just, 1982a), wheat or oat bran (Just, 1982b) gross energy digestibility fell by 2.1 or 3.5 units respectively and the efficiency of use of ME fell by 0.7 units in each case. These decreases corresponded to increases in the proportion of the dietary energy being digested in the large intestine. A general linear relationship between the percentage of dietary energy disappearing from the large intestine (X) and the net energy value (as a percentage of metabolizable energy in the diet) (Y) was expressed by Just, Fernandez and Jorgensen (1983) as:

$$Y = 74.5 + 0.49X$$

EFFECTS OF DIETARY FIBRE ON BODY COMPOSITION

From the discussion in several sections of this review, it can be seen that increasing the dietary fibre content of diets results in trends towards greater faecal nitrogen loss largely through increased output of bacteria and endogenous matter (Mason, Kragelund and Eggum, 1982). Conversely the urinary output of nitrogen is usually reduced, with a greater amount of urea excretion into the large intestine, providing a substrate for the bacteria (Mosenthin and Henkel, 1983). The net effect is thus for nitrogen retention and therefore carcass lean or protein content to be relatively unaffected by increasing the dietary fibre content of the diet, although instances of both increases and decreases can be found, but the reasons for these effects remain unclear.

The effect of an increased percentage of dietary fibre in the diet on fat deposition is almost invariably to decrease it in growing pigs: a reduction of approximately 0.5 mm in backfat thickness for every 1 per cent increase in the crude fibre content was calculated by Elsley (1969) from the literature, with a corresponding increase in the days of growth before slaughter. More recent information supports these conclusions. Concomitant reductions in carcass weight are consistently found as a result of increasing the dietary fibre content of the diet in many reports.

DIETARY FIBRE AND SOWS

Though breeding pigs have often been fed diets with a high content of dietary fibre, few detailed studies have been made on this topic. Problems in the interpretation of some published work include lack of definition of the types of fibre used and failure to allow for the often considerable consumption of straw bedding. Højgaard-Olsen and Nielsen (1966) observed that sows given supplementary straw gave birth to significantly heavier piglets, which consumed more milk and creep feed and thus had a greater weight at weaning. Münchow *et al.* (1982) found that partially hydrolysed straw gave rise to improved reproductive performance compared with unhydrolysed straw; in particular 1.5 more piglets were born per litter, for as yet unknown reasons. It was concluded that partially hydrolysed straw could replace about 45 per cent of the concentrates in sow diets without detrimental effects.

When sows were given either a control diet on a restricted basis, or the same diet with substitution by oat husks (400 g/kg) or barley straw (300 g/kg), both fed on an *ad libitum* basis, daily digestible energy intakes were 70.1, 85.0 and 60.4 MJ respectively (Zoiopoulos, English and Topps, 1982). Corresponding nitrogen balances (g/day) were 18.3, 25.5 and 3.5. The liveweight changes during lactation were −9.8, 5.1 and −16.8 kg. These results indicate that there is potential for *ad libitum* feeding of sows on diets with a high content of dietary fibre provided that the cost is sufficiently low: they also indicate that different sources of dietary fibre have very different effects. Further studies on the effects of barley straw on heat production and energy use in sows have been made by Müller and Kirchgessner (1983).

Several studies on gestating sows have suggested that the digestion of dietary fibre increases during gestation (for example Zivkovic and Bowland, 1970). Hemicellulose digestion improved while cellulose digestion remained constant in sows given alfalfa or tall wheatgrass during gestation by Pollman, Danielson and Peo (1979). However, Zivkovic and Bowland (1970) found reduced gestation weight gains in pigs fed diets with a high dietary fibre content.

There appears to be potential for the use of fibre in improving the satiety and behaviour of sows. Significant increases in the time spent eating (from 15.8 to 52.0 min) and lying down (monitored by video recording) were found by Mroz, Partridge, Broom and Mitchell when a barley–soya diet was supplemented with oat hulls (personal communication).

INTERACTIONS BETWEEN DIETARY FIBRE AND ANTIBIOTICS

At present the effects of antibiotics on the nutritional value of diets with a high content of dietary fibre is only partly understood. Bohmann, Hunter and McCormick (1955) showed that the addition of alfalfa to young pig diets led to decreased daily gain, but this effect was reversed by aureomycin. However, Powley *et al.* (1981) found no consistent improvement in the use of high-alfalfa diets in pigs after antibiotic supplementation. On the other hand Sherry, Harrison and Fahey (1981) observed that supplementation of maize–soya diets with cellulose (80 g/kg) and antibiotic resulted in a significant fibre × antibiotic interaction, which depressed the resting metabolic rate of weaning pigs, i.e. heat production fell. This was accompanied by higher growth and improved feed:gain. It appeared that the microbial population was on the one hand enhanced by the additional fibre and on the other hand suppressed by the antibiotic, leading to changes in its size or composition, or predominant metabolic pattern. This work suggests that more knowledge of the interactions between the microbial population and dietary fibre could lead to the development of effective practical systems of using feedstuffs with an increased content of dietary fibre.

DIETARY FIBRE AND WEANING

The role of dietary fibre in the weaning phase of piglets remains uncertain. Creep feeds are usually of relatively low dietary fibre content, but intakes are both variable and often low. At weaning diets of rather higher fibre content are offered, but appetites are often poor, and diarrhoea is a frequent problem. Drochner *et al.* (1978) suggested that a supplement of wood cellulose can depress bacterial activity and help reduce diarrhoea. Diets which combine such potentially beneficial effects with high digestibility and palatability are needed in order for maximal growth potential to be achieved.

POSSIBLE BREED EFFECTS ON USE OF DIETARY FIBRE

The possibility that some breeds of pigs may use dietary fibre more efficiently than others deserves more investigation; Laurentowska (1959) noted higher cellulose and lignin digestibility in Pulawy than in Large White Pigs. Pekas, Yen and Pond (1983) found that lean and obese genotypes grew at the same rate and efficiency on low or high dietary fibre diets, but gut dimensions differed.

PROCESSING OF FEEDSTUFFS

Processing of dietary fibre for pigs has received little attention. Pelleting of timothy–red clover diet (Cameron, 1960), oats (Seerley, 1962), lucerne and bran (Kracht *et al.*, 1975) led to improved feed intake and performance. Particle size may also be important: Nutzback, Pollmann and Behnke (1984) found that gravid pigs digested finely-ground (6.25 mm) alfalfa-containing diets better than normally ground diets (12.5 mm). Cellulose digestion was also improved by pelleting.

Chemical treatment of straw has been practised for many decades but Bergner (1981) has refined this procedure and has thoroughly investigated its nutritional and physiological effects in growing and also in breeding pigs, for which it seems suitable. Chemical treatment of other feedstuffs for pig nutrition is certainly merited.

Conclusions

A wide variety of fibrous feedstuffs is currently available for pig nutrition (Van Es, 1981), and in particular 'bulky' feeds, popular in the past, such as potatoes, fodder beet, brassicas, young grass, grass silage dried beet pulp, and the entire maize plant have attractions (Thomke, 1981; Livingstone, 1983). Future research priorities in this field should include much more detailed knowledge of the chemical and physical composition of each of these sources of dietary fibre in relation to physiological studies on their mode of action, processing methods and their nutritive value at all stages of life in pigs. Until this information is available the use of feedstuffs with a high content of dietary fibre cannot be made on a sound scientific basis. The question of how to express practical responses of pigs to such feedstuffs is very difficult because all types of dietary fibre probably exert both indirect effects on other nutrients and direct effects as nutrient sources in their own right. Herein lies a complex and challenging problem for the animal nutritionist.

References

AGRICULTURAL RESEARCH COUNCIL (1967). In *The Nutrient Requirements of Farm Livestock No 3: Pigs*, pp. 56–63. Agricultural Research Council; London

AGRICULTURAL RESEARCH COUNCIL (1981). In *The Nutrient Requirements of Pigs*, pp. 41–44. Commonwealth Agricultural Bureaux; Farnham Royal

ALBERS, N. and HENKEL, H. (1979). *Zeitschrift für Tierphysiologie, Tierernährung und Futtermittelkunde*, **42**, 113–121

ARGENZIO, R.A. (1982). *Les Colloques de l'INRA*, **12**, 207–215

ARGENZIO, R.A. and SOUTHWORTH, M. (1975). *American Journal of Physiology*, **228**, 454–460

ASP, N.G., JOHANSSON, C.G., HALLMER, H. and SILJESTROM, M. (1983). *Journal of Agricultural and Food Chemistry*, **31**, 476–482

BAKER, D.H., BECKER, D.E., JENSEN, A.H. and HARMON, B.G. (1968). *Journal of Animal Science*, **27**, 1332–1335

BARCROFT, J., MCANALLY, R.A. and PHILLIPSON, A.T. (1944). *Journal of Experimental Biology*, **20**, 120–129

BARDON, T. and FIORAMONTI, J. (1983). *British Journal of Nutrition*, **50**, 685–690

BEHM, G. (1954). *Archives für Tierernährung*, **4**, 197–218

BELL, J.M. and SHIRES, A. (1982). *Canadian Journal of Animal Science*, **62**, 557–565

BELL, J.M., SHIRES, A. and KEITH, M.O. (1983). *Canadian Journal of Animal Science*, **63**, 201–212

BERGNER, H. (1981). *Pig News and Information*, **2**, 135–140

BERGNER, H., SIMON, O. and BERGNER, U. (1980). In *Protein Metabolism and Nutrition*, pp. 198–204. Ed. H.J. Oslage and K. Rohr. European Association of Animal Production, Braunschweig

BOHMANN, V.R., HUNTER, J.E. and MCCORMICK, J. (1955). *Journal of Animal Science*, **14**, 499–506

CAMERON, C.D.T. (1960). *Canadian Journal of Animal Science*, **40**, 126–133

CAMPBELL, R.G., TAVERNER, M.R. and CURIC, D.M. (1983). *Animal Production*, **36**, 193–199

CANGUILHEM, R. and LABIE, C. (1977). *Revue de Medécine Vétérinaire*, **128**, 1669–1681

CLEMENS, E.T., STEVENS, C.E. and SOUTHWORTH, M. (1975). *Journal of Nutrition*, **105**, 759–768

COOPER, P.H. and TYLER, C. (1959). *Journal of Agricultural Science (Cambridge)*, **52**, 332–339

COEY, W.E. and ROBINSON, K.L. (1954). *Journal of Agricultural Science (Cambridge)*, **45**, 41–47

CRANWELL, P.D. (1968). *Nutrition Abstracts and Reviews*, **38**, 721–730

CUNNINGHAM, H.M., FRIEND, D.W. and NICHOLSON, J.W.G. (1961). *Canadian Journal of Animal Science*, **41**, 120–125

CUNNINGHAM, H.M., FRIEND, D.W. and NICHOLSON, J.W.G. (1962). *Canadian Journal of Animal Science*, **42**, 167–175

DE GOEY, L.W. and EWAN, R.C. (1975). *Journal of Animal Science*, **40**, 1045–1057

DIERICK, N., VERVAEKE, I., DECUYPERE, J. and HENDERICKX, H.K. (1983). *Revue de l'Agriculture (Brussels)*, **36**, 1691–1712

DROCHNER, W., HAZEM, A.S., MEYER, H. and RENSMANN, F.W. (1978). *Fortschritte der Veterinärmedizin*, **28**, 220–225

EHLE, F.R., JERACI, J.L., ROBERTSON, J.B. and VAN SOEST, P.J. (1982). *Journal of Animal Science*, **55**, 1071–1080

ELSLEY, F.W.H. (1969). In *Third Nutrition Conference for Feed Manufacturers*, pp. 126–152. J. and A. Churchill; London

ENGLYST, H.N., ANDERSON, V. and CUMMINGS, J.H. (1983). *Journal of the Science of Food and Agriculture*, **34**, 1434–1440

ENGLYST, H.N., WIGGINS, H.S. and CUMMINGS, J.H. (1982). *Analyst (London)*, **107**, 307–318

ES, A.J.H. VAN (1981). *Agriculture and Environment*, **6**, 195–204

FARRELL, D.J. (1973). *Animal Production*, **16**, 43–47

FARRELL, D.J. and JOHNSON, K.A. (1972). *Animal Production*, **14**, 209–217

FIORAMONTI, J. and BUENO, L. (1980). *British Journal of Nutrition*, **43**, 155–162

FORBES, R.M. and HAMILTON, T.S. (1952). *Journal of Animal Science*, **11**, 480–490

FRANK, G.R., AHERNE, F.X. and JENSEN, A.H. (1983). *Journal of Animal Science*, **57**, 645–654

FRIEND, D.W., NICHOLSON, J.W.G. and CUNNINGHAM, H.M. (1964). *Canadian Journal of Animal Science*, **44**, 303–308

GARGALLO, J. and ZIMMERMAN, D.R. (1981a). *Journal of Animal Science*, **53**, 395–402

GARGALLO, J. and ZIMMERMAN, D.R. (1981b). *Journal of Animal Science*, **53**, 1286–1291

HENRY, Y. (1970). *Annales de Zootechnie*, **19**, 117–141

HØJGAARD-OLSEN, N.J. and NIELSEN, H.E. (1966). In *Forsøgslaboratoriets Aarbog*, pp. 12–15. National Institute of Animal Science; Copenhagen

HORSZCZARUK, F. (1962a). *Roczniki Nauk Rolniczych*, **80B2**, 115–125

HORSZCZARUK, F. (1962b). *Roczniki Nauk Rolniczych*, **80B2**, 5–22

HORSZCZARUK, F. and SLJIVOVACKI, K. (1971). *Rocznini Nauk Rolniczych*, **93B**, 143–147

HUANG, W.Y. and KUMMEROW, F.A. (1976). *Lipids*, **11**, 34–41

IMOTO, S. and NAMIOKA, S. (1978a). *Journal of Animal Science*, **47**, 479–487

IMOTO, S. and NAMIOKA, S. (1978b). *Journal of Animal Science*, **47**, 467–478

IMOTO, S. and NAMIOKA, S. (1983a). *Journal of Animal Science*, **56**, 858–866

IMOTO, S. and NAMIOKA, S. (1983b). *Journal of Animal Science*, **56**, 867–875

JAMES, W.P.T. and THEANDER, O. (Ed.) (1981). *The Analysis of Dietary Fiber in Food*. Marcel Dekker; New York

JENTSCH, W., SCHIEMANN, R. and HOFFMANN, L. (1968). *Archives für Tierernährung*, **18**, 352–357

JUST, A. (1982a). *Livestock Production Science*, **9**, 717–729

JUST, A. (1982b). *Livestock Production Science*, **9**, 569–580

JUST, A., ANDERSEN, J.O. and JØRGENSEN, H. (1980). *Zeitschrift für Tierphysiologie, Tierernährung und Futtermittelkunde*, **44**, 82–90

JUST, A., FERNANDEZ, J.A. and JØRGENSEN, H. (1983). *Livestock Production Science*, **10**, 171–186

JUST, A., JØRGENSEN, H. and FERNANDEZ, J.A. (1983). *Livestock Production Science*, **10**, 487–506

JUST, A., SAUER, W.C., BECH-ANDERSEN, S., JØRGENSEN, H. and EGGUM, B.O. (1980). *Zeitschrift für Tierphysiologie, Tierernährung und Futtermittelkunde*, **43**, 83–91

KASS, M.L., VAN SOEST, P.J., POND, W.G., LEWIS, B. and MCDOWELL, R.E. (1980). *Journal of Animal Science*, **50**, 175–191

KENNELLY, J.J. and AHERNE, F.X. (1980). *Canadian Journal of Animal Science*, **60**, 717–726

KENNELLY, J.J., AHERNE, F.X. and SAUER, W.C. (1981). *Canadian Journal of Animal Science*, **61**, 349–362

KEYS, J.E. and DEBARTHE, J.V. (1974). *Journal of Animal Science*, **39**, 53–57

KIRCHGESSNER, M., ROTH-MAIER, D.A. and ROTH, F. (1975). *Zuchtungskunde*, **47**, 96–103

KRACHT, W., SCHRODER, H., RINNE, W. and FRANKE, M. (1975). In *Tierernährung und Futterung-Erfahrungen, Ergebnisse, Entwicklungen-9*, pp. 250–259. VEB Deutscher Landwirtschaftsverlag; Berlin

KUAN, K.K., STANOGIAS, G. and DUNKIN, A.C. (1983). *Animal Production*, **36**, 201–209

KUPKE, B. and HENKEL, H. (1977). *Zeitschrift für Tierphysiologie Tierernährung und Futtermittelkunde*, **38**, 330

LATYMER, E.A. and LOW, A.G. (1984). *Proceedings of the Nutrition Society*, **43**, 12A

LATYMER, E.A. and WOODLEY, S.C. (1984). *Proceedings of the Nutrition Society*, **43**, 22A

LAURENTOWSKA, C. (1959). *Roczniki Nauk Rolniczych*, **74B**, 567–578

LIVINGSTONE, R.M. (1983). *Pig Farming*, **31**, 61–62, 65

LLOYD, L.E., DALE, D.G. and CRAMPTON, E.W. (1958). *Journal of Animal Science*, **17**, 684–692

LOW, A.G. and KEAL, H.D. (1981). *12th International Congress of Nutrition, San Diego*, p. 56

LOW, A.G., PARTRIDGE, I.G. and SAMBROOK, I.E. (1978). *British Journal of Nutrition*, **39**, 515–526

LOW, A.G. and RAINBIRD, A.L. (1984). *British Journal of Nutrition*, **52**, 499–505

MASON, V.C., KRAGELUND, Z. and EGGUM, B.O. (1982). *Zeitschrift für Tierphysiologie, Tierernährung und Futtermittelkunde*, **48**, 241–252

MOHME, H., MOLNAR, S. and LENKHEIT, W. (1970). *Zeitschrift für Tierphysiologie, Tierernährung und Futtermittelkunde*, **21**, 138–146

MORGAN, C.A., WHITTEMORE, C.T. and COCKBURN, J.H.S. (1984). *Animal Feed Science and Technology*, **11**, 11–34

MOSENTHIN, R. and HENKEL, H. (1983). *Les Colloques de l'INRA*, **16**, 447–450

MOSER, R.L., PEO, E.R., MOSER, B.D. and LEWIS, A.J. (1982a). *Journal of Animal Science*, **54**, 800–805

MOSER, R.L., PEO, E.R., MOSER, B.D. and LEWIS, A.J. (1982b). *Journal of Animal Science*, **54**, 1181–1195

MÜLLER, H.L. and KIRCHGESSNER, M. (1983). *Zeitschrift für Tierphysiologie, Tierernährung und Futtermittelkunde*, **49**, 127–133

MUNCHOW, H., BERGNER, H., SEIFERT, H., SCHONMUTH, G. and BRABAND, E. (1982). *Archiv für Tierernährung*, **32**, 483–491

MURRAY, A.G., FULLER, M.F. and PIRIE, A.R. (1977). *Animal Production*, **24**, 139

NEWTON, G.L., HALE, O.M. and PLANK, C.O. (1983). *Canadian Journal of Animal Science*, **63**, 399–408

NUZBACK, L.J., POLLMANN, D.S. and BEHNKE, K.C. (1984). *Journal of Animal Science*, **58**, 378–385

OWEN, J.B. and RIDGMAN, W.J. (1967). *Animal Production*, **9**, 107–113

OWEN, J.B. and RIDGMAN, W.J. (1968). *Animal Production*, **10**, 85–91

PARTRIDGE, I.G. (1978). *British Journal of Nutrition*, **39**, 539–545

PARTRIDGE, I.G., KEAL, H.D. and MITCHELL, K.G. (1982). *Animal Production*, **35**, 209–214

PEKAS, J.C., YEN, J.T. and POND, W.G. (1983). *Nutrition Reports International*, **27**, 259–270

POLLMANN, D.S., DANIELSON, D.M. and PEO, E.R. JR. (1979). *Journal of Animal Science*, **48**, 1385–1393

POTKINS, Z.V., LAWRENCE, T.L.J. and THOMLINSON, J.R. (1984). *Animal Production*, **38**, 534

POWLEY, J.S., CHEEKE, P.R., ENGLAND, D.C., DAVIDSON, T.P. and KENNICK, W.H. (1981). *Journal of Animal Science*, **53**, 308–316

RAINBIRD, A.L. and LOW, A.G. (1983). *Proceedings of the Nutrition Society*, **42**, 88A

RAINBIRD, A.L., LOW, A.G. and ZEBROWSKA, T. (1983). *British Journal of Nutrition*, **52**, 489–498

RAINBIRD, A.L., LOW, A.G. and SAMBROOK, I.E. (1984). *Proceedings of the Nutrition Society*, **43**, 28A

REEDS, P.J., CADENHEAD, A., FULLER, M.F., LOBLEY, G.E. and MCDONALD, J.D. (1980). *British Journal of Nutrition*, **43**, 445–455

RERAT, A., VAISSADE, P. and VAUGELADE, P. (1979). *Annals de Biologie Animale Biochimie Biophysique*, **19**, 739–747

SAMBROOK, I.E. (1981). *Journal of the Science of Food and Agriculture*, **32**, 781–791

SAMBROOK, I.E., RAINBIRD, A.L. and LOW, A.G. (1982). In *Fibre in Human and Animal Nutrition* (Abstract). Royal Society of New Zealand; Wellington

SAUER, W.C., STOTHERS, S.C. and PARKER, R.J. (1977). *Canadian Journal of Animal Science*, **57**, 775–784

SCHNABEL, E., BOLDUAN, G. and GULDENPENNING, A. (1983). *Archives für Tierernährung*, **33**, 371–378

SEERLEY, R.W. (1962). *Dissertation Abstracts*, **22**, 4143

SHERRY, P.A., HARRISON, P.C. and FAHEY, G.C. JR. (1981). *Journal of Animal Science*, **53**, 1309–1315

SIMON, O., MÜNCHMEYER, R., BERGNER, H. and ZEBROWSKA, T. (1978). *British Journal of Nutrition*, **40**, 243–252

SOEST, P.J. VAN (1963a). *Journal of Association of Official Agricultural Chemists*, **46**, 825–828

SOEST, P.J. VAN (1963b). *Journal of Association of Official Agricultural Chemists*, **46**, 829–835

SOEST, P.J. VAN and MCQUEEN, R.W. (1973). *Proceedings of the Nutrition Society*, **32**, 123–130

SOUTHGATE, D.A.T. (1969). *Journal of the Science of Food and Agriculture*, **20**, 331–335

TAVERNER, M.R., CAMPBELL, R.G. and BIDEN, S. (1984). *Proceedings of the Australian Society of Animal Production*, **15**, 757

TAVERNER, M.R., HUME, I.D. and FARRELL, D.J. (1981). *British Journal of Nutrition*, **46**, 149–158

THOMKE, S. (1981). *Livestock Production Science*, **8**, 188–189

TROWELL, H., SOUTHGATE, D.A.T., WOLEVER, T.M.S., LEEDS, A.R., GASSULL, M.A. and JENKINS, D.J.A. (1976). *Lancet*, **1**, 967

TULLIS, J.B. and WHITTEMORE, C.T. (1981). *Animal Production*, **32**, 395

WHITING, F. and BEZEAU, L.M. (1957). *Canadian Journal of Animal Science*, **37**, 106–113

WOODMAN, H.E. and EVANS, R.E. (1947). *Journal of Agricultural Science (Cambridge)*, **37**, 202–210

YOSHIMOTO, T. and MATSUBARA, N. (1983). *Japanese Journal of Zootechnical Science*, **54**, 748–754

ZEBROWSKA, T. (1973). *Roczniki Nauk Rolniczych*, **95B1**, 115–123

ZEBROWSKA, T. (1982). *Les Colloques de l'INRA*, **12**, 225–236

ZEBROWSKA, T., LOW, A.G. and ZEBROWSKA, H. (1983). *British Journal of Nutrition*, **49**, 401–410

ZEBROWSKA, T., SIMON, O., MUNCHMEYER, R., WOLF, E., BERGNER, H. and ZEBROWSKA, H. (1982). *Archives für Tierernährung*, **32**, 431–444

ZIVKOVIC, S. and BOWLAND, J.P. (1970). *Canadian Journal of Animal Science*, **50**, 177–184

ZOIOPOULOS, P.E., ENGLISH, P.R. and TOPPS, J.H. (1982). *Animal Production*, **35**, 25–33

ZOIOPOULOS, P.E., ENGLISH, P.R. and TOPPS, J.H. (1983a). *Zeitschrift für Tierphysiologie, Tierernährung und Futtermittelkunde*, **49**, 210–218

ZOIOPOULOS, P.E., TOPPS, J.H. and ENGLISH, P.R. (1983b). *Zeitschrift für Tierphysiologie, Tierernährung und Futtermittelkunde*, **49**, 219–228

5

EFFECT OF FIBRE IN COMPOUND FEEDS ON THE PERFORMANCE OF RUMINANTS

A. STEG, Y. VAN DER HONING AND H. DE VISSER
Institute for Livestock Feeding and Nutrition Research, Lelystad, The Netherlands

Introduction

To meet the increasing production potential of (particularly dairy) cattle, the animals concerned have to consume the required amount of nutrients. With limited world supplies of food and feedstuffs it should be best to fully exploit the specific capacity of the ruminant to digest fibrous materials, and in particular roughages. A higher ingestion of nutrients from roughages is promoted by increasing the feeding value per unit quantity as well as by increasing the quantity ingested. In many cases, considerable improvements in these aspects still seem possible, for example by attention to the choice of the type of forage, the cutting regime, the harvesting and preservation procedure, the feeding technique, etc. However, a more detailed analysis of these aspects of roughage feeding lies beyond the scope of this chapter.

For the high producing ruminant, even the best quality forage (e.g. fresh grass, lucerne or forage maize) fed *ad libitum* provides insufficient nutrients. To fully meet the energy and protein requirements, concentrate supplements are therefore needed. Traditionally, these supplements were primarily based upon cereals and some oil cakes. This situation has remained unchanged in a number of countries. However, as production levels have increased, concentrate need has increased substantially. The use of high amounts of cereals gave doubts about animal well-being and the optimal utilization of ingested nutrients for animal production, with the result that concern was expressed about the optimal feeding strategy for high producing dairy cows (Broster and Swan, 1979).

It may be of interest at this point to consider the Dutch situation. The Netherlands is a small country (2 million hectares of land used for agriculture), but one with a considerable number of livestock. Animal density/ha, calculated in livestock units, is almost four times the average of the European Economic Community. To feed the steadily increasing number of pigs, poultry and dairy cows in the last 25 years, only limited amounts of home-grown feedstuffs like roughages or cereals were available. As a result, the usage of compound feeds has increased about threefold in a 20 year period to reach 15 300 tonnes in 1980. By far the greatest proportion of the ingredients had to be imported. The Feed Manufacturers and Trade Industry have been active in selecting the ingredients with the best price per unit feeding value and this has led to a very interesting shift in the type of ingredients used, as is shown in *Table 5.1*. The amount of cereals (two-thirds of it

Table 5.1   AVAILABLE CONCENTRATE INGREDIENTS USED FOR THE PRODUCTION OF CONCENTRATES IN THE NETHERLANDS. THE RELATIVE PROPORTIONS OF THE DIFFERENT RAW INGREDIENTS USED ARE COMPARED TO AN INDEX VALUE OF 100 FOR THE TOTAL LEVEL OF CONCENTRATES PRODUCED

	1960	*1970*	*1980*
Concentrates produced (t)	5566 (= 100)	9270 (= 100)	15 300 (= 100)
Cereals + pulses	69	36	18
Cereal by-products	7	15	17
Oil seed by-products	13	20	19
Dried beet pulp	3	7	5
Citrus pulp		1	7
Molasses + condensed mol.sol.	2	4	4
Cassava		6	15
Miscellaneous	6	11	15

(Jaarstatistiek van de Veevoeders, 1983)

Table 5.2   PERCENTAGE COMPOSITION OF BRITISH (1978) AND DUTCH (1980) COMPOUND FEEDS FOR DAIRY CATTLE

	Netherlands	*UK*
Cereals	1	28
Cereal by-products: maize gluten	25	6
other	3	24
Vegetable proteins	19	14
Animal proteins		4
Molasses/condensed mol.sol.	7	7
Cassava	3 ⎱	10
Beet and citrus pulp	36 ⎰	
Minerals	2	3
Miscellaneous	4	4

(Wilson, Brigstocke and Cuthbert, 1981; Jaarstatistiek van de Veevoeders, 1983)

being maize) has decreased, and cereals are almost exclusively used nowadays in non-ruminant feeding. Cassava has filled part of the gap, but the use of the by-product feeds rich in fibre has increased the most (e.g. cereal by-products like maize gluten feed, oil seed by-products, beet pulp and citrus pulp, brewers' grains, etc). Most of these fibre-rich by-products are used for ruminants. Indeed ruminants now have to produce on mixtures mainly consisting of beet and citrus pulps, maize gluten feed and the more cellulose-rich types of oil seed by-products, as is shown in *Table 5.2*. When compared with the data of Wilson, Brigstocke and Cuthbert (1981) for British compound feeds, differences are striking, the more so since these authors remark that the cereals figures for 1978 were very low. These differences in ingredient composition are also reflected in differences in chemical characteristics of the compounds, and in particular the ratio between plant cell walls and cell contents. For example, on the basis of the figures presented in *Table 5.2*, the crude fibre contents of the British and Dutch compounds would be about 65 and 115 g/kg, respectively.

In the following sections of this chapter comments will be made about the effect of (large) differences in compound composition on intake, rumen fermentation, feeding value and level of production in dairy cows. Because De Visser and co-workers in the Netherlands have studied this subject for a number of years on a wide range of compound feeds, intensive reference will be made to their results. However, more recently information has also been gathered in the UK (Sutton *et al.*, 1984; Thomas *et al.*, 1984).

Feed intake and rumen fermentation

To achieve maximum energy intake in high-producing dairy cattle it is important to know which factors limit feed intake and their interactions. Feed intake regulation in ruminants is complex and not fully understood. The traditional opinion that the main physical factors in limitation of feed intake from roughage-rich diets are rumen capacity and rate of disappearance of digesta from the digestive tract is well-known (Conrad, Pratt and Hibbs, 1964). Metabolic factors are said to play a more important role in the regulation of intake of highly digestible forages and diets rich in concentrates (Baumgardt, 1970; Baile and Forbes, 1974). A considerable number of papers on feed intake regulation suggest, however, that metabolic control of feed intake may also interact with physical regulation. Bines (1979), in a review on voluntary feed intake by high-yielding dairy cows, followed a different approach. Factors controlling intake were divided in groups, either attributable to the animal, to the feed or to the management and environment.

In the scope of this chapter interest is focused on feed factors in particular. The ruminant can utilize the major part of bulky, fibrous materials only via microbes. Voluntary intake of rations rich in roughages is generally restricted by the limited capacity of the digestive tract, the reticulorumen in particular. Disappearance of digesta from the reticulorumen is possible either by microbial degradation and absorption of end-products (VFA, etc.) or by passage to the lower digestive tract of undigested residues, after sufficient reduction of particle size, and of microbial mass. In addition to the effect of chewing and ruminating, rumen fermentation plays an important role in particle size reduction.

Thus factors limiting reduction of particle size or microbial degradation will generally reduce the voluntary feed intake. For maximum feed intake, the rate of disappearance of digesta from the rumen has to be optimized. Important factors in this respect are feed particle size and rate of degradation in the rumen.

GROUND FORAGES

Intake generally increases after reduction of particle size by chopping, wafering, grinding or pelleting of forages. These smaller particles, due to their increased surface area, allow a more rapid microbial attack and an increased rate of passage. The effect on intake seems greater in more mature and less digestible forages and with smaller particles (Van der Honing, 1975). Although intake increases, however, digestibility of ground and pelleted forages compared to the unprocessed material tends to be lower. These effects on intake and digestibility are mainly attributed to an increased rate of passage through the forestomachs and the reduced time for microbial fermentation. In most cases the lower digestibility is compensated for by an improved utilization of digestible energy (Blaxter, 1973; Van der Honing, 1975).

The forage pellets can be fed as such (Van der Honing, 1975) or included in the concentrate-mixture (Westerhuis and De Visser, 1974; De Visser, 1977).

Information about the effect on intake of incorporating ground forage in the concentrate-mixture is limited. De Visser (1977) observed no significant differences in dairy cows when comparing compound feeds containing up to 60 per cent of grass pellets with compound feeds based on by-products. However, the lower energy value of compounds with grass pellets resulted in a slightly lower net energy intake. For high producing cattle, grinding of forage will be of limited value for a higher energy intake, unless animals have to produce mainly from forage of moderate quality. Nevertheless, substituting ground forage for rapidly fermenting feed ingredients can be of importance for maintaining an optimum rumen fermentation.

CONCENTRATES AND RUMEN FERMENTATION

The activity of the microbes in the rumen depends upon sufficient substrate and nitrogen supply in the rumen contents, and its intensity is important for the fermentation and the rate of degradation. Feed factors involved in rate of degradation and type and extent of microbial fermentation are: the forage-to-concentrate ratio, the proportion of fibrous roughages in long form in the ration, the concentration and quantity of easily fermentable substances in the ration, supplementation of the diet with fats or fatty acids, etc. (Tamminga, 1982). Besides these factors, level of feeding, changing the feeding procedure, processing such as grinding, pelleting, chemical or heat treatment, coating, inclusion of active agents (e.g. monensin), salts and mineral buffers may also affect microbial degradation.

Rate of fermentation varies between different sources of carbohydrates (Johnson, 1976; Sutton, 1980). The highest rate is found with soluble sugars, starch has an intermediate rate varying with type of starch, but cell-wall constituents (hemicellulose, cellulose, lignin) have the lowest rate of fermentation, often not commencing until after a lag phase.

High levels of easily fermentable substances, such as soluble sugars, starch, some proteins, etc., in a ration tend to decrease rumen pH and increase concentrations of VFA and lactate in the rumen fluid, resulting in a lower cellulolytic activity of the microbes in the rumen (Porter *et al.*, 1972; Counotte, 1981). Moreover, erratic day-to-day fluctuations in VFA-proportions and unstable fermentation were reported by Barry, Thompson and Armstrong (1977) with sheep. Lower cellulolytic activity causes a slower degradation of cell-wall constituents, which lowers the rate of breakdown of fibrous particles in the reticulorumen. As a result the increased fill of the rumen with undigested residues will restrict intake of new feed.

Preventing a suboptimal fermentation and a too rapid formation of VFA and lactic acid can be achieved by decreasing the amount of readily fermentable substances in the diet. If such changes are not possible or insufficient, incorporation of water-soluble buffers into the diet will help to reduce the fluctuation in ruminal pH and enhance fibre digestion (Rogers, Davis and Clark, 1982). However, feed intake may be lower due probably to a palatability effect, although increase of feed intake was shown by Erdman *et al.* (1980).

Feeding system, time available for feed consumption and frequency of feeding may also influence feed intake and affect microbial fermentation. Increased frequency of feeding of (starchy) concentrates prevented extreme low pH and high peaks of VFA and lactate (Kaufmann *et al.*, 1975; Sutton, Hart and Broster, 1982).

COMPOUND FEEDS BASED ON BY-PRODUCTS

To maximize nutrient and energy intake, De Visser (1978, 1980, 1982) studied the effect of the ingredient composition of concentrate mixtures on the voluntary intake of concentrates in a ration with a restricted amount of forage. He did so by using different kinds of by-products, such as beet and citrus pulps, wheat feed, linseed expeller, or soya bean hulls in the formulation of concentrate-mixtures to arrive at different concentrations of starch and sugars (S+S).

Table 5.3 presents examples of such mixtures; some of these were used in the trials indicated in *Table 5.4*. In the trials depicted in *Table 5.4* the effect on feed intake, rumen fermentation and milk yield and composition in the first 13 weeks of lactation was studied for the different concentrate mixtures fed as a supplement to a basal diet providing a DM intake of 7.5 kg/day from hay, wilted grass silage or maize silage.

In 1978 and 1979 de Visser and de Groot (1980) fed concentrates with 20, 30, 40 or 50 per cent S+S in the dry matter during the last four weeks of pregnancy and for the first 13 weeks of lactation to a total of 103 cows. Lower S+S concentrations

Table 5.3 EXAMPLES OF EXPERIMENTAL CONCENTRATE MIXTURES, DIFFERING IN PERCENTAGE OF STARCH AND SUGARS

| | *Content of starch + sugars in dry matter (%)* | | | | |
| | *10* | *20* | *30* | *40* | *50* |
Ingredient			*(% inclusion rate)*		
Cassava	—	—	14.8	29.7	35.0
Wheat	—	—	—	—	18.0
Hominy feed	—	—	11.3	22.6	—
Cane molasses	3.5	2.6	4.8	6.6	5.0
Soya bean meal, solv. extr.	7.0	10.7	13.9	16.7	15.0
Maize gluten feed	20.0	24.6	22.6	20.6	25.0
Linseed	—	3.8	1.8	—	—
Citrus pulp, dried	5.0	20.0	10.0	—	—
Beet pulp, dried	—	20.0	10.0	—	—
Wheat bran	—	14.5	7.0	—	—
Tallow	2.0	1.8	1.8	1.8	—
Linseed expeller	10.0	—	—	—	—
Soya bean hulls	50.0	—	—	—	—
Minerals and vitamins	2.5	2.0	2.0	2.0	2.0

(De Visser and De Groot, 1980; De Visser, 1984)

Table 5.4 DETAILS OF DIETS USED IN FEEDING TRIALS WITH DAIRY COWS IN 1978–1982. THE TYPE OF CONCENTRATE WAS VARIED BY USING BY-PRODUCTS WHICH GAVE RISE TO THE DIFFERENT % SOLUBLE STARCH AND SUGARS IN THE DRY MATTER (DM). ALL CONCENTRATES WERE FED TO COWS IN WHICH THE PROVISION OF ROUGHAGE WAS DESIGNED TO PROVIDE AN INTAKE OF 7.5 kg DM/DAY

Year of experiment	*Type of roughage*	*% Starch + sugars in concentrate DM*
1978[a]	Hay	50; 40; 30; 20
1979[a]	Wilted grass silage	40; 30; 20
1981[b]	Hay (H) or maize silage (M)	H20; M10; M20
1982[b]	Hay (H) or maize silage (M)	H20; M10; M20

[a]De Visser and De Groot (1980)
[b]De Visser (1984)

Table 5.5   EFFECT OF VARIOUS LEVELS OF STARCH PLUS SUGARS (S+S) OF
CONCENTRATE MIXTURES ON DAILY DRY MATTER AND ENERGY INTAKE OVER THE
FIRST 13 WEEKS OF LACTATION

| | *% S + S in concentrate DM* | | | |
	20	*30*	*40*	*50*
Number of animals	30	30	30	13
Roughage intake (kg DM/day)	7.4	7.4	7.5	7.5
Concentrate intake (kg DM/day)	11.2	10.4	9.3	8.3
Total intake (kg DM/day)	18.6	17.7	16.8	15.8
Net energy intake[a] (MJ/day)	127	122	115	100
Net energy requirement[a] (MJ/day)	139	135	131	120

[a]Net-energy lactation according to Van Es (1978)
(See *Table 5.4*; 1978, 1979; De Visser and De Groot, 1980)

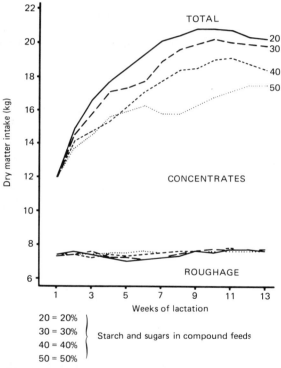

Figure 5.1   Effect of % starch and sugars in the compound feed on daily dry matter
intake of dairy cows—trials 1978/79 (De Visser and De Groot, 1980)

resulted in higher total dry matter intakes (*Table 5.5*, *Figure 5.1*). The incidence of
off-feed periods also increased with higher S+S contents. At and above 40 per cent
S+S there was a sudden increase in the number of digestive disturbances, with
two-thirds of the cows showing one or more serious off-feed periods. Rumen
fermentation studies in fistulated cows receiving different quantities of concentrate
in their diets showed that pH remained higher with lower S+S content and with a
lower amount of concentrates fed (*Figure 5.2*). VFA concentrations of rumen fluid
increased mainly due to the amount of concentrates ingested; significant differences

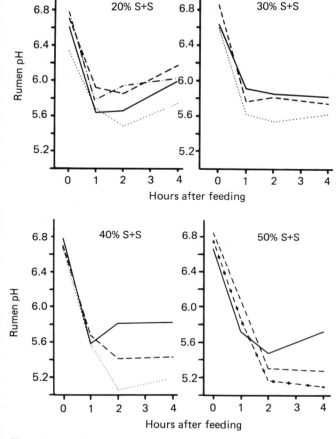

Figure 5.2 pH measurements in rumen fluid as affected by the quantity and composition of the concentrate mixture (De Visser and De Groot, 1980). Amount of concentrates; — 10 kg; – ◆ – 12.5 kg; –·–·– 16 kg; – – – 12 kg; ······ 14 kg

Table 5.6 EFFECT OF FEEDING TWO TYPES OF CONCENTRATES MIXTURES (10 AND 20% S+S) IN ADDITION TO HAY (H) OR MAIZE SILAGE (M) ON DAILY DRY MATTER AND ENERGY INTAKE OVER THE FIRST 13 WEEKS OF LACTATION (EXPERIMENTS 1981 AND 1982)

Treatment	M10	M20	H20
Number of animals	32	32	32
Roughage intake (kg DM/day)	7.4	7.1	7.2
Concentrate intake (kg DM/day)	12.1	11.6	11.5
Total intake (kg DM/day)	19.5	18.7	18.7
Net energy intake[a] (MJ/day)	139	134	129
Net energy requirement[a] (MJ/day)	147	144	142

(De Visser, 1984; See *Table 5.4*)
[a]Net energy lactation according to Van Es (1978)

between concentrate mixtures were not found. High peaks of lactate accumulation were observed for some hours after feeding with large quantities of concentrates containing 40 or 50 per cent S+S.

Experiments conducted in 1981 and 1982 included 40 or 50 per cent soya bean hulls in the concentrate mixture to obtain 10 per cent S+S (see *Table 5.4*). Highest intake of total dry matter and energy was observed with this treatment compared to those with higher S+S contents (*Table 5.6*). Supplementation of a basal ration of approximately 7 kg DM from maize silage with this mixture did not result in any increase in the incidence of off-feed periods or digestive disorders, as might be expected from supplementation of a forage with a low level of structural constituents.

Sutton *et al.* (1984) fed two levels of either starchy or fibrous concentrates to dairy cows and allowed *ad libitum* access to hay. Cows given the fibrous concentrate ate about 1 kg more hay. Reducing the level of concentrate feeding from 14.0 to 10.6 kg raised hay intake by about 2 kg for both types of concentrates.

When using by-products with a lower digestibility than cereals in concentrate mixtures, compensation with energy-rich feedstuffs such as (saturated) fat may be appropriate to maintain high energy intakes. In the literature, several authors have reported a decrease in fibre digestion, although of variable size, due to including fat in the mixture. However, most of these experiments were done with ruminants at low levels of feeding (see review of Palmquist, 1984). The supplementation with fat might therefore be another interacting factor in digestion of fibre by ruminants. However, in high-yielding dairy cows Palmquist and Conrad (1980) and van der Honing *et al.* (1981, 1983) observed none or only a minor effect of fat supplementation of concentrates on the digestibility of ADF or crude fibre.

Digestibility and energetic feeding value

Most feed evaluation systems are based on the prediction of metabolizable or net energy from digested nutrients, determined in sheep at the maintenance level of feeding. Equations, with additional corrections for influence of feeding level and subsequently calculated requirements, are based upon and so hold true for rations, with concentrates containing high levels of inclusion of cereals. When compound feeds mainly based on by-products are fed instead of cereal–soya bean meal mixtures, more attention has to be given to

(1) the prediction of digestible components in sheep;
(2) the effect of feeding level and proportion of concentrates on digestibility and metabolizability in cattle, and
(3) the utilization of digested nutrients.

DIGESTIBILITY IN SHEEP

Specific problems when using concentrates based on by-products are that chemical characteristics of by-products are normally much more variable than those of primary products (Steg, 1975) and that information on average digestibility of such ingredients and their variation tends to be limited. In addition, a large spectrum of feedstuffs can be used, but fluctuating market prices can cause rather drastic changes in actual utilization.

Some years ago, trials were done at Lelystad to increase the amount of information about digestibility in relation to composition of several related concentrate ingredients (Steg, 1976a,b; Steg and Rijpkema, 1976). As a result, in the Dutch Table of Feedingstuffs (Veevoedertabel, 1983) separate equations are given to estimate the feeding value of by-products from maize, wheat and cassava from their chemical composition. In fact, the equations were derived from relationships between chemical components and digestible components, determined in sheep at maintenance feeding level. For related products, reasonably accurate prediction of digestibility appears to be possible with a knowledge of cell-wall characteristics such as crude fibre. So, in the Dutch Tables, differences in digestibilities of by-products like maize-, wheat- and rice bran, beet pulp, cassava, soya bean meal and maize gluten feed are primarily based upon relationships between digestibility and crude fibre content. Unfortunately, limited information on digestibility of ingredients in sheep hampers the progress of this type of approach for several other by-products. For more accurate prediction of digestibility, more work is needed to study the possibilities of using methods of analysis other than crude fibre.

In addition to the study of the influence of compound composition on dairy cattle performance in the last ten years (De Visser, 1978, 1980, 1982, 1984), digestibility of a wide range of compounds was studied in sheep (*Table 5.7*). From the amounts

Table 5.7 RANGE IN SOME CHEMICAL CHARACTERISTICS AND OF ORGANIC MATTER DIGESTIBILITY OF 34 COMPOUND FEEDS STUDIED

Organic matter (g/kg DM)	812–946
Crude protein (g/kg DM)	143–404
Lipids (g/kg DM)	26–89
Crude fibre (g/kg DM)	55–238
Neutral detergent fibre[a] (g/kg DM)	202–488
Sugars (g/kg DM)	60–147
Starch (g/kg DM)	32–420
Digestibility of organic matter (%)	73.4–88.1

[a]Some data missing

and type of ingredients used to formulate a compound, it was possible to compare digestibility and feeding value predicted from data in feed tables with those of digestion trials with sheep. Results were given partly by Van Donselaar and Steg (1980). They concluded that predicted and measured organic matter digestibility (OMD %) of the mixtures studied were in agreement (the difference being 0.2 ± 1.5 percentage units). In some cases, however, predicted and measured energetic feeding values differed substantially, because of differences between expected and measured chemical composition. When a correction was made for differences between measured and calculated chemical composition, a fairly accurate estimation of energy value was possible from the data given in the Dutch Table of Feedingstuffs, the difference being 0.6 ± 2.0 per cent. In this approach, mixtures containing artificially dried grass were excluded as no accurate prediction of that ingredient's digestibility and feeding value could be done.

When no information about ingredient composition is available, prediction of feeding value of compound feeds is very difficult. Several attempts have been made to relate the feeding value of compound feeds with laboratory data (Kirchgessner and Kellner, 1981; Wainman, Dewey and Boyne, 1981; Cottyn *et al.*,

1984). However no sufficiently accurate prediction of digestibility of compound feeds from cell-wall analyses such as crude fibre, neutral detergent fibre or acid detergent fibre seems feasible, because the relationship between cell walls and digestibility differs from one ingredient to another. The inaccuracy of compound feed predictions increases with products containing high levels of cell-wall constituents. It is evident that the relationship between cell-wall content and OMD is quite different for soya bean hulls, beet pulp, artificially dried grass or lucerne, treated straw, untreated straw, coffee waste and grape follicle.

The poor relationship between fibre and organic matter digestibility is demonstrated in *Figure 5.3*, suggesting that crude fibre is a poor predictor of

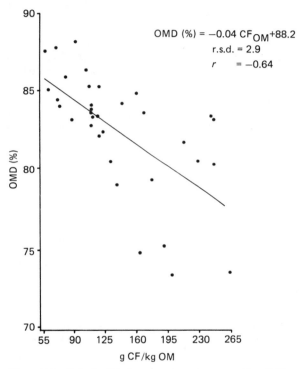

$$OMD\ (\%) = -0.04\ CF_{OM} + 88.2$$
$$r.s.d. = 2.9$$
$$r = -0.64$$

Figure 5.3 Relationship between organic matter digestibility and crude fibre content of the organic matter for 34 compound feeds

digestibility, particularly when its content is above 150 g/kg OM. NDF seems slightly better, but a direct comparison was frustrated by missing data for mixtures containing grass pellets (up to 40 per cent in some cases), because of a fire in the laboratory. Wainman, Dewey and Boyne (1981), Schöner and Pfeffer (1981) and Cottyn *et al.* (1984) demonstrated that, for a reasonably accurate estimation of feeding value, information is needed on digestibility in rumen fluid *in vitro* or *in sacco* or eventually by cellulase digestibility. This will be more so in feedstuffs with higher cell-wall contents than those studied by Cottyn *et al.* (1984) and Wainman, Dewey and Boyne (1981). It is, however, very important to standardize the analytical procedure to get more reproducible data (Blaxter, 1982). Accuracy of prediction of *in vivo* digestibility will be improved when raw *in vitro* data are corrected for differences between *in vivo* and *in vitro* digestibilities of standard samples of compound feeds measured in the same *in vitro* series (Van Es and Van der Meer, 1981; Zwart, 1984). Although this makes procedures somewhat more complex, such an approach should be recommended routine for all types of *in vitro* incubations, aiming at predicting what will happen at the animal level.

DIGESTIBILITY IN SHEEP VERSUS CATTLE

In most feed evaluation systems it is assumed that, at the maintenance level of feeding, digestibility of feedstuffs in sheep and cattle hardly differs. The effect of higher feeding level on digestibility in cattle is in some energy systems incorporated into the equations to calculate feeding values, and in the tabulated requirements (Van Es, 1978; Van der Honing and Steg, 1984), while in other systems it is simply neglected.

At Lelystad several of the compound feeds previously mentioned were also tested in digestibility trials with dairy cows. Information on some of the concentrates tested is given in *Table 5.8*. In the dairy cow trials, in addition to 6–9 kg grass hay, 7–16 kg of concentrates were fed to three to six cows. Some data on the results are given in *Table 5.9*. Data are given for cows at feeding levels above

Table 5.8 DATA OF SOME COMPOUND FEEDS TESTED IN DAIRY COW DIGESTIBILITY TRIALS

	Concentrate mixture[a]				
	K50	*K40*	*K20*	*D20*	*D10*
	Chemical composition (g/kg DM)				
Crude protein	200	202	211	187	188
Lipids	21	35	56	51	53
Crude fibre	57	83	124	103	229
Neutral detergent fibre	173	184	279	304	468
Sugars	128	128	125	118	60
Starch	420	298	101	91	53
OMD sheep (%)	85.1	83.2	80.5	83.4	83.3
Net energy lactation content[b] (MJ/kg DM)	7.4	7.3	7.4	7.4	7.5

[a]The ingredient composition of D20 and D10 is given in *Table 5.3*; the ingredient composition of K50, K40 and K20 resembled the data given in *Table 5.3*.
[b]According to Van Es (1978).

Table 5.9 ORGANIC MATTER DIGESTIBILITY (OMD %) IN DAIRY COWS OF RATIONS CONSISTING OF 7–9 kg HAY AND VARIABLE QUANTITIES OF DIFFERENT CONCENTRATES. DETAILS OF THE COMPOSITION OF THE CONCENTRATES ARE GIVEN IN *TABLE 5.8*.

Compound type	*Concentrate allowance* (kg/day)	*Feeding level*[a]	*OMD* (%)	*Differences in OMD between cows and sheep* (OMD % cow − OMD % sheep)
K50	7	2.7	78.1	+0.8
K50	12	3.6	76.7	−2.8
K40	11	3.0	76.1	−4.0
K20	7	2.7	75.9	+0.6
K20	12	3.5	75.4	−1.4
K20	12	3.3	74.6	−3.7
K20	16	4.1	76.3	−1.6
D20	14	3.5	74.3	−5.9
D10	14	3.6	71.0	−9.3

[a]Feeding level expressed as multiples of maintenance requirement

maintenance with those calculated from sheep at the maintenance level of feeding. Differences in OMD between cows and sheep were rather small for rations containing K50, K40 and K20. For these rations some influence of feeding level was evident, but not beyond what was expected (Van der Honing and Wieman, 1983). Differences in OMD between cows and sheep were, however, fairly large for D20 and large for D10. It appeared that in these trials, fibre digestibility was lower than expected. As far as D10 is concerned, the ingredient composition with 50 per cent soya bean hulls was very extreme, but the composition of D20 resembled greatly that of K20.

Thomas *et al.* (1984) compared two extreme concentrates (barley + fish meal: 591 g S+S/kg DM and beet pulp + rice bran, fat and soya bean meal; 136 g S+S/kg DM) at inclusion rates of 6 and 12 kg dry matter daily in a ration with grass silage fed *ad libitum*. Increasing the level of concentrates did depress ADF-digestibility considerably with the high-starch concentrate, but had little effect with the low-starch one. Mayne and Gordon (1984), comparing a barley-based concentrate (506 g starch/kg DM) with a sugar beet pulp based concentrate (175 g starch/kg DM) at 7 and 10 kg inclusion per animal per day together with grass silage fed *ad libitum*, found no significant differences in OMD. Sutton *et al.* (1984) on the other hand, mentioned, that in cows the DM digestibility of rations containing starchy concentrates (barley, wheat, cassava) was 2–3 per cent greater than that of fibrous concentrates (citrus pulp, beet pulp, wheat feed), although digestibility of the concentrate organic matter as measured in sheep was essentially identical.

This information causes some confusion about the validity of using sheep digestibility data for prediction of dairy cow digestibility of extremely fibrous compound feeds. Additional information in this respect will be needed.

UTILIZATION OF DIGESTED NUTRIENTS

Very limited data are available from energy balance trials on compound feeds differing extremely in fibre content. Energy losses as methane and urine, and utilization of metabolizable energy were studied in two separate trials by Van der Honing and Wieman (1983) for rations containing 12–14 kg of compound types K40, K20, D20 or D10 and 7 or 8 kg of hay. A summary of the results is given in *Table 5.10*. Differences between rations in losses of energy through methane and urine were small and not significant. Energy in milk was similar for all of the rations

Table 5.10   ENERGY LOSSES IN METHANE AND URINE, UTILIZATION OF METABOLIZABLE (k_1) AND OF GROSS ENERGY (e_1) OF DAIRY COW RATIONS[a]

| | Type of concentrate fed | | | |
	K40	K20	D20	D10
Energy losses as methane[b]	6.1	6.2	5.4	5.4
Energy losses in urine[b]	3.7	4.0	4.2	4.1
Energy in milk (MJ/kg $W^{0.75}$)	670	734	685	694
Retained in body (MJ/kg $W^{0.75}$)	−11	−16	77	65
k_1 (%)	61	62	62	64
e_1 (%)	39	38	38	37

[a]All values are the means from four to six animals. Details of the composition of concentrates are given in *Table 5.8*.
[b]Losses expressed as a % of GE

concerned. While the animals fed concentrates K40 and K20 lost some body energy and those on D20 and D10 retained some energy, the variability between cows was considerable.

Utilization of metabolizable energy for milk production and energy retention (k_1) was, surprisingly, better for D10, compensating partly for the lower digestibility of that ration. As a result, the overall utilization of gross energy (e_1) was not significantly different for the rations concerned.

Additionally, a comparison was made between net energy lactation predicted from sheep digestibility data (Van Es, 1978) and net energy determined in dairy cows. On average, dairy cows did 2, 3 and 6 per cent better on D20, K40 and K20 and 1 per cent worse on D10 than predicted, but these differences were not significant. Van der Honing and Wieman (1983) concluded that the results were within the range expected for normal diets. So, based on this limited information, sheep digestibility data can also be used for net energy prediction in dairy cows for fibrous compounds, confirming the results obtained from the feeding trials.

Milk production and milk composition

When the production potential of the animal is not limiting, the level of milk production in dairy cows is highly related to the energy and protein intake, although some energy reserve can be mobilized, especially in early lactation.

Milk composition, however, will be dependent on the availability of sufficient amounts of precursors, needed for the production of fat, lactose and protein, respectively. *Table 5.11* gives some information about the partitioning of energy in milk and the necessary precursors.

Table 5.11 PARTITIONING OF THE TOTAL ENERGY REQUIREMENTS FOR MILK PRODUCTION INTO THE RELATIVE PROPORTIONS REQUIRED FOR THE VARIOUS MILK CONSTITUENTS

	%	*Precursors*
1 kg milk	100	
40 g fat	49	long chain fatty acids, acetate, butyrate
46 g lactose	25	glucose, propionate, glucogenic amino acids
33 g protein	26	amino acids

The quantity and ratio in which different precursors are available to the animal depend on the type and amount of feed offered. Increasing the energy intake of dairy cows by increasing the consumption of starchy concentrates, such as rolled barley or ground maize, will increase the level of milk production, provided no off-feed problems occur (Broster, Sutton and Bines, 1979; Sutton, 1980). If at the same time, however, the ratio of acetate to propionate in the rumen is reduced, a decrease of the milk fat content is likely. Depending on the net result of these opposing effects, even lower total milk-fat yields can be observed. Digestion of fibre in the rumen will promote the production of acetic acid. Therefore, the utilization of fibrous compound feeds might, by maintaining a more favourable rumen fermentation, ensure a more stable composition of the milk.

This influence of the level of fibre on levels of milk production and milk composition was studied in some of the experiments of De Visser and co-workers mentioned above.

Table 5.12 AVERAGE MILK-YIELD AND COMPOSITION IN THE FIRST 13 WEEKS OF LACTATION OF COWS FED CONCENTRATES CONTAINING DIFFERENT LEVELS OF STARCH + SUGARS (EXPERIMENTS 1978 AND 1979)

	% S + S in concentrate DM			
	20	*30*	*40*	*50*
Milk yield (kg/day)	32.0	31.0	30.3	27.7
4% Fat-corrected milk yield (kg/day)	32.6	31.5	30.3	26.9
Fat content (g/kg)	41.5	41.2	40.3	38.1
Protein content (g/kg)	31.8	31.9	31.9	32.0

For full details of the diets fed and levels of intake see *Tables 5.4* and *5.5*.

Table 5.13 AVERAGE MILK-YIELD AND COMPOSITION IN THE FIRST 13 WEEKS OF LACTATION OF COWS FED CONCENTRATES CONTAINING DIFFERENT LEVELS OF STARCH + SUGARS (10 or 20%) IN CONJUNCTION WITH HAY (H) OR MAIZE SILAGE (M) (EXPERIMENTS 1981 AND 1982)

	M10	*M20*	*H20*
Milk yield (kg/day)	34.5	33.5	33.2
4% Fat-corrected milk yield (kg/day)	34.2	33.6	33.2
Fat content (g/kg)	39.9	40.5	40.5
Protein content (g/kg)	30.9	31.2	30.2

For full details of the diets fed and levels of intake see *Tables 5.4* and *5.5*.

Some data concerning feed intake have already been given (*Tables 5.5* and *5.6*). Data on milk production in the 1978 and 1979 trials are given in *Table 5.12*. In these trials, in addition to an intake of 7.5 kg DM from grass hay or wilted grass silage, compound feeds containing 20, 30, 40 and 50 per cent S+S were fed according to milk production. Volume of milk, as well as fat content, tended to increase with increasing cell-wall (fibre) content in both trials. The higher milk output from low S+S% mixtures could be explained by the higher energy intake, as given in *Table 5.5* and *Figure 5.1*.

Thomas *et al.* (1984) and Lees, Garnsworthy and Oldham (1982) recently published results showing similar tendencies. Sutton (1985), however, reported a lower milk yield on low-starch diets. After correction for differences in milk-fat content, milk yields were similar. The data presented in *Table 5.12* show no effect of compound composition on milk-protein content, although Sutton (1980) and Thomas *et al.* (1984) found higher milk-protein content with high-starch diets. This might be attributed to the increased availability of propionic acid (Sutton, 1985).

Table 5.13 gives the results on milk-yield and composition in trials performed in 1981 and 1982 (De Visser, 1984), when feeding 7.5 kg DM of grass hay (H) or maize silage (M) and extremely fibrous compounds. As is evident, level of milk production was excellent for each treatment tested. Small differences in production could be attributed to differences in energy intake (*Table 5.6*). Somewhat surprisingly, milk-fat content was similar for rations with hay and maize silage, even though there were differences in the starch content of these roughages. These results seem to suggest that the rate of fermentation of both diets was similar. In all probability this was due to a combination of the high digestibility of the hay, and the low solubility of maize starch added to the fact that the ensiling process may affect degradation.

Conclusions

Possibilities have been demonstrated to manipulate rumen fermentation, feed intake and milk production by substitution of starchy ingredients in concentrate mixtures with fibrous ingredients, containing a high proportion of digestible cell walls. Fewer off-feed periods and less incidence of digestive disorders result from a more stable and balanced rumen fermentation due to a lower amount and proportion of soluble sugar and starch consumed per unit of time. The improvement of nutrient and energy' intake in the case of optimal rumen fermentation results in higher milk energy output, if cows have the genetic capability for high yields.

Our ability to predict the effects of individual feedstuffs as components of different rations with high precision is still limited, in particular with by-products with high cell-wall contents. Work on digestibility *in sacco* or *in vitro*, and measuring the rate of digestion may enable us to increase our knowledge and create more reliable prediction equations in the near future.

References

BAILE, C.A. and FORBES, J.M. (1974). *Physiological Review*, **54**, 160–214

BARRY, T.N., THOMPSON, A. and ARMSTRONG, D.G. (1977). *Journal of Agricultural Science*, **89**, 183–195

BAUMGARDT, B.R. (1970). In *Physiology of digestion and metabolism in the ruminant*, pp. 235–253. Ed. A.T. Philipson. Oriel Press Ltd; Newcastle-upon-Tyne

BINES, J.A. (1979). In *Feeding strategy for the high yielding dairy cow*, pp. 23–48. Ed. W.H. Broster and H. Swan. Granada Publishing; London

BLAXTER, K.L. (1973). In *Proceedings of the first international green crop drying congress*, pp. 64–72. Ed. C.L. Skidmore. E. and E. Plumridge; Cambridge

BLAXTER, K. (1982). In *Recent Advances in Animal Nutrition*, pp. 217–232. Ed. W. Haresign. Butterworths; London

BROSTER, W.H., SUTTON, J.D. and BINES, J.A. (1979). In *Recent Advances in Animal Nutrition*, pp. 99–105. Ed. W. Haresign and D. Lewis. Butterworths; London

BROSTER, W.H. and SWAN, H. (1979). In: *Feeding Strategy for the High Yielding Dairy Cow*, p. 432. Ed. W.H. Broster and H. Swan. Granada; London

CONRAD, H.R., PRATT, A.D. and HIBBS, J.W. (1964). *Journal of Dairy Science*, **47**, 54–62

COTTYN, B.G., AERTS, J.V., VANACKER, J.M., MOERMANS, R.J. and BUYSSE, F.X. (1984). *Animal Feed Science and Technology*, **11**, 137–147

COUNOTTE, G.H.M. (1981). *Regulation of lactate metabolism in the rumen*, pp. 1–171. Dissertation, State University; Utrecht

DONSELAAR, B. VAN and STEG, A. (1980). *IVVO-Report 132*. Institute for Livestock Feeding and Nutrition Research; Lelystad

ERDMAN, R.A., BOTTS, R.L., HEINKEN, R.W. and BALL, L.S. (1980). *Journal of Dairy Science*, **63**, 923

ES, A.J.H. VAN (1978). *Livestock Production Science*, **5**, 331–345

ES, A.J.H. VAN and MEER, J.M. VAN DER (1981). *Methods of Analysis for Predicting the Energy and Protein Value of Feeds for Farm Animals*. Institute for Livestock Feeding and Nutrition Research; Lelystad

ES, A.J.H. VAN (1983). In *Recent advances in animal nutrition*, pp. 13–22. Ed. D.J. Farrell and Pran Vohra. University of New England; Armidale

HONING, Y. VAN DER (1975). *Agricultural Research Reports*, **836**, pp. 1–156. Centre for Agricultural Publishing and Documentation; Wageningen

HONING, Y. VAN DER and STEG, A. (1984). *IVVO-Report*, **160**. Institute for Livestock Feeding and Nutrition Research; Lelystad

HONING, Y. VAN DER and WIEMAN, B.J. (1983). *IVVO-Report*, **145**. Institute for Livestock Feeding and Nutrition Research; Lelystad

HONING, Y. VAN DER, TAMMINGA, S., WIEMAN, B.J., STEG, A., DONSELAAR, B. VAN and GILS, L.G.M. VAN (1983). *Netherland Journal of Agricultural Science*, **31**, 27–36

HONING, Y. VAN DER, WIEMAN, B.J., STEG, A. and DONSELAAR, B. VAN (1981). *Netherland Journal of Agricultural Science*, **29**, 79–92

Jaarstatistiek van de Veevoeders (1983). Ministry of Agriculture and Fisheries; The Hague

JOHNSON, R.R. (1976). *Journal of Animal Science*, **43**, 184–191

KAUFMANN, W., ROHR, K., DAENICKE, R. and HAGEMEISTER, H. (1975). *Berichte über Landwirtschaft*, **191**, Sonderheft 269–295

KIRCHGESSNER, M. and KELLNER, R.J. (1981). *Zeitschrift für Tierphysiologie, Tierernährung und Futtermittelkunde*, **45**, 9–16

LEES, J.A., GARNSWORTHY, P.C. and OLDHAM, J.D. (1982). In *Occasional Publication of the British Society of Animal Production*, **6**, 157–159

MAYNE, C.S. and GORDON, F.J. (1984). *Animal Production*, **39**, 65–75

MERTENS, D.R. (1979). In *Regulation of Acid-Base Balance*, pp. 65. Ed. W.H. Dale and P. Meinhardt. Church and Dwight Co. Inc; New York

PALMQUIST, D.L. (1984). In *Fats in animal nutrition*, pp. 357–381. Ed. J. Wiseman. Butterworths; London

PALMQUIST, D.L. and CONRAD, H.R. (1980). *Journal of Dairy Science,* **63**, 391–395

PALMQUIST, D.L. and JENKINS, T.C. (1980). *Journal of Dairy Science*, **63**, 1–14

PORTER, J.W.G., BALCH, C.C., COATES, M.E., FULLER, M.E., LATHAM, M.J., SHARP, M.E., SMITH, R.H., SUTTON, J.D. and JAYNE-WILLIAMS, D.J. (1972). In *Biennial Reviews*, pp. 13–36. NIRD; Reading

ROGERS, J.A., DAVIS, J.A. and CLARK, J.H. (1982). *Journal of Dairy Science*, **65**, 577–583

SCHÖNER, F.J. and PFEFFER, E. (1981). *Zeitschrift für Tierphysiologie, Tierernährung und Futtermittelkunde*, **46**, 139–144

STEG, A. (1975). Personal communication

STEG, A. (1976a). *IVVO-Report*, **10**. Institute for Livestock Feeding and Nutrition Research; Lelystad

STEG, A. (1976b). *IVVO-Report*, **21**. Institute for Livestock Feeding and Nutrition Research; Lelystad

STEG, A. and RIJPKEMA, Y.S. (1976). *IVVO-Report*, **22**. Institute for Livestock Feeding and Nutrition Research; Lelystad

SUTTON, J.D. (1980). *IDF-Bulletin*, **125**, 126–134

SUTTON, J.D. (1985). Personal communication

SUTTON, J.D., BINES, J.A. and NAPPER, D.J. (1985). *Animal Production*, **40** (in press)

SUTTON, J.D., BINES, J.A., NAPPER, D.J., WILKS, J.M. and SCHULLER, E. (1984). In *Annual Report National Institute for Research in Dairying*, pp. 74

SUTTON, J.D., HART, I.C. and BROSTER, W.H. (1982). In: *Energy Metabolism of Farm Animals*, pp. 26–29. Eds. A. Ekenn and F. Sundstøl. Agricultural University of Norway; Aas-NLH

SUTTON, J.D., OLDHAM, J.D. and HART, I.C. (1980). In *Energy Metabolism*, pp. 302–306. Ed. L.E. Mount. Butterworths; London

TAMMINGA, S. (1980). In *Proceedings Fifth International Symposium for Fish Meal Manufacturers*, pp. 4–17. Ed. Miller and Pike, Amsterdam

TAMMINGA, S. (1982). In *Protein and energy supply for high production of milk and meat*, pp. 15–31. Pergamon; Oxford

THOMAS, L., ASTEN, K., BASS, J., DALEY, S.R. and HUGHES, P.N. (1984). *Animal Production*, **38**, 519–522

VEEVOEDERTABEL (1983). Centraal Veevoederbureau; Lelystad

VISSER, H. DE (1977). Personal communication

VISSER, H. DE (1978). *IVVO-Report*, **40**. Institute for Livestock Feeding and Nutrition Research; Lelystad

VISSER, H. DE (1980). *Bedrijfsontwikkeling*, **11**, 1041–1047

VISSER, H. DE (1982). In *World Congress on diseases of cattle*, pp. 415–420. Koninklijke Nederlandse Maatschappij voor Diergeneeskunde; Utrecht

VISSER, H. DE (1984). *Bedrijfsontwikkeling*, **5**, 383–388

VISSER, H. DE and GROOT, A.M. DE (1980). In *Proceedings of the Fourth International Conference on Production Diseases in Farm Animals*, pp. 41–48. Ed. D. Giesecke, G. Dirksen and M. Stangassinger. München.

WAINMAN, F.W., DEWEY, P.J.S. and BOYNE, A.W. (1981). *Third Report Feedingstuffs Evaluation Unit*. Rowett Research Institute; Aberdeen

WESTERHUIS, J.H. and VISSER, H. DE (1974). *IVVO-Report*, **74**. Institute for Livestock Feeding and Nutrition Research; Lelystad

WILSON, P. (1979). In *Feeding strategy for the high yielding dairy cow*, pp. 374–397. Ed. W.H. Broster and H. Swan. Granada Publishing; London

WILSON, P.N., BRIGSTOCKE, T.D.A. and CUTHBERT, N.H. (1981). *Animal Feed Science and Technology*, **6**, 1–13

ZWART, S. (1984). Personal communication

III

Pig Nutrition

6

STRATEGIES FOR SOW NUTRITION: PREDICTING THE RESPONSE OF PREGNANT ANIMALS TO PROTEIN AND ENERGY INTAKE

I.H. WILLIAMS*, W.H. CLOSE
National Institute for Research in Dairying, Shinfield, Reading, Berks, UK
and
D.J.A. COLE
University of Nottingham School of Agriculture, Sutton Bonington, UK

Introduction

Since nutrition is the primary factor influencing sow productivity it follows that the establishment of a successful feeding strategy to ensure optimum productivity must be based on a sound knowledge of the response of the animal to specified nutritional inputs. Productivity of the breeding herd is commonly measured as the number of pigs born, weaned or sold per unit time, for example, per year or throughout the breeding lifetime. It can be optimized by mating gilts at a young age to minimize the time between selection from the bacon pens and first conception, and then by keeping them in the breeding herd reproducing regularly for as long as possible.

Traditional feeding strategies have often utilized the body reserves of the gilt and sow to buffer short-term deficits in nutrient intake with minimum effect on the fetus or suckling piglets. For example, animals which are allowed to make large gains in body weight during pregnancy compensate by eating less food during lactation, often losing large amounts of body weight. Modern sows are managed differently from their counterparts of 20 years ago. They begin their reproductive life with fewer body reserves because they are mated younger and at a lighter body weight, and the amount of food is rationed during pregnancy so that they gain less body weight. As a consequence with modern sows it may be necessary to consider nutritional responses much more precisely. For example, weight loss during lactation may be associated with fewer ova at the next oestrus (Hardy and Lodge, 1969) and extended intervals between weaning and oestrus particularly in first-litter sows (Reese *et al.*, 1982; King and Williams, 1984). Cole (1982) has suggested that 'a strategy of maximum conservation' is more appropriate for current-day sows. The main aim of this strategy is to maintain body condition during lactation, and implies a high level of feeding during lactation (the period of maximum production) preceded by a carefully controlled and limited weight gain during pregnancy.

*Permanent address: Faculty of Agriculture (Animal Science), University of Western Australia, Nedlands, Western Australia 6009.

In devising any feeding strategy it is important that any allowances established are within the appetite limits of the animal, since low feed intake is frequently a problem with lactating sows. Although environment and genotype influence food intake, both previous and current nutritional regimens may have a profound effect. For example, it is well established that increasing the level of nutrition in pregnancy is associated with decreased appetite in lactation (Salmon-Legagneur and Rerat, 1961). In addition the quality of the diet is also of importance. Mahan and Mangan (1975) have shown that low levels of dietary protein during both pregnancy and lactation have been associated with low intake during the suckling period.

Responses to nutrients are not always obvious and often difficult to demonstrate, depending on the extent of body reserves of the sow and hence her ability to compensate during times of nutrient shortage when metabolic demand exceeds nutrient intake. It is evident that there is a whole complex of interrelationships which will influence the feeding strategy to be adopted. To understand these effects it is necessary to establish detailed relationships and requirements for both energy and protein to meet specified targets at various stages of the reproductive cycle.

Several models of growth based on empirical equations describing nutrient utilization have been developed and used successfully to predict the rate and composition of bodyweight gain in growing pigs (Whittemore and Fawcett, 1976; Fowler, 1979; Phillips and MacHardy, 1982). This chapter describes a simple model for the partition of nutrients during pregnancy as an aid to the establishment of feeding strategies for breeding animals. The model predicts maternal and conceptus weight gain and their composition from given amounts of dietary protein and energy fed to animals of specified body weight in a thermoneutral environment.

Partition of nutrients

Dietary energy can be partitioned between the costs of maintenance, the energy contained in the products of conception, and the deposition of protein and fat in the maternal tissue, provided that relationships can be established between the retention and intake of nitrogen (N) and energy at various body weights.

FACTORS INFLUENCING NITROGEN DEPOSITION DURING PREGNANCY

Amount and quality of dietary nitrogen

Relationships between the intake and retention of N of gilts fed different levels of energy intake during gestation, derived from the data of Kemm (1974), are shown in *Figure 6.1*. An approach similar to that of Black and Griffiths (1975) with lambs was used to evaluate the data in which the response was described in two phases. In the first phase, N retention was limited by N intake. When animals of a given body weight were fed increasing amounts of N under conditions of adequate energy supply, N retention increased linearly with N intake until it reached a maximum value. Diets in this phase will be referred to as diets which are deficient or limiting

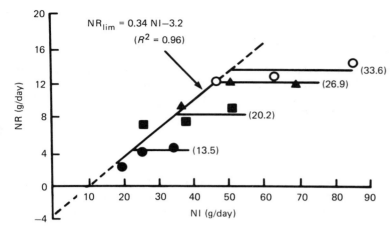

Figure 6.1 The effect of nitrogen intake (NI) and digestible energy (DE) intake on the N retention (NR) of pregnant gilts (adapted from Kemm, 1974). Values in parentheses are the DE intakes (MJ/day) at which maximum NR occurs. The equation describing the N-limiting phase of the relationship is also given

in N or in crude protein (CP). N retention in this N-limiting phase (NR_{lim}) is described by equation (1).

$$NR_{lim} = 0.34\,NI - 3.2 \tag{1}$$

$$(R^2 = 0.96)$$

where NI is the intake of dietary N. The slope of the line was 0.34 and is a direct measure of the biological value of dietary protein during pregnancy.

Additional data from several experiments where sows were fed diets limiting in N are given in *Figure 6.2*. From this it appears that sows retain N with a similar efficiency to gilts and equation (2) describes the pooled data for all animals.

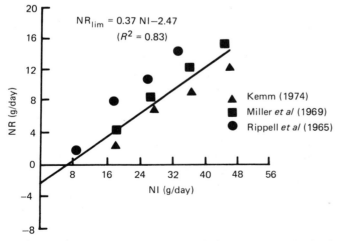

Figure 6.2 The effect of nitrogen intake (NI) on the N retention (NR) of gilts and sows from a number of sources. The equation describing the relationship is given

$$NR_{lim} = 0.37\,NI - 2.47 \tag{2}$$

$$(R^2 = 0.83)$$

The relationship between the retention and intake of N given in equation (2) was used in all subsequent calculations and, although the estimate of total endogenous N was approximately half (68 mg/kg$^{0.75}$/day) that proposed by Carr, Boorman and Cole (1977), no adjustment was made.

Energy intake

In the second phase N retention was independent of N intake and, in animals of similar body weight, was determined by energy intake. This is clearly illustrated in *Figure 6.1* by the data of Kemm (1974). N retention was dependent on, and linearly

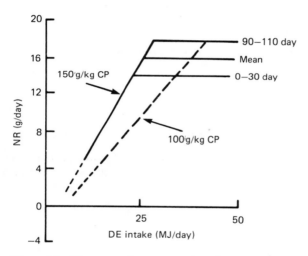

Figure 6.3 Diagrammatic representation of the effects of digestible energy (DE) intake and crude protein content of the diet (100 and 150 g/kg) on the nitrogen retention (NR) of gilts (120 kg body weight at mating) at two stages of gestation (0–30 days and 90–110 days). The mean value throughout pregnancy is also indicated

related to, digestible energy (DE) intake between 13.5 and 27 MJ/day. Above this higher level of intake, which represents approximately 1.6 times the animal's maintenance energy requirement, there was no further increase in N retention. Hereafter diets in this phase will be termed sufficient or adequate in N or CP. *Figure 6.3* shows, diagrammatically, the relationships between N retention and DE intake used in the calculations for diets which contained adequate N ($\geq$150g CP/kg) or were limiting in N (100g CP/kg).

In addition to the effect of N and energy intake, N retention is also influenced by the stage of pregnancy and body weight.

Stage of pregnancy

W.H. Close (unpublished data) showed that maximum N retention in gilts increased from 14 g/day at day 30 of gestation up to 18 g/day at day 110. Two-thirds of this increase was accounted for by N deposition within the gravid uterus.

Body weight

Body weight has a large effect on N retention as shown by the data of Carr, Boorman and Cole (1977). Their derived equation and some additional data, selected on the basis that neither DE nor N intake were limiting N deposition, are shown in *Figure 6.4*. Although there is considerable variation, the data indicate that

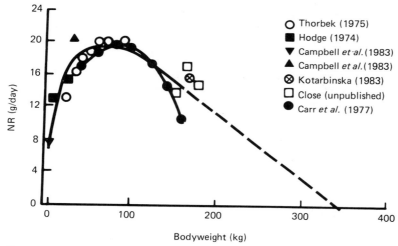

Figure 6.4   The influence of body weight on the maximum rate of nitrogen retention (NR) in pigs. Only values for gilts and castrates have been included above 40 kg body weight. −−−− is the line extrapolated to a mature body weight of 340 kg

N retention increases after birth, reaches a maximum value between 30 and 100 kg body weight and then begins to decline, approaching zero when mature body weight has been reached. There is no information on the mature body weights of modern sows and, from inspection of sow records at the National Institute for Research in Dairying at Shinfield, the value of 340 kg was chosen to represent the mature body weight of a modern sow at zero N retention.

THE PARTITION OF ENERGY INTAKE

Deposition of fat and protein

After making an appropriate allowance for the animal's maintenance energy requirement, the remaining DE was partitioned between protein and fat deposition according to the amount of N retained. The maintenance energy requirement was taken as 430 kJ metabolizable energy (ME)/kg$^{0.75}$/day (452 kJ DE/kg$^{0.75}$/day),

Table 6.1 CALCULATION OF BODYWEIGHT GAINS TO DAY 110 OF PREGNANCY FOR GILTS WEIGHING 120 kg AT MATING AND FED A DIET CONTAINING 150 g CRUDE PROTEIN/kg AT VARIOUS DIGESTIBLE ENERGY (DE) INTAKES

DE (MJ/day)	ME for maintenance (ME_m)[a] (MJ/day)	Nitrogen retention (g/day)	Protein deposited (P) (g/day)	ME for protein (P_E)[b] (MJ/day)	ME for fat deposition (F_E)[c] (MJ/day)	Fat deposited (F) (g/day)	Lean tissue deposited (L)[d] (g/day)	Fat + lean deposited (g/day)	Daily gain (ΔW)[e] (g/day)	Total gain (kg/110 day)
18	16.6	10.9	68	2.7	−2.2	−69	296	227	252	27.7
24	17.5	15.3	96	3.8	1.5	30	415	445	494	54.3
30	18.4	16.0	100	4.0	6.1	123	435	558	620	68.2
36	19.3	16.0	100	4.0	10.9	219	435	656	729	80.2
42	20.2	16.0	100	4.0	15.7	317	435	752	836	92.0
48	21.1	16.0	100	4.0	20.5	413	435	848	942	103.6

[a] $ME_m = 430 \, kJ/kg^{0.75}/day$
[b] $P_E = P \times (0.0238 \div 0.60)$
[c] $F = F_E \div (0.0397 \times 0.80)$ when $(ME_M + P_E) > 0.95 \, DE$ and $F = F_E \div (0.0397 \div 0.8)$ when $(ME_M + P_E) < 0.95 \, DE$
[d] $L = P \div 0.23$
[e] $\Delta W = (F + L) \div 0.9$

calculated from the mean of several recent estimates (Agricultural Research Council, 1981; Burlacu, Iliescu and Cărămidă, 1982; Close, Noblet and Heavens, 1985). Unlike estimates derived by the Agricultural Research Council (1981), no increase in the maintenance energy requirement with the progress of gestation was allowed, since recent experimentation (Burlacu, Iliescu and Cărămidă, 1982; W.H. Close, unpublished) indicated that it did not significantly increase during gestation. The efficiencies of utilization of ME for the deposition of protein and fat were taken as 0.6 and 0.8, respectively, with the corresponding energy values of 23.8 and 39.7 MJ/kg (Agricultural Research Council, 1981; Close, Noblet and Heavens, 1985).

As an example a calculation is described for a sow weighing 120 kg at mating and receiving 22.8 MJ ME (24 MJ DE) per day on a protein-adequate diet. Of the daily ME intake, 17.5 MJ ($0.43 \times 140^{0.75}$, where 140 kg represents the mean body weight of the animal throughout gestation) was required for maintenance. Protein deposition was 96 g/day (15.3 g N $\times$ 6.25), requiring 3.8 MJ ME [(0.096 $\times$ 23.8) $\div$ 0.6], thus leaving 1.5 MJ ME/day for the synthesis and deposition of fat. Hence the daily retention of fat was 30 g/day [(1.5 $\times$ 0.8) $\div$ 39.7] (*Table 6.1*).

Calculation of bodyweight gain

Total bodyweight gain was calculated on the basis that lean and fat gain represents 90 per cent of the total gain; the remaining 10 per cent represents ash and gut fill. The lean tissue growth rate was calculated from the protein gain on the criterion that the protein gain represents 23 per cent of the combined protein plus water gain (Walach-Janiak *et al.*, 1983; Shields and Mahan, 1983). Thus in the example cited above, the daily lean tissue gain was 415 g (96 $\div$ 0.23) and, since the gain in fat was 30 g/day, the total bodyweight gain was 494 g/day [(415 + 30) $\div$ 0.90], that is a total

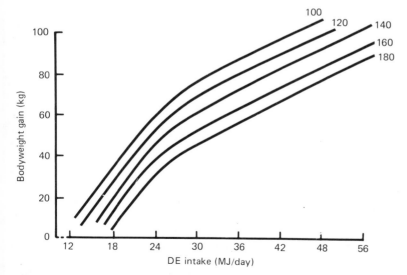

Figure 6.5 Predicted effect of body weight at mating (100, 120, 140, 160 and 180 kg) and digestible energy (DE) intake on bodyweight gain of pregnant animals fed diets containing adequate nitrogen

of 54.3 kg throughout a 110-day gestation period. A more detailed account of the effect of energy intake on the rate and composition of the bodyweight gain of sows mated at 120 kg is given in *Table 6.1*, whereas *Figure 6.5* shows the effect of energy intake on the bodyweight gain of sows of different body weights at mating and fed protein-adequate diets.

Partition of nutrients between maternal and conceptus tissue

The accretion of fat and protein in both the conceptus and maternal tissue depends upon nutrient supply and the priority for tissue deposition. In early gestation the needs of the conceptus tissue are small and nutrients are predominantly deposited in the maternal tissue. In late gestation, on the other hand, most nutrients are directed towards the conceptus tissue since its maximum rate of growth and development occurs at this stage. However, from the results of Kotarbinska (1983) and Noblet *et al.* (1985) it would appear that maximum N retention throughout gestation in both the conceptus and maternal tissue occurs at approximately similar energy intakes, that is, 25 MJ DE/day for a protein-sufficient diet (150 g CP/kg) or 37 MJ DE/day for a diet deficient in protein (100 g CP/kg). For a protein-sufficient diet, N retention in the conceptus tissue was calculated to be 1.7 g/day, at 18 MJ DE/day and increased linearly to a maximum of 2.7 g/day at 25 MJ DE/day.

Increases in both fresh weight and dry matter accompany the increase in N in the conceptus tissue, but the amount of fat is independent of energy intake and remains nearly constant at approximately 12 per cent of the dry matter content of the conceptus.

Since the rate of gain and composition of the total body and conceptus tissue is known, the gain in the maternal body can be calculated by difference. *Figure 6.6* therefore shows the effect of dietary energy and CP content of the diet on the partition of weight gain and its tissue composition into conceptus and maternal components for gilts and sows mated at 120 and 180 kg body weight, respectively (*Figure 6.6a* and *b*).

Validation of the model

Predicted values of bodyweight gains during pregnancy are shown in *Figure 6.7* for gilts weighing 120 kg at mating and fed diets either adequate (150 g/kg) or deficient (100 g/kg) in CP at levels of DE between 18 and 48 MJ/day and compared with data from several experiments not used in deriving the basic relationships of the model. There was excellent agreement between the predicted and observed values. Both the magnitude and direction of the response to changes in DE intake were well predicted for all the available data. Prediction of the response to dietary CP was also in good agreement with the limited data available (Greenhalgh *et al.*, 1977, 1980). Thus at a constant DE intake of 25 MJ/day, increasing the dietary CP from 90 to 140 g/kg was associated with an 11 kg increase in body weight during pregnancy, and this compared favourably with the predicted change of 14 kg.

Multiparous animals of heavier body weight did not follow the predicted response nearly as closely as the gilts. For example, the data of Lee and Mitchell (1984) in *Figure 6.8* show that the predicted response of gilts is very close to experimental values but that the response of sows is underpredicted by nearly 30

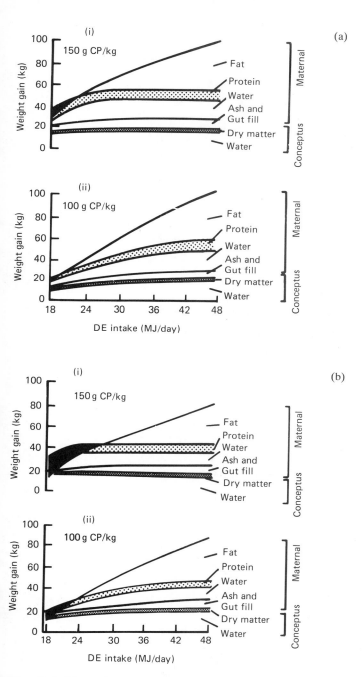

Figure 6.6 The predicted effect of digestible energy (DE) intake on the partition of total bodyweight gains to 110 days of gestation, of gilts and sows, into maternal and conceptus components. The animals were mated at different body weights and fed diets containing either (i) 150 or (ii) 100 g crude protein/kg. ■, denotes loss of maternal body fat. (a) Gilts mated at 120 kg body weight; (b) Sows mated at 180 kg body weight

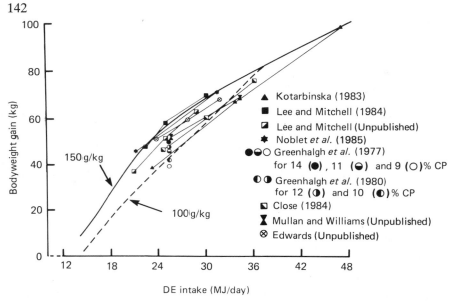

Figure 6.7 Comparison of predicted and observed changes in the bodyweight gains of pregnant gilts (120 kg body weight at mating) in relation to digestible energy (DE) intake when fed diets supplying 100 g (– – – –) and 150 g (——) of crude protein/kg

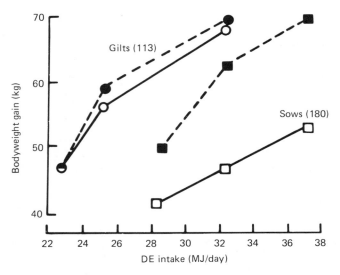

Figure 6.8 Predicted (——) and observed (– – – –) gains in body weight of gilts and sows in relation to digestible energy (DE) intake. (Values in parentheses are the body weights of the animals at mating) (Lee and Mitchell, 1984)

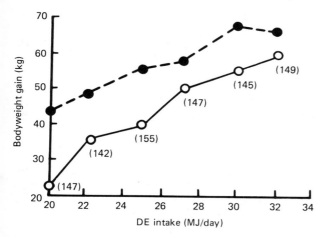

Figure 6.9 Predicted (——) and observed (————) gains in body weight of sows during their second parity in relation to digestible energy (DE) intake. (Values in parentheses are the body weights of the sows at mating) (A.J. Harker and D.J.A. Cole, unpublished data)

per cent, especially at the higher energy intakes. Similarly, data from the University of Nottingham for second parity sows (A.J. Harker and D.J.A. Cole, unpublished) show a similar degree of underprediction (*Figure 6.9*). Despite these differences there was reasonable agreement in both the direction and magnitude of the response of sows to a change in feed intake.

Differences between observed and predicted values

There are several possible reasons why the model is less successful in predicting the weight gains of heavy sows than gilts.

(1)   In all calculations a constant value for the maintenance energy requirement of 430 kJ ME/kg$^{0.75}$/day has been assumed, regardless of body weight. If the maintenance energy requirement decreases with increase in body weight then more energy would become available for production giving a greater weight gain at any given energy intake. For example, from the experiments of Lee and Mitchell (1984) the weight gain of sows throughout pregnancy has been underestimated by 15 kg (*Figure 6.8*). This is equivalent to a growth rate throughout pregnancy of 144 g/day and, assuming that N retention is maximum and cannot increase, would represent a gain in fat deposition of 120 g/day. The ME required for this gain in fatty tissue is 6 MJ/day. For a sow weighing 180 kg, its maintenance energy would need to decrease by nearly 30 per cent to give a sufficient increase in productive energy.

   On theoretical grounds there are reasons why maintenance may not be constant and might vary with body weight. Protein turnover per unit of metabolic body weight decreases as animals approach maturity and should reduce maintenance energy requirements. However, given that protein turnover accounts for a relatively small proportion of maintenance (Reeds *et al.*, 1980), large changes would be needed to reduce maintenance sufficiently to give the required increase in productive energy.

(2)   The phenomenon of compensatory gain or pregnancy anabolism might explain the difference between the actual and predicted weight gains of sows. Such effects have been demonstrated in heavy sows (Salmon-Legagneur and Rerat, 1961) but not in gilts. Compensatory gain is well known in many species, particularly sheep, and generally occurs following a period of food restriction. The loss of body weight during lactation could be a predisposing factor for such compensatory gains in the subsequent pregnancy and might explain its occurrence in sows but not in gilts. Apart from increased food intake, several mechanisms have been suggested to explain compensatory growth including reduced basal metabolic rate, more efficient accretion of protein and/or fat, and increased amounts of water in the carcass. Since older, heavier sows are relatively lean compared with gilts, small changes in the ratio of water to protein in the body could have a large effect on weight gain.

(3)   The most likely possibility to explain underprediction of weight gain in sows is that maximum N retention has been underestimated. There are very few published values of N retention for pigs above 100 kg body weight and, consequently, extrapolation was made from younger animals having set the mature body weight of modern sows at 340 kg. Since fat is energetically more expensive to deposit than lean (49.6 MJ/kg compared with 9.1 MJ/kg), it may be calculated for a sow weighing 180 kg at mating, that an extra 15 kg of body gain during pregnancy could be achieved by a 5–6 g/day increase in N retention.

Predictions from the model and possible consequences

Energy is required during pregnancy by the developing conceptus and by the sow to maintain her own body tissues. It is common practice to ration sows to achieve set target gains of body weight on the basis that growth of the conceptus will not be retarded provided that some maternal gain is made. Suggested targets vary but one growth path which seems to be well accepted is that the sow should be given sufficient food to gain 15 kg in body weight per reproductive cycle for the first four cycles and then maintained at that body weight thereafter (Hillyer, 1980). Sows do not frequently consume sufficient food to gain weight during lactation and, therefore, most or all of the weight gain required in each cycle must be made during pregnancy.

The model described clearly demonstrates the consequences of such target changes in body weight on maternal body reserves. For example, a gilt beginning her reproductive life at a body weight of 120 kg and fed sufficient of a protein-adequate diet to give a maternal gain during pregnancy of 15 kg (total gain of maternal + conceptus tissue of 15 + 20 = 35 kg) would require a DE intake of approximately 18 MJ/day (see *Figure 6.7*). At this level of intake the net gain of 15 kg would be entirely lean tissue and would be accompanied by a loss in body fat of approximately 5 kg (see *Figure 6.6a(i)*, *Figure 6.10*). Bigger sows making similar gains in maternal weight would lose even more fat as a consequence of a lower energy intake relative to maintenance. Thus a gilt weighing 120 kg at mating and fed a protein-adequate diet in sufficient amounts to give a maternal gain of 15 kg in each pregnancy would lose approximately 5, 7, 8 and 8 kg of body fat in the first

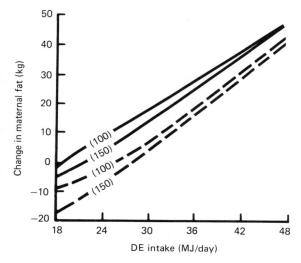

Figure 6.10   The predicted changes in maternal fat in gilts (——, 120 kg body weight at mating) and sows (————, 180 kg body weight at mating) in relation to digestible energy (DE) intake, when fed diets supplying 100 or 150 g crude protein/kg

four reproductive cycles, that is, a total of 28 kg. Modern gilts weighing 120 kg at mating are unlikely to have sufficient body fat to cover losses of this magnitude. Furthermore, the predicted loss of 28 kg is likely to be an underestimate. Although some sows consume sufficient food to maintain body weight during lactation the majority lose body weight and most of this loss will be fat. In addition, it is likely that the model underestimates the amount of energy retained as protein in heavier sows and, therefore, overestimates the amount stored as fat.

Feeding a diet deficient in protein can result in the alternative outcome where body fat is gained rather than lost during pregnancy. For example, feeding a diet containing 100 g CP/kg in sufficient amounts to achieve a maternal gain of 15 kg or a total gain of 35 kg would require a DE intake of 22.5 MJ/day rather than the 18.0 MJ/day on a protein-adequate diet. Under this feeding regimen sows would be predicted to gain approximately 4 kg of fat per cycle or a total of 16 kg in the first four reproductive cycles.

The concentration of dietary protein has a very profound influence on body fat reserves of the sow since the animal is normally fed at a much lower level relative to its maintenance energy requirement when compared with the growing pig. As indicated above, feeding protein-adequate diets will reduce body fat to zero within four parities assuming that a gilt of 120 kg contains approximately 30 kg of body fat at mating and that there is no loss of fat during lactation. Depletion of body fat can however be prevented by increasing feed intake. For example, increasing DE intake of a protein-adequate diet to 22 MJ/day would maintain fat reserves during the first pregnancy (*Figure 6.10*). The gain in maternal body weight corresponding to this intake would be approximately 25 kg, that is 10 kg higher than the current target recommendations.

Clearly the components forming the basis of the model proposed here have not been the subject of sufficient research. However, in addition to providing a working hypothesis for nutrition in pregnancy, the model highlights the areas of inadequacy in our knowledge.

Acknowledgements

We are most grateful to the following people for providing us with results of unpublished data: Sandra Edwards, MAFF, Terrington Experimental Husbandry Farm, Kings Lynn, Norfolk; A.J. Harker, University of Nottingham, School of Agriculture, Sutton Bonington, Loughborough, Leics; Pauline A. Lee and K.G. Mitchell, National Institute for Research in Dairying, Shinfield, Reading, Berks; B.P. Mullan, University of Western Australia, Nedlands, Western Australia.

References

AGRICULTURAL RESEARCH COUNCIL (1981). *The Nutrient Requirements of Pigs*, p. 50. Commonwealth Agricultural Bureaux; Slough

BLACK, J.L. and GRIFFITHS, D.A. (1975). *British Journal of Nutrition*, **33**, 399–413

BURLACU, GH., ILIESCU, M. and CĂRĂMIDĂ, P. (1982). European Association for Animal Production Publication No. 29, 222–224

CAMPBELL, R.G. and DUNKIN, A.C. (1983). *British Journal of Nutrition*, **49**, 221–230

CAMPBELL, R.G., TAVERNER, M.R. and CURIC, D.M. (1983). *Animal Production*, **36**, 193–199

CARR, J.R., BOORMAN, K.N. and COLE, D.J.A. (1977). *British Journal of Nutrition*, **37**, 143–155

CLOSE, W.H., NOBLET, J. and HEAVENS, R.P. (1985). *British Journal of Nutrition*, **53**, 267–279

COLE, D.J.A. (1982). In *Control of Pig Reproduction*, p. 603. Ed. D.J.A. Cole and G.R. Foxcroft. Butterworths; London

FOWLER, V.R. (1979). In *Recent Advances in Animal Nutrition–1978*, p. 73. Ed. W. Haresign and D. Lewis. Butterworths; London

GREENHALGH, J.F.D., BAIRD, BARBARA, GRUBB, D.A., DONE, S., LIGHTFOOT, A.L., SMITH, P., TOPLIS, P., WALKER, N., WILLIAMS, D. and YEO, M.L. (1980). *Animal Production*, **30**, 395–406

GREENHALGH, J.F.D., ELSLEY, F.W.H., GRUBB, D.A., LIGHTFOOT, A.L., SAUL, D.W., SMITH, P., WALKER, N., WILLIAMS, D. and YEO, M.L. (1977). *Animal Production*, **24**, 307–321

HARDY, B. and LODGE, G.A. (1969). *Animal Production*, **11**, 505–510

HILLYER, G.M. (1980). In *Recent Advances in Animal Nutrition–1979*, p. 69. Ed. W. Haresign and D. Lewis. Butterworths; London

HODGE, R.W. (1974). *British Journal of Nutrition*, **32**, 113–126

KEMM, E.H. (1974). A study of the protein and energy requirements of the pregnant gilt (*Sus scrofa domesticus*). PhD Thesis, University of Stellenbosch

KING, R.H. and WILLIAMS, I.H. (1984). *Animal Production*, **38**, 241–247

KOTARBINSKA, MARIA (1983). *Pig News & Information*, **4**, 275–278

LEE, PAULINE, A. and MITCHELL, K.G. (1984). *Animal Production*, **38**, 528 (abstract)

MAHAN, D.C. and MANGAN, L.T. (1975). *Journal of Nutrition*, **105**, 1291–1298

MILLER, G.M., BECKER, D.E., JENSEN, A.H., HARMON, B.G. and NORTON, H.W. (1969). *Journal of Animal Science*, **28**, 204–207

NOBLET, J., CLOSE, W.H., HEAVENS, R.P. and BROWN, D. (1985). *British Journal of Nutrition*, **53**, 251–265

PHILLIPS, P.A. and MACHARDY, F.V. (1982). *Canadian Journal of Animal Science*, **62**, 109–121

REEDS, P.J., CADENHEAD, A., FULLER, M.F., LOBLEY, G.E. and MCDONALD, J.D. (1980). *British Journal of Nutrition*, **43**, 445–455

REESE, D.E., MOSER, B.D., PEO, E.R. JR., LEWIS, A.J., ZIMMERMAN, D.R., KINDER, J.E. and STROUP, W.W. (1982). *Journal of Animal Science*, **55**, 590–598

RIPPEL, R.H., RASMUSSEN, A.H., JENSEN, A.H., NORTON, H.W. and BECKER, D.E. (1965). *Journal of Animal Science*, **24**, 209–215

SALMON-LEGAGNEUR, E. and RERAT, A. (1961). In *Nutrition of Pigs and Poultry*, p. 207. Ed. J.T. Morgan and D. Lewis. Butterworths; London

SHIELDS, R.G. and MAHAN, D.C. (1983). *Journal of Animal Science*, **57**, 594–603

THORBEK, GRETE (1975). In *Studies on Energy Metabolism in Growing Pigs*, p. 100. Beretning fra Statens Husdyrbrugs forsøg no. 424

WALACH-JANIAK, M., RAJ, S., FANDREJEWSKI, H., KOTARBINSKA, MARIA and LASSOTA, M. (1983). Paper no. 5.31. 34th EAAP Annual Meeting, Madrid

WHITTEMORE, C.T. and FAWCETT, R.H. (1976). *Animal Production*, **22**, 87–96

7

NUTRITIONAL MANIPULATION OF CARCASS QUALITY IN PIGS

C.T. WHITTEMORE
Edinburgh School of Agriculture, Scotland, UK

Introduction

The business of producing meat from pigs requires that the producer has a clear view of his target end-product, has an adequate definition of that target, and has a means of manipulating the production system to achieve the stated goal. Usually, but not invariably, the pig buyer and meat packer will have some means of grading meat pigs received from producers; payment for the pigs will be related to the achievement of grading standards. This does not mean, however, that the grading target set by the producer to optimize his business should necessarily be the same as the grading standards set by the buyer. A market preferring, and paying premium rates for, a high standard of blockiness in the carcass (as would be attained with Pietrain or Belgian Landrace type pigs) may be best exploited, not by obtaining all pigs of premium grade from the use of pure bred animals, but by a lower percentage achieving the premium grade by the use of cross-bred Large White animals which would be more prolific, faster growing and less prone to stress. A market preferring and paying premium rates for pigs of less than 15 mm backfat depth at the P2 site (65 mm from the mid-line at the last rib), may often be best exploited by achieving less than 80 per cent top grade in circumstances where mixed groups of pigs require the castrated males to be grown so slowly that the naturally leaner females are unnecessarily held back.

Discrimination by a meat buyer against entire male pigs may be resolved by the producer castrating his animals, or by acceptance of the price penalty. Optimum tactics will depend upon cost benefit analysis and the ability of the producer to attain high feed intakes and rapid growth.

Pig producing businesses must therefore identify their target grading standards in the light of, but not necessarily identical with, grading and payment schemes set up by meat buyers and processors. The means by which producers can identify appropriate grading targets for pigs grown for meat are complex but becoming established (for example, the Edinburgh Model Pig (Whittemore, 1980 and 1983) and others). This chapter will discuss the ways in which producers can achieve those targets once the optimum grading standard for any particular production unit in any particular trading environment has been decided.

Aspects of grading standards

Grading schemes usually contain a range of standards. In some the standard (such as level of fatness) may be the prime controller of value and payment received by the producer, whilst in others the standard (such as quality of fat) may be of considerable importance to carcass quality but not yet play a functioning part in the payment schedule.

In some markets conformation is a functional aspect of the grading standard. Shape is almost entirely dependent upon breed, and not much open to nutritional manipulation other than through the creation of over-fatness. Most aspects of meat quality, other than amount of fat, are also not open to nutritional control. For example, muscle quality (in particular PSE and DFD) is influenced primarily by breed and physical treatment around the time of slaughter. Soft fat in pigs is associated, in any breed or sex, with leanness itself, but there may also be a tendency for entire males to have slightly softer fat than females even at the same degree of fatness. Unsaturated fatty acids in the diet, especially linoleic (C18:2) may influence the type of fat deposited in the body, rendering it softer. Extreme leanness in pigs can also lead to the fat becoming lacey and splitting away from the lean. Splitting fat can be a problem where the packer wishes to prepare cuts with some fat left on, as for example with bacon, but is less of a problem where the joint is sold as lean alone (as would be the case for continental pig loins comprising solely longissimus dorsi (eye) muscle).

Important as the quality of the lean and fat is to meat consumers, grading standards take little account of them at present, although the imposition of minimum, rather than maximum, fatness levels would reduce problems associated with over-leanness. In the United Kingdom, good carcass shape may even be discriminated against. At equal percentage lean, the blocky breeds carry more backfat than conventional Large White and Landrace breeds. The consequence is that although some breeds of good conformation may contain more lean meat, having deeper hams and eye muscles, less bone (as well as an improved carcass yield of about 3 percentage units), and smaller heads, they are liable to be down-graded for overfatness at the P2 site. At equal P2 fat depth, total body fat may be 6 per cent less. As an approximation:

$$\text{Lean in carcass } (\%) = (B) \, P2^{-0.21}$$

where B is the degree of blockiness and ranges from 90 for Large White and Landrace pigs to 100 for pure Pietrain/Belgian Landrace types. J.D. Wood (personal communication) estimates Pietrain pigs to have some 4 percentage units more lean meat than Large Whites (61 *vs.* 57 per cent), and to have a considerably more favourable lean:bone ratio (6:1 *vs.* 5:1).

Most grading standards and payment schedules relate to fatness grades within a given weight band. For example, one scheme may limit carcass weight to between 60 and 75 kg, and pay premium price for pigs of less than 15 mm P2 and impose a maximum price penalty for pigs of more than 20 mm. Equivalent schemes might pertain for pork carcasses of below 60 kg carcass weight and cutter and heavy pig carcasses of above 75 kg. There may be additional requirements, perhaps that the length of the carcass be greater than 775 mm, or that the fat measurements at shoulder, mid-back and loin each be contained within a certain limit. It follows from the natural growth pattern of the pig that lighter animals have a lower fat thickness, thus, as the potential value of the carcass increases with its weight, the likelihood of it being down-graded because of over-fatness is also increased. The consequence would be a diminished price paid for each kilogram of lean meat provided. This inconsistency would be ameliorated by a grading scheme which paid for the kilograms of lean meat yielded. This could be calculated from knowledge of the carcass weight and the P2 measurement (together with perhaps the breed, if of the blocky type). Some suggested predictions of percentage lean in the carcass side have been 63–0.51 P2 (Wood, J.D., personal communication); 61–0.52 P2 (Tullis, 1982); Rook, A.J. (unpublished data) examined a number of data sets for which the average multiplier for P2 was −0.58. Kempster and Evans (1979) presented three equations for 47, 72 and 93 kg carcasses. These were respectively; 60–0.73 P2, 60–0.63 P2 and 57–0.54 P2.

The phenomenon of increased fatness with increased weight would also indicate that the correct slaughter weight for the fatter castrated males should be towards the lighter end of the market, whilst that for entire males should be towards the heavier end. It is germane to production tactics that the natural tendency is for fatness to increase faster than body weight, thus fatness accelerates disproportionately rapidly. This has been well illustrated by Rook who gave the following prediction from one population of pigs:

Subcutaneous fat (kg) $= 0.0002\ X^{2.54}$
where X = carcass weight (kg)

Strict weight limits for any particular grading scheme are often not needed in effectively integrated producer/retailer organizations. Nevertheless, many buyers will take in pigs over a range of, say, 50–80 kg carcass weight, but do this through the medium of not one, but perhaps three, separate grading schedules; each penalizing producers for underweights and overweights. Achievement of maximum allowable weight consistent with an adequately low depth of backfat and an adequately low number of outgrades due to overweight, within any one scheme, is clearly a realistic producer target.

Standards of over-fatness (say a maximum of 15 mm P2) may come to be matched by standards of under-fatness. Minimum fat levels (about 10 mm P2) are required for the eating quality of the lean meat, as well as to help maintain the quality of the fat itself. Given modern techniques for measurement of carcass fatness in the live animal, pigs could, if required, be sent off to slaughter at a given target fatness of 10 mm P2. Targetting for sale within a given weight range can be antagonistic to targetting for sale within a given backfat depth range; the narrower these ranges become, the more difficult it is to meet both simultaneously.

Fatness is considered as being normally distributed through the population. However, as average fatness reduces, then so the possibility of normal distribution lessens and that for skewness increases. With a skewed distribution the likelihood of over-lean pigs rises disproportionately. Given the perceived biological distributions for fatness and for weight at any given age, it is difficult to see how producers could supply pigs to ever-decreasing ranges of weight, fatness and age. The benefits to the producer of sale for slaughter at pre-selected calendar dates may override the benefits of closely meeting arbitrary standards for weight and fatness.

Nutrition and fatness

Whilst for many pigs there are few or no grading standards and for others the standards include measures such as conformation, pig grading standards at present in the UK can be considered as primarily dependent upon the thickness of backfat. Backfat depth is greatly influenced by breed and genetic merit; Large White pigs are leaner than Pietrain, and over the past 20 years of selection in the Large White breed some 10 mm of backfat has been removed from pigs slaughtered at 90 kg. The primary determinant of grade is the quality or the strain of the pig in use; genetically fat pigs will tend to be always fat within the feasible range of nutritional and environmental variation. However, whilst the long-range strategy for fatness reduction and meeting grading standards must be genetic, the tactics with animals of any given genetic composition must depend upon the knowledge that fatness is greatly influenced by both quality and quantity of food. The major mechanism open to producers to manipulate grade and achieve grading standards is therefore through the control of the nutrition of the growing pig.

PROTEIN

Diets which do not adequately provide for the requirement of absolute amounts of ideal protein (ARC, 1981) fail to allow maximum lean tissue growth. Energy thus freed from protein synthesis is diverted to fatty tissue growth. Excess protein, on

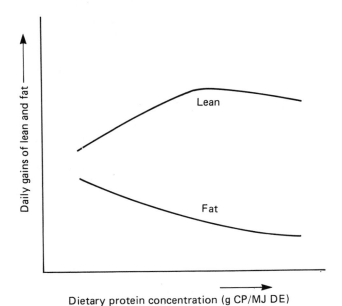

Figure 7.1   The influence of increasing protein concentration (g CP/MJ DE) upon daily gains of lean and fat. The figure relates to an optimum level of feed intake; at lower levels the total growth response is less, while at higher levels of feed intake lean tissue growth will not increase above the potential limit of the pig but fatty tissue growth will increase markedly, and a lower ratio of lean to fat will be seen at all protein concentrations

the other hand, reduces energy status. The energy yielded from protein by deamination is about half of the assumed DE of protein. The effective energy value of a diet containing excess protein will therefore fall as deamination rate rises, with a resultant diminution of energy available for fat deposition. Excess supply of total protein over the requirements for protein maintenance and protein growth will have the consequence of enhancing leanness. Increasing diet protein therefore first reduces fat in the carcass by diverting energy into lean tissue growth and away from fatty tissue growth as a frank protein deficiency is reduced. Second, further increments of protein above the requirement will continue to increase leanness by effectively reducing the available energy yielded from the diet and thus pre-empting the conversion of energy to fat. This second method, of reducing carcass fatness by the supply of excess protein, while explaining linear responses of percentage lean to dietary crude protein, can be expensive to execute and also bring about a reduction in pig growth rate. This latter is consequent not only upon a reduction in the rate of fat gains; if the general level of feeding is not sufficiently generous, then lean growth itself may be curtailed through an inadequate energy supply to drive the metabolic motors of protein anabolism. The role of protein (CP) concentration is illustrated in *Figure 7.1*.

LEVEL OF FEED (ENERGY SUPPLIED)

As the amount of feed (balanced for protein, vitamins and minerals) consumed daily by the pig increases, then initially the daily gains of both lean and fat respond

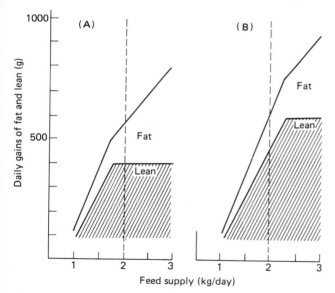

Figure 7.2 Daily lean and fatty tissue growth responses of pigs to increases in daily feed supply. Increments of balanced feed induce linear growth of lean until the maximum potential daily lean growth is achieved. Up to that point fat growth proceeds at a lower rate determined by the minimum fat:lean ratio (*see also Table 7.1*). After maximum daily lean growth is achieved further increases in feed supply generate rapid growth of fatty tissue. Pigs differ genetically in their ability to grow lean, and this influences the level of feed intake at which fattening commences

linearly (*Figure 7.2*). Lean growth will cease to respond to increasing feed supply when the maximum lean tissue growth rate potential is reached; for pig A this is at 400 g, for pig B at 600 g. At this point the excess energy will be channelled to fat deposition with the consequence that, while total growth rate increases at a slower rate, the proportion of growth that is fat rapidly increases. This will mitigate against the achievement of a high percentage of pigs in the premium low-fat grades.

Even while feed supply is inadequate to maximize lean tissue growth there is nevertheless always some deposition of a minimum level of fat commensurate with normal positive daily gains. This minimum may be expressed in terms of a ratio to lean. This minimum fat:lean ratio gives the level of fatness in the pig which can only be undercut by creating abnormal conditions of fat catabolism such as would occur at very slow rates of growth. Should this minimum give backfat depths at slaughter weight that are in excess of the premium grade standard, then only considerable reduction in feed supply and growth rate could place carcasses in the top grade (such might be the case for castrated pigs of low genetic merit). Equally, should the minimum ratio give backfat depths at slaughter weight that are below a minimum fatness standard (as might be the case with entire males of high genetic merit), then adequate fatness can only be achieved by feed intake levels in excess of those that will maximize lean tissue growth rate. The higher the potential for lean tissue growth rate, the more difficult such a feed intake level would be to achieve.

Pigs of high genetic merit may have higher lean tissue growth rate potentials, lower minimum fat ratios, or both. Such animals will be thinner at low feed intakes and more difficult to fatten as feed level increases. Excessive fatness is feasible for all pigs, but only provided that voluntary feed intake is sufficient to put the maximum limit to potential lean tissue growth rate into range. The position as it relates to likely appetite and weight of pig is described in *Figure 7.3*, while some

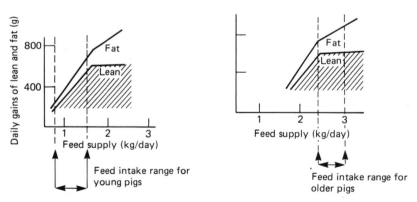

Figure 7.3   Influence of age and appetite upon perceived rates of lean and fatty tissue growth

average values for maximum lean tissue growth rates and minimum fat:lean ratios are given in *Table 7.1*. It is evident that, in order to optimize production and achieve grading targets, the feed supply that will maximize lean tissue growth without generating excessive fat is crucial. It is likely that this point is out of appetite range for many young pigs, unless they are managed well and encouraged to eat; equally, for many older pigs a ration may need to be imposed unless the animal is either of high genetic merit or has a low appetite.

Table 7.1 VALUES FOR MAXIMUM DAILY LEAN TISSUE GROWTH RATES (g)[a] AND FOR MINIMUM FAT:LEAN RATIOS. (THESE VALUES DETERMINE THE FORM OF THE RESPONSE TO FEED SUPPLY AS ILLUSTRATED IN *FIGURE 7.2*)

Genetic strain	Entire male		Female		Castrate male	
	Max. lean growth	Min. fat ratio	Max. lean growth	Min. fat ratio	Max. lean growth	Min. fat ratio
Improved	630	0.12	540	0.16	495	0.18
Commercial	585	0.16	520	0.20	475	0.22
Utility	540	0.20	475	0.24	405	0.26

[a]These values relate to the whole live pig, and not to the carcass alone; the latter values are usually about 60 per cent of the former.

ENERGY VALUE OF FEEDS

Achievement of target grading standards by alteration of the level of feeding implies knowledge of the energy density of the feed. Digestible energy values for compounded diets may be calculated from the known DE value of the ingredients, or where these are unknown from the chemical analysis of the mixed diet. The equations in *Table 7.2* have been proposed by Morgan and co-workers (1984).

Table 7.2 EQUATIONS TO PREDICT DE (MJ/kg DM) FROM THE CHEMICAL COMPOSITION OF COMPOUNDED FEEDS (g/kg DM)

	r.s.d.[a]
$DE^b = 3.8 - 0.019\,NDF^c + 0.76\,GE^d$	0.38
$DE = 17.0 + 0.016\,EE^e - 0.018\,NDF$	0.44
$DE = 17.0 + 0.011\,EE - 0.041\,CF^f$	0.66
$DE = 18.0 + 0.016\,EE - 0.017\,NDF - 0.016\,Ash$	0.41
$DE = 17.5 + 0.016\,EE - 0.008\,CP^g - 0.033\,Ash - 0.015\,NDF$	0.32

[a]r.s.d. = Residual standard deviation
[b]DE = Digestible energy
[c]NDF = Neutral detergent fibre
[d]GE = Gross energy
[e]EE = Oil by petroleum spirit extraction
[f]CF = Crude fibre
[g]CP = Crude protein

Conclusion

The nutritional manipulation of carcass fatness is a major element in optimizing pig meat production tactics. First, the inherent genetic makeup of the animal must not predispose it to unacceptable levels of fatness even at low food intakes. This is becoming increasingly unlikely with the continued selection of improved strains of pigs and with the use of entire, rather than castrated, males. Second, the protein level in the diet must meet the appropriate energy:protein ratio. Third, the amount of food given should relate to the point at which daily lean tissue growth rate is maximized. Below that point pigs grow at less than optimum speed, but will not be fatter than the minimum fatness inherently pre-determined. Above the point of maximization of lean tissue growth rate, increments of food are diverted solely to the deposition of surplus fatty tissue with no benefit to lean growth. Invariably, limited voluntary feed intake levels dictate that maximum lean tissue growth rates are usually not achieved in commercial pigs of below 40 kg live weight. This situation can be eased by improving both the feed and the feeding method. Once voluntary feed intake no longer limits lean tissue growth rate, as may often be the case above 50 kg live weight, then the producer can restrict feed intake to maintain minimum fatness, or feed more to exceed it. Reduction of feed input will slow down growth rate, reduce fatness, and may improve grade and individual pig value. But the cost benefit of reduced feed inputs require careful assessment, particularly where throughput and overall feed efficiency is important to production optimization. Where problems of over-leanness pertain, there is a clear indication for enhancing feed intake to the highest possible level. Pigs of high genetic merit will also carry the potential for high daily lean tissue gains. Again, the consequence is that higher feed levels can be consumed with positive responses to growth rate without forgoing leanness.

Achieving grading standards or grading targets by nutritional manipulation is therefore relatively straightforward. However, to decide in the first place upon which of all the possible targets and standards is appropriate for an individual producer to optimize the production process is rather more complex.

References

ARC (1981). *The Nutrient Requirements of Pigs.* Commonwealth Agricultural Bureaux; Farnham Royal, Slough, England

KEMPSTER, A.J. and EVANS, D. (1979). *Animal Production,* **28**, 87–96

MORGAN, C.A., WHITTEMORE, C.T., PHILLIPS, P. and CROOKS, P. (1984). *The Energy Value of Compound Foods for Pigs.* Edinburgh School of Agriculture; Scotland

TULLIS, J.B. (1982). PhD Thesis, University of Edinburgh

WHITTEMORE, C.T. (1980). *Pig News and Information,* **1**, 343–346

WHITTEMORE, C.T. (1983). *Agricultural Systems,* **11**, 159–186

8

CONSEQUENCES OF CHANGES IN CARCASS COMPOSITION ON MEAT QUALITY

J.D. WOOD
AFRC Food Research Institute Bristol, Bristol, UK

Introduction

Although the national consumption of pigmeat has remained high during the last ten years, particularly in relation to that of beef and lamb, some meat traders have said that the reduction in average fat thickness levels that has occurred in the same period has lowered meat quality. This chapter considers the role of fat in different aspects of meat quality, the changes in structure and composition of lean and fat tissues which occur as overall fatness is reduced and the consequences of these for changes in quality. Before proceeding however, it should be remembered that the recent success of pigmeat in consumption terms is closely linked with its relatively low price compared with other meats (Clark, 1984) which in turn is explained by high levels of feed efficiency, only possible in lean, rapidly-growing animals. Also, recent reports that the dietary intake of animal fat should be reduced for health reasons (e.g. DHSS, 1984) are likely to put even more emphasis on low-fat meats in the future.

Definition of meat quality and the role of fat

There are three components of meat quality: visual, handling and eating quality. Visual quality is determined mainly by the relative proportions of lean and fat, all surveys showing that pigmeat with high ratios of lean to fat is most preferred and most likely to be bought (Baron and Carpenter, 1976).

Handling quality, which is possibly more important to butchers than consumers, refers to the firmness and cohesiveness of the tissues and meat when handled and cut. Fat tissue has a role in binding the muscles together and the fatty acid composition of lipid determines the firmness of fat tissue which is an important factor in overall firmness. The third and most important aspect of meat quality is eating quality. In this case, fat provides flavour components, prevents drying out during cooking and has a role in tenderness.

Most butchers agree that leaner meat is most likely to be bought and reserve their critical comments mainly for the handling and eating characteristics of lean pigmeat. Changes in these characteristics must be due to changes in the composition and structure of lean and fat tissues associated with differences in the overall fat content of the carcass.

COMPOSITION AND QUALITY OF LEAN TISSUE

The individual muscles of the pig carcass differ widely in lipid (intramuscular fat) content (Lawrie, Pomeroy and Cuthbertson, 1963; Davies and Pryor, 1977). *M. longissimus*, which is the heaviest muscle in the body (approximately 11 per cent of lean in the side) and is most frequently sampled, has a relatively low lipid content. For example, in the study of Davies and Pryor (1977) it varied from 2.1 (*m. adductor*) to 25.4 (*m. cutaneous omobrachialis*) per cent lipid with a mean value of 5.0. The lipid content of *m. longissimus* was 4.2 per cent. In general, lipid content was highest in the most superficial muscles.

As the fat content of the carcass increases so does the lipid content of individual muscles. The results in *Table 8.1* are taken from studies conducted at the Food

Table 8.1   LIPID CONTENT OF *M. LONGISSIMUS* IN RELATION TO CARCASS COMPOSITION. THREE EXPERIMENTS INVOLVING RELATIVELY HIGH AND LOW LEVELS OF FEEDING

	Level of feeding			
	High	*Low*	*S.E.D.*	*Significance of difference*
Experiment 1[a] (47.0 kg carcass weight)				
C fat thickness (mm)[d]	13.2	11.8	0.79	NS
Lean (% of side)	53.8	54.5	0.84	NS
Lipid in *m. longissimus* (%)	2.05	1.97	0.17	NS
Experiment 2[b] (50 kg carcass weight)				
C fat thickness (mm)[d]	12.3	7.6	0.65	***
Lean (% of side)	54.7	59.6	0.70	***
Lipid in *m. longissimus* (%)	3.36	2.62	0.23	***
Experiment 3[c] (66 kg carcass weight)				
C fat thickness (mm)[d]	11.8	9.7	0.81	**
Lean (% of side)	56.8	60.6	0.65	***
Lipid in *m. longissimus* (%)	1.85	1.56	0.13	*

[a]Results of Wood, Dransfield and Rhodes (1979); 48 gilts (12 from each of four breeds)
[b]Unpublished results from 21 gilts, 13 boars and ten castrated males
[c]Results of Wood and Enser (1982); 64 pigs (32 boars and 32 gilts)
[d]Thickness of fat above deepest part of *m. longissimus* at last rib. Measured cold and excluding skin thickness

Research Institute Bristol (FRIB). When feeding at a low level reduced the thickness of backfat and increased the lean content of the carcass (experiments 2 and 3) it also reduced the concentration of lipid in *m. longissimus*. However, the relationship between muscle lipid and carcass fatness was quite variable, correlation coefficients of 0.61 and 0.40 between percentage lipid and C fat thickness being found in experiments 2 and 3, respectively.

Lipid is only obvious in *m. longissimus* as streaks of 'marbling fat' at high levels of carcass fatness. This does not mean that intramuscular fat is a 'late developing' fat depot, however, since studies in sheep by Broad and Davies (1981a and b) and in pigs by Davies and Pryor (1977 *Table 8.2*), showed that it is relatively slow growing compared with the other fat depots. The storage triglyceride component, approximately 80 per cent of the total in pigs of commercial weights, grows more rapidly than phospholipid, located in the cell membranes (Broad and Davies, 1981b).

Table 8.2 GROWTH OF FAT DEPOTS IN THE SIDE (*Y*) RELATIVE TO TOTAL SIDE FAT (*X*) (SUBCUTANEOUS + INTERMUSCULAR + CAVITY) USING EQUATION $Y = aX^b$

Y	Growth coefficient[b]	*S.E.*
Subcutaneous fat	1.007	0.043
Intermuscular fat	0.972	0.038
Cavity fat	1.077	0.057
Intramuscular fat	0.910	0.045

(Davies and Pryor, 1977)

Genetic differences in the association between intramuscular fat and carcass fat would have important consequences for meat quality. Reports in the literature showing wide variations in muscle lipid content between individual animals (e.g., Lawrie, Pomeroy and Cuthbertson, 1963) and between groups of animals of the same fat thickness (*see Table 8.1*, experiments 1 and 2) suggest that such differences might exist. It has also been suggested that wild pigs have inherently less muscle lipid than domesticated pigs (Crawford, Hare and Whitehouse, 1984). However, there is no good evidence for clear genetic effects in pigs and it may well be that different lipid extraction and dissection procedures are the cause of much of the variation found between studies.

INTRAMUSCULAR FAT AND EATING QUALITY

The importance of intramuscular (marbling) fat in the meat industry is epitomized in the USDA quality grading scheme for beef carcasses where carcasses with high levels of marbling are placed in the highest grade. In all species, including pigs (where concentrations of muscle lipid are lower than in beef), intramuscular fat affects the juiciness, flavour and tenderness of meat. The effect on juiciness is associated with the lubricating action of melted lipid during cooking; flavour is affected by the release of volatile compounds during cooking, some of which react with components from lean; and tenderness may be affected by the replacement of some fibrous protein by softer lipid. Early work at FRIB (e.g. Rhodes, 1970) showed that the measurable effect of fat thickness or intramuscular fat content on these aspects of eating quality, as determined in taste panel tests, was extremely

Table 8.3 EATING QUALITY OF PORK LOINS IN 56 kg CARCASSES OF DIFFERENT FATNESS AS ASSESSED BY TASTE PANEL

	Fat thickness at 'C' (mm)		S.E.D.	Significance of difference
	12	6		
Tenderness[a]	1.8	0.9	0.69	NS
Flavour[a]	2.4	2.5	0.22	NS
Juiciness[b]	1.4	0.9	0.14	*
Toughness (*J*)[c]	0.14	0.16	0.02	NS

(Wood, Mottram and Brown, 1981)
[a]Scores −7 to +7 in steps of 2 where −7 is extremely tough or disliked extremely and +7 is extremely tender or liked extremely
[b]Scores 0 (dry) to 3 (extremely juicy)
[c]Measured by Instron materials testing instrument

small and led to the conclusion that 'selection programmes aimed at reducing fatness are in little danger of producing a less acceptable meat on the plate' (Rhodes, 1970). Similar conclusions were drawn in more recent studies (Wood, Dransfield and Rhodes, 1979; Wood, Mottram and Brown, 1981) although in the 1981 report a statistically significant difference in the taste panel score for juiciness was found between carcasses having C fat thickness measurements of 6 and 12 mm (10 and 16 mm P2 respectively) in carcasses of 56 kg (*Table 8.3*). These results for juiciness may be compared with those in the 1979 study in which four breeds had mean juiciness scores of 1.2 (these are the pigs described in *Table 8.1*, experiment 1; the comparison between studies is valid because the same panellists were involved in the two studies). There is therefore a hint that 6 mm C (10 mm P2) may represent a level of fat thickness below which some slight deterioration in eating quality is observed in carcasses of this weight. However, many more samples are required before this point can be established. A large-scale study currently being conducted by FRIB and the Meat and Livestock Commission should provide more information both on trained taste panel and consumer attitudes to lean pigmeat.

Danish studies suggest that around 2.0 per cent of lipid in *m. longissimus* is required for good eating quality (Buchter and Zeuthen, 1971; Jul and Zeuthen, 1980). A recent report (*Table 8.4*) showed that tenderness, flavour and juiciness

Table 8.4 EFFECT OF LIPID (INTRAMUSCULAR FAT) CONTENT OF *M. LONGISSIMUS* ON EATING QUALITY[a] OF PORK CHOPS

Number of pigs	Intramuscular fat (%)	Flavour	Tenderness	Juiciness	Overall acceptability
24	1.47[b]	2.5[b]	1.3[b]	1.7[b]	0.6[b]
43	2.89[c]	2.9[c]	3.1[d]	3.2[d]	2.0[c]
51	4.34[d]	2.8[c]	2.4[c]	2.5[c]	2.0[c]

(Bejerholm, 1984)
[a]Taste panel scores for each aspect on a scale of −5 to +5 in steps of 1 where −5 is poor and +5 ideal
[bcd]Means in a column with different superscripts are significantly different (*P*<0.01)

were scored higher in fried chops with 2.9 per cent lipid in *m. longissimus* than in those with 1.5 or 4.3 per cent. The pigs were Danish Landrace, Hampshire and Duroc but unfortunately no fat thickness measurements were given.

Few studies have attempted to define the exact role of lipid in eating quality. An exception is that of Mottram and Edwards (1983) which partitioned the characteristic aromas and flavours of cooked beef between the storage component triglyceride and the cellular component phospholipid. The conclusion was that phospholipids alone were required for the development of aroma and flavour. Translated into pig *longissimus* lipid values this suggests that less than 1 per cent of lipid is necessary for optimal flavour development.

PALE SOFT EXUDATIVE (PSE) MUSCLE

Pigs which are homozygous for the gene which confers sensitivity to the anaesthetic halothane (*nn*) also produce PSE muscle which has poor visual and handling qualities (Webb, 1981). Their carcasses produce a lower yield of bacon after curing (Taylor, Dant and French, 1973) and are more likely to produce tough meat (e.g.

Table 8.5   CARCASS COMPOSITION IN ENTIRE MALE PIETRAIN AND LARGE WHITE PIGS OF 90 kg LIVE WEIGHT

	Pietrain	*Large White*
Lean[a]	61.1	57.0
Fat[a]	22.6	25.6
Bone[a]	10.0	11.1
Lean:bone ratio	6.1	5.1
Depth of *m. longissimus* (mm)[b]	55.9	48.0
Carcass length (mm)	723	798

(Fortin, Wood and Whelehan, 1985)
[a] Percentage of side
[b] At last rib

Bejerholm, 1984). A high incidence of the halothane gene is found in pigs of the Pietrain breed which are lean, have 'blocky conformation' and a correspondingly high ratio of lean to bone (*Table 8.5*). Such results suggest a genetic link between PSE incidence and carcass lean and fat content although within breeds the genetic correlations are low (McGloughlin and McLoughlin, 1975; Kempster, Evans and Chadwick, 1984). It therefore cannot be said that the reported increase in PSE incidence in Britain during the last ten years (Chadwick and Kempster, 1983) is associated directly with the trend towards leaner pigs. Since the correlation with carcass conformation score is higher than that with carcass lean content, it may be that increased use of blocky breeding pigs partly accounts for the increased incidence of PSE muscle. The commercial breeding companies have suggested that *nn* sire lines (with above average leannesss and conformation) and *NN* dam lines (homozygous for the gene conferring halothane resistance) should be used to produce *Nn* slaughter progeny, which have some of the advantages in terms of carcass quality of the *nn* parent and none of the disadvantages in terms of stress sensitivity and meat quality (they do not react to halothane). However there are possible dangers in this approach. Apart from the possibility that some *Nn* progeny will be used for breeding rather than meat, thereby producing some *nn* progeny when mated to other *Nn* individuals, it has also been shown that *Nn* pigs are intermediate in muscle quality between the two extreme homozygotes (Frøystein *et al.*, 1981). A recent Danish report shows that *Nn* pigs are also intermediate in their reactions to pre-slaughter handling conditions (*Table 8.6*). Abattoir A had poor conditions with a high incidence of PSE muscle in *NN* and *Nn*. Abattoir C, on the other hand, had better (more considerate) conditions, resulting in a zero incidence in *NN*. However in all cases *Nn* pigs produced some PSE meat.

The results show that there is likely to be some penalty (in terms of meat quality) inherent in the promotion of the halothane gene in Britain. Other countries, e.g. Norway, have elected to reduce the incidence of the gene at the cost, in their case, of extremes in conformation and possibly leanness.

Table 8.6   INCIDENCE OF PSE MUSCLE (% OF CARCASSES) IN 259 DANISH LANDRACE PIGS WITH KNOWN HALOTHANE GENOTYPE SLAUGHTERED AT THREE ABATTOIRS

	Abattoir		
	A	*B*	*C*
nn	100	74	79
Nn	33	17	13
NN	33	8	0

(Barton-Gade, 1984)

Composition and quality of fat tissue

FACTORS CONTROLLING FAT QUALITY

The most important aspects of fat quality in pigmeat are firmness (i.e. hardness or softness), colour and cohesiveness (i.e. whether the elements of the tissue are bound together or show separation). Firm, white fat showing no separation is desired by butchers and consumers. This combination of characteristics is found in thick fat which is well developed but is more difficult to achieve in thin, underdeveloped fat because of the structural and chemical changes which occur as fattening proceeds (Wood, 1984).

During the development of fat tissue the concentration of lipid increases and the concentrations of water and connective tissue fall, although these changes are more gradual beyond about 30 days of age (10 kg live weight) than before (Wood, 1984). At the same time the lipid, more than 90 per cent of which is triglyceride, becomes more saturated. This is largely due to a decrease in the concentration of linoleic acid (C18:2), which is derived from the diet, and an increase in the concentration of stearic acid (C18:0) which is synthesized. Also the fat cells increase in size and become more turgid. All these factors contribute to the improvement in fat quality which occurs as the fat tissue develops but several studies show that fatty acid composition is the most critical (Enser, 1984; Wood *et al.*, 1984).

Similarly in pigs of a particular carcass weight the concentration of stearic acid provides the best prediction of instrumentally-measured firmness and lipid melting point (Enser, 1984) and directly affects colour through changing the opacity of lipid. Stearic acid and linoleic acid are important in explaining variation in cohesiveness (Wood *et al.*, 1984) although this is probably an indirect effect. Observation shows that separation occurs between the lobules of fat cells that are surrounded by sheaths of connective tissue (*Figure 8.1*). As yet very little work has

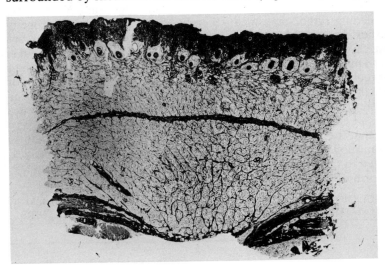

Figure 8.1   Pig subcutaneous fat (backfat) is a highly organized tissue in which the fat cells are arranged in groups (lobules) surrounded by connective tissue. Connective tissue is concentrated in a band separating the outer and inner layers and in the skin dermis. (×10)

been done on factors affecting the strength of the connective tissue matrix in fat tissue.

EFFECT OF FAT THICKNESS ON FAT QUALITY

The above suggests that the thickness of backfat is itself an important factor in fat quality, at least in subcutaneous fat. Recent results, collected in a joint study between FRIB and the Meat and Livestock Commission show that this is so (*Table 8.7*). Three hundred pork-weight pigs, half boars and half gilts, were sampled in ten abattoirs. The 30 pigs per abattoir were from five producers, each supplying three boars and three gilts falling into different fat thickness categories, respectively 8, 12 and 16 mm P2. There were significant effects of fat thickness on firmness assessed by experienced operators and by an instrumental method. Twenty-four per cent of

Table 8.7 EFFECTS OF FAT THICKNESS ON FAT QUALITY IN 300 PORK-WEIGHT PIGS (58 kg CARCASS WEIGHT)

	Fat thickness at P2 (mm)			S.E.D.	Significance of difference
	8	12	16		
Sensory firmness[a]					
Assessor 1	2.8	3.9	5.3	0.16	***
Assessor 2	2.8	3.8	5.3	0.13	***
Instrumental firmness (g)[b]	432	637	913	46.7	***
Loin fat samples exhibiting separation (%)	52	23	4		

(Wood *et al.*, 1985)
[a]Using an 8-point scale to assess loin samples where 1 is very soft and 8 is very hard
[b]Loin fat samples assessed using materials testing instrument at 0 °C.

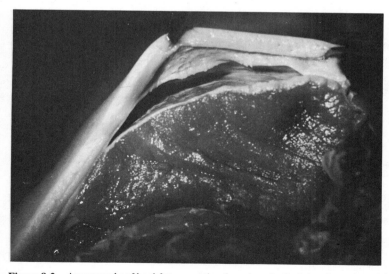

Figure 8.2 An example of backfat separation from lean in the loin of a pork-weight carcass (58 kg) having 8 mm P2 fat thickness

loin samples were placed in categories 1 and 2 on the 8-point sensory scale and it may be that these samples are unsatisfactorily soft. More than half the samples in the 8 mm P2 group exhibited fat separation as determined by the physical separation of fat from lean when pulled upwards, away from *m. longissimus* (*Figure 8.2*).

The relevance of these findings to consumers in terms of overall satisfaction following eating cannot be assessed at present. Preliminary results suggest that consumers are less concerned with fat quality than butchers.

EFFECTS OF SEX AND DIET ON FAT QUALITY

The study described in *Table 8.7* contained equal numbers of boars and gilts. Both groups had similar fat thickness (12 mm P2) and yet boars had significantly softer fat which tended to separate from lean more easily than that of gilts. However the differences were smaller than those between fatness categories. For example, the scores for sensory firmness of loin fat showed that boars with 12 mm P2 had fat as firm as all pigs (boars and gilts) with 11.5 mm P2. Gilts had fat as firm as all pigs with 12.5 mm P2. Previous work showed that boar backfat contains a higher percentage of water and a lower percentage of lipid than that of gilts or castrates (Wood and Enser, 1982) although no difference between the sexes in fat quality at the same fat thickness has been found before (also Wood *et al.*, 1984).

The fatty acid composition of the diet has long been recognized as an important factor in pig fat quality. For example, early American work showed that pigs which had eaten large quantities of soya beans produced soft oily fat because of incorporation of linoleic acid into body fat (Ellis and Isbell, 1926a and b). The more recent practice of incorporating high levels of vegetable oils in pig diets to increase energy density produces the same effect and has a particularly detrimental effect on fat quality if the diet is underfed or the pigs are lean, since thin backfat has a high ratio of linoleic to stearic acid anyway. Recent results show the consequences for fat quality of increasing the proportion of dietary energy derived from linoleic acid (*Table 8.8*). Boars and castrates were included in the experiment and although the results for both sexes were in the same direction, the effects of diet were more marked in the castrates. A number of FRIB studies summarized by Prescott

Table 8.8   EFFECT OF CHANGING THE PROPORTION OF DIETARY ENERGY DERIVED FROM LINOLEIC ACID ON FAT QUALITY IN BACON-WEIGHT CASTRATE PIGS (90 kg LIVE WEIGHT)

| | Percent of DE from linoleic acid | | S.E.D. | Significance of difference |
	2	5		
Fat thickness at P2 (mm)	15.4	11.1	0.93	***
Stearic acid (% of fatty acids)[a]	14.6	12.5	0.45	***
Linoleic acid (% of fatty acids)[a]	9.3	24.3	1.01	***
Firmness of backfat (N)[b]	7.3	2.8	0.98	***
Cohesiveness of backfat ($Nm^{-2} \times 10^3$)[c]	6.4	3.8	0.70	**

(Wood *et al.*, 1984)
[a]Dorsal mid-line at last rib (inner layer)
[b]Instrumental method
[c]Instrumental method

(personal communication) suggests that the linoleic acid concentration in backfat is directly proportional to the ratio of linoleic acid energy to total energy consumed.

The effect of the concentration of a fatty acid in the diet on its concentration in backfat is more marked for linoleic acid than for the other fatty acids (Wood, 1984). Therefore, increasing the dietary concentration of stearic acid, apart from possibly reducing digestibility, does not have the same effect of 'hardening' fat as linoleic acid has in 'softening' it. Diets high in carbohydrate and protein and low in lipid which rely on synthesis rather than dietary incorporation for lipid deposition are a possible option for the retention of high fat quality in lean pigs.

Conclusions

The recent reduction in fat thickness which has occurred in British pigs has produced a more attractive product in terms of appearance (visual quality) and puts pigmeat in a favourable position compared with other meats in the light of recent reports that consumers should reduce their intake of animal fat for health reasons. However as the fat tissue content of the carcass is reduced, the lipid content of lean and fat tissues also inevitably declines and becomes more unsaturated, thus changing handling and eating characteristics.

Lipid in muscle affects eating quality, but early British studies showed no clear association between the concentration of lipid in muscle and taste panel scores for tenderness, juiciness or flavour within the range of fat levels studied. More recent work with leaner pigs suggests that juiciness may be slightly reduced below 10 mm P2 fat thickness.

The incidence of PSE muscle has increased recently and this will have reduced tenderness in the 13 per cent or so of carcasses affected. There is no evidence that selection for leaner pigs has brought this about, rather, greater use of particular breeds which have good conformation and carry the halothane gene is implicated and further use of these types should be carefully controlled.

The firmness and cohesiveness of backfat decline with fat thickness, due mainly to a reduction in the saturation of fatty acids. Results of a recent study suggest that 8 mm P2 fat thickness in pork-weight pigs represents the point at which butchers' complaints of handling quality increase although there is doubt about the significance of this to consumers. Some of the problems can be overcome by manipulating the amount and type of dietary fat.

Taken together the information available at present shows no cause for concern over meat quality in lean pigs and there is wide variation at each fat thickness level. Rather than applying price penalties to pigs with thin backfat (perhaps less than 8 mm P2) the industry should seek solutions to particular problems and encourage the development of objective methods for evaluating each aspect of quality.

References

BARON, P.J. and CARPENTER, E.M. (1976). *Report No. 23*. Department of Agricultural Marketing, University of Newcastle upon Tyne; Newcastle upon Tyne

BARTON-GADE, P. (1984). *Proceedings of 30th European Meeting Meat Research Workers*, pp. 8–9

BEJERHOLM, A.C. (1984). *Proceedings of 30th European Meeting Meat Research Workers*, pp. 196–197

BROAD, T.E. and DAVIES, A.S. (1981a). *Animal Production*, **31**, 63–71

BROAD, T.E. and DAVIES, A.S. (1981b). *Animal Production*, **32**, 234–243

BUCHTER, L. and ZEUTHEN, P. (1971). *Proceedings of 2nd International Symposium Condition and Meat Quality of Pigs*, pp. 247–254. Centre for Agricultural Publishing and Documentation; Wageningen, The Netherlands

CHADWICK, J.P. and KEMPSTER, A.J. (1983). *Meat Science*, **9**, 101–111

CLARK, A.G. (1984). In *Matching Production to the Markets for Meat*, pp. 35–38. Ed. A. Cuthbertson and R.G. Gunn. British Society of Animal Production Occ. Publ. No. 8; Edinburgh

CRAWFORD, M.A., HARE, W.R. and WHITEHOUSE, D.B. (1984). In *Fats in Animal Nutrition*, pp. 471–479. Ed. J. Wiseman. Butterworths; London

DAVIES, A.S. and PRYOR, W.J. (1977). *Journal of Agricultural Science*, **89**, 257–266

DEPARTMENT OF HEALTH AND SOCIAL SECURITY, (1984). *Diet and cardiovascular disease*. Report on Health and Social Subjects, No. 28. Her Majesty's Stationery Office; London

ELLIS, N.R. and ISBELL, H.S. (1926a). *Journal of Biological Chemistry*, **69**, 219–238

ELLIS, N.R. and ISBELL, H.S. (1926b). *Journal of Biological Chemistry*, **69**, 239–248

ENSER, M. (1984). In *Fat Quality in Lean Pigs*, pp. 53–57. Ed. J.D. Wood. Document No. EUR8901 EN, Commission of the European Communities; Brussels

FORTIN, A., WOOD, J.D. and WHELEHAN, O.P. (1985). *Animal Production* (in press)

FRØYSTEIN, T., NØSTVOLD, S.O., BRAEND, M., STORSETH, A. and SCHIE, K.A. (1981). In *Porcine Stress and Meat Quality*, pp. 161–176. Ed. T. Frøystein, E. Slinde and N. Standal. Agricultural Food Research Society; As, Norway

JUL, M. and ZEUTHEN, P. (1980). *Progress in Food and Nutrition Science*, **4**, 1–132

KEMPSTER, A.J., EVANS, D.G. and CHADWICK, J.P. (1984). *Animal Production*, **39**, 455–464

LAWRIE, R.A., POMEROY, R.W. and CUTHBERTSON, A. (1963). *Journal of Agricultural Science*, **60**, 195–209

MCGLOUGHLIN, P. and MCLOUGHLIN, J.V. (1975). *Livestock Production Science*, **2**, 271–280

MOTTRAM, D.S. and EDWARDS, R.A. (1983). *Journal of the Science of Food and Agriculture*, **34**, 517–522

RHODES, D.N. (1970). *Journal of Science of Food and Agriculture*, **21**, 572–575

TAYLOR, A.A., DANT, S.J. and FRENCH, J.W.L. (1973). *Journal of Food Technology*, **8**, 167–174

WEBB, A.J. (1981). In *Porcine Stress and Meat Quality*, pp. 105–124. Ed. T. Frøystein, E. Slinde and N. Standal. Agricultural Food Research Society, As, Norway

WOOD, J.D. (1984). In *Fats in Animal Nutrition*, pp. 407–435. Ed. J. Wiseman. Butterworths; London

WOOD, J.D., DRANSFIELD, E. and RHODES, D.N. (1979). *Journal of the Science of Food and Agriculture*, **30**, 493–498

WOOD, J.D. and ENSER, M. (1982). *Animal Production*, **35**, 65–74

WOOD, J.D., JONES, R.C.D., BAYNTUN, J.A. and DRANSFIELD, E. (1984). *Animal Production*, **40** (in press)

WOOD, J.D., JONES, R.C.D., DRANSFIELD, E. and FRANCOMBE, M.A. (1985). *Animal Production*, (in press)

WOOD, J.D., MOTTRAM, D.S. and BROWN, A.J. (1981). *Animal Production*, **32**, 117–120

IV

Poultry Nutrition

9

RECENT DEVELOPMENTS IN THE FIELD OF ANTICOCCIDIAL AGENTS FOR POULTRY

A.C. VOETEN

Gezondheidsdienst voor Dieren in Noord-Brabant, Boxtel, The Netherlands

Introduction

Before discussing the use of anticoccidial agents it is appropriate to consider recent developments in our knowledge of the field of coccidiosis.

Coccidiosis occurs in mammals and avian species. Almost all avian species are susceptible; in domestic poultry the disease is caused by the protozoan, *Eimeria* and is characterized by intestinal lesions. These intestinal lesions are the result of different developmental stages of *Eimeria* in the gut wall, which reproduce there both sexually and asexually. The disease can vary from a mild, subclinical form to a very severe clinical form with a high mortality rate. Coccidiosis is more prevalent in younger chicks and current husbandry practices with broiler chicks promotes the occurrence of the disease. Coccidiosis in broiler chicks can be prevented by the use of anticoccidial products incorporated in the feed. Furthermore both clinical and subclinical coccidiosis outbreaks can be either acute or chronic.

Although broiler chicks can be affected by all types of coccidiosis, under most practical conditions one usually finds *Eimeria acervulina, E. maxima* and *E. tenella*. The species *E. acervulina* and *E. maxima* are generally responsible for subclinical cases which can occur as both acute and chronic outbreaks. *E. tenella* is usually associated with clinical cases; it is not known whether this species can cause subclinical forms of the disease, and if so what level of damage results.

Broiler chicks with coccidiosis shed large numbers of oocysts in the faeces. These are the forms of *Eimeria* that live outside the body, and can remain viable for several years. On the farm they may be found both inside and outside the building with a considerable cross infection between the two. The carry-over effects of oocysts from one batch of birds to the next therefore poses a recurring danger, with that species of *Eimeria* which was allowed to propagate during the previous batch posing the greatest danger to incoming birds. However, since oocysts can be carried by man and materials from farm to farm, other *Eimeria* spp. can also occur.

The manner of coccidiosis occurrence in broiler chicks

As mentioned earlier, small intestinal coccidiosis, caused by both *E. acervulina* and *E. maxima* infections, generally occurs subclinically, in both the acute and chronic

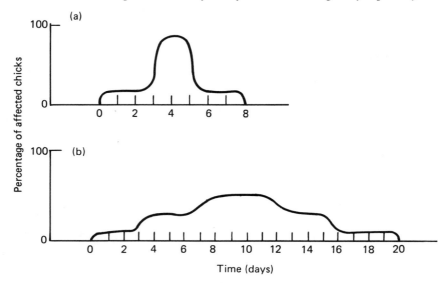

Figure 9.1   Pattern of infection with *E. acervulina* or *E. maxima* in broiler chicks with acute (a) or chronic (b) forms of the disease

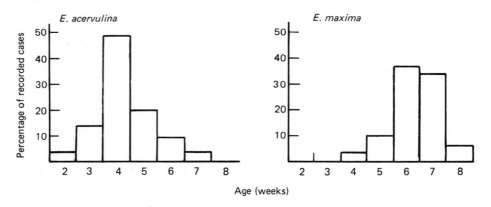

Figure 9.2   Effect of age of chick on the incidence of acute infections of subclinical coccidiosis, caused by either *E. acervulina* or *E. maxima*

form. In the acute subclinical form, almost all birds can be affected within a few days, but with the chronic form the rate of build-up and the proportion of infected birds are much lower (*Figure 9.1*).

If the coccidiosis can occur unhindered, i.e. in the absence of any effective treatment, then *E. acervulina* infections generally occur in the third, fourth or fifth week of life, while those associated with *E. maxima* generally occur in the fifth, sixth or seventh week of life (*Figure 9.2*). Chronic coccidiosis usually occurs in the same weeks of life, but takes a longer course.

Effect of coccidiosis on growth rate and feed conversion efficiency

Although *E. acervulina* infections predominantly occur during the fourth week of life, chicks can be artificially infected at other ages. The reductions in growth rate and feed conversion efficiency were assessed at the end of the growing phase (six weeks age) in chicks subjected to acute subclinical coccidiosis at different ages. In the case of *E. acervulina*, the greatest influence on feed conversion efficiency occurred when the birds were affected during the third week of life, but this had only a small detrimental effect on the growth rate. The reduction in growth rate was most severe when the birds were affected towards the end of their growing phase (*Figure 9.3*). Similar results were obtained with subclinical infections of *E. maxima* (*Figure 9.3*).

The actual extent and time course of damage from chronic forms of subclinical coccidiosis are not known, although it is known that the damage is appreciable. As

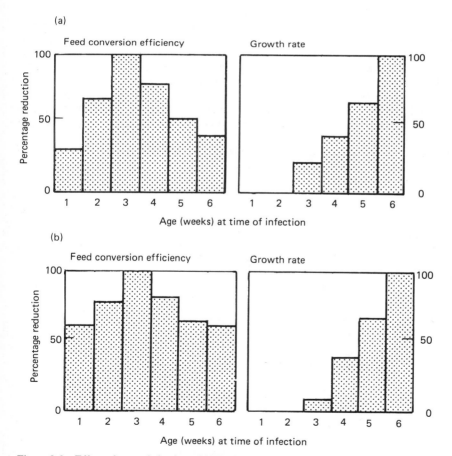

Figure 9.3 Effect of age at infection with *E. acervulina* (a) or *E. maxima* (b) on the reduction in feed conversion efficiency and growth rate up to the end of six weeks of age in broiler chicks. The vertical axis represents the relative reduction in performance expressed as a percentage of the maximum levels recorded

indicated above, the damage from subclinical coccidiosis manifests itself in an increased feed conversion ratio, which can amount to an extra 0.1 kg feed/kg liveweight gain by the end of the growing period. In such case the broilers can be 100 g lighter at slaughter.

For preventive measures, isolation and disinfection can be considered, but it would be difficult to be optimistic about this at present. Furthermore, preventive vaccinations for broiler chicks are not yet available, although the weapons to combat coccidiosis totally may well be obtained in time from such areas of molecular biology. Consequently, the only means of combatting the problem at the moment is the recourse to pharmaceutical materials.

Pharmaceuticals for the prevention of coccidiosis

Pharmaceuticals which are used for the prevention of coccidiosis can be either coccidiostatic or coccidiocidal in their mode of action. Those products which are coccidiostatic in effect prevent the multiplication of *Eimeria* spp. in the gut. On the other hand, coccidiocidal products kill the development stage within the gut. This classification is somewhat artificial as it is not definitely known for many products whether their effect is coccidiocidal or coccidiostatic. Furthermore, experience has indicated that products which were initially coccidiocidal have a static effect after long use, and with time a reduced activity results. Consequently, within this discussion we shall limit ourselves to the term anticoccidial products which encompasses both modes of action.

Numerous anticoccidial products have been developed in the past 25 years, and these are listed in *Table 9.1*. Some are single products while others are combinations of products.

Table 9.1 LIST OF AVAILABLE ANTICOCCIDIAL AGENTS AUTHORIZED FOR USE WITH POULTRY

	Trade name	*Chemical name*
Single products		
chemical	Amprolium	amprolium
products	Arpocox	arprinocid
	Coyden	metichlorpindol
	Cycostat	robenidine
	Deccox	quinoline
	Nicrazin	nicarbazine
	Stenerol	halofuginone
	Zoalene	3,5 dinitro-*o*-toluamide (DOT)
ionophore	Avatec	lasalocid sodium
preparation	Elancoban	monensin sodium
	Monteban	narasin
	Saccox	salinomycin sodium
	Cygro	ammonium prinicin
Combination products		
	Aprol plus	amprolium and ethopabate
	Lerbek	metichlorpindol and methylbenzoquate
	Pancoxin plus	amprolium, ethopabate, sulphaquinoxaline and pyrimethamine

The development of resistance to anticoccidiosis products

In the event that an anticoccidial product is used continuously on the farm for any given period of time, then there is a great chance that the *Eimeria* spp. will become partially or totally resistant to it. This does not have to occur simultaneously with all *Eimeria* spp. For example, a resistance may develop against an *E. acervulina* strain, but not against an *E. maxima* strain. In practice, it appears that the development of resistance to *E. necatrix* and *E. brunetti* usually does not pose a problem. However, a great number of *E. acervulina* and *E. maxima* strains have developed resistance to many of the available products, while the development of resistance by *E. tenella* strains varies from product to product.

When an *Eimeria* spp. develops resistance to an anticoccidial product this can occur either in a 'one step' fashion or in a 'step by step' manner (*Figure 9.4*). An

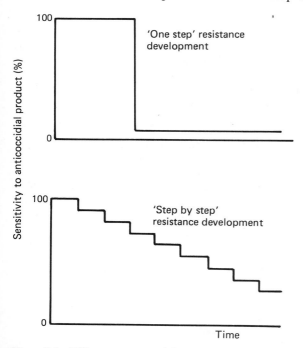

Figure 9.4 Different patterns of change with time in the sensitivity of *Eimeria* spp. to anticoccidial products

example of an anticoccidial product against which 'one step' resistance has developed is Deccox. When an *Eimeria* strain on a farm has developed resistance, then the presence of the anticoccidial product in question is of little or no use. An *E. acervulina* or E. maxima infection in this case would behave as if the product was not present, with the result that subclinical acute coccidiosis would occur.

In the case where an *Eimeria* strain develops 'step by step' resistance the situation is different. Examples of products against which such a pattern of resistance has developed are the ionophores and nicarbazine. In this instance the *Eimeria* spp. will suddenly be in the state to start multiplying, with the result that subclinical, chronic coccidiosis may occur. This can be of a mild or more serious nature, resulting in varying degrees of impairment in performance. Such changes in resistance are typical of those observed with ionophore anticoccidial products.

When the occurrence of coccidiosis in a large number of closed integrated broiler farms was analysed it was possible to draw several conclusions. The continual use of monensin over several years was initially associated with hardly any coccidiosis. After one or two years' use, coccidiosis did occur fairly regularly, but the impairment in performance was minimal. After more extensive use, coccidiosis occurred on almost all farms, and on numerous farms an effect on performance could be determined. At an even later stage the damage became more severe with the frequent occurrence of subclinical coccidiosis, which tended to be chronic in its course. Although the time course of the development of resistance varied from farm to farm, the same series of stages listed below occurred in all cases:

Stage 1 almost no cases of subclinical coccidiosis.
Stage 2 regular cases of subclinical, chronic coccidiosis, but the influence on feed conversion efficiency and growth rate was minimal.
Stage 3 many cases of subclinical, chronic coccidiosis; the influence on feed conversion efficiency and growth rate was quite large.
Stage 4 almost no efficacy attained with the anticoccidial preparation/product and any cases of coccidiosis remained chronic and were therefore difficult to treat; the effect on performance was severe.

The problems of continual use of ionophore anticoccidial products

The various stages of damage listed above occur when the same ionophore is used over several years on the same farm. If a second ionophore is used its behaviour and effect is different from the previous one. Although we can be confident that a 100 per cent cross-resistance does not exist, a certain degree of cross-tolerance is

Table 9.2 THE EFFECT OF CHANGING FROM MONENSIN TO SALINOMYCIN ON THE INCIDENCE OF COCCIDIOSIS IN BROILERS. THE INCIDENCE OF SUBCLINICAL COCCIDIOSIS WAS ASSESSED THREE TIMES THROUGHOUT THE GROWING PHASE IN THE LAST TWO CROPS OF BIRDS FED MONENSIN AND THE FIRST TWO CROPS FED SALINOMYCIN

| Unit | Monensin | | | | | | Salinomycin | | | | | |
	Previous crop 2			Previous crop 1			Trial crop 1			Trial crop 2		
1	—	M	—ª	—	M	A	—	M	A	—	A	M
2	—	—	—	—	—	—	—	A	—	—	—	—
3	—	T	—	—	T+M	—	—	M	—	—	M	—
4	—	—	—	—	—	—	—	—	—	—	—	M
5	—	T	—	—	—	—	—	—	—	—	—	—
6				—	M	—	—	M	—	—	—	—
7	—	M	—	—	—	—	—	M+A	—	—	M	—
8	—	—	—	—	—	—	—	—	—	—	A	—
9	—	—	—	—	T	—	—	A	—	—	M	—
10	—	—	—	—	—	—	—	—	—	—	—	—
11	—	—	—	—	M	—	—	M	—	—	—	—
12	—	—	—	—	—	—	—	A	A	—	—	—
13	—	A	—	—	M	—	—	—	—	—	T	—
14	—	M	—	—	M+A	—	—	M	M	—	M	—

ªA = *Eimeria acervulina*; M = *Eimeria maxima*; T = *Eimeria tenella*; — None recorded

Table 9.3 THE EFFECT OF CHANGING FROM MONENSIN TO SALINOMYCIN ON THE PERFORMANCE OF BROILERS. ALL VALUES RELATE TO THE EUROPEAN BROILER INDEX (SEE TEXT) AND ARE GIVEN FOR THE FINAL TWO CROPS FED MONENSIN AND THE FIRST TWO CROPS FED SALINOMYCIN

Unit	Monensin		Salinomycin	
	Previous crop 2	Previous crop 1	Trial crop 1	Trial crop 2
1	139	155	156	149
2	166	168	174	162
3	184	179	188	164
4	173	151	166	155
5	183	188	193	195
6	—	144	196	164
7	172	157	194	176
8	125	135	163	160
9	153	138	178	176
10	163	157	176	158
11	167	167	165	164
12	157	140	188	184
13	133	139	178	166
14	129	155	166	149
Mean ± s.e.	156 ± 17.9		172 ± 13.3	

Table 9.4 THE EFFECT OF CHANGING FROM MONENSIN TO LASALOCID ON THE INCIDENCE OF COCCIDIOSIS IN BROILERS. THE INCIDENCE OF SUBCLINICAL COCCIDIOSIS WAS ASSESSED THREE TIMES THROUGHOUT THE GROWING PHASE IN THE LAST TWO CROPS OF BIRDS FED MONENSIN AND THE FIRST TWO CROPS FED LASALOCID

Unit	Monensin						Lasalocid					
	Previous crop 2			Previous crop 1			Trial crop 1			Trial crop 2		
1	—[a]	AT	—	—	A	—	—	—	—	—	T	—
2	—	—	—	—	—	—	—	—	—	—	—	—
3	—	—	—	—	TM	—	—	A	—	—	M	—
4	—	A	T	—	T	—	—	A	—	—	A	—
5	—	—	—	—	—	—	—	A	—	—	A	—
6	—	—	M	—	—	M	—	—	M	—	—	A
7	—	—	M	—	—	M	—	A	—	—	—	—
8	—	T	M	—	AT	M	—	A	—	—	M	A
9	—	A	—	—	—	—	—	A	—	—	—	A
10	—	T	—	—	—	—	—	M	—	—	A	T
11	—	—	—	—	—	—	—	—	—	—	—	—

[a]A = *Eimeria acervulina*; M = *Eimeria maxima*; T = *Eimeria tenella*; — None recorded

bound to have developed. The experiments presented below were designed to investigate the extent to which this cross-tolerance existed.

On two separate integrated broiler operations monensin, which had been used on all farms for some four to five years, was replaced by another ionophore in the feed. With one operation this was salinomycin and with the other it was lasalocid. Coccidiosis examinations were carried out three times during the growing phase on the last two crops of birds fed monensin, and this was repeated with the first two crops which received the new ionophore. Data of the performance for all four crops of birds were also collected. *Tables 9.2* and *9.3* show the results for the changeover from monensin to salinomycin, and *Tables 9.4* and *9.5* give the results for the changeover from monensin to lasalocid.

Table 9.5   THE EFFECT OF CHANGING FROM MONENSIN TO LASALOCID ON THE PERFORMANCE OF BROILERS. ALL VALUES RELATE TO THE EUROPEAN BROILER INDEX (SEE TEXT) AND ARE GIVEN FOR THE FINAL TWO CROPS FED MONENSIN AND THE FIRST TWO CROPS FED LASALOCID

Unit	Monensin		Lasalocid	
	Previous crop 2	*Previous crop 1*	*Trial crop 1*	*Trial crop 2*
1	200	137	184	172
2	—	173	193	186
3	—	176	171	177
4	163	142	171	171
5	180	170	151	173
6	175	163	163	171
7	153	154	166	155
8	154	146	—	175
9	153	197	166	161
10	136	172	185	178
11	—	—	187	164
Mean ± s.e.	163.6 ± 18.5		172.5 ± 10.8	

From the data of both field trials it is apparent that the occurrence of coccidiosis was hardly reduced by changing to the new ionophore, although it was noted that the impairment in performance was markedly reduced. This was manifest in a higher European Broiler Index (EBI = growth per animal per day × per cent survival:feed conversion factor × 10), together with a decrease in the variation of performance between farms. This improvement in EMI could be traced back to a better feed conversion efficiency and an improved growth rate. Since the number of coccidiosis cases was hardly reduced it is apparent that the extent of the disease was reduced from stage 3 to stage 2. Since then the damage from coccidiosis has increased again and returned to the stage 3 level.

The interrupted use of anticoccidial products

Since the continuous use of any one anticoccidial product is not possible, it is necessary to interrupt their use. The number of farms contaminated with coccidiosis is of fundamental importance and this can be determined in several ways. For a good coccidiosis management programme it is essential to be up to date with such information because it is important that the use of any anticoccidial product be terminated prior to it losing all of its efficacy.

Furthermore, it is more important that some anticoccidial products are used during certain times of the year. For example, an anticoccidial product with a water-sparing effect, such as monensin, would preferably be used during those months when there is the greatest chance of wet litter problems (summer months).

The efficacy of several anticoccidial products increases when they have not been used for a period of time. For example, the activity of the ionophores, after not being used for 12 months or more, improves and allows the incidence of subclinical coccidiosis to be reduced from stage 3 to stage 2. Other products, such as Coyden, Nicarbazine or Cycostat, also regain some of their activity if they have not been used for a period of time (up to several years). However, this restoration of activity does not always happen; practical experience has indicated that the re-use of biquinolates after many years of non-use still gives disappointing results.

Unfortunately precise data relating to this phenomenon for all anticoccidial products are not available.

The influence of anticoccidial products on the growth rate is also an important factor for consideration in any coccidiosis management programme. The use of some materials will actually reduce growth rate and this is especially true with nicarbazine, and less so with monensin. Once these products are withdrawn there is a compensatory effect on growth rate. Indeed in cases where nicarbazine is used for three to four weeks the growth rate may be decreased by as much as 10 per cent. However, experience has shown that this initial loss in growth rate is totally regained by compensatory growth after its withdrawal, so much so in fact that the compensatory growth achieved after the product has in several cases been greater than the initial growth depression during the period when the material was included in the diet.

When choosing an anticoccidial product one will also have to take price into consideration. A great variation in price exists between the various products available. In the Netherlands there is as much as a tenfold difference in price.

Finally, there may be technical problems of incorporating anticoccidial products into the feed. These can be related to the facilities available to the feed compounder, or the fear of accidental cross-contamination of other feeds produced in the mill.

An action plan for the use of anticoccidial products

On the basis of experience from the interrupted use of anticoccidial products it is possible to develop an appropriate strategy for coccidiosis management. In principle, such a programme will be based on rotation, in which, after a period of use, one anticoccidial product will be exchanged for another. In addition a shuttle programme can be employed in which two different anticoccidial products are used at different growth stages with the same crop of birds.

There is only one reason for using a shuttle programme, and that is when nicarbazine is used. In such cases nicarbazine is used for three to four weeks, and thereafter another material is used. Furthermore it is recommended that the use of ionophorous anticoccidial products are alternated with chemical products and that within each category the actual materials used are also rotated.

There are particular reasons for using ionophorous products in the summer. The ionophore, monensin, has a water-sparing effect, which makes it particularly useful for use in the summer. Secondly, despite the use of ionophores, subclinical chronic coccidiosis still occurs. This is of less concern in the summer as the higher external house temperature allows an increase in ventilation rate, which in turn results in a reduction in the potential risk from viral infection. The combination of coccidiosis, a high NH_4 content in the house and virus infection frequently results in an *E. coli* infection.

A quick change of chemical products offers most benefits during the winter months. There are a number of chemical anticoccidial products which, when not having been used for some one to two years, are very effective for two to three months. A rotation involving two or three such materials has many advantages in the winter months. To afford a higher degree of protection to the birds, these can even be incorporated into a shuttle programme with nicarbazine. Experience has shown that nicarbazine can be used in this manner for several years without

Table 9.6   A SUGGESTED MANAGEMENT PROGRAMME FOR THE CONTROL OF COCCIDIOSIS INVOLVING IONOPHORES, TOGETHER WITH EITHER A SHUTTLE PROGRAMME OR A ROTATIONAL PROGRAMME INVOLVING CHEMICAL PRODUCTS

Summer period (6–8 months)	*Winter period* (4–6 months)
Annual changeover of ionophore:	Chemical products used[a] in either (a) a shuttle programme with nicarbazine or (b) a rotational programme
Salinomycine	Coyden (lerbek)
Avatec	Cycostat
Monensin	Arpocox
	Stenerol

[a]Chemical products used for two months at a time in either programme

problems. A satisfactory suggested management programme for the use of anticoccidial products which incorporates many of these points is given in *Table 9.6*.

It must be emphasized that if one does have a management schedule, it is unwise to leave it too readily. Feed compounders are extremely sensitive to complaints, and, in the cases where there is an accumulation in the incidence of complaints among customers, compounders frequently take panic-orientated decisions to change the anticoccidial product being used. All too often a sudden deterioration in food conversion efficiency, bad litter conditions or an increase in the variation of time to slaughter are blamed on loss of effectiveness of the anticoccidial agent. Generally, these problems cannot be correlated with an increased resistance to the products being used, and are likely to be the result of some other nutritional, environmental or management problem.

In order to keep abreast of coccidiosis prevention it is useful to use routine coccidiosis examinations. This can be done by using indicator animals, that is by checking five birds per 10 000 for the presence of *Eimeria*. On those farms where coccidiosis is not a problem this examination can be conducted once, during the fourth week of life. On those farms that have a history of coccidiosis problems the examination should be conducted twice, during the third and fifth week of life. Severely affected farms may need to conduct a weekly examination. Instead of using indicator animals one can conduct an examination of the litter. This has the disadvantage that it requires a large amount of laboratory work. Furthermore, the oocysts in the litter frequently do not survive for long, with the result that the findings are not always easy to interpret. A reduction in the number of oocysts in the litter by a factor of 50 to 100 per week is quite usual.

An example of the results from an operation which has been conducting coccidiosis examinations over the last ten years on its farms are given in *Figure 9.5*. Also shown in this figure are the anticoccidial products which were used over different portions of the overall period, and in many instances there was a reduction in the incidence of infected birds when there was a change in the anticoccidial product employed.

If, despite all preventive measures, there is a coccidiosis outbreak the animals can be treated with 60 mg sulphadimidine sodium per kg bodyweight per day. The medication must be given in the drinking water for a period of 5 h/day for three days. Two comments must be made here. Such treatment will have an immediate and beneficial effect on the feed conversion efficiency and growth rate in cases of

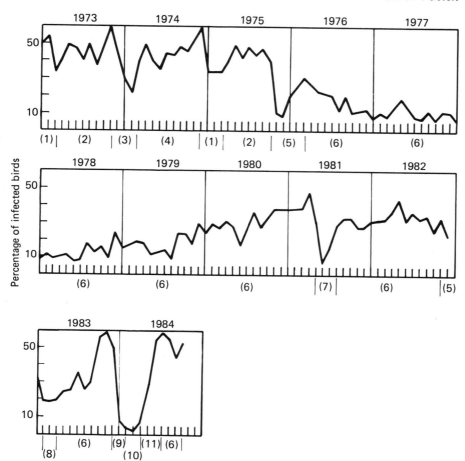

Figure 9.5   Incidence of coccidiosis in indicator broiler chicks from one operation over a ten-year period. Figures in parenthesis beneath the horizontal axis indicate the anticoccidial product being used as follows: (1), Coyden; (2), Zoalene; (3), Deccox; (4), Amprol plus; (5), Cycostat; (6), Monensin; (7), Arpocox; (8), Lerbek; (9), Shuttle programme of Nicarbazine and Stenerol; (10), Shuttle programme of nicarbazine and Narasin; (11), Narasin

subclinical acute coccidiosis, at least when treatment is initiated during the peak of the infection and for some days thereafter. However, it will have little or no effect when ionophorous anticoccidial products are being administered and the chronic forms of subclinical coccidiosis is present.

10

EGGSHELL FORMATION AND QUALITY

K.N. BOORMAN, J.G. VOLYNCHOOK
University of Nottingham School of Agriculture, Sutton Bonington, UK
and
C.G. BELYAVIN
Harper Adams Poultry Husbandry Experimental Unit, Edgmond, Newport, England, UK

Introduction

The problems associated with eggshells have been much reviewed (see for example Beuving, Scheele and Simons, 1981; Washburn, 1984) and much is known about the shell and its formation in fundamental terms (see for example Simkiss and Taylor, 1971; Taylor and Dacke, 1984). Much of the work aimed at redressing the problems has however been essentially empirical, i.e. applying a likely treatment and observing the outcome. While this approach has been successful in identifying the gross nutritional and management needs for producing eggs, a high proportion of which are well enough shelled to be marketable, it is less likely to be successful in identifying remaining problems and ameliorating new problems which may arise. In the case of nutritional treatments, for example, response will be related to the degree to which the nutrient is involved in the problem, the extent of the problem and the initial dietary concentration of the nutrient. Thus nutrient treatments which produce promising results in one circumstance may not do so elsewhere and equivocal results are common in studies on shell quality (see for example Belyavin and Boorman, 1981). Although there has been application of fundamental knowledge to speculation about limiting processes in shell formation (see for example Mongin, 1968; Hurwitz, Bar and Cohen, 1973; Buss and Guyer, 1981), relationships between such observations and shell faults as they occur in practice are not clear.

The studies described in this chapter started from the idea of trying to observe shell quality in essentially commercially-kept flocks and trying to relate the quality of the shell to the individual bird which produced it. This has developed into deeper studies of individuals and causes of variation in shell quality within an individual and between individuals. Some of these observations are described in the context of relevant observations of others, together with some comments on their implications in a broadly nutritional context.

'Shell quality' is used as a convenient term for the attributes measured by specific gravity, deformation, breaking strength, shell mass and density and in this sense relates mostly to the mineral components. It is recognized that quality in its fullest sense means more than this. In addition, it is not intended to imply that current problems in shell quality all stem from this one cause.

Variation in shell quality

The variation in shell quality as the laying year progresses is well enough known, especially the accelerated decline which usually occurs in the last quarter. This curve for a flock is an integration of the trends for individuals. Belyavin (1979) isolated 48 individuals *in situ* in a flock of about 1000 Warren SSL hens and studied their characteristics over a laying year. Eggs were sampled, as far as possible, on a regular weekly basis. The mean trend in egg specific gravity for the flock and the patterns for three individuals are shown in *Figure 10.1a*. Although some individuals (bird 41) showed a fair degree of similarity with the mean trend, others showed sudden large differences (bird 12) or consistent smaller differences (bird 33). It is evident that the flock curve is not a simple integration of similar curves for individuals or of sudden thresholds in shell quality at different times in individuals. It is also evident that shell quality in an individual may be largely unrelated to the mean of the flock and that an individual's shell quality at one time may (bird 33) or may not (bird 12) be generally characteristic of that bird's relation to the mean. It is of interest that a sudden decline, at least in the middle period, is not necessarily irredeemable (bird 12). The individuals illustrated are not typical in that the final decline in shell quality is not incontrovertibly evident in any. It was usually evident and became clear as soon as trends were combined for several individuals. Its apparent inevitability is illustrated by the fact that, if the five best individuals with respect to production characteristics and shell quality are selected, their average trend shows this decline despite their overall superiority when compared with the flock mean (*Figure 10.1b*).

These data can also be used to show that there are no simple rules for predicting which individuals are likely to produce poor shells. *Table 10.1* shows mean characteristics of production, together with various attributes of shell quality, of the five best birds and of five which were among the worst. It cannot be concluded that it is the highest producers which produce the worst shells and, although there are more birds producing heavier eggs among the group producing poor shells, there is no simple relationship between these characteristics. Belyavin (1979) investigated correlations between the main production characteristics and shell quality and demonstrated using data for all individuals that there were no simple relationships.

Since eggs are laid in sequences, separated by pauses, and eggs are laid later in the day as the sequence progresses, it became evident that if there were structured changes in shell characteristics and/or egg mass during a sequence, some of the variation seen in individuals would arise from this cause. The monitoring described above was made without any knowledge of positions of sampled eggs in their respective sequences. However, there are indications of such structured changes. Early studies showed that the last egg of the sequence has a thicker shell than eggs laid earlier in the sequence (Wilhelm, 1940; Berg, 1945) and that the first egg of a sequence is heavier than subsequent eggs (Atwood, 1929). More recently Roland, Sloan and Harms (1973) found that eggs laid in the afternoon were of higher specific gravity than those laid in the mornings and the several subsequent observations from that laboratory culminated in the report of Choi *et al.*(1981) which identified and substantiated several important trends. This report is contrasted with our own findings below.

Belyavin (1979) carried out a limited examination of sequence effects in 12 Warren SSL hens isolated among a larger flock. He was not able to establish any trends with statistical significance but found good indications that the first egg of the

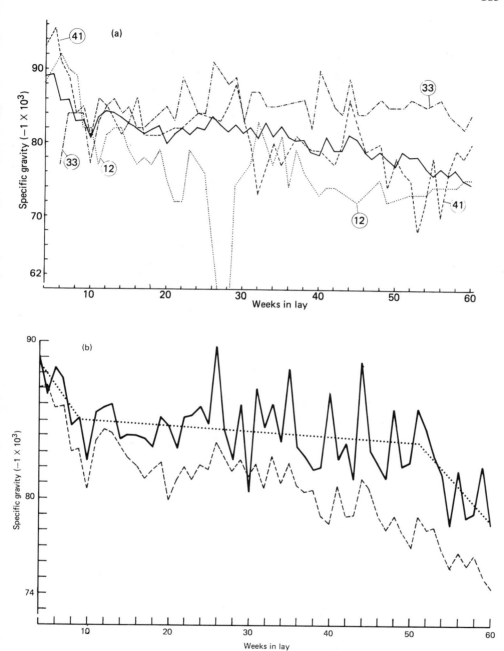

Figure 10.1 Variation in egg specific gravity among individual Warren hens distributed within a commercially-kept flock. (a) For three individuals (as numbered), together with the mean (solid line) of 48 birds. (b) Mean of the five best birds (solid line), together with the best-fit line (dotted) allowing two nodes, compared with the overall mean of 48 birds (broken line). From Belyavin (1979)

Table 10.1 SOME PRODUCTION CHARACTERISTICS OF TEN WARREN LAYING HENS HAVING ABOVE OR BELOW AVERAGE SHELL QUALITY (MEANS FOR 20 TO 80 WEEKS OF AGE)

	Above average birds						Below average birds					
	1	2	3	4	5	Mean	6	7	8	9	10	Mean
Mean food intake (g/bird daily)	111	110	123	125	137	121	122	119	141	115	124	124
Eggs produced	341	306	342	314	335	328	294	269	366	314	329	314
Mean egg mass	52.7	52.4	59.3	64.1	69.3	59.6	57.9	63.5	65.6	62.6	65.8	63.1
Total egg mass produced (kg)	18.0	16.0	20.3	20.1	23.2	19.5	17.0	17.1	24.0	19.7	21.6	19.9
Mean egg specific gravity (-1×10^3)	91	89	88	87	86	88	57	73	73	77	77	71
Mean dry shell mass per egg (g)	5.00	5.02	5.51	5.86	6.21	5.52	2.20	4.49	4.41	4.98	5.06	4.23
Total shell produced (kg)	1.71	1.54	1.88	1.84	2.08	1.81	0.65	1.21	1.61	1.56	1.66	1.34
Shell (mg) as proportion of egg mass (g)	97	98	95	94	92	95	40	73	69	82	79	69

Examples of individuals distributed randomly in a commercially-housed flock under conventional feeding (38 g Ca/kg) and lighting (17 h light/24 h) conditions.

Table 10.2 EFFECT OF POSITION OF THE EGG IN THE SEQUENCE ON ITS MASS AND SHELL QUALITY IN 24 SHAVER 585 HENS IN LATE LAY

	$Slope^a$	$Difference^b$	
		First egg	*Last egg*
For individuals:			
mass (g)	-4.59×10^{-3} (2.58×10^{-3})*	1.452 (0.522)**	-1.241 (0.406)***
specific gravity	2.32×10^{-5} (1.61×10^{-5})	-4.1×10^{-3} (1.0×10^{-3})****	5.2×10^{-3} (1.2×10^{-3})****
shell density^c (mg/cm^3)	2.29×10^{-2} (1.71×10^{-3})	-3.66 (0.920)****	4.77 (1.083)****
For all sequences:			
mass (g)	-3.13×10^{-3} (3.06×10^{-3})	1.553 (0.205)****	-1.089 (0.174)****
specific gravity	3.20×10^{-5} (1.07×10^{-5})***	-4.0×10^{-3} (3.2×10^{-4})****	4.9×10^{-3} (2.0×10^{-4})****
shell density (mg/cm^3)	3.24×10^{-2} (1.22×10^{-2})***	-3.49 (0.262)****	4.43 (0.252)****

*$P<0.1$, **$P<0.05$, ***$P<0.01$, ****$P<0.001$.

Only data for sequences of three or more eggs were analysed and values (with standard errors in parentheses) refer to means of averages for individuals or means of all sequences (867 analysed).

^{a}Slope refers to rate of change in egg characteristic with respect to number of the egg in the sequence.

^{b}Difference refers to difference in egg characteristic between first or last egg and the mean for that characteristic of the rest of the sequence.

^{c}Shell density (DN) from a relationship developed with these birds: $DN = -1098.76 + 1062.58SG + 0.4062M$, where SG is specific gravity and M is egg mass (g).

sequence was more poorly shelled than subsequent eggs. Volynchook, Boorman and Belyavin (1982) studied a much larger number of sequences (867) in 24 individually-caged Shaver 585 hens from 57 to 81 weeks of age in an experimental facility. When data for all sequences were combined there were highly significant positive changes in specific gravity and a derived measure, shell density, with position of the egg in the sequence (*Table 10.2*). It should be stressed that for one sequence the change from egg to egg will be very small and may not be consistent. For their identification these trends require measurement of large numbers of sequences. Much more consistently observed in any sequence however was that the first egg was poorly shelled, relative to the mean of the rest of the sequence, while the last egg was relatively well shelled (*Table 10.2*). There was a tendency towards a decrease in weight of egg with sequence, which could not be identified with statistical significance, although differences between first eggs (heavier) and last eggs (lighter) and the means of the sequences were clearly evident.

Choi *et al.* (1981) measured laying times, egg weight and shell characteristics in 552 eggs from 184, 50-week-old Babcock B-300 hens which laid eggs on three consecutive days. Thus the first day's collection included a proportion of first eggs of sequences, while the subsequent days' collections included none. Trends in egg weight with time of lay showed the heavier nature of first eggs, although there was no clear indication of a decrease in egg weight subsequently in the sequence. Trends in shell characteristics showed that shell mass and proportion of shell (100 × shell mass/egg mass) are not at their minimum values at the start of the day, but decline during the morning before increasing to much higher values in the afternoon. There were steady linear increases on the second and third days. These trends indicate that first eggs of the sequence do not have the poorest shells, as our observations indicate, but that shell quality declines from that of the first egg before improving later. The difference between the two studies cannot be resolved yet; it may be that our simple linear analysis ignored a small curvilinear effect, there may be differences in intensities of such trends due to strain or age (although both flocks were post-peak) and the methods of approach and measurement were different in the two studies. However, both studies show clearly that there are structured changes in shell deposition and egg mass.

Shell formation and calcium supply

Hens have the ability to store extra calcium (and phosphorus) in the skeleton to augment dietary supply during shell formation. This extra calcium, in the form of medullary ('spongy') bone, is deposited especially within the hollow interiors of the limb bones in response to the hormonal changes arising from stimulatory lighting patterns and sexual maturation. It is maintained, more or less, during laying (see Taylor and Dacke, 1984 for a recent review). During laying each egg is formed over a period which, for the average hen in a traditional lighting pattern, will be an hour or two longer than 24 h. Somewhat less than one-quarter of the formation time is spent in the upper tract (see Melek, Morris and Jennings, 1973), while the remainder is spent in the shell gland, although active shelling probably doesn't start until about 3 h after the egg enters the gland (Simkiss and Taylor, 1971). The first egg of a sequence is usually laid about the time of the dark–light change ('lights on'), and thus virtually all of the later shelling of this egg occurs in the following dark period. As the sequence progresses for each egg a greater proportion of shelling will occur after the lights come on. Roland, Sloan and Harms (1973) invoked this gradual change during the sequence as an explanation of the better shell quality later in the day, on the basis that calcium can be derived directly from the diet in the light whereas it must be mobilized from the skeleton in the dark when the bird does not feed. This explanation, its assumptions and consequences are explored further below.

Whether the large proportion of late shelling in the dark is sufficient to explain the special nature of the shell of the first egg of the sequence, or whether there is a more fundamental explanation is not known. It is clear that simple progression through the sequence does not entirely explain the curvilinear response described by Choi *et al.* (1981). The better shell of the last egg is consistent with the large proportion of its shelling which occurs in the light. It is also known that the last egg of the sequence is retained longer in the body—a feature first documented by Fraps (1955) and since incorporated into a model of the ovulatory cycle by Etches and Schoch (1984)—so that there is a longer interval (for example, about 2 h) between penultimate and final ovipositions than between earlier ovipositions. It is tempting to speculate that the extra time is spent in the shell gland and that this is reflected in shell quality. Longer residence in the shell gland is thought to account for the improved shell quality induced by ahemeral patterns of more than 24 h (Melek, Morris and Jennings, 1973). However, there is an inconsistency here; such ahemeral patterns also induce greater egg size, whereas in the case of the last egg of the sequence the size is usually less than that of the rest of the sequence. Indeed, the question of change in size during the sequence has not been much considered: why should the first egg be heavier, why should there be a change as the sequence progresses and what is the nature of the change in mass in terms of egg components?

The idea that the shell is better if calcium can be supplied from the diet directly *via* the gut, whereas it is poorer if calcium is provided from the skeleton, is based on an assumption; there is no direct proof that supplying calcium from the skeleton is less 'efficient' in some way. As described above, however, if the assumption is accepted it explains the gradual change in shell quality within the sequence and would also underlie possible mechanisms for differences between individuals. Scott, Hull and Mullenhorf (1971) suggested that mobilization of calcium from the skeleton might be a limiting factor in shell formation in the dark, to explain their observation that forms of calcium which persist in the gut ('grit') tend to improve shell quality. It is also possible to imagine that some individuals would be more affected by this constraint than others, leading to differences in shell quality.

Volynchook and Boorman (unpublished), have measured plasma total calcium at the end of the dark period, when skeletal mobilization should be most intense, in birds during complete sequences and have not found any correlation with shell mass. There is, however, a large flux of calcium through the plasma during shell formation and plasma concentration may be a poor indicator of rate of delivery to the shell gland. We have also attempted to measure plasma ionic ('free') calcium, but the variation in the measurement is very large, which defeats the object of trying to detect small differences between individuals. A difference between individuals in respect of the ability to mobilize calcium from the skeleton or to utilize such calcium once mobilized cannot therefore be excluded and provision of a form of calcium which persists in the gut should assist shelling in such individuals. It may also be that relationships are more complex and that the phosphorus released during skeletal mobilization is important.

Phosphorus and shell formation

Phosphorus is an important element for shell formation, not because eggshell contains much phosphorus (there is about 100 times as much calcium as phosphorus in eggshell), but because of the special relationship between calcium and phosphorus in bone formation. Calcium is stored in the skeleton probably almost entirely as calcium phosphate and therefore synthesis of medullary bone requires dietary phosphorus. This phosphorus is however involved in an essentially 'futile' process, because if the calcium is used for shell formation the phosphorus must be excreted.

The pattern of change in plasma inorganic phosphate during egg formation has been described by Miller, Harms and Wilson (1977a,b) and Mongin and Sauveur (1979). There are differences of detail between the findings, but they are essentially similar and the pattern found by the latter authors is shown in *Figure 10.2*. In hens receiving a conventional diet (ground limestone included in mash) phosphate starts to increase in the plasma prior to the dark period, increases to a maximum during the dark period and is declining to its normal concentration by the end of the dark period (*Figure 10.2a*). Since skeletal mobilization is necessary to provide calcium during the dark period and release of calcium must be accompanied by release of phosphate, this rising tide of phosphate is to be expected. However, as Mongin and Sauveur rightly emphasized, the start of this increase before onset of the dark period is not explained simply by skeletal mobilization during the dark period. They favoured increased intestinal absorption of phosphate as the mechanism of this initial increase. Mongin and Sauveur also showed that if a persistent source of

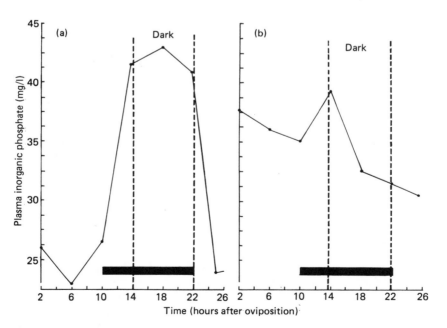

Figure 10.2   Plasma phosphate in relation to shelling (represented by solid bar) where birds were fed on a conventional diet (a) or a calcium-low diet with access to calcareous grit (b). Redrawn after Mongin and Sauveur (1979), and reproduced with permission

calcium ('sea shell' grit) was made available to hens, the response in plasma phosphorus was modified (*Figure 10.2b*). In this condition the initial increase in plasma phosphorus occurred, demonstrating its inevitability, but enhancement during the dark period did not occur and the concentration declined rapidly. This the authors explained on the basis that the continuing supply of calcium from the gut would obviate the need for skeletal mobilization.

One other feature commented upon by these authors and reflected in our own findings was the marked variation there was in the plasma phosphate response among individuals.

Nutritional interest in phosphorus has been stimulated by the several observations that dietary excesses of this element have a detrimental effect on shell quality (Arscott *et al.*, 1962; Taylor, 1965) and Harms and colleagues have studied this phenomenon intensively recently (*see* Harms, 1982a and b). It is not clear whether this phosphorus excess, by accumulating in the blood, interferes with mobilization of skeletal reserves of calcium phosphate during shelling in the dark or whether there is a direct antagonistic effect of the blood phosphorus on the shelling process. Whatever the mechanism however, there is no doubt that dietary treatments which lead to increases in plasma phosphate cause a decline in egg specific gravity. Miles and Harms (1982) showed a clear linear negative correlation between specific gravity and plasma phosphate over a range of treatments.

The involvement of phosphorus in shell formation is now thought to underlie the sometimes beneficial effect of dietary sodium bicarbonate on shell formation (Howes, 1966; Harms, 1982b; Washburn, 1984). Earlier interpretation of this effect concentrated more on possible effects of the bicarbonate ion in relation to the carbonate need for shell, but more recently the effect of the addition of the sodium ion has been seen as important. The data of Miles and Harms (1982) show clearly that dietary treatments without added sodium bicarbonate produce higher plasma phosphate concentrations (with consequent effects on specific gravity) than comparable treatments with added bicarbonate. It is assumed that the sodium exerts its effect by facilitating the renal loss of phosphate, as a balancing cation.

Unfortunately, involvement of sodium in calcium–phosphate relationships cannot be studied in isolation from the whole subject of ion ('acid–base') balance, especially with respect to dietary Na^+, K^+ and Cl^-. There are limits to the amounts of one of these ions which can be included in the diet without adjustment to the intakes of the other ions. Thus dietary additions of $NaHCO_3$ represent additions of Na^+ without balancing additions of Cl^-. A high $Na^+ : Cl^-$ ratio, especially at very low chloride intakes can cause severe overall effects on laying hens and their production (Junqueira *et al.*, 1984), while high dietary chloride, without concomitant increases in sodium, can have a deleterious effect on shell quality (see Harms, 1982b). The proposed effect of sodium, as $NaHCO_3$, in decreasing blood phosphorus cannot necessarily be reproduced by additions of sodium with other anions (Harms, 1982b; Washburn, 1984).

It is evident that the nature and extent of any effect of dietary sodium bicarbonate on shell quality will depend on the extent to which phosphorus is in excess, and whether the sodium bicarbonate can be added without disturbances to the overall ion balance ($Na^+ + K^+ - Cl^-$; see Saveur and Mongin, 1978). Ionic balance in laying hens is a complex subject (Sauveur and Mongin, 1978) and Washburn (1984) has cautioned against too simple an interpretation of the relationship between sodium and phosphate. Gross disturbances of ionic balance will affect egg production severely, while Harms (1982b) has pointed out that smaller effects seen on shell quality should be interpreted on the basis of the effects of other ions on calcium and phosphorus metabolism.

In studies on individual hens Volynchook (unpublished) measured plasma ions in ten 60-week-old Hubbard hens, fed on a conventional diet. Plasma was sampled about 30 min before the end of the dark period, this time being chosen as reflecting the period when the contribution of the skeleton would be clearest and the contribution of the diet would be absent. Hens were sampled for complete sequences. Multiple regression analysis indicated a significant negative relationship between shell weight and plasma phosphate concentration. When the relationship between plasma phosphate and shell weight of the first egg of the sequence was examined it was much more marked (*Figure 10.3*). These data indicate that, for first eggs in these birds at least, at low plasma phosphate (0.4 mM) shell mass is independent of phosphate concentration, but as plasma phosphate increases a decline in shell mass occurs. It must be stressed that these birds were all receiving the same diet containing about 6.5 g total phosphorus and about 4.5 g available phosphorus with 38 g calcium per kg. These variations therefore represent

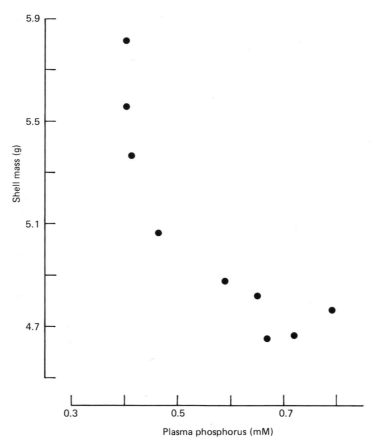

Figure 10.3   Relationship between shell mass of first egg of the sequence and plasma phosphorus concentration at the end of the dark period in Hubbard hens in late lay receiving a diet containing about 4.5 g available P and 38 g Ca/kg

variations between individuals (see above) and the relationship shown indicates that some of the variation among individuals in respect of shell mass is explained by variations in plasma phosphate.

These data may be interpreted in two ways. One interpretation would be based on the assumption that a higher plasma phosphorus 'causes' a weaker shell and that the problem in such individuals is the elimination of excess phosphorus. The other interpretation would be based on the assumption that some individuals require larger amounts of calcium to produce a shell, because, possibly, they are inefficient utilizers of calcium, and the high plasma phosphorus is an indication of the extent of skeletal mobilization necessary in such cases. The former interpretation suggests that shell mass is the dependent variable while plasma phosphorus is the independent, while the latter suggests the converse. Unfortunately, correlative data of this type do not allow distinction of these alternatives.

Finally it must be emphasized that these observations were made on very few hens and data for one were excluded as atypical. There is an evident need to confirm these observations and extend measurement to include younger birds.

Vitamin D

The eluciation of the metabolism of vitamin D and the role of this vitamin in calcium and phosphorus metabolism has been one of the phenomena of nutritional research over the last two decades. The subject is reviewed frequently and Taylor and Dacke (1984) and Soares (1984) have summarized salient features of relevance to poultry. These will not be repeated here. Assuming that ample vitamin D is included in the diet, is there any evidence that its metabolism might sometimes limit its effectiveness? Soares (1984) reported an investigation of the plasma concentration of the active metabolite, 1,25-dihydroxycholecalciferol (1,25 $(OH)_2D_3$), in lines of hens selected for production of thick or thin shells. There was a higher concentration of the metabolite in the plasma of birds producing thick shells. There are also observations which suggest insufficient production of 1,25 $(OH)_2D_3$ in late lay when shell quality is likely to decline (see Taylor and Dacke, 1984). Unfortunately the feeding studies on the effect of vitamin D metabolites on shell quality have been concerned with 25-hydroxycholecalciferol, the substrate for 1,25 $(OH)_2D_3$, which is unlikely to compensate for a deficiency of the latter because it seems that decline in the activity of the enzyme involved (1-hydroxylase) is more likely to be the limiting factor.

This area may be another cause of variation between individuals or may be one linked to those already discussed. The relationship between vitamin D metabolism and individuals in late lay seems worthy of further investigation, although techniques for measurement of vitamin D metabolites are complex.

Implications

VARIATION AND EXPERIMENTATION

Even allowing that the original examination of variation among individuals reported in an earlier section was confounded by structured variation within sequences, there is considerable variation in patterns of change in shell quality among individuals. There are some individuals that produce poor shells for large proportions of the laying year. This raises the question of whether these birds are more likely to respond to remedial treatments such as higher intakes of calcium or separate calcium feeding. This remains to be tested, but it should be noted that eggs from such birds will be a small proportion of those in a random sample, a situation exacerbated, if, as can be the case, the birds involved are also poor producers. If the effects of a remedial treatment, therefore, are tested on means of random samples of eggs, detection of response is likely to be difficult.

The structured variation in shell quality during the sequence imposes further constraints. Ideally, eggs similar in their position in the sequence must be compared in the evaluation of treatments. This means that eggs must be related to the individuals which laid them and those individuals must be sampled for complete sequences or large parts thereof. This applies not only to studies of remedial treatments, but also to correlation studies for the selection of individuals in breeding experiments. Although this seems to demand much more monitoring and effort in experiments, it is likely that understanding this structured variation and using individuals, possibly in cross-over designs, will allow fewer birds to be used in experiments. The approach of Choi *et al.* (1981) could be extended as a compromise. If eggs from individuals were collected for five days, eggs collected during the middle three days of the period could be characterized at least as far as first eggs, last eggs and 'mid-sequence' eggs.

CALCIUM SUPPLY

It is well known that calcium need for maximizing production rate in hens is less than that for maximizing shell quality (see for example, ARC, 1975). An intake of about 3.5 g calcium/day might satisfy the former, while responses in the latter occur up to 5 g/day, although the response above 4 g/day is small and diminishing. With respect to feeding practice, the use of discrete sources of calcium in combination with a low-calcium mash has not recommended itself much in this country. Evidence from empirical trials is equivocal (Belyavin and Boorman, 1981), possibly for reasons of experimental design (*see above*), but the theoretical basis for such practice is sound. In providing a dietary source of calcium during much of shelling this should obviate much of the need for skeletal mobilization. This might improve the situation in birds where such mobilization is a limiting factor, has implications for the unwanted accumulation of phosphate (*see below*), and should reduce the variation within the sequence since this effect is seen as partly the result of the proportion of shelling which is dependent upon such mobilization (*see above*). Limited experience with some birds late in lay does suggest exercise of some caution in this respect. Contrary to general experience it was noted that a significant minority of birds offered low-calcium mash and oyster shell failed 'to eat for calcium' and ceased laying (Volynchook, unpublished). This observation was made with three different groups of Hubbard hens and incidence increased with age. It seems that in late lay (about 60 weeks of age) the 'drive' to lay may not be strong enough to cause a bird to eat an unpalatable source of calcium.

An alternative way of effecting more continuous supply of dietary calcium is to use modified lighting patterns. Sauveur and Mongin (1983) showed substantial improvements in shell quality (7.7 per cent increase in shell weight in conventionally-reared birds) associated with 6 h repeating light–dark cycles. The authors postulated that this effect was due to the more regular supply of dietary calcium allowed by the repeated short light periods. Such patterns do however allow the adoption of ahemeral cycles and the improvement in shell quality is of the same order as that reported in response to 27 or 28 h conventional ahemeral patterns (Melek, Morris and Jennings, 1973; Yannakopoulos and Morris, 1979). It is notable that the effects on egg production rate and egg weight observed by Sauveur and Mongin (1983) using repeating short cycles were typical of those observed in conventional ahemeral patterns of longer than 24 h. Possibly therefore eggshell quality benefits from the longer residence in the shell gland typical of such ahemeral patterns and the supply of calcium is not the main effect. Raine (1984) has commented recently that nutritional treatments can be expected to produce improvements in shell quality of about 1 to 2 per cent, while lighting patterns may produce much larger improvements such as those described above. The interaction between lighting patterns and nutritional treatments has not been much studied and there is a need for the exploration of potential in this direction.

PHOSPHORUS AND ITS INTERACTIONS

Nutritional and economic considerations demand that careful attention be paid to the phosphorus requirement of the laying hen. As with any nutrient there will be a minimum demand for the productive process, but as discussed earlier, there may be deleterious effects on the shell from relatively small excesses. One of the complicating difficulties is the availability of phosphorus from plant sources; total phosphorus has little meaning when comparing diets differing greatly in ingredient composition, while the generality of published values for available phosphorus from ingredients is not known. Current assessments of needs for hens (Harms, 1982b; Raine, 1984; Said *et al.*, 1984) in agreement with earlier assessments (ARC, 1975; Belyavin, 1979) suggest that the requirement for maintaining production and shell quality in caged birds is about 400 mg available phosphorus/day. In experimental work significant decline in shell quality has not usually been observed until intakes of available phosphorus are in excess of 500 mg/day, often considerably. There have been reports to the contrary however; Ousterhout (1980) showed a significant decline in shell quality when increasing dietary available phosphorus from about 3.5 to 4.5 g/kg.

The relationship between plasma phosphorus and shell quality means that nutritional and management practices tending to minimize the former will tend to have a beneficial effect on shell quality. In this context correct ionic balance is important, but it is not clear how large a margin for error there is in the recommendation of 200 mEq $(K^+ + Na^+ - Cl^-)$/kg diet (Sauveur and Mongin, 1978) usually used. Two aspects are of especial note in respect of shell formation. First, strongly acidotic diets (eg. high Cl^-) are likely to cause poor shells and second, sodium bicarbonate can decrease high plasma phosphorus. High concentrations of chloride, without the balancing ion sodium, are unlikely to occur in natural diets, but since such diets always contain excess potassium, additions of sodium bicarbonate without compensatory decrease in sodium from other sources will alter the balance $K^+ + Na^+ - Cl^-$. In light of this complexity it is not surprising that results of experiments on additions of sodium bicarbonate are often equivocal.

Another approach to minimizing plasma phosphorus during shelling is to minimize skeletal mobilization of calcium and phosphate. It is clear from the data of Mongin and Sauveur (1979) that feeding calcareous grit can prevent the large enhancement of plasma phosphorus usually seen during the dark period (*see Figure 10.3*). If skeletal stores are not depleted, their replenishment will not be necessary and the need for phosphorus in this role will largely disappear. Thus, as Mongin and Sauveur pointed out, discrete persistent sources of calcium should decrease the need for phosphorus. If short repeated light–dark cycles also allow more continuous supply of calcium from the gut and thereby prevent skeletal mobilization, they should have the same effect on phosphorus requirement. Possibly, therefore, in such treatments a small excess of phosphorus is being supplied and further improvements in shell quality would accrue from decreasing dietary phosphorus.

Results on individual birds, described above, show that some of the variation among individuals in shell quality is due to individual variation in phosphorus metabolism. Thus even at normal dietary phosphorus content, some birds are showing effects of phosphorus 'excess'. This is assumed to arise because of skeletal mobilization primarily, and it may be predicted that treatments which minimize such mobilization would tend to decrease the variation among individuals in shell quality.

ACKNOWLEDGEMENTS

Our studies reported herein were supported by grants from the British Egg Marketing Board Research and Education Trust and the Agriculture and Food Research Council.

References

AGRICULTURAL RESEARCH COUNCIL (1975). *The Nutrient Requirements of Farm Livestock. No. 1, Poultry.* Agricultural Research Council; London

ARSCOTT, G.H., RACHAPAETAYAKOM, P., BENIER, P.E. and ADAMS, F.W. (1962). *Poultry Science*, **41**, 485–488

ATWOOD, H. (1929). *Poultry Science*, **8**, 137–140

BELYAVIN, C.G. (1979). *Egg-shell quality in the older hen.* PhD thesis. University of Nottingham

BELYAVIN, C.G. and BOORMAN, K.N. (1981). In *Quality of Eggs*, pp. 165–174. Ed. G. Beuving, C.W. Scheele and P.C.M. Simons. Spelderholt Institute for Poultry Research; Beekbergen, The Netherlands

BERG, L.R. (1945). *Poultry Science*, **24**, 555–563

BEUVING, G., SCHEELE, C.W. and SIMON, P.C.M. (1981). *Quality of Eggs.* Spelderholt Institute for Poultry Research; Beekbergen, The Netherlands

BUSS, E.G. and GUYER, R.B. (1981). In *Quality of Eggs*, pp. 239–249. Ed. G. Beuving, C.W. Scheele and P.C.M. Simons. Spelderholt Institute for Poultry Research; Beekbergen, The Netherlands

CHOI, J.H., MILES, R.D., ARAFA, A.S. and HARMS, R.H. (1981). *Poultry Science*, **60**, 824–828

ETCHES, R.J. and SCHOCH, J.P. (1984). *British Poultry Science*, **25**, 65–76

FRAPS, R.M. (1955). In *Progress in the Physiology of Farm Animals*, Vol. II, pp. 671–740. Ed. J. Hammond. Butterworths; London

HARMS, R.H. (1982a). *Feedstuffs*, May 10, pp. 25–26

HARMS, R.H. (1982b). *Feedstuffs*, May 17, pp. 25–28

HOWES, J.R. (1966). *Poultry Science*, **45**, 1092–1093

HURWITZ, S., BAR, A. and COHEN, I. (1973). *American Journal of Physiology*, **225**, 150–154

JUNQUEIRA, O.M., COSTA, P.T., MILES, R.D. and HARMS, R.H. (1984). *Poultry Science*, **63**, 123–130

MELEK, O., MORRIS, T.R. and JENNINGS, R.C. (1973). *British Poultry Science*, **14**, 493–498

MILES, R.D. and HARMS, R.H. (1982). *Poultry Science*, **61**, 175–177

MILLER, E.R., HARMS, R.H. and WILSON, H.R. (1977a). *Poultry Science*, **56**, 586–589

MILLER, E.R., HARMS, R.H. and WILSON, H.R. (1977b). *Poultry Science*, **56**, 1501–1503

MONGIN, P. (1968). *World's Poultry Science Journal*, **24**, 200–230

MONGIN, P. and SAUVEUR, B. (1979). *British Poultry Science*, **20**, 401–412

OUSTERHOUT, L.E. (1980). *Poultry Science*, **59**, 1480–1484

RAINE, H. (1984). *Poultry World*, 29 November, pp. 10–11

ROLAND, D.A., SLOAN, D.R. and HARMS, R.H. (1973). *Poultry Science*, **52**, 506–510

SAID, N.W., SULLIVAN, T.W., SUNDE, M.L. and BIRD, H.R. (1984). *Poultry Science*, **63**, 2007–2019

SAUVEUR, B. and MONGIN, P. (1978). *British Poultry Science*, **19**, 475–485

SAUVEUR, B. and MONGIN, P. (1983). *British Poultry Science*, **24**, 405–416

SCOTT, M.L., HULL, S.J. and MULLENHORF, P.A. (1971). *Poultry Science*, **50**, 1055–1063

SIMKISS, K. and TAYLOR, T.G. (1971). In *Physiology and Biochemistry of the Domestic Fowl*, Vol. 3, pp. 1331–1343. Ed. D.T. Bell and B.M. Freeman. Academic Press; London

SOARES, J.H. (1984). *Poultry Science*, **63**, 2075–2083

TAYLOR, T.G. (1965). *British Poultry Science*, **6**, 79–87

TAYLOR, T.G. and DACKE, C.G. (1984). In *Physiology and Biochemistry of the Domestic Fowl*, Vol. 5, pp. 125–170. Ed. B.M. Freeman. Academic Press; London

VOLYNCHOOK, J.G., BOORMAN, K.N. and BELYAVIN, C.G. (1982). *World's Poultry Science Journal*, **38**, 138

WASHBURN, K.W. (1984). In *Proceedings and Abstracts of 17th World's Poultry Congress and Exhibition, Helsinki (Finland)*, pp. 43–46

WILHELM, L.A. (1940). *Poultry Science*, **19**, 246–253

YANNAKOPOULOS, A.L. and MORRIS, T.R. (1979). *British Poultry Science*, **20**, 337–342

V

Ruminant Nutrition

11

SEASONAL VARIATION OF APPETITE IN RUMINANTS

R.N.B. KAY
Physiology Department, Rowett Research Institute, Aberdeen, Scotland

Introduction

Under natural conditions most grazing ruminants, wild or domesticated, have to contend with enormous seasonal changes in the amount and quality of herbage available to them. In cool temperate countries such as the British Isles plant growth is confined to the spring and summer months; during autumn and winter only dormant and dead vegetation is available, declining progressively in quality and abundance. *Figure 11.1* shows that on Scottish hill pastures, plant growth is largely limited to the four summer months when the mean air temperature exceeds 10 °C. Judging by the faecal nitrogen concentration of red deer grazing such hill pastures, the quality of the herbage selected declines rapidly once the peak of the growth season in July has passed. (Nitrogen in faecal dry matter serves as an index of herbage quality because as the digestibility of the herbage increases faecal N content, reflecting microbial synthesis, will increase and indigestible dry matter will decrease, although the relationship will differ numerically between plant species and parts and so be influenced by changing grazing behaviour.)

Animals must adapt to this uncomfortable fact of life if they are to survive and reproduce successfully. They do so in various ways. Winter scarcity may be avoided to some extent by moving to better pastures, either locally (sheep, red deer) or by migrating over long distances (caribou). Energy requirements may be reduced by economies ranging from reduced activity and heart rate in winter (sheep, deer) to intermittent torpor or full hibernation. The direct effects of environmental chill may be reduced by sheltering behaviour and by growing an insulating coat. The problem can be fought by conserving food (man) or by laying down fat reserves (sheep, deer). But, most effectively of all, many herbivores, ruminants especially, have learned to live with the seasons by confining their most productive activities—late gestation and lactation, juvenile growth and adult fattening—to summer when the climate is kind and food is abundant. A mixture of these strategies is likely to be employed, the combination depending on the habitat and nutritional niche of the animal and on its size, longevity and reproductive rate.

Our domesticated sheep, goats and cattle are probably derived from ancestral types that were strongly seasonal, for primitive breeds and related wild species retain this characteristic. Provision of shelter and conserved food in winter will have reduced the selective pressure that maintains seasonality while deliberate

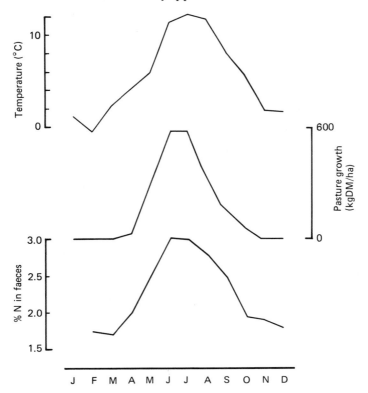

Figure 11.1   Annual cycles of growth of herbage on unimproved Scottish hill pasture
(Newbould, 1971–73), and of its digestibility as indicated by faecal nitrogen
concentration in red deer on a hill farm (Blaxter *et al.*, 1974), in relation to mean
monthly air temperature recorded at Braemar, Scotland

selection for year-round productivity, of offspring, milk, meat and wool, has nearly
eliminated it from many lowland breeds. However, the price of continuous
production is continuous nutrition, and this calls for added expense on conserved or
bought-in food in winter. Increasingly, continuity of the supply of animal products
to the market is aided by storing the products for a time, so lessening the need to
maintain continuous production at the cost of supplementary winter food. Allden
(1970), in reviewing the compensatory growth that follows a period of nutritional
deprivation, emphasized that the compensation mechanisms at pasture may offset
the apparent advantages of fodder conservation. Though the mechanisms involved
in compensation following a period of deprivation imposed by man or by seasonal
deterioration of the pasture may not be identical with those that underlie the
annual cycle of growth and appetite seen in seasonally adapted animals, the
consequences are very similar. It is thus important, as mentioned previously (Kay,
1979), to be aware of the extent to which our various breeds are seasonal and to
understand the physiological mechanisms concerned so that we can take advantage
of these characteristics when seeking to optimize productivity under different
environmental and economic conditions. Sometimes it will be better to go along
with the animal's deep-rooted adaptations to the seasonal cycle of scarcity and
plenty than to override them.

Seasonal cycles

Many seasonal cycles are endogenous, determined by the nature of the animal. It is evident that they are not simple responses to present climate or food supply, for they are seen in animals that are sheltered and fed to appetite. Sheep and deer that are penned indoors and offered a standard diet *ad libitum* all year round still breed in autumn so their young are born in spring, their coats grow seasonally, voluntary intake of food rises to a peak in summer and falls abruptly during the autumn rut and midwinter period, and metabolic rate, activity and heart rate similarly increase during summer and fall during winter. The various hormones underlying these effects—melatonin, hypothalamic releasing factors, gonadotrophins and gonadal hormones, prolactin and thyroid hormones—also show seasonal cycles.

Some seasonal cycles have a circannual period in the absence of external annual cues, though whether this natural period is innate or acquired in early life is not clear. An external cue, usually changing daylength, then serves to entrain the endogenous cycle so as to attune it to the season of the year. While some hormonal changes can be detected within a few days of operation of the external cue, the behavioural response of the animal may take many weeks to appear for this depends on the slow unfolding of a sequence of physiological responses. For example, sudden reduction in daylength reduced plasma prolactin in Soay rams within six days but growth and secretion by the testes took 100 days to develop fully (Lincoln and Short, 1980).

The appetite cycle

The appetite cycle is of particular interest to the nutritionist. It may perhaps be regarded as reflecting the nutrient demands arising not only from seasonal reproductive activities (gestation, lactation) but also from photoperiodic growth cycles as suggested by Forbes (1982). Appetite may thus be thought of as a consequence of growth, rather than its cause. At the Rowett Research Institute recent studies of the appetite cycles of red deer and Soay sheep have been made by Simpson (1976), Suttie (1981) and Argo (1985). The red deer, our largest native wild ruminant, is well adapted to the hazards of the British climate. The Soay is a small ancestral breed of sheep, long isolated on the St Kilda Islands 40 miles west of the Hebrides, and looking rather like the mouflon of the Mediterranean basin. It is intensely seasonal in its behaviour, fitting it well to the rigours of its northern island home (Jewell, Milner and Boyd, 1974). Yet in captivity it is easy to handle and so makes an excellent subject for studies of photoperiodism.

The voluntary food intake of adult red deer stags and Soay rams falls abruptly at the onset of the rut. This fall takes place even though the animals are individually penned, and so not competing for food, and no females are present; sometimes the animals virtually stop eating for days at a time. Appetite then recovers somewhat but remains low throughout winter. From late February onwards, food intake increases, reaching an irregular plateau in summer.

Mature black-tailed and red deer hinds, which have an eight-month gestation and often suckle their calves through the rut, show little loss of appetite during the rut and less inappetence during winter than the stags (Bandy *et al.*, 1970; Suttie and Simpson, 1985). On the other hand mature Soay ewes, whose five-month gestation allows them to wean their lambs before the next rut, display an appetite cycle that

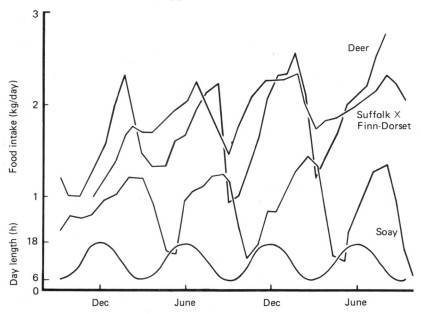

Figure 11.2   Voluntary food intake by red deer stags, Suffolk × (Finnish Landrace × Dorset Horn) rams and Soay rams. The animals, all intact males, were penned for two years while about 0.5 to 2.5 years old, given standard complete pelleted diets, and illuminated with artificial lighting that provided a six-month photoperiod (after Kay, 1979)

resembles that of the rams in declining sharply at the onset of the breeding season (Argo, 1985).

Other breeds of sheep have also been shown to exhibit clear seasonal cycles of food intake when penned and offered standard diets to appetite. These include Shetland wethers and Scottish Blackface ewes (Gordon, 1964), Suffolk × (Border Leicester × Scottish Blackface) wethers (Greenhalgh and Reid, 1974), and Suffolk × (Finnish Landrace × Dorset Horn) wethers and rams (Blaxter, Fowler and Gill, 1982; Simpson, Suttie and Kay, 1984). However, the appetite cycle in the Suffolk × Finn–Dorset, a lowland cross selected for its rapid growth and extended breeding season, is considerably less than that of the primitive Soay or the wild red deer (*Figure 11.2*). Lowland cattle also show a distinct though moderate decline in growth and food conversion efficiency in late autumn under stall-feeding conditions (Kilkenny, 1974). While this was tentatively ascribed to subclinical disease, the growth, appetite and lactation of cows can be improved by extended daylength (Peters *et al.*, 1980), so it seems that seasonal cycles of growth and appetite may occur in cattle.

What is the nature of the appetite cycle and how does it relate to other seasonal cycles? Is the underlying mechanism similar to that responsible for the better-known breeding cycle? Sheep and deer are aroused from sexual quiescence by the lengthening nights of late summer so as to achieve breeding condition in midautumn (Lincoln and Short, 1980). During daytime, impulses from the retina activate a neural centre in the hypothalamus, the suprachiasmatic nucleus, whose diurnal activity allows it to serve as an internal clock (*Figure 11.3*). This centre in

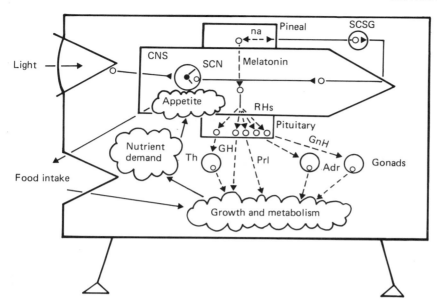

Figure 11.3 Neurohormonal mechanisms concerned with the photoperiodic control of growth, appetite and food intake and of reproduction. Abbreviations: Adr, adrenal glands; CNS, central nervous system; GH, growth hormone; GnH, gonadotrophic hormones; na, noradrenaline; Prl, prolactin; RHs releasing hormones from hypothalamus; SCN, suprachiasmatic nucleus; SCSG, superior cervical sympathetic ganglion; Th, thyroid glands

turn projects by way of the cervical sympathetic nerve to the pineal gland, suppressing the formation of melatonin during daytime. As nights lengthen the pattern of melatonin secretion changes, leading to the production of gonadotrophin releasing hormone in the hypothalamus, the secretion of gonadotrophins by the pituitary gland, and so the growth and activity of the ovaries and testes. Administration of melatonin, which can be given by mouth, is now used to produce a well-orchestrated advance of the breeding season both in sheep (Kennaway, Gilmore and Seamark, 1982) and in red deer (Adam and Atkinson, 1984).

At the Rowett Research Institute, red deer and sheep were confined to pens whose artificial lighting was regulated to provide a daylength cycle of only six months' duration. The animals, male and female, duly showed a six-month breeding cycle. The appetite cycle also adopted the six-month period (Simpson, Suttie and Kay, 1984; Suttie and Simpson, 1985) (*Figure 11.2*) as did the moulting cycle (Kay and Ryder, 1978), the cycle of metabolic rate (Argo and Smith, 1983), and cycles of testosterone, oestradiol, prolactin and thyroid hormones (Simpson, Suttie and Kay, 1984; Argo, 1985). Denervation of the pineal gland (and the head generally) by removal of the anterior cervical sympathetic ganglion has been shown to cause a gradual abolition of all these responses; the breeding cycle ceases, leaving rams in a continuous state of moderate sexual activity (Lincoln and Short, 1980), and the appetite cycle is reduced (Suttie, Kay and Goodall, 1984). Although entrainment of the breeding, appetite and moulting cycles by a shortened photoperiod can still occur immediately after sympathetic denervation of the pineal (Argo, 1985), the cycles eventually peter out. Thus all these physiological responses are entrained by the same stimulus and share a common control mechanism at least as far as the pineal; to this extent they form an indivisible package.

Appetite and breeding cycles

It seemed possible that the appetite cycle might largely be secondary to the breeding cycle. This is obviously true for the enhanced appetite of the lactating female. However, is it true also for the elevated food intake seen in non-reproductive adults in summer that is associated with replenishment of their fat reserves? After all, in nature these reserves are used mainly in support of reproduction. In red deer the fat depots of the stag are mobilized during the rut, allowing attention to be focused on seeking and holding a mate rather than on grazing, while the reserves of the female are retained in part through the winter to be of service in late gestation (Mitchell, McCowan and Nicholson, 1976). The castration of stags and rams has been shown to cause a substantial reduction in the amplitude of the appetite cycle, due to a reduction of the summer peak as well as to a lessening of the fall during the rut (Simpson, 1976; Kay, 1979). However, prepubertal deer show a sharp reduction in growth and appetite during their first winter (Kay, 1979; Suttie *et al.*, 1983), and Argo (1985) has shown that when adult Soay rams are reduced to a prepubertal condition by immunocastration (immunization against their own gonadotrophin releasing hormone) they show only a small reduction of their appetite cycle. Thus although the appetite cycle of the non-reproductive animal may require low levels of gonadal hormones for its full expression, it is not simply a consequence of the breeding cycle.

A more practical question concerns the appetite of animals breeding out of season. Ewes that naturally would lamb in March or April may be brought into oestrus early by administration of hormones so that they lamb in January. At this time their appetite would normally be low. Does this winter inappetence persist, to the detriment of late fetal growth and lactation? This question was studied by Argo (1985). Soay ewes maintained on a six-month photoperiod came into breeding condition at six-month intervals and showed a sharp reduction in food intake; during intervening periods they passed into sexual quiescence and their appetite increased. When bred they lambed normally five months later. They went on to lactate quite successfully, as judged by yield and composition of milk and by lamb growth, despite the fact that all this occurred during the period when photoperiod would otherwise have led to sexual activity and reduced appetite. Evidently the demands of gestation and lactation over-ride photoperiodic responses.

Appetite and metabolism cycles

Metabolic rate follows an annual cycle in various species of deer, being lowest in winter. In the white-tailed deer, for example, fasting heat losses, expressed on a metabolic body size basis, were substantially lower in winter than in summer (Silver *et al.*, 1969) and this cycle is paralleled by a reduction in activity and heart rate in winter (Moen, 1978).

Sheep show a similar cycle. Argo and Smith (1983) showed that the intake of metabolizable energy (ME) required for maintenance of energy balance in Soay rams confined to calorimeter chambers varied by 28 per cent with the daylength cycle. Blaxter and Boyne (1982) found a similar cycle in the calculated fasting metabolic rate of mature wether sheep used in feed evaluation trials and held to a constant level of ME intake.

A seasonal cycle in voluntary food intake is, of course, bound to be associated with a cycle in metabolic rate, for diet induced thermogenesis will cause heat losses to vary with food intake. What is interesting about the studies referred to above is the indication that an additional component of metabolic rate varies with season independently of food intake. Forbes and his colleagues (Forbes, 1982) have shown that lamb growth may be accelerated by extended daylength, even when food intake is restricted. Possibly photoperiodically controlled cycles of hormone balance and growth are reflected in changes in metabolic rate, independently of food intake. Further research is needed.

Although the influence of seasonal cycles of metabolism and growth on food intake are clearly revealed in studies on penned non-reproductive sheep and deer, the requirements of grazing farm animals may be dominated by reproduction and lactation and by activity and the demands of the environment. In New Zealand the ME requirements of stags fed out of doors were almost as high in winter as in summer (Fennessy, Moore and Corson, 1981), the increased grazing activity on sparse pasture and environmental chill evidently counterbalancing photoperiodically depressed appetite and metabolism.

Appetite and growth

The seasonal appetite cycle seen in many species native to temperate and high latitudes is associated with a seasonal cycle of growth. The black-tailed deer buck, when fed to appetite, is typical. The suckled calf grows rapidly during summer and autumn but its growth declines in the first winter; rapid growth resumes in spring and summer but ceases at the autumn rut and during the following winter. This pattern moderates during the next two or three years to give a balanced annual cycle of weight gain and loss of about 20 per cent amplitude in the mature animal (Wood *et al.*, 1962). The red deer follows a similar seasonal pattern of growth (Blaxter *et al.*, 1974).

COMPENSATORY GROWTH

In some respects the seasonal cycle of voluntary weight loss and gain may be regarded as an example of compensatory growth. If the winter growth check of young red deer stags was exacerbated by further restriction of their food intake, their growth rate and appetite in summer, when food was made freely available, became much greater than that of unrestricted controls, allowing them partially to catch up (Suttie *et al.*, 1983). The carcass fat content of each group was similar at the same empty body weight. A similar compensatory growth surge following restricted winter nutrition is seen in reindeer calves (Ryg and Jacobsen, 1982), another intensely seasonal species.

Ryg (1982) noted that weight changes in 1-year-old reindeer bulls during a midsummer growth check and again during the rut were inversely related to the weights recorded at the beginning of these periods, so that live weights tended towards a set point of about 72 kg. Watkins and Hudson (1984) showed that in Canadian wapiti, a large subspecies of the red deer, weight changes during winter also varied with autumn weight, while those in summer showed a similar dependence on spring weight. The set point in summer exceeded 300 kg and presumably represented the target weight each sex would eventually reach at maturity under the nutritional conditions provided. In winter animals that received a pelleted barley–alfalfa supplement to appetite showed much the same set point, 340 kg, as in summer, whereas those that had to subsist without supplement in aspen parkland tended towards a much lower set point, about 120 kg.

COMPOSITION OF SEASONAL WEIGHT GAIN

Much work has been done on the composition of body weight gain in continuously growing farm animals and this has recently been reviewed (Agricultural Research Council, 1980). A considerable amount is also known of the composition of weight gain in sheep and cattle showing compensatory growth after a period of imposed dietary restriction (Agricultural Research Council, 1980; O'Donovan, 1984). However, information concerning the composition of annual weight gain in seasonal animals seems largely limited to deer.

The composition of carcass gain depends on many factors. The most important is stage of maturity, as reflected by empty body weight rather than age; other factors include breed, sex, plane of nutrition and growth rate, the energy and protein contents of the diet, frequency of feeding and activity (Agricultural Research Council, 1980). Once empty body weight has exceeded a certain value, about 30 kg in the precocious sheep, carcass gain is of fairly constant composition; it contained about 68 per cent of fat (solvent extractable lipid) in the Suffolk × Finn–Dorset sheep, wethers and rams, that Blaxter, Fowler and Gill (1982) studied to mature weights of about 130 kg. In earlier studies, summarized in The Nutrient Requirements of Ruminant Livestock (Agricultural Research Council, 1980), the fat content of liveweight gain by sheep and cattle was shown to rise from around 100 g/kg gain in the very young animal to about 500–700 g/kg in the adult, there being considerable effects of breed, sex and rate of gain.

O'Donovan (1984) reviewed the composition of compensatory weight gains. Animals that were released from imposed dietary restriction at first restored their level of hydration and gut fill towards normality. After this adjustment, however, the composition of their weight gain was usually found to be similar to that seen in continuously growing controls, though different experiments have yielded quite a range of results.

At first glance one might suppose that the composition of seasonal weight gain in animals showing an annual cycle of growth might resemble that of compensatory growth and of continuous growth. However, the hormonal and metabolic mechanisms underlying seasonal growth and its associated changes of voluntary food intake may well differ from those resulting from imposed dietary restriction of experimental or environmental origin. In seasonal animals, growth occurs during sexual quiescence when prolactin levels are high, while weight loss occurs mainly during sexual activity when gonadal hormones are at their peak. In non-seasonal animals continuous growth or compensatory growth following dietary restriction occurs throughout the year and against a more constant hormonal background.

Forbes (1982) reviewed the results of experiments in which sheep and cattle were subjected to periods of extended day length. Lambs that were fed to appetite and were exposed to long days (16 h light : 8 h dark) increased their food intake and growth rate compared to animals on short days, though part of the increase in growth rate was due to increased gut fill. Even if restricted to a constant level of food intake, the lambs on long days still grew faster and again much of this was due to increased gut fill (Forbes *et al.*, 1979). When lambs on the two daylength treatments were pair-fed, those subjected to long days produced larger and leaner carcasses than those on short days (Jones *et al.*, 1982), suggesting that when food is limited the lean tissue growth caused by long days is maintained in preference to deposition of fat. Cattle also respond to increased daylength. In the experiment of Peters *et al.* (1980) for example, a group of heifers exposed to 16 h light : 8 h dark showed increased growth followed by an increase in food intake when compared to other groups that had normal winter daylength or were continuously illuminated.

The growth surges associated with long daylength in ruminants are often accompanied by raised concentrations of prolactin, but not always (Peters *et al.*, 1980), and the evidence that prolactin is required for such growth is equivocal (Forbes, 1982).

Some information is now available on the growth of the conspicuously seasonal red deer. The deer calf does not begin to lay down substantial adipose reserves until it reaches 100 kg empty body weight, about a half of its mature size (Blaxter *et al.*, 1974), a much later stage of development to start fattening than in sheep or cattle. Thereafter, however, about 55 per cent of its empty body weight gain is due to accretion of fat (Suttie *et al.*, 1983), a value similar to that for sheep and cattle (Agricultural Research Council, 1980). In a summary of observations on red deer stags in New Zealand, Suttie (1982) recorded that fat deposition accounted for only 14 per cent of the summer gain in empty body weight in one year old stags and 23 per cent in two year olds, but accounted for 63 per cent of the summer growth of mature stags. It thus appears that although red deer only begin to accumulate fat late in development, and then show a seasonal pattern of accretion and loss of fat, the fat content of mature weight gain in deer is about as large as in sheep or cattle. Indeed Suttie (1982) recommends that in order to uphold the lean character of venison established from the sale of young animals, mature stags should be slaughtered in winter, after losing most of their fat during the rut. Adam (1983) found that 16-month-old stags slaughtered during the rut had even less fat plus connective tissue in their dressed carcass (4.7 per cent) than five-month-old stag calves of much smaller size (6.3 per cent).

WINTER INAPPETENCE

It is common experience that ruminant farm animals are less easy to fatten in winter than in summer, but only recently has it been appreciated that this is due not only to poor food, poor housing and chilling temperatures but also to a seasonal decline in growth and appetite. The reduced growth of deer calves in winter is one of the main obstacles to the profitable development of intensive deer farming (Adam, 1983). Various ways of overcoming the problem have been examined and these are reviewed by Kay, Milne and Hamilton (1984).

Provision of additional light to mimic the summer photoperiod produced either no growth response or one that was small and delayed. A liberal supply of concentrates throughout the winter allows deer calves to maintain a moderate growth rate, though at a prohibitive cost (Adam, 1983). Even on such good diets, growth ceases altogether for a few weeks in midwinter (Adam and Moir, 1985). At this time a calf may be able to meet its reduced growth target from a poorer and more economical diet, provided that rumen capacity, and so ability to consume coarse roughage, has not declined along with growth rate.

Improvements in growth during winter tend to be balanced by a reduced rate of growth during the following summer (Suttie and Hamilton, 1983; Adam and Moir, 1985). This partially frustrates attempts to improve yearling slaughter weights by good winter nutrition and management, and decreases the proportion of gain obtained from cheap summer pasture. Adam (1983) has suggested that on intensive deer farms the problem of poor winter growth should be avoided by the slaughter of surplus calves in late autumn, advancing the rut and so the calving season by hormonal treatment (Adam and Atkinson, 1984) to allow a longer summer period for lactation and calf growth.

Conclusion

Ruminant animals have adapted to natural environmental and nutritional conditions so as to survive and reproduce. Prominent among the difficulties they must face is the seasonal cycle of climate and herbage growth. The development of physiological responses to photoperiod allows them to time their growth and reproduction to occur during summer when climate and food supply are most favourable.

Farmers are not concerned simply with the survival of their stock, but rather with the surplus production their animals can give, and so they have learned how to protect, feed and genetically transform their domesticated breeds in order to increase their productivity. To the extent that many of our farm animals, ruminants in particular, remain affected by our climate and are dependent on seasonal forage crops, it is necessary to consider carefully their deeply seasonal nature and how to make best use of this characteristic.

References

ADAM, C.L. (1983). *British Deer Farmers Association Newsletter*, **12**

ADAM, C.L. and ATKINSON, T. (1984). *Journal of Reproduction and Fertility*, **72**, 463–466

ADAM, C.L. and MOIR, C.E. (1985). *Animal Production*, **40**, 135–141

AGRICULTURAL RESEARCH COUNCIL (1980). *The Nutrient Requirements of Ruminant Livestock*. Commonwealth Agricultural Bureaux; Slough

ALLDEN, W.G. (1970). *Nutrition Abstracts and Reviews*, **40**, 1167–1184

ARGO, C.M. (1985). *Photoperiodic Control of Nutritional and Reproductive Cyclicity in the Soay Sheep*. PhD thesis, University of Aberdeen; Scotland

ARGO, C.M. and SMITH, J.S. (1983). *Journal of Physiology, London*, **343**, 23–24 P

BANDY, P.J., COWAN, I. MCT. and WOOD, A.J. (1970). *Canadian Journal of Zoology*, **48**, 1401–1410

BLAXTER, K.L. and BOYNE, A.W. (1982). *Journal of Agricultural Science, Cambridge*, **99**, 611–620

BLAXTER, K.L., FOWLER, V.R. and GILL, J.C. (1982). *Journal of Agricultural Science, Cambridge*, **98**, 405–420

BLAXTER, K.L., KAY, R.N.B., SHARMAN, G.A.M., CUNNINGHAM, J.M.M. and HAMILTON, W.J. (1974). *Farming the Red Deer*. Her Majesty's Stationery Office; Edinburgh

FENNESSY, P.F., MOORE, G.H. and CORSON, I.D. (1981). *Proceedings of the New Zealand Society of Animal Production*, **40**, 158–162

FORBES, J.M. (1982). *Livestock Production Science*, **9**, 361–374

FORBES, J.M., EL SHAHAT, A.A., JONES, R., DUNCAN, J.G.S. and BOAZ, T.G. (1979). *Animal Production*, **28**, 33–42

GORDON, J.G. (1964). *Nature, London*, **204**, 798–799

GREENHALGH, J.F.D. and REID, G.W. (1974). *Animal Production*, **19**, 77–86

JEWELL, P.A., MILNER, C. and BOYD, J.M. (1974). *Island Survivors: The Ecology of the Soay Sheep of St Kilda*. Athlone Press, University of London; London

JONES, R., FORBES, J.M., SLADE, C.F.R. and APPLETON, M. (1982). *Animal Production*, **35**, 9–14

KAY, R.N.B. (1979). *ARC Research Review*, **5**, 13–15

KAY, R.N.B., MILNE, J.A. and HAMILTON, W.J. (1984). *Proceedings of the Royal Society of Edinburgh*, **82B**, 231–242

KAY, R.N.B. and RYDER, M.L. (1978). *Journal of Zoology, London*, **185**, 505–510

KENNAWAY, D.J., GILMORE, T.A. and SEAMARK, R.F. (1982). *Endocrinology*, **110**, 1766–1772

KILKENNY, J.B. (1974). In *Handbook No. 2, Meat and Livestock Commission*, Chapter 9. Ed. M. Kay, J.B. Kilkenny, J.E. Sutherland, H. Swan and R. Tallack. Rowett Research Institute; Aberdeen

LINCOLN, G.A. and SHORT, R.V. (1980). *Recent Progress in Hormone Research*, **36**, 1–51

MITCHELL, B., MCCOWAN, D. and NICHOLSON, I.W. (1976). *Journal of Zoology, London*, **180**, 107–127

MOEN, A.N. (1978). *Journal of Wildlife Management*, **42**, 715–738

NEWBOULD, P. (1971–73). In *Hill Farming Research Organisation, Sixth Report*. Plants to improve hill pastures, pp. 74–85. HFRO; Penicuik, Scotland

O'DONOVAN, P.B. (1984). *Nutrition Abstracts and Reviews B*, **54**, 389–410

PETERS, R.R., CHAPIN, L.T., EMERY, R.S. and TUCKER, H.A. (1980). *Journal of Animal Science*, **51**, 1148–1153

RYG, M. (1982). *Endocrine Components in the Control of Annual Cycles of Growth and Fattening in Male Cervidae*. PhD thesis, University of Oslo; Norway

RYG, M. and JACOBSEN, E. (1982). *Canadian Journal of Zoology*, **60**, 15–23

SILVER, H., COLOVOS, N.F., HOLTER, J.B. and HAYES, H.H. (1969). *Journal of Wildlife Management*, **33**, 490–498

SIMPSON, A.M. (1976). *A Study of the Energy Metabolism and Seasonal Cycles of Captive Red Deer*. PhD thesis, University of Aberdeen; Scotland

SIMPSON, A.M., SUTTIE, J.M. and KAY, R.N.B. (1984). *Animal Reproduction Science*, **6**, 291–299

SUTTIE, J.M. (1981). *The Influence of Nutrition and Photoperiod on the Growth, Development and Endocrine Status of Captive Red Deer and Soay Rams*. PhD thesis, University of Aberdeen; Scotland

SUTTIE, J.M. (1982). *British Deer Farmers Association Newsletter*, **10**, 8–10

SUTTIE, J.M., GOODALL, E.D., PENNIE, K. and KAY, R.N.B. (1983). *British Journal of Nutrition*, **50**, 737–747

SUTTIE, J.M. and HAMILTON, W.J. (1983). *Journal of Zoology, London*, **201**, 153–159

SUTTIE, J.M., KAY, R.N.B. and GOODALL, E.D. (1984). *Livestock Production Science*, **11**, 529–534

SUTTIE, J.M. and SIMPSON, A.M. (1985). In *The Biology of Deer Production*. Ed. P.F. Fennessy and K.R. Drew. *Royal Society of New Zealand*, Bulletin 22. Wellington, New Zealand

WATKINS, W.G. and HUDSON, R.J. (1984). In *63rd Annual Feeder's Day Report*, pp. 60–61. University of Alberta; Edmonton, Canada

WOOD, A.J., COWAN, I. MCT. and NORDAN, H.C. (1962). *Canadian Journal of Zoology*, **40**, 593–603

12

PHOTOPERIODIC INFLUENCES ON MILK PRODUCTION IN DAIRY COWS

H.A. TUCKER

Department of Animal Science, Michigan State University, East Lansing, MI, USA

Introduction

Physiologically, dairy cattle are non-seasonal breeders. Perhaps for this reason, relatively little research has been devoted to studies of the effects of season on lactation in this species, and most research of seasonal effects on mammary function of the cow has focused on ambient temperature. From such studies it is clear that milk yield is generally lowest in summer. The inhibitory effects of summer on milk yield occur when ambient temperatures exceed the upper critical temperature of the cow's thermoneutral zone. Under these conditions, feed intake is suppressed to curtail endogenous heat production, and milk yields consequently decline (Fuquay, 1981; Morrison, 1983). High relative humidity, thermal radiation and low air movement exacerbate the effects of high ambient temperatures on milk yield. When ambient temperatures plunge below the lower critical temperature, dairy cattle consume more feed, but produce less milk because a greater proportion of intake is used to meet greater maintenance requirements (Young, 1981; 1983). European-type dairy cattle are relatively cold-tolerant but they are heat-susceptible. As a result of a complex interaction between ambient temperature, photoperiod and rainfall some seasonal effects on milk yield may also be mediated indirectly via alteration in quality and quantity of available feed.

Until the late 1950s there had been little study of the effects of photoperiod on lactation of the dairy cow. But in recent years several experiments have shown that photoperiod affects milk yield, feed intake, eating patterns and hormone secretion in dairy cattle. The purpose of this chapter is to summarize such findings.

Milk yield response to photoperiod

Initial research results on the effects of photoperiod on milk yield conflicted. Sarchet, Ward and Hansen (1958) reported that exposure of lactating dairy cows to 20 h of light per day for six weeks had no effect on daily milk yields. Subsequently, Murrill *et al.* (1969) exposed three herds of lactating dairy cows to either mercury vapour lamps, incandescent floodlights or fluorescent lights throughout the night in summer and in winter in California. Herdmate controls received no supplemental light. The herd exposed to supplemental fluorescent light produced approximately

0.5 kg/day more milk in summer, and also tended to produce more milk in winter. Milk yield responses to supplemental mercury vapour or incandescent lighting in the other two herds were inconclusive. However, fluorescent lighting is not necessarily superior to other types of lighting because there was wide variation in management and feeding practices which could account for the different responses among the three herds.

Bourne and Tucker (1975) and Leining, Bourne and Tucker (1979) showed that repeated exposure of cattle to 16 h of light (L) and 8 h of dark (D) each day increased serum concentrations of prolactin, a hormone associated with milk yield in cattle (Koprowski and Tucker, 1973; Akers, Goodman and Tucker, 1980). It was therefore decided to re-investigate the effects of photoperiod on milk yield of dairy cattle. In an initial experiment (Peters *et al.*, 1978), 46 multiparous, lactating dairy cows were subjected to natural duration photoperiods of approximately 12 to 9 h of light per day (the experiment began 15 September and continued for 100 days). Concurrently, a second group of 46 similar cows received supplemental cool-white fluorescent light between 05.00 and 21.00 h each day. Light-supplemented cows produced 10 per cent more milk than controls through 100 days

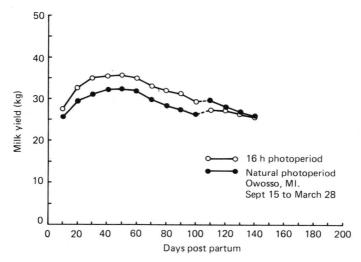

Figure 12.1   Milk production of Holstein cows exposed to 16 h (○) or natural duration (●) photoperiods between September and March in Owosso, Michigan (From Peters *et al.*, 1978)

of lactation (*Figure 12.1*). When treatments were reversed between groups on day 100 of lactation, the animals receiving 16L:8D tended to be more persistent than non-supplemented cows. In confirmation of these results, Bodurov (1979) obtained a 13 per cent increase in milk yield from cows in two herds exposed to 16L:8D during autumn–winter–spring seasons in Bulgaria.

Subsequently, Peters *et al.* (1981) exposed 12 cows in early lactation (37 to 74 days after parturition) and nine cows in late lactation (94 to 204 days after parturition) to 16L:8D beginning on 25 October in Michigan. Similar numbers of control cows were exposed to natural photoperiods of 9–12 h duration per day plus minimal supplemental light for routine management practices. During the 19 weeks of exposure to 16L:8D treated cows produced an average of 6.7 per cent (1.4 kg)

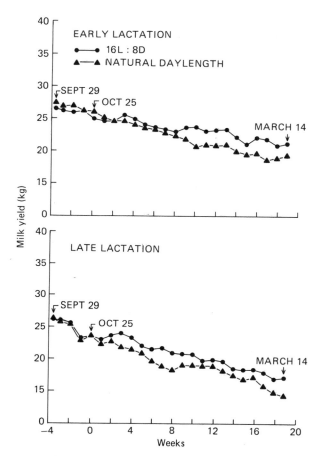

Figure 12.2 Effect of daylength on milk production of Holstein cows. Between 29 September and 24 October, 24 cows in early lactation (37 to 74 days post partum) and 18 cows in late lactation (94 to 204 days post partum) were exposed to natural photoperiods of approximately 12 h of light per day and standardized dietary conditions. From 25 October to 14 March, the 12 control cows in early lactation and nine control cows in late lactation were exposed to natural photoperiod (9 to 12 h of light daily). The remaining 12 cows in early lactation and nine cows in late lactation were exposed daily to fluorescent lighting between 03.00 and 19.00 h, superimposed on a natural photoperiod. Pooled standard errors of average milk yields of cows in early and late lactation were 1.1 and 1.5 kg respectively. Mean daily milk yields under the 16-h photoperiod for cows in early and late lactation were 6 and 7 per cent greater, respectively, than yields for cows exposed only to the natural photoperiod. (From Peters *et al.*, 1981)

more milk per day (adjusted for parity and pretreatment milk yield) than controls. Increases in yield of milk were similar for cows in early or late stages of lactation (*Figure 12.2*).

More recently, Stanisiewski *et al.* (1985) tested the effects of supplemental light in 13 commercial dairy herds in Michigan in the autumn–winter seasons. Approximately one-half of each herd received natural duration photoperiods plus supplemental light (total light, 16 to 16.25 h duration each day). Controls received natural photoperiod exposures plus minimal duration supplemental light to permit routine management activities such as milking and feeding (total daily light did not exceed 13.5 h each day). After adjustment for differences in stage of lactation, lactation number, mature equivalent and pretrial milk yield, cows exposed to supplemental lighting produced 2.2 kg per day more milk than herdmate controls.

Marcek and Swanson (1984) observed that 18L:6D photoperiods stimulated 4 per cent fat-corrected-milk yields of multiparous cows, but not in primiparous cows. The physiological basis for this difference associated with parity is unknown. In other studies, Tanida, Swanson and Hohenboken (1984) showed that cows exposed to 18L:6D or 24L:0D produced similar amounts of milk over a three-month period, although by the third month of exposure cows given 18L:6D produced 12 per cent more milk (a non-significant trend) than cows under 24L:0D. Perhaps differences would have been detected if the exposures were continued. Comparisons between continuous lighting photoperiods and photoperiods containing long or short exposures to darkness each day have not been made. Although the effectiveness of a 4-h interval of darkness on milk yield responses has not been tested, 16L:8D and 20L:4D were equally effective in stimulating secretion of the hormone, prolactin (Leining, Bourne and Tucker, 1979). Thus, to maximize milk yield our current recommendation is to provide lactating cows with 4 to 8 h of darkness each day (or conversely, 20 to 16 h of light per day).

Milk fat response to photoperiod

Response of milk fat secretion to photoperiod has not been consistent across experiments. Initially, Bodurov (1979) reported that in comparison with short days, 16L:8D increased milk fat by a total of 0.3 percentage units. Peters *et al.* (1981) reported that long-day photoperiods did not affect percentage of fat in milk. In more recent work in 13 commercial dairy herds, which utilized over 2600 observations, cows exposed to 16L:8D produced 0.16 percentage units less milk fat than cows exposed to less than 13.5 h of light each day (Stanisiewski *et al.*, 1985). Generally, milk yield is inversely related to milk fat per cent (Rook and Campling, 1965); thus, one might expect that as milk yield increases in response to supplemental light, milk fat per cent may decline.

Mammary growth response to photoperiod

Recently, Petitclerc *et al.* (1985) discovered that in comparison with an 8L:16D photoperiod, 16L:8D stimulated the mammary parenchyma to grow into the fat pad of the mammary gland of pre- and postpubertal dairy heifers. Whether increased daily exposure of heifers to light subsequently leads to increased milk yields has not yet been tested. Since longer daylight exposure produces leaner carcasses in heifers (Petitclerc *et al.*, 1983; Tucker, Petitclerc and Zinn, 1984), and stimulates mammary development, it would be of interest to determine if supplemental light would prevent the harmful effects of high levels of nutrition on mammary development of prepubertal heifers (Sjersen *et al.*, 1982).

Feed intake and eating pattern response to photoperiod

Dry matter intake increased by 6.1 per cent in lactating cows exposed to 16L:8D relative to controls given short-day photoperiods (Peters *et al.*, 1981). The increase in dry matter intake was associated with greater yields of milk. In fact, estimates of energetic efficiency of milk yield, corrected for maintenance and body weight gain, were similar regardless of photoperiod. Thus, gains in efficiency are achieved by maintaining milk production with fewer cows. Petitclerc *et al.* (1983) showed that in comparison with an 8L:16D photoperiod, 16L:8D stimulated body weight gain in Holstein heifers even when feed intake was restricted to equal quantities in both groups of heifers. Thus, feed efficiency for growth increased in the 16L:8D group. Photoperiod-induced increments in milk yields of lactating cows fed moderately restricted quantities of energy has not been reported.

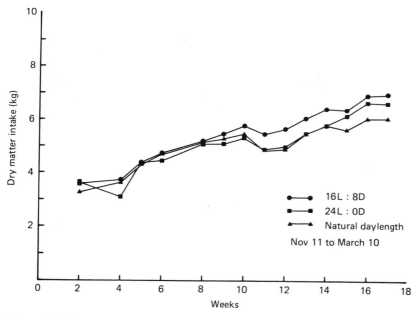

Figure 12.3 Dry matter intake of Holstein heifers exposed to 16L:8D, 24L:0D and natural photoperiods between November 11 and March 10; 16 heifers per treatment. (From Peters *et al.*, 1980)

One presumptive reason continuous lighting of cattle at night has been used for many years, has been to stimulate eating activity and feed intake. However, evidence to support the value of this practice for stimulating intake is equivocal. For example, Holstein heifers exposed to a 16L:8D photoperiod consumed 6.9 per cent more dry matter than heifers given continuous lighting (*Figure 12.3*; Peters *et al.*, 1980). Furthermore, lactating cows given an 18L:6D photoperiod had similar numbers of eating events per day compared with cows given continuous lighting (Tanida, Swanson and Hohenboken, 1984). Although continuous lighting may be required for security and managerial activities, it may not be effective in stimulating an increase in feed intake.

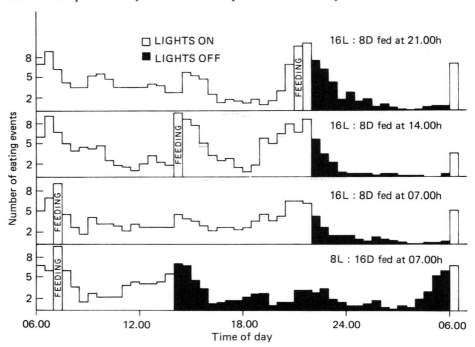

Figure 12.4 Number of eating events of Holstein heifers exposed to 16L:8D photoperiods. (From Zinn, Chapin and Tucker, 1983)

Photoperiod affects eating patterns. For example, growing Holstein heifers given a 16L:8D photoperiod had more eating events and performed more of these events in lighted hours of the day than heifers exposed to 8L:16D (*Figure 12.4*; Zinn, Chapin and Tucker, 1983). Heifers exposed to 8L:16D increased their eating activity 1 to 2 h before lights came on, whereas heifers given 16L:8D did not commence eating until lights were actually on. Feeding also stimulated eating activity. To date, the pattern of eating of lactating cows in response to short *versus* long daylight photoperiods has not been reported.

Economics of milk yield response to photoperiod

Cost effectiveness of supplementing the lactating herd with 16 h of light per day in autumn, winter and spring seasons is likely to be beneficial (Stanisiewski *et al.*, 1985). Based on daily milk yields of 22.7 kg and the economy of the USA in 1983 an increase of 8 per cent in milk yield promoted by the installation of fluorescent light fixtures and time clocks, will increase net income by approximately $0.17 per day per cow. At that rate, the installation costs of a new lighting system could be paid for in approximately four months.

Reproduction and photoperiod

Secretion of luteinizing hormone (LH), follicle stimulating hormone (FSH), oestradiol, progesterone and testosterone changes dramatically with changes in photoperiod in seasonal breeding species (Tucker and Ringer, 1982). Since dairy cattle are non-seasonal breeders, changes in secretion of these reproduction-associated hormones in response to photoperiod are generally muted. For example, in sexually mature heifers neither photoperiod (8 *versus* 16 h of light per day) nor season (autumn *versus* winter) affected the timing, amplitude or pattern or pre-ovulatory surges of LH or FSH or length of oestrous cycles (Rzepkowski *et al.*, 1982). Nonetheless, a few reproductive responses to photoperiod have been noted in cattle and these are outlined below.

Heifers born in seasons of increasing daylight reached puberty about two months earlier than heifers born when daylight is decreasing (Roy *et al.*, 1980). Similarly, six-month-old Angus × Holstein heifers exposed to spring–summer–autumn conditions of photoperiod (and ambient temperatures) reached puberty earlier than heifers exposed to autumn–winter–spring conditions (Schillo *et al.*, 1983). In addition, Holstein heifers reared under 16 to 18 h of light per day reached puberty earlier and at a smaller weight than heifers reared under short daylight conditions (Peters *et al.*, 1978; Petitclerc *et al.*, 1983; Hansen, Kamwanja and Hauser, 1983). Since increasing the length of the light phase from 8 to 16 h per day increases average daily bodyweight gains in peripubertal Holstein cattle (Tucker, Petitclerc and Zinn, 1984), these effects of photoperiod on puberty may be associated with changes in growth rate and (or) body composition, but the hormonal mediator(s) has not been clearly established.

Hormonal mediation of photoperiodic signals

The specific hormones that mediate photoperiod-induced changes in milk yield or feed intake in dairy cattle have not been identified. Only a few studies have reported hormonal response of lactating cows to change in photoperiod. The following description of hormonal mediation of photoperiodic signals will utilize data from lactating cows where possible, but the majority of the data were collected from prepubertal bulls or heifers.

Concentrations of insulin, thyroid stimulating hormone and thyroxine in the serum of heifers, and growth hormone and glucocorticoids concentrations in lactating cows do not change in response to photoperiod (Peters *et al.*, 1981; Tucker, Petitclerc and Zinn, 1984); thus, these hormones are probably not directly involved in hormonal regulation of photoperiod-induced changes in milk yield or feed intake.

In cattle, prolactin is most responsive to changes in photoperiod. For example, gradual increases in light exposure from 8 to 16 h per day increased concentrations of serum prolactin approximately fourfold (Bourne and Tucker, 1975). Conversely, a gradual reduction of light from 16 to 8 h per day reduced prolactin by 86 per cent. In addition, abrupt increases in light exposure from 8 to 16 h or from 8 to 20 h per day increases basal concentrations of prolactin in serum two- to tenfold (Leining, Bourne and Tucker, 1979; Petitclerc *et al.*, 1983; Stanisiewski, Chapin and Tucker, 1984). An example of the response is shown in *Figure 12.5*. A skeleton-long photoperiod of 6L:8D:2L:8D increases basal concentrations of serum prolactin as effectively as 16L:8D (Petitclerc *et al.*, 1983), but the use of skeleton-long photoperiods to increase milk yields of cows has not been tested. However, a photoperiod of 24L:0D was not as effective as 16L:8D or 20L:4D in stimulating secretion of prolactin (Leining, Bourne and Tucker, 1979) or average daily

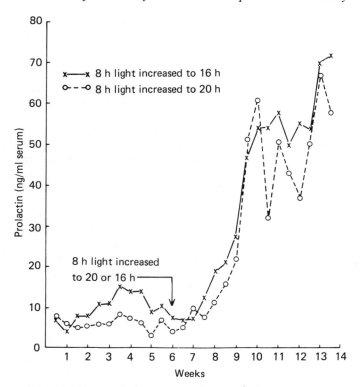

Figure 12.5   Average serum prolactin of prepubertal bulls during daily light exposure which was increased from 8 to 16 h (X) or from 8 to 20 h (O per day). There were four bulls per observation. Overall pooled SE was 3 ng/ml between weeks 1–6 and 6 ng/ml between weeks 7–14. (From Leining, Bourne and Tucker, 1979)

liveweight gains (Peters *et al.*, 1980). As discussed previously, it appears also that to maximize milk yields, cows should be exposed to a period of 4 to 8 h darkness each day.

A variety of lamps with different spectral properties have been shown to be equally as effective as cool-white fluorescent lamps in stimulating secretion of prolactin. These include red, blue and Vita-Lite® fluorescent, incandescent, mercury vapour and high pressure sodium lamps (Leining, Bourne and Tucker, 1979; Stanisiewski, Chapin and Tucker, 1984). Whether all of these types of lamps will stimulate milk yields has not been determined, although there is some evidence that Vita-Lite® may be slightly superior to cool-white fluorescent in stimulating yield of milk and average daily gain (Stanisiewski *et al.*, 1985; Zinn, S.A. and Tucker, H.A., unpublished observations).

Intensities of light between 200 and 600 lux effectively stimulate secretion of prolactin (Peters and Tucker, 1978; Leining, Bourne and Tucker, 1979), and intensities of approximately 100 to at least 300 lux stimulate yield of milk (Peters *et al.*, 1978; Stanisiewski *et al.*, 1985). Forbes (1982) suggests that intensities of light as great as 100 lux may be required to stimulate body growth and lactation, although milk yield responses to lower intensities than 100 lux have not been examined.

Whether or not prolactin is actually involved in photoperiod-induced increments of milk yield remains uncertain. For example, administration of 2-Br-α-ergokryptin to cattle during established lactation markedly suppresses prolactin secretion but does not affect secretion of milk (Karg, Schams and Reinhardt, 1972; Smith *et al.*, 1974). Similarly, decreasing ambient temperatures will suppress basal secretion of prolactin in the face of 16L:8D photoperiods (Peters and Tucker, 1978), but these cool temperatures did not reduce the secretion of milk (Peters *et al.*, 1978; Peters *et al.*, 1981). These latter reports should be interpreted with caution, however, because unrecorded temporary increases in ambient temperature could have permitted photoperiod-induced increments in secretion of prolactin, which may have been sufficient to stimulate secretion of milk. Milking-induced release of prolactin tends to be greater in cattle subjected to long duration photoperiods than those exposed to short duration photoperiods (Peters *et al.*, 1981), and cold temperatures did not inhibit photoperiod-induced increments in secretion of prolactin during milking. Therefore, despite cold ambient temperatures, cows given long duration photoperiods are still likely to be exposed to more prolactin than cows subjected to short daylight conditions. Unfortunately, the effects of increased concentrations of prolactin in blood on lactation in cattle have not been clearly established. Thus, additional research will be needed to understand the hormonal mechanisms involved in photoperiod-induced changes in secretion of milk.

Some unsolved problems

Increases in milk yield have been obtained with average light intensities in barns of 100 to 300 lux. Greater intensities are also effective, but we do not yet know the minimal effective intensity. Furthermore, are gradual changes in light intensity which mimic dawn and dusk more effective in stimulating milk yield than abrupt changes in intensity? Recent results from our own laboratory (Zinn, Chapin and Tucker, unpublished data) strongly suggest that gradual changes in intensity of light at dawn and dusk stimulate a greater increase in growth rates of dairy heifers than abrupt changes, but similar trials with lactating cows have yet to be undertaken.

The optimal duration of daily exposure to light for maximal production of milk has not been clearly determined. Furthermore, the milk yield response to the addition to natural photoperiods of only a few hours of supplemental light before dawn or after dusk (or both) has not been reported, and, as previously discussed, milk yield responses to skeleton-long photoperiods have not been described.

Where cattle were housed unrestrained, we arbitrarily made the decision to place lamps over the areas where cows spend the most time resting, rather than placing them directly over the feed bunk area. Placement of lamps is obviously another aspect in need of additional research. Our experiments designed to investigate the effect of daylength on milk yield have used fluorescent lamps. (It should be noted that fluorescent light fixtures should be equipped with high output, −20 °C ballasts to insure maximal function of lights during cold ambient temperatures.) Although many lamp types effectively increase secretion of prolactin (Stanisiewski, Chapin and Tucker, 1984), few have been tested for their ability to stimulate milk yield.

Animals subjected to 16 h of light during the autumn–winter seasons will lose their long winter hair coats and grow a summer length hair coat. This change in hair coat requires two to three months of exposure to 16L:8D photoperiods. Although we have had no health problems in our cattle in enclosed unheated barns, the effect of short hair length on the health of cattle directly exposed to outside winter conditions has not yet been studied.

Conclusion

Supplemental lighting (16L:8D) of lactating dairy cows stimulates an increase in milk yield of 6 to 10 per cent, but decreases milk fat by a total of approximately 0.16 percentage units. Increased feed intake is associated with photoperiod-induced increases in yield of milk. Supplementation of the lactating herd with 16 h of light per day in autumn–winter–spring seasons is likely to be beneficial. It is estimated that the use of supplemental light may increase net income by approximately $0.17 per cow per day. Installation of a lighting system could be paid for in approximately four months. Thereafter, it is profit! There is no irrefutable proof that enhanced secretion of prolactin is responsible for the increased milk yields or feed intakes when cattle are supplemented with light. Thus, the hormonal mechanisms involved in photoperiod-induced alterations of the economically important traits remain to be established.

Acknowledgements

Michigan Agricultural Experimental Station Journal Article No. 11437. This research was supported in part by USDA Grants 901-15-2 and 59-2261-02-072-0 and USPHS Grant HD09883.

References

AKERS, R.M., GOODMAN, G.T. and TUCKER, H.A. (1980). *Proceedings of the Society for Experimental Biology and Medicine*, **164**, 115–119
BODUROV, N. (1979). *Veterinarnomeditsinski Nauki*, **16**, 58–65
BOURNE, R.A. and TUCKER, H.A. (1975). *Endocrinology*, **97**, 473–475
FORBES, J.M. (1982). *Livestock Production Sciences*, **9**, 361–374
FUQUAY, J.W. (1981). *Journal of Animal Science*, **52**, 164–174
HANSEN, P.J., KAMWANJA, L.A. and HAUSER, E.R. (1983). *Journal of Animal Science*, **57**, 985–992
KARG, H., SCHAMS, D. and REINHARDT, V. (1972). *Experientia*, **28**, 574–576
KOPROWSKI, J.A. and TUCKER, H.A. (1973). *Endocrinology*, **93**, 645–651
LEINING, K.B., BOURNE, R.A. and TUCKER, H.A. (1979). *Endocrinology*, **104**, 289–294
MARCEK, J.M. and SWANSON, L.V. (1984). *Journal of Dairy Science*, **67**, 2380–2388
MORRISON, S.R. (1983). *Journal of Animal Science*, **57**, 1594–1600
MURRILL, F.D., EIDE, R.N., LEONARD, R.O. and BATH, D.L. (1969). *Journal of Dairy Science*, **52**, 947 (abstract)
PETERS, R.R., CHAPIN, L.T., EMERY, R.S. and TUCKER, H.A. (1980). *Journal of Animal Science*, **51**, 1148–1153
PETERS, R.R., CHAPIN, L.T., EMERY, R.S. and TUCKER, H.A. (1981). *Journal of Dairy Science*, **64**, 1671–1678

PETERS, R.R., CHAPIN, L.T., LEINING, K.B. and TUCKER, H.A. (1978). *Science,* **199**, 911–912

PETERS, R.R. and TUCKER, H.A. (1978). *Endocrinology,* **103**, 229–234

PETITCLERC, D., CHAPIN, L.T., EMERY, R.S. and TUCKER, H.A. (1983). *Journal of Animal Science,* **57**, 892–898

PETITCLERC, D., CHAPIN, L.T., HARKINS, P.A. and TUCKER, H.A. (1983). *Proceedings of the Society for Experimental Biology and Medicine,* **172**, 478–481

PETITCLERC, D., KINEMAN, R.D., ZINN, S.A. and TUCKER, H.A. (1985). *Journal of Dairy Science,* **68**, 86–90

ROOK, J.A.F. and CAMPLING, R.C. (1965). *Journal of Dairy Research,* **32**, 45–55

ROY, J.H.B., GILLIES, C.M., PERFITT, M.W. and STOBO, I.J.F. (1980). *Animal Production,* **31**, 13–36

RZEPKOWSKI, R.A., IRELAND, J.J., FOGWELL, R.L., CHAPIN, L.T. and TUCKER, H.A. (1982). *Journal of Animal Science,* **55**, 1125–1131

SARCHET, J., WARD, G. and HANSEN, R. (1958). *Colorado Agric. Exp. Stn. Colorado Farm Power Council Pamphlet*

SCHILLO, K.K., HANSEN, P.J., KAMWANJA, L.A., DIERSCHKE, D.J. and HAUSER, E.R. (1983). *Biology of Reproduction,* **28**, 329–341

SEJRSEN, K., HUBER, J.T., TUCKER, H.A. and AKERS, R.M. (1982). *Journal of Dairy Science,* **65**, 793–800

SMITH, V.G., BECK, T.W., CONVEY, E.M. and TUCKER, H.A. (1974). *Neuroendocrinology,* **15**, 172–181

STANISIEWSKI, E.P., CHAPIN, L.T. and TUCKER, H.A. (1984). *Proceedings of the Society for Experimental Biology and Medicine,* **175**, 226–232

STANISIEWSKI, E.P., MELLENBERGER, R.W., ANDERSON, C.R. and TUCKER, H.A. (1985). *Journal of Dairy Science,* **67** (in press)

TANIDA, H., SWANSON, L.V. and HOHENBOKEN, W.D. (1984). *Journal of Dairy Science,* **67**, 585–591

TUCKER, H.A., PETITCLERC, D. and ZINN, S.A. (1984). *Journal of Animal Science,* **59**, 1610–1620

TUCKER, H.A. and RINGER, R.K. (1982). *Science,* **216**, 1381–1386

YOUNG, B.A. (1981). *Journal of Animal Science,* **52**, 154–163

YOUNG, B.A. (1983). *Journal of Animal Science,* **57**, 1601–1607

ZINN, S.A., CHAPIN, L.T. and TUCKER, H.A. (1983). *Journal of Dairy Science,* **66** (Suppl. 1), 275

13

FACTORS AFFECTING THE NUTRITIVE VALUE OF GRASS SILAGES

C. THOMAS
Animal and Grassland Research Institute, Hurley, Maidenhead, Berks, UK
and
P.C. THOMAS
Hannah Research Institute, Ayr, Scotland

Introduction

Although ensilage is an age-old method of forage conservation, it is less than 20 years since farmers in the UK began widely to accept and adopt ensilage technology and to make silage crops a central part of their forage conservation programmes. Moreover, it is even more recent that scientists and farmers alike have begun to regard 'silage' as more than simply 'preserved grass' and to appreciate that under the generic name there lies a wide spectrum of prefermented feeds, the composition and nutritional characteristics of which vary substantially. In this chapter it is intended briefly to review the ensilage of grass crops and the utilization of silages as feeds for ruminant livestock. The main topics considered will be under the headings silage production, nutritive value of silages, and animal production from silage diets, and there will be a final section for conclusions and for some thoughts on prospects for the future. With a subject so large the approach adopted is necessarily selective and particular emphasis is given to topics of current interest to ruminant nutritionists. It should be pointed out that in some instances the summary views presented are qualified because of the paucity or inadequacy of the information available, and it should also be recognized that, while individual factors influencing silage composition and nutritive value are discussed under separate headings, there is considerable potential for interaction between factors under field conditions.

Silage production

The composition of silage is governed by the composition of the standing crop at the time of cutting and by modifications which take place during field drying (wilting) and ensilage.

COMPOSITION OF GRASS CROPS

For a given species and variety of grass the composition is influenced by the rate and type of fertilizer application and by climatic environment, but under most

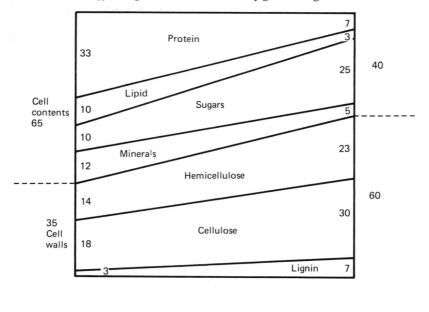

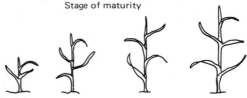

Stage of maturity

Figure 13.1   Schematic representation of the changes in chemical composition of grasses which accompany advancing maturity. All values are in percentages (Osbourn, 1980)

circumstances the major determinant of composition is the stage of maturity of the crop. As grass plants mature the proportion of cell wall increases while that of cell contents is reduced, and within both the cell wall and cell content components there are changes in chemical composition and structure (*Figure 13.1*).

Three aspects of crop composition require further comment. First, the increases in amount and degree of lignification of the cell wall with maturity inevitably reduce the digestibility of the crop and consequently its metabolizable energy (ME) value. Second, as the crop matures its crude protein (N × 6.25) content invariably falls and, while soluble proteins of a relatively constant amino acid composition continue to make up 0.75 to 0.85 of the crude protein (Lyttleton, 1973), the susceptibility of those proteins to attack by proteolytic enzymes increases (Chamberlain and Thomas, 1984), and this may have consequences during ensilage. Third, the ease with which crops can be satisfactorily ensiled depends in part on their content of water-soluble carbohydrates (WSC), consisting mainly of glucose, fructose and sucrose (Waite, Johnston and Armstrong, 1964; Smith, 1973), and fructosans, which are present in relatively high concentrations in the plant stem and inflorescence (Mackenzie and Wylam, 1957). Though the water-soluble carbohydrate content increases as the plant matures it is also positively related to light intensity (Deinum, 1966) and negatively related to the rate of fertilizer nitrogen application (Smith, 1973), and when this is taken in conjunction with the large inherent differences in WSC which occur between grass species it is understandable that values vary over a wide range.

POST-CUTTING CHANGES IN COMPOSITION

In many cases cut crops are subjected to a period of wilting prior to ensilage and during this period there are major changes in crop composition. Continuing respiration in the plant leads to the oxidation of carbohydrate, though the changes in WSC content may be relatively small since the oxidized soluble sugars may be compensated for by sugars released from the hydrolysis of polysaccharide. For example, Carpintero, Henderson and McDonald (1979) noted little change in the WSC content of herbage over a 48 h period of wilting. Plant proteolysis also occurs and as outlined in *Table 13.1* there are increases in the proportions of non-protein N, amino-N, amide-N and ammonia-N.

Table 13.1 NITROGEN REDISTRIBUTION IN RYEGRASS WILTED FOR DIFFERENT PERIODS OF TIME AND IN SILAGE[a]

	Wilting time (h)	*Dry matter* (g/kg)	*Total nitrogen* (g/kg DM)	*Nitrogen (g/kg total nitrogen)*				
				Protein	*Non-protein*	*Amino*	*Amide*	*Ammonia*
Grass	0	161	20.2	911	89	26	8	1
	2.5	192	18.3	886	114	59	8	2
	6.5	268	17.3	873	127	71	7	2
	26.5	390	17.9	827	173	92	13	6
Silage	(26.5)[b]	390	19.6	452	548	274	5	69

[a]Data is based on the results of Brady (1960). Values for protein N have been calculated as the difference between total N and the non-protein nitrogen extracted in 0.1 N HCl.
[b]Time in parenthesis is the period that grass was wilted before ensilage.

The changes in composition during wilting naturally depend on the length of the wilting period (see *Table 13.1*, for example) and the temperature, humidity and wind conditions under which wilting takes place. Where the period is short and the rate of moisture loss is high, changes in crop composition are minimized and there may be advantages for ensilage because the sugars in the fresh crop are concentrated by the water loss. However, under adverse conditions and particularly where cut crops are wetted by dew or rain, losses of soluble constituents are increased and effects due to plant enzyme activity are exacerbated by the effects of leaching.

Attempts to analyse and rationalize experiments in the literature on the effects of wilting on silage composition are hampered by the lack of quantitative information about the wilting treatments applied. In few experiments are details other than the wilting period and the general weather conditions recorded, and only rarely is there any assessment of fluctuations in drying rate and the chemical changes that have occurred in the crop between cutting and ensilage.

FERMENTATION IN THE SILO

The principles of conservation by ensilage leading to the anaerobic storage of crops at low pH are well understood and the microbiology and biochemistry of the process has been reviewed in detail by McDonald (1981) and Woolford (1984). The rate of fermentation is dependent on the availability of substrate but is also influenced by buffering capacity. In this respect Weissbach, Schmidt and Hein (1974) proposed the ratio of WSC to buffering capacity as an index of the probable fermentation pattern. However, Wilkinson *et al.* (1983) have recently found that variation in WSC alone is more important.

In the initial period after the crop has been placed in the silo, the aerobic metabolism of soluble carbohydrates continues. However, provided the silo is satisfactorily compacted and sealed to exclude air, anaerobiosis is achieved within hours and homolactic and heterolactic bacteria begin to proliferate to the relative exclusion of the yeasts, clostridia and fungi that are potential competitors for the same biological niche.

Fermentation of carbohydrates by the homolactic and heterolactic bacteria produces lactic acid and acetic acid and this reduces the pH in the silo. Fermentation is progressively inhibited until a stable silage is achieved. During the aerobic and fermentative phases of ensilage there is also a considerable hydrolysis of plant proteins, and even when fermentation has ceased protein hydrolysis may continue, albeit at a reduced rate (Carpintero, Henderson and McDonald, 1979). The lactic acid bacteria have limited capacities for deamination and decarboxylation of amino acids and therefore produce only small amounts of ammonia and amines.

Under adverse ensilage conditions, where the exclusion of air from the silo is inadequate or where wet, highly buffered crops of low sugar content slow the initial fall in pH, clostridial bacteria begin to thrive. These organisms metabolize sugars and lactic acid to produce butyrate and a mixture of lesser products including acetate, propionate, ethanol, butanol and formate. They also degrade amino acids extensively, yielding ammonia and a range of amines which tend to slow or reverse the normal reduction in pH in the silo. In extreme cases this leads to prolonged fermentation of the crop, excessive nutrient losses and spoilage, and a silage of exceptionally low nutritive value and acceptability to animals.

Clearly the rapid attainment of a low pH and anaerobic conditions are crucial to the conservation of nutrients. Indeed it can be argued that the rate of pH decline is more important than the final pH of the silage. However, certain modifications in crop composition are inevitably associated with the ensilage process. There is hydrolysis of plant proteins (*Table 13.1*), hemicellulose (Dewar, McDonald and Whittenbury, 1963; Morrison, 1979) and glycerides (Jackson and Anderson, 1971; Lough and Anderson, 1973), a reduction in WSC content and an accumulation of fermentation end-products, which reflects the nature and extensiveness of the fermentation process. With modern equipment and ensilage techniques, silages dominated by clostridial fermentation are avoidable. However, the composition of the crop harvested, the logistics of making silage on a large scale, and the limitations in technical expertise or experience of the silage-maker often result in silages being made under less than perfect conditions. Most farm scale silages show evidence in their composition of a spectrum of fermentation activity, with greater or smaller concentrations of the wide range of fermentation end-products that can be formed through bacterial and yeast fermentations of plant carbohydrates and

Table 13.2 CLASSIFICATION OF SILAGES

Well fermented	{	A	High lactic, low acetic
		B	Medium lactic, high acetic
Badly fermented	{	C	Low lactic, high acetic
		D	Low lactic, high acetic, high butyric
		E	High acetic, high butyric
Restricted	{	F	Restricted fermentation—wilted
		G	Restricted fermentation—acid
		H	Restricted fermentation—formaldehyde

(Modified from Wilkinson *et al.*, 1983)

amino acids. Attempts to classify silages are necessarily over-simplistic but the classification in *Table 13.2*, based on the analysis of Wilkinson *et al.* (1983) serves to illustrate the wide range that can be encountered.

Many factors apart from those ensuing from the standing crop have the ability to modify fermentation. They include the oxygen-content in silo mass, density and temperature. However, it is intended here only to examine the influence of wilting and additives on the fermentation process.

Wilting

Recently there have been major coordinated experiments on wilting ('Eurowilt') conducted throughout Europe, and while the results of these studies illustrate the variations that occur from experiment to experiment they also show some consistent trends. Reducing the moisture content of the crop retards the activity of all micro-organisms, but in particular that of clostridia and, to a lesser extent, heterofermentative organisms. Thus, in a review of the studies Wilkins (1984) concluded that wilting, on average, reduces the concentration of fermentation acids

Table 13.3 THE EFFECT OF WILTING ON FERMENTATION CHARACTERISTICS

	DM content (g/kg fresh)	*pH*	*Fibre* (g/kg DM)	*Lactic acid* (g/kg total acid)	*Total acid* (g/kg DM)	*NH_3-N* (g/kg total N)	*DM digestibility*
Unwilted	209	4.3	313	520	125	128	0.698
Wilted	349	4.5	293	680	82	102	0.681

(Wilkins, 1984)

but also increases the proportion of lactic acid and reduces ammonia-N concentration (*Table 13.3*). However, there appears to be little change in the proportion of N appearing as protein-N (Jackson and Forbes, 1970) although this must clearly depend on the extent of clostridial activity in the unwilted silages. Wilting tends to reduce digestibility of silage (*Table 13.3*) despite a reduction in fibre content. Similar effects on digestibility have been reported in other reviews (Marsh, 1979), and Donaldson and Edwards (1976) observed a reduction in ME content. The depression in digestibility is likely to be a reflection of changes occurring during field drying rather than during ensiling.

Silage additives

The classification of additives and their mode of action has been reviewed recently by McDonald (1981) and Woolford (1984). It is intended here to discuss only the effect of acids and their salts, the use of formaldehyde either alone or in combination with acids and inoculants.

Acids and their salts
There has been considerable research effort on the influence of formic acid on fermentation and the data were extensively reviewed by Waldo (1978) (*Table 13.4*). The results show that use of formic acid induced a reduction in fermentation combined with a decrease in the proportion of total acids as acetic and butyric and a reduction in proteolysis.

Table 13.4 SUMMARY OF THE EFFECTS OF FORMIC ACID, FORMALDEHYDE AND FORMIC ACID/FORMALDEHYDE ADDITIVES ON FERMENTATION IN DIRECT-CUT SILAGES

Component	Untreated	Formic acid	Formaldehyde	Formic acid + formaldehyde
pH	4.7	4.2	4.7	4.4
Acetic acid (g/kg)	30	18	24	23
Butyric acid (g/kg)	15	1	7	4
Lactic acid (g/kg)	46	45	39	46
Total acids (g/kg)	101	71	78	77
Ammonia N (g/kg total N)	157	63	96	70
Insoluble N (g/kg total N)	420	510	550	630
Residual sugar (g/kg)	12	36	12	28

(From Waldo, 1978)

Table 13.5 A COMPARISON OF THE EFFECTS OF FORMIC ACID WITH SULPHURIC ACID IN SILAGE PRODUCTION

	Control	Formic acid	Sulphuric acid
DM content (g/kg)	168	190	188
pH	5.1	4.2	4.2
Ammonia-N (g/kg total N)	233	74	71
DM digestibility	0.544	0.658	0.675

(Flynn and O'Kiely, 1984)

Formic acid, unlike inorganic acids, has specific antimicrobial properties apart from its effects mediated via acidity *per se* (Woolford, 1975). Nevertheless, there has been a renewed interest in the use of sulphuric acid as an alternative to the more expensive organic acids. Flynn and O'Kiely (1984) reported similar improvements in fermentation characteristics with formic acid (850 g/kg) and with sulphuric (450 g/kg) when both were applied at 2.3 litres/t (*Table 13.5*). It must be noted that the use of mineral acid here is essentially different from that adopted for AIV silage, where large volumes (55–70 litres/t) of 2 N HCl were applied immediately to lower pH to 3.6 in order to stop rather than reduce proteolysis (See Watson and Nash, 1960).

The corrosive nature of strong organic and inorganic acids has prompted research into the use of salts of acids as additives. For example, Wilson *et al.* (1979) noted that sodium acrylate applied at 3.3 litres/t was only slightly less effective than formic acid in restricting fermentation. Also initial results from experiments conducted by Drysdale and Berry (1980), indicate that ammonium tetraformate is about as effective as formic acid.

Formaldehyde and acid/formaldehyde

Although the use of acids results in restriction of fermentation and inhibition of clostridial activity, these additives cannot improve the nutritional value of the silage above that of the original forage. In contrast, formaldehyde has an ability firstly to restrict fermentation (Wilkins, Wilson and Cook, 1974) and secondly to bind with plant proteins (Barry, 1976) so that the supply of amino acids to the animal is greater from the silage than from the original herbage. This latter aspect will be discussed later.

The effect of formaldehyde (as formalin) on fermentation when applied either alone or with formic acid is indicated in *Table 13.4*, though the mean data presented take no account of the rate of application of formalin nor of the fermentation quality of the control silage. Wilkins, Wilson and Cook (1974) examined a wide range of application rate of formalin and showed an almost complete restriction of fermentation above 8 litres/t fresh weight. However, there is evidence that at lower rates of application (<4 litres formalin/t fresh wt) clostridial fermentation may be encouraged (Wilson and Wilkins, 1978), although no such effect is observed with paraformaldehyde. The inclusion of an acid permits a reduction in the amount of formaldehyde required to inhibit fermentation and also reduces the risk of clostridial activity. There is some evidence of a synergistic effect between the components of the mixture in that in two experiments formalin tended to be more effective in reducing fermentation acids and N degradation in the presence of formic acid (Valentine and Brown, 1973; Barry, 1976). Non-fermented silages have been produced consistently in laboratory silos using a combination of 2.3 litres/t formalin and 4.6 litres/t formic acid or 4.5 litres/t formalin and 1.3 litres/t formic acid. Lower total volumes than this are generally applied when commercial silage additives are used (rates are about 4 to 5 litres/t) but with ratios of formalin:formic acid in the range 2:1 to 1:2. However, evidence from Kaiser *et al.* (1981) suggests that low levels of acid (2 litres/t) combined with intermediate levels of formalin result in elevated concentrations of butyric acid in wet silages made in large scale silos.

Inoculants

There has been considerable interest recently in the use of microbial cultures as additives. Criteria for a successful inoculum (see Woolford, 1984) include:

    High growth rate and ability to dominate other organisms;

    Homofermentative;

    Tolerance of acid;

    Ability to ferment fructose, glucose, frutosans and pentosans;

    Inability to produce dextrans;

    Absence of proteolytic enzymes.

The importance of attaining a rapid fall in pH has been mentioned already in this review and, given that within the silage microflora inefficient acid-producing bacteria may be in the majority (Langston, Bouma and Conner, 1962), there is clearly a case for inoculation with efficient homofermentative organisms. However these organisms have to compete with the indigenous microflora and, since sterilization (as in the brewing industry) is impractical, high rates of addition (about 10^6/g fresh weight) are required. Further, since research on the progress of fermentation has highlighted the role of *Streptococci* in initiating fermentation to be superseded by species of *Lactobacillus* and *Pediococcus*, an innoculation consisting of a single strain of organism is unlikely to be successful (see Woolford, 1984). On the basis of these criteria Woolford and Sawczyc (1984a) selected three strains from *Streptococcus durans*, *Lactobacillus acidophilus* and *Lactobacillus plantarum* as having potential. These were subsequently tested alone or in combination on a crop of perennial ryegrass (200 g DM/kg) in 100 g silos (*Table 13.6*).

The formic acid silage sustained the least loss of WSC at day 16 and had the lowest concentration of ammonia-N. Residual WSC tended to be higher with *L. acidophilus* and *S. durans* and *L. acidophilus*. None of the treatments favoured the production of lactic acid at the expense of other products. Further, only the use of formic acid had any effect on the composition of the final silage after 128 days of storage. Recently, however, experiments at Edinburgh School of Agriculture (Seale and Henderson, 1984), again with laboratory-scale silos, showed that, compared with an untreated control, a commercial preparation of *L. plantarum* promoted a more rapid drop in the pH of perennial ryegrass and resulted in a silage

Table 13.6   FERMENTATION CHARACTERISTICS OF SILAGE AT DAY 16 OF STORAGE WHEN pH WAS AT ITS LOWEST

Treatment	Water soluble carbohydrate (g/kg day 0)	Lactic acid (g/kg acetic + ethanol)	Ammonia-N (g/kg total N)
Control	0.19	1.84	62
Formic acid	0.35	1.19	50
S. durans	0.18	2.00	75
L. acidophilus	0.24	2.11	60
L. plantarum	0.21	1.18	86
S. durans + L. acidophilus	0.25	1.75	80
S. durans + L. plantarum	0.20	1.44	92

(Woolford and Sawczyc, 1984b)

Table 13.7   EFFECT OF ADDITIVES ON SILAGE FERMENTATION (MEANS OF SIX TRIALS CONDUCTED BY ADAS)

	Control	Inoculant ± enzyme	Acid mixture	Formic acid ± formalin
Herbage ensiled				
DM content (g/kg)	157	162	152	165
Crude protein (g/kg DM)	173	176	178	171
WSC (g/kg DM)	79	96	90	90
Silage				
DM content (g/kg)	172	176	169	184
pH	4.8	4.8	4.8	4.2
Lactic acid (g/kg DM)	41	34	47	56
VFA (g/kg DM)	97	85	100	66
Ammonia-N (g/kg total N)	270	260	280	140
WSC (g/kg DM)	8	6	7	10

(Haigh, Appleton and Clench, 1984)

of lower ammonia-N content. Results from large scale studies are shown in *Table 13.7*. With the wet crops used the inoculants had no effect on fermentation and only formic acid additives alone or in mixture with formaldehyde resulted in a reduction in pH and ammonia-N and an increase in concentration of lactic acid.

Differences between experiments may arise from the use of different strains of bacteria. Further, there can be considerable genetic instability within strains; Lindgren (1984) has noted that spontaneous variants of *L. plantarum* with altered metabolic properties could be isolated at high frequencies. Furthermore, the effectiveness of inoculants depends on the availability of soluble carbohydrate substrates in the crop and in practice variability in fermentation quality will arise from differences in crop composition. In this respect, the development of additives containing hemicellulolytic and cellulolytic enzymes could have potential provided that the hydrolytic activities of these enzymes are maintained in the silo environment.

In summary, it would appear that only strong acids, either alone or in combination with formaldehyde, have the potential consistently to modify fermentation. Results from the use of inoculants show considerable variability particularly with wet silages. These latter data are derived in the main from laboratory silos and there is considerable concern about the applicability to the large scale in the absence of satisfactory techniques to simulate non-ideal conditions.

Nutritive value of silages

VOLUNTARY INTAKE

Relationship to silage composition

There is considerable evidence that DM intake is less with silage than with corresponding fresh or dried herbage (Moore, Thomas and Sykes, 1960; Harris and Raymond, 1963). However the extent of the depression varies greatly. Demarquilly (1973) noted a range from −1 to −64 per cent.

In an analysis of a restricted population of experiments which involved the feeding of well-fermented silages of different digestibilities to dairy cows, Thomas (1980) noted a positive response in intake to increased digestibility within experiments but marked differences in intake between experiments. The results of individual studies showed that differences between silages in fermentation pattern had an important effect in modifying the response in intake to increased digestibility in accord with the view of earlier workers. On the basis of a regression analysis of data from feeding experiments with a wide range of silages, Harris and Raymond (1963) and Wilkins *et al.* (1971) concluded that relatively little of the total variance in silage intake was associated with the digestibility and that intake was more closely related to the products of silage fermentation. In the studies of Wilkins *et al.* (1971), voluntary intake of silage by sheep was positively correlated with the contents of DM, nitrogen, lactic acid (per cent total acid) and Flieg index. Negative correlations were obtained with acetic acid and ammonia-N (per cent total N). No overall relationship was found with pH but when lactic acid (per cent total acid) was constrained to be constant then there was a positive relationship

Table 13.8 THE EFFECT OF PARTIAL NEUTRALIZATION OF SILAGES WITH SODIUM BICARBONATE ON THE VOLUNTARY INTAKE OF CALVES, SHEEP AND COWS

Type of silage	Test animals	Addition to silage	Rate of addition (g/kg silage DM)	pH of the silage at feeding	Organic matter intake (g/kgW$^{0.75}$ per day)	Response to NaHCO$_3$ (proportion of control intake)	Source of data[a]
Unwilted grass silage made without additive	Calves	None	—	4.0	66.2		1
		NaHCO$_3$	67	5.5	78.0	+0.151	
Unwilted grass silage made without additive	Calves	None	—	4.1	80.0		
		NaHCO$_3$	67	5.4	84.4	+0.055	
Maize silage	Calves	None	—	3.9	68.9		2[c]
		NaHCO$_3$	72	5.4	70.5	+0.022	
Maize silage made with added urea (20 g/kg)	Calves	None	—	4.0	70.5		
		NaHCO$_3$	72	5.5	79.7	+0.130	
Unwilted grass silage made without additive	Sheep	None	—	4.1	51.3		1
		NaHCO$_3$	67	5.3	54.6	+0.064	
Unwilted grass silage made without additive	Sheep	None	—	4.1	47.5		1
		NaHCO$_3$	84	5.4	52.4	+0.103	
Unwilted grass silage made without additive	Sheep	None	—	3.9	47.6[b]		3
		NaHCO$_3$	120	6.1	46.3	-0.027[b]	
Unwilted grass silage made without additive	Sheep	None	—	4.1	43.3[b]		3
		NaHCO$_3$	120	7.7	47.6	+0.099[b]	
Wilted grass silage made with formic acid as additive	Sheep	None	—	3.8	44.3		4
		NaHCO$_3$	34	4.2	46.4	+0.047	
		NaHCO$_3$	68	5.0	46.6	+0.052	
Unwilted grass silage made without additive	Cows	None	—	3.9	70.3[b]		3[d]
		NaHCO$_3$	120	7.0	63.5	-0.097[b]	
Wilted grass silage made with formic acid as additive	Cows	None	—	3.8	81.5		4
		NaHCO$_3$	32	4.3	75.7	-0.075	
		NaHCO$_3$	63	4.9	69.3	-0.149	

[a]1, McLeod et al. (1970); 2, Thomas and Wilkinson (1975); 3, Lancaster and Wilson (1975); 4, Farhan and Thomas (1978)

[b]Values are DM intake

[c]For presentation of results data have been normalized to a live weight of 100 kg

[d]For presentation of results the Jersey cows used have been assumed to have an average live weight of 350 kg

between intake and silage pH. In a subsequent analysis Wilkins *et al.* (1978) confirmed the correlations with nitrogen (positive) and ammonia-N (negative) but the coefficients of determination were markedly lower and no relationships could be found with fermentation acids or with Flieg index. This latter study included silages with restricted fermentations and in general the range in silage composition was less than that observed in the first analysis.

Care should be taken in the interpretation of the relationships established by regression analysis and it should not be assumed that significant relationships imply causal effects. For example, recent information from the 'Eurowilt' experiments (Rohr and Thomas, 1984) has shown that the response in intake to silage DM content is small (9 per cent) when low dry matter silages are well-fermented. Moreover, this difference might have been reduced further if the alcohols, generally present in wet formic-acid silages, had been included in the DM analysis.

Mechanisms of intake regulation

Attempts to relate the low intakes of silages to their pH or contents of specific fermentation end-products have given variable and equivocal results. McLeod, Wilkins and Raymond (1970) and Thomas and Wilkinson (1975) observed that the ingestion of low pH silages leads to disturbances in acid–base balance and reduction in blood and urine pH, with little effect on pH within the rumen. However, responses in intake to dietary supplements of sodium bicarbonate, designed to overcome any problems of acidity from low pH silages, have been far from consistent (*see Table 13.8*). The most pronounced increases in intake have been observed with calves and sheep and in cows the effects have been negative. There are increases in silage intake in cows given bicarbonate supplements included in the dairy concentrate (Kassem *et al.*, 1984), but that probably relates to the influence of the buffer on ruminal cellulolysis. Cottrill *et al.* (1976) noted that, while partial neutralization of maize silage increased intake, the response was not evident when the diet contained a supplement of fishmeal.

Intraruminal infusions or dietary additions of silage acids have also been investigated without a clear picture emerging. Ulyatt (1965) noted a reduction in the intake of herbage when acetic acid was given, whereas Hutchinson and Wilkins (1971) could detect no effect independent of the effect of pH *per se*. Similarly, McLeod, Wilkins and Raymond (1970) found silage intake to be reduced by dietary additions of lactic acid but Morgan and L'Estrange (1977) did not detect a significant reduction in intake when lactic acid was added to dried grass diets. There is evidence that the depressant effect of lactic acid on silage intake is overcome by use of fishmeal to increase dietary protein supply (Thomas, Gill and Austin, 1980), though the protein has no associated effects on digestive efficiency or acid–base balance. The mechanism involved in this interaction and that reported by Cottrill *et al.* (1976) (see above) has not been elucidated and indeed the mechanism through which lactic acid itself reduces silage intake remains to be established. Recent studies of lactic acid metabolism (Chamberlain, Thomas and Anderson, 1983; Gill *et al.*, 1984) have shown that in silage-fed animals both $L(+)$ and $D(-)$ isomers are rapidly fermented in the rumen to acetate, propionate and butyrate, the proportions of the acids formed varying with the relative numbers of bacteria and protozoa in the rumen.

Studies on the effects of nitrogenous silage-fermentation products have indicated that intake is not reduced by dietary or intraruminal administration of tyramine, tryptamine (Neumark, Bondi and Volcani, 1964; Thomas *et al.*, 1961), histamine (McDonald, MacPherson and Watt, 1963) or γ-amino butyric acid (Clapperton and Smith, 1983). On the other hand intraruminal infusions of ammonium salts have reduced silage intake (Thomas *et al.*, 1961) and in animals given high-concentrate diets resulted in shorter and less frequent meals (Conrad, Baile and Mayer, 1977). These intake effects appear to relate to an excessive uptake of ammonia from the rumen and could be important when silages with a high N content and proportion of non-protein N are consumed. With these diets there may be a substantial net loss of N between the feed and the duodenum.

The utilization of N in the rumen may also be important in another regard since silage intake may be influenced by the balance between energy and amino acid supply to the tissues (*cf.* Egan, 1977). Intake has been increased by dietary supplements of fishmeal (Gill and England, 1983) but whether this reflects an interaction with lactic acid (see above) or an influence on amino acid supply is uncertain. Thus, while marked intake responses to postruminal or parenteral supplements of methionine have been noted in some experiments, they are by no means invariably obtained (Barry, Fennessy and Duncan, 1973; Kelly and Thomas, 1975; Gill and Ulyatt, 1977; Barry, Cook and Wilkins, 1978; Shamoon, 1984), and intra-abomasal infusion of casein was without effect (Hutchinson, Wilkins and Osbourn, 1971).

In work with a highly digestible silage of high fermentation quality Farhan and Thomas (1978) found that intake was reduced by the insertion of water-filled bladders into the rumen and concluded that a 'rumen-fill' mechanism was in operation. Consistent with this, intake has been shown to be increased when silage is minced before feeding (Thomas, Kelly and Wait, 1976; Deswysen, Vanbelle and Focart, 1978) and a similar response has been obtained with grass chopped short during silage-making (Castle, Retter and Watson, 1979; Castle, Gill and Watson, 1981) although it is important here to separate the influence of chop-length *per se* from the indirect effect through silage fermentation quality. Animals receiving silage have a low rumination activity and a long 'latency period' after feeding (Deswysen, Vanbelle and Focart, 1978) and this may impose special limitations on the physical breakdown of silages in the rumen. Clancy, Wangsness and Baumgardt (1977) showed that intraruminal infusions of silage juice reduced rumen motility and rate of eating but the results have not been reproduced with consistency (Phillip, Buchanan-Smith and Grovum, 1981a, 1981b; Smith and Clapperton, 1981).

Supplementation of silages

Silage is rarely offered as a sole feed but rather in combination with a concentrate supplement. When silage is given *ad libitum* the addition of supplement depresses forage intake but increases total intake. The factors influencing replacement or substitution rate were discussed by Broster and Thomas (1981) and generalized hypotheses have been described by Blaxter (1980) and Osbourn (1980). They suggest that one feed substitutes for another in proportion to the amounts voluntarily consumed when given alone (i.e. not necessarily digestibility *per se*). This occurs within limits imposed by metabolic constraints on intake and the effect

Table 13.9 THE EFFECT OF THE PROTEIN CONTENT OF THE SUPPLEMENTARY CONCENTRATE ON THE INTAKE OF SILAGE DRY MATTER IN LACTATING COWS GIVEN SILAGES WITH HIGH OR LOW CONCENTRATIONS OF DIGESTIBLE ORGANIC MATTER AND CRUDE PROTEIN

Classification of silage	Source of data	Silage composition			Concentrate		Silage intake (kg DM/day)	Response in silage intake (%)[b]
		Dry matter (g/kg)	Digestible organic matter (g/kg DM)	Crude protein (g/kg DM)	Crude protein (g/kg DM)[a]	Feeding (kg DM/day)		
High-digestibility, high protein	1	226	707	181	150	8.8	9.1	
					250	8.8	9.4	+3.2
	2	219	712	182	155	5.6	6.6	
					201	5.8	7.6	+15.1
Low-digestibility, low protein	1	259	624	119	150	8.8	8.2	
					250	8.8	9.0	+9.8
	2	232	625	128	155	5.8	6.7	
					201	5.9	6.5	−2.9

1 Results from Gordon (1980) for cows in their second or later lactation
2 Results from Thomas et al. (1984) for cows in their first lactation
[a] All concentrates contained soya bean meal as protein concentrate
[b] Response is expressed as a percentage of the intake with the lower protein supplement. Positive sign indicates an increase

of supplements on cellulolytic activity in the rumen. The concepts were recently examined by Thomas, C. *et al*. (1984c). Early and late cut silages were given either alone or with four supplements differing in their ratios of starch, fibre and fat. The supplements were also offered alone with chopped straw at 50 g/kg total DM. The intake of silage could be described by separate equations for the early and late-cut silage diets with respective substitution rates of −0.98 and −0.76 kg silage DM/kg of additional supplement. There was little evidence that substitution rate was influenced by the type of supplement although a mixture consisting of beet pulp, rice bran and fat had the highest intake when given as the sole feed. More detailed examination revealed that the differences in substitution rate between silages of differing digestibility occurred below an inclusion level of 400 g/kg total DM with little effect thereafter. However, between 400 and 600 g/kg there was a trend for silage intakes to be higher with a supplement containing fibre and fat despite a similarity in substitution rate between supplements. This effect was confirmed subsequently with dairy cows (Thomas, C. *et al*. 1984a). In these experiments neither the unifying concepts of constancy of energy intake nor faecal organic matter output explained the variation in silage intake.

A topic much discussed in recent years has been the protein content of cereal based supplement for silage diets. Early experiments with dairy cows indicated that protein levels above those indicated by current feeding standard could be justified on the basis that the high-protein supplements gave low substitution rates (see for example Castle and Watson, 1976). However, more recent research has shown that while large effects on silage intake can occur, they lack predictability and do not appear to be correlated with the energy or protein content of the silage (*see Table 13.9*). There is also some evidence that the response in intake is modulated by the dietary protein source, being greater with fishmeal than with vegetable protein sources like soya bean meal.

Prediction of silage intake

The data presented so far indicate that both attributes of the crop and the conservation process influence voluntary intake of silage and the rate at which silage will be substituted for by supplements. However the majority of equations to predict voluntary intake of diets by dairy cows do not take into account differences in the composition of silages. These equations were recently examined by Neal, Thomas and Cobby (1984) in relation to observed intakes by a dairy herd offered silage based diets at the Grassland Research Institute (*Table 13.10*). Only the equations derived by Lewis (1981) and INRA (1978) include aspects of fermentation quality and physical characteristics of the forage. However the equation of Lewis (1981) was not markedly different in its predictive ability from others which relied primarily on attributes of the cow rather than the forage. The most extensive description of silage is encompassed in the INRA (1978) equation and yet this equation gave the greatest errors of prediction, although much of this was in the form of bias as a result of an inadequate description of the influence of stage of lactation.

Given the inadequate description of silage characteristics it is not surprising that the best equations outlined in *Table 13.10* result in an error of prediction of ± 1.7 kg/DM equivalent to ± 4.0 kg milk at zero energy balance. Where silages have undergone a clostridial fermentation then indices of fermentation quality such as

Table 13.10   RANKING OF EQUATIONS TO PREDICT THE VOLUNTARY INTAKE OF DIETS BY DAIRY COWS

Source	Prediction error (kg DM^2)	Independent variables
Vadiveloo and Holmes (1979) (equation 1)	2.1	Milk yield, LW, lactation week, concentrate intake
Lewis (1981)	2.5	Silage characteristics, milk yield, LW, concentrate intake
Vadiveloo and Holmes (1979) (equation 3)	2.8	As in equation 1
MAFF (1975)	3.3	Milk yield, LW
ARC (1980)	4.0	Milk yield, LW, lactation month
INRA (1978)[a]	4.9	Milk yield, LW, lactation week, silage characteristics, concentrate intake, substitution rate

[a]From Report of Joint Working Party on the Prediction of the Voluntary Intake of Ruminants

acetic acid, lactic acid (per cent total acids), Flieg index and ammonia-N provide a guide to silage intake. However, where the fermentation is dominated by homofermentative organisms and the fermentation is restricted, then physical factors increasingly become involved. When silages have undergone extensive fermentation then acidity itself can influence intake. In this respect, the use of sodium bicarbonate to neutralize silages can induce increases in intake by calves but not by cows. Further, there is evidence that an increase in protein supply overcomes the depression in intake. It is clear from the foregoing that a single index such as ammonia-N is unlikely to provide an accurate prediction of silage intake. Indeed, even in studies where ammonia-N has proved to be a significant factor it has only accounted for 38 per cent of the variation in intake when considered alone. The commonly-assessed additional indices of DM content and pH are unlikely to contribute to any increase in predictive ability. Further the qualitative rather than quantitative descriptions of silage as used in the INRA system do not appear to increase precision

PROTEIN AND AMINO ACID SUPPLY

As has been pointed out already, grass contains a large proportion of soluble protein and in the silo this is extensively degraded to non-protein nitrogen (NPN) compounds. With well-preserved silages the NPN consists mainly of free amino acids, small peptides and a little ammonia but with clostridial silages deamination and decarboxylation reactions begin to dominate and ammonia and amines form a substantial part of the total NPN. Clostridial fermentations have a major impact on the utilization of silage N. In experiments by Barry, Cook and Wilkins (1978) silages with clostridial fermentations resulted in reduced DM intake, N retention and apparent biological value (BV); deamination reactions in the silo appeared to be less important than decarboxylation reactions in determining nutritive value. Consistent with this, ammonia-N was a poorer index of N retention and BV than were products of decarboxylation reactions such as α-amino butyrate, γ-aminobutyrate and alanine (Barry *et al.*, 1978).

Most detailed studies on N digestion and utilization have been conducted solely with well-preserved silages and the following sections briefly outline some of the information available. The subject has recently been reviewed more fully by Beever (1980), Thomas (1982) and Thomas and Chamberlain (1982a).

Rumen-degradability of silage N

The rate of degradation of silage NPN and soluble-protein N in the rumen is characteristically high and the ingestion of silage is followed by a pronounced peak in rumen ammonia concentration. Formaldehyde additives, which chemically link the grass protein and protect it from breakdown, reduce silage NPN content and rumen ammonia concentration (Beever *et al.*, 1977), but high rates of acid additives, which suppress proteolysis in the silo have a less consistent action (see below). Quantitative estimates of the ruminal-degradability of silage N have been made using the *in sacco* incubation of feeds in polyester bags suspended in the rumen. Values obtained lie in the range 0.75–0.85 (Agricultural Research Council, 1980; Brett, Dawson and Armstrong, 1981; Crawshaw *et al.*, 1981) and are consistent with the high rumen ammonia concentrations observed with silage diets. However, a feature of the values is that determined degradabilities appear to be little reduced for formaldehyde-treated silages. Siddons, Beever and Kaiser (1982) compared *in sacco* incubations and various laboratory tests based on solubility in buffers, *in vitro* incubation with rumen fluid and incubations with acid or neutral proteases. Without exception the laboratory methods gave lower degradability values for silage N than those measured *in sacco*, and the difference was particularly pronounced for silage made with high levels of formaldehyde additive. For this silage, buffer and *in vitro* incubation tests gave a degradability of 0.2, while *in sacco* tests gave a degradability of 0.75. Based on a survey of data from the literature, Thomas (1982) estimated that the rumen-degradability of silage N *in vivo* was 0.78–0.86 for three silages made without additive, 0.54–0.81 for seven formic-acid silages and 0.31–0.51 for four silages made with the addition of formaldehyde or formic acid/formaldehyde (35–60 g formaldehyde/kg protein). However, these values should be interpreted with caution. In an experiment with four silages made from the same grass with formic acid applied at rates of 0, 2.3, 4.6 or 5.9 litres/t, Chamberlain, Thomas and Wait (1982) found that soluble proteins saved from hydrolysis in the silo were susceptible to attack in the rumen and protein degradability values were in the range 0.74–0.83. Similarly, with silage made with formic acid/formaldehyde additive, but supplying only 15 g formaldehyde/kg protein, Rooke, Greife and Armstrong (1983) measured a protein degradability value of 0.80.

At present it would appear that the *in sacco* tests may overestimate the degradability of formaldehyde-treated silages. However, there are also indications that some of the degradability values determined *in vivo* for formic acid silages may be underestimates. This may be an example of a more general problem, since Beever and Siddons (1984) have pointed out that many *in vivo* estimates for the ruminal degradability of fresh herbages similarly lie in the range 0.5–0.75 though the herbages contain a high proportion of soluble protein which would be expected to be highly degradable.

Microbial protein synthesis

There is unequivocal evidence that diets containing a high proportion of silage support a low rate of microbial protein synthesis in the rumen. The Agricultural Research Council (ARC, 1984) adopted a value of 23 g microbial N/kg organic matter digested in the rumen (DOMR) for silages as compared with a value of 32 g N/kg DOMR for hays and grasses. For mixed silage and concentrate diets the information is more limited and rather variable, but for diets containing 0.3 concentrates or more, a value of 30 g N/kg DOMR is probably applicable (Thomas and Chamberlain, 1982a; ARC, 1984). The reason for the low efficiency of synthesis is not entirely resolved but in great part it must reflect the poor ATP yield obtained in the rumen from the silage fermentation products. Thus it can be argued that extensively fermented silages will be associated with reduced rates of microbial protein production, and further, that the effect is mediated via energy substrates in the rumen rather than proteolysis *per se*.

The relative deficiency in 'energy' supply and the rapidity of release of ammonia from silage N compounds in the rumen argues that silages should be supplemented with readily-fermented carbohydrate sources to promote the microbial fixation of ammonia. Starch supplements, like barley, reduce amonia concentration (Durand, Zelter and Tisserand, 1968), increase microbial protein synthesis (Thomas *et al.*, 1980) and enhance N retention in sheep and cattle (Griffiths, Spillane and Bath, 1973; Kelly and Thomas, 1978). However, their introduction into silage diets leads to a pronounced increase in rumen protozoal numbers (Chamberlain *et al.*, 1985) and the benefits of improved 'energy' supply are partly offset by an increased intraruminal recycling of N, via the protozoa. Sugars are more effective than starch in reducing postprandial concentrations of ammonia in the rumen and they are without effect on rumen protozoal numbers (Syrjala, 1972; Chamberlain *et al.*, 1985) but the quantitative benefits in microbial protein synthesis have yet to be assessed.

Amino acid supply from the small intestine

The N content of grass varies widely and independently of the D-value. Thus, even when grass is cut at the immature silage-stage of growth, the crude protein content of the silage may range from 120–200 g/kg DM. Not unexpectedly, this has an influence on the supply of amino acids to the postruminal gut, though the quantitative relationship between amino acid supply and diet crude protein content is not straightforward. In *Table 13.11* the relationship has been described by means of a summary of results taken from digestion experiments with sheep and dairy cows given silages conserved by natural fermentation or with the application of acid silage additives. The information is more comprehensive for sheep than for cows and the diets that have been examined cover the full range of protein content, albeit rather incompletely. As can be seen, with diets of moderate or low protein content, sheep show little net loss of N between the mouth and the duodenum; duodenal non-ammonia nitrogen (NAN) flow approximately equals dietary N intake. However, at higher dietary protein level, net losses of N are considerable, amounting to one-third of the total N ingested. A similar relationship is evident in the results for cows but it should be noted that net losses of N across the rumen become significant at lower dietary protein concentrations. The reason for this

Table 13.11   MEAN VALUES FOR THE RATIO OF DUODENAL NON-AMMONIA NITROGEN (NAN) FLOW TO DIETARY NITROGEN INTAKE FOR SHEEP AND DAIRY COWS GIVEN SILAGES OF DIFFERENT CRUDE PROTEIN CONTENT (MEAN VALUES ARE BASED ON DATA FOR SILAGES MADE WITHOUT ADDITIVES OR WITH NON-FORMALDEHYDE ADDITIVES

Range of crude protein contents (g/kg DM) in diets contributing to duodenal values	Duodenal NAN flow/dietary N intake	
	Sheep	*Dairy cows*
125–134	0.97 ± 0.03 (2)[a]	0.95 ± 0.02 (2)
138–139	1.01 ± 0.01 (2)	0.85
140–148	0.93 ± 0.04 (3)	0.75 ± 0.03 (2)
151–157	0.95 ± 0.01 (2)	—
195–200	0.69 ± 0.07 (4)	—

Taken from Beever *et al.* (1977); Gill and Ulyatt (1977); Gill, Ulyatt and Barry (1979); Siddons, Evans and Armstrong (1982); Thomas *et al.* (1980); Chamberlain, Thomas and Wait (1982); Rooke, Brooks and Armstrong (1982); Chamberlain and Thomas (1983); Rooke, Brookes and Armstrong (1983); Rooke, Griefe and Armstrong (1983); Siddons *et al.* (1984)
[a]Mean ± mean deviation. Figures in parenthesis indicates the number of diets contributing to the mean

difference is not known but it does not appear to be a methodological artefact. In nutritional terms the difference is of immense importance since the indication is that even with silages of moderate protein content, dairy cows may 'lose' up to one-quarter of the N ingested through absorption of ammonia in the rumen.

There appears to be little effect on amino acid supply from using acid additives to reduce proteolysis in the silo since Chamberlain, Thomas and Wait (1982) observed that the increase in the proportion of true protein in the silage merely resulted in an increase in the true protein degradation in the rumen, with no net benefit in passage of protein to the small intestine. However, nitrogen losses between the mouth and the duodenum can be reduced through the use of an additive containing formaldehyde (or paraformaldehyde) or glutaraldehyde during the conservation process. However, for such additives to be effective, the rate of application must be sufficient not only to restrict decarboxylation and deamination of amino acids in the silo but also to protect silage protein from microbial attack in the rumen. At low rates of formaldehyde application silage NPN, soluble-N and ammonia-N levels are reduced but there is no associated increase in duodenal protein flow (*see Table 13.12*).

Because of the degradation of dietary protein and synthesis of microbial protein in the rumen, the amino acid composition of duodenal digesta tends to resemble that of bacterial protein and differences in duodenal amino acid composition between diets tend to be small. Silage diets are somewhat of an exception in that, associated with the low rates of microbial protein synthesis in the rumen, there are low duodenal concentrations of methionine and lysine. It has been calculated that where the supply of protein to the small intestine is restricted, methionine and lysine are likely to be among the first limiting amino acids for both growth and lactation (Thomas and Chamberlain, 1982a).

The coefficients of digestibility of total amino acids in the small intestine of animals receiving silage diets normally lie in the range 0.65–0.75, while values for individual essential amino acids may be 0.60–0.80. Silage made with formaldehyde additives may give values at the lower end of these ranges, indicating that formaldehyde can impair the absorption of amino acids in the small intestine (see Beever *et al.*, 1977). The effect does not appear to become severe until application

Table 13.12 THE EFFECT OF FORMALDEHYDE APPLICATION AT ENSILAGE ON SILAGE COMPOSITION AND ON THE DIGESTION OF SILAGE NITROGEN IN THE RUMEN

Experiment no.[a]	1		2		3		4		5	
Rate of formaldehyde[b] application (g/kg crude protein)	0[c]	15	0	30	0[c]	35	0	50	0[c]	60
Silage total N (g/kg DM)	19.9	19.6	32.0	29.9	32.0	30.7	26.4	26.7	31.3	31.3
Silage NPN (g/kg total N)	—	512	578	431	769	388	—	—	—	—
Silage water-soluble N (g/kg total N)	615		600	451	737	404	462	494	820	776
Silage ammonia-N (g/kg total N)	95	61	53	47	134	36	98	Tr.	—	—
Total N intake (g/day)	91.3	90.7	27.9	24.7	32.3	30.1	66.3	70.6	32.6	32.3
Duodenal N flow (g/day)	92.4	94.1	19.3	22.9	21.6	35.5	61.9	84.0	27.8	35.5
Duodenal N flow (kg/kg N intake)	1.01	1.04	0.69	0.93	0.67	1.18	0.93	1.19	0.85	1.10
Response to formaldehyde (% of control duodenal flow)[d]	+3.0		+34.7		+76.1		+27.9		+29.4	

[a]Expt. 1 with cows from Rooke, Greife and Armstrong (1983). Expt. 2 with sheep from Siddons et al. (1984). Expt. 3 with sheep from Siddons, Evans and Beever (1979). Expt. 4 with cattle from Thomson et al. (1981). Expt. 5 with sheep from Beever et al. (1977).
[b]Additives also contained formic acid except in Expt. 5.
[c]Control silage made without additive, other control silages made with application of formic acid.
[d]Values have been adjusted to equalized N intakes.

rates are above 50 g formaldehyde/kg grass crude protein (see Thomson *et al.*, 1981). However, it may be important that the first and most affected amino acid is lysine and that, even at application rates of 50 g formaldehyde/kg crude protein, absorption of lysine is depressed.

ENERGY SUPPLY

Direct evaluation of silages made under experimental conditions have shown that well-made grass silages typically contain 10.0–12.5 MJ ME/kg DM depending on their maturity at cutting and method of conservation. Similar values apply for many individual silages made on commercial farms though the average value for samples submitted to the advisory service is much lower. For advisory purposes ME is routinely estimated from laboratory analysis or from *in vitro* digestibility determinations, though it is important to note that none of these procedures accounts for more than 40 per cent of the variance in ME content between silages. In the near future the analyses and equations used for these calculations are to be updated. As a result the determined DM contents of silages will be higher and calculated ME concentrations will be increased. The overall effect will be to raise calculated ME intake for a given weight of silage by 7–10 per cent (Barber, 1984).

Calorimetric determinations of the efficiency of utilization of silage ME for maintenance (k_m) and fattening (k_f) have been made with a range of silages but all have been of high-fermentation quality. Determined k_m values are consistently lower than those predicted from the metabolizability of the diet using the equation of Agricultural Research Council (1980); on average the difference is about 0.04 or approximately 5.5 per cent of the calculated value (*Table 13.13*). Determined k_f values are also on average lower than those predicted, the difference being 0.09 or 17.3 per cent of the calculated value (*Table 13.14*). The size of the discrepancy in the k_f values varies, however, and while determined and calculated values are in agreement for some silages, for others they are widely divergent (*Table 13.14*). Where low determined k_f values are recorded, they reflect an abnormally high dietary-induced thermogenesis, the cause of which remains to be explained. The

Table 13.13   THE PARTIAL EFFICIENCY OF UTILIZATION OF METABOLIZABLE ENERGY FOR MAINTENANCE (k_m) DETERMINED CALORIMETRICALLY AND CALCULATED BY THE EQUATION OF AGRICULTURAL RESEARCH COUNCIL (1980) FOR EIGHT SILAGES

Silage	Determined k_m	Calculated k_m[a]	Source of data
1	0.69	0.75	
2	0.71	0.74	Kelly and Thomas (1978)
3	0.68	0.70	
4	0.66	0.70	Ekern and Sundstøl (1974)
5	0.71	0.71	Smith *et al.* (1977)
6	0.68	0.70	Sundstøl *et al.* (1980)
7	0.65	0.74	
8	0.66	0.74	McLellan and McGinn (1983)
Mean	0.68	0.72	
S.E. of difference	0.01[b]		

[a] $k_m = 0.35$ ME/GE + 0.503
[b] Difference between determined and calculated values is significant at $P<0.01$ level

Table 13.14 THE PARTIAL EFFICIENCY OF UTILIZATION OF METABOLIZABLE ENERGY FOR FATTENING (k_f) DETERMINED CALORIMETRICALLY AND CALCULATED BY THE EQUATION OF AGRICULTURAL RESEARCH COUNCIL (1980) FOR SILAGES

Silage	Determined k_f	Calculated $k_f{}^a$	Silage	Determined k_f	Calculated $k_f{}^a$
1	0.21	0.44	8	0.43	0.49
2	0.51	0.56	9	0.39	0.47
3	0.42	0.42	10	0.34	0.53
4	0.41	0.45	11	0.23	0.61
5	0.49	0.43	12	0.61	0.61
6	0.54	0.51	13	0.52	0.61
7	0.40	0.53	14	0.45	0.58
Mean k_f determined	0.43				
Mean k_f calculated	0.52				
S.E. of the difference	0.03[b]				

(After McDonald, 1983)
[a]Calculated from $k_f = 1.32$ ME/GE $- 0.318$
[b]Difference between determined and calculated values is significant at $P<0.05$ level

effect may arise because of a nutritional imbalance in silage diets, resulting from the poor utilization of silage nitrogen in the rumen. Consistent with this, the agreement between determined and predicted k_f values for silage–barley diets appears to be better than for diets of silage alone (see Thomas and Chamberlain, 1982b) and there is evidence that k_f is higher for silage–barley diets than for silage only diets of corresponding metabolizability (Beever *et al.*, 1984; see later). Alternatively, the effects on thermogenesis could relate to the activity of specific components which are present in silages. In this regard, ingestion of dried silage extracts increases the basal metabolic rate of rats, apparently through effects of specific flavonoid compounds on the animal's metabolism (McLaren *et al.*, 1964; Qasim and Stelzig, 1973; Stelzig and Qasim, 1973).

For rationing purposes, the efficiency of utilization of ME for lactation (k_{l0}) is assumed to be constant at 0.62 (Ministry of Agriculture, Fisheries and Food, 1975), though determined values vary over a range of 0.56–0.66 (ARC, 1980). Very few calorimetric determinations have been made with cows receiving grass silage diets, but in a recent experiment (Unsworth, Wylie and Anderson, 1984) with wilted and direct-cut silages given with dairy concentrates (approximately 40 per cent of the DM intake), k_{l0} values of 0.58 and 0.56, respectively, were recorded. These compared with values of 0.64 and 0.65 estimated from the ARC (1980) equation $k_{l0} = 0.35\,qm + 0.42$ (Unsworth, 1984). On the basis of an analysis of data from feeding experiments carried out at the Hannah Research Institute, Thomas and Castle (1978) estimated that k_{l0} values varied between 0.39 and 0.64. These estimates are subject to considerable errors but it is worthwhile noting that within experiments k_{l0} was consistently higher for diets containing supplementary protein feeds.

Animal production from silage

Major changes in nutrient supply from silage to the ruminant should be achieved by altering the date of cut of the crop (digestibility) and by modifying and restricting fermentation through wilting or the use of additives. The extent to which these factors influence animal production will now be discussed.

DIGESTIBILITY OF SILAGE

In a review of the experiments which examined the influence of digestibility of silage on milk output Thomas (1980) derived an average response of $+0.29\,kg$ milk/unit rise in D-value. This is slightly higher than value of $+0.23\,kg/\Delta D$ derived by Castle (1975) based on data from the Hannah Research Institute. However, there is a wide range in response from 0 to $+0.7\,kg/\Delta D$ which may in part be associated with the modifying effect of fermentation characteristics on intake, as has been discussed previously. There may also be important effects on milk composition. Extensive studies by Murdoch and Rook (1963) and Murdoch (1965) indicated that earlier cutting of grass for silage resulted in a depression in both fat and snf (solids-not-fat) content in milk, the latter principally associated with the protein fraction. The depression in milk protein content was not influenced by the fermentation characteristics of the silage. More recent information reviewed by Thomas (1984) suggests that milk protein concentration increases with increased digestibility of silage. The causes of the variability in protein responses between experiments are not clear. However, it must be noted that, even in the experiments where protein content in milk was reduced by earlier cutting, the yield of protein and snf was enhanced. Similarly, reduced milk fat contents were accompanied by maintained or increased milk fat yields.

Silage of uniform quality is rarely available and silages of two or more digestibilities may be present on the farm for winter feeding. Strategies for feeding silages of 60 and 70 D were recently examined by Rae, Thomas and Reeve (1985). Three treatments were imposed over a 172 day winter feeding period. Strategy HL was 70 D silage offered from days 14 to 84 and subsequently 60 D silage until turnout; strategy M was an equal mixture of the two silages for the whole period; strategy LH was 60 D for the first period followed by 70 D silage until turnout. Milk yields for the whole experiment were 20.0, 20.3 and 20.1 kg/day for treatments HL, M and LH respectively indicating no differences between the strategies. Further, the response to increased digestibility was the same in mid as in early lactation. In this experiment the supplement was offered at a flat rate. It is not known whether the effects would be different if the supplement was fed to yield.

Thomas, C. *et al.* (1984b) compared the response of beef cattle to increased digestibility of silage with that achieved by enhancing the proportion of barley supplement (*Table 13.15*). Higher gains were achieved by steers given silage of high

Table 13.15 INTAKE AND GAIN BY BEEF CATTLE GIVEN EARLY-CUT SILAGE ALONE OR LATE-CUT SILAGE ALONE OR WITH ROLLED BARLEY

	Treatments			
	Late-cut silage			Early-cut silage
Barley (g/kg DM)	0	280	560	0
Digestibility of gross energy	0.619	0.668	0.705	0.735
ME intake (kJ/kg $W^{0.75}$ per day)	758	834	871	932
Gains				
empty body (g/day)	292	552	800	696
fat (g/day)	121	189	302	260
protein (g/day)	31.1	76.0	116.1	86.9
energy (MJ/day)	5.48	9.23	14.58	12.24

(Thomas, C. *et al.* 1984b)

rather than low digestibility, but although these steers consumed the most ME their gains were lower than those achieved by the animals receiving the mixture of late-cut silage and the high level of barley. It can be calculated that 20 per cent more ME above maintenance was required by steers given the early-cut silage in order to achieve the same energy retention as those given the silage/barley mixtures. This difference in efficiency was confirmed in concurrent calorimetric studies (Beever *et al.*, 1984) which derived k_f values of 0.49 and 0.54 for the silage alone and mixed silage/barley diets respectively.

MODIFICATION OF FERMENTATION

Effect of wilting

In a review of the effect of wilting on animal performance Wilkins (1984) noted that, on average, milk yield was no higher with wilted than unwilted silage but when the analysis was restricted to include only the unwilted silages made with additive, milk yield was 0.9 kg/day higher for the unwilted silages. Although liveweight gains by beef cattle were higher, on average, with wilted silages, these cattle consumed more silage DM and the gain per kg DM intake was higher with unwilted silages. In a subsequent analysis of the 'Eurowilt' experiments Rohr and Thomas (1984) found little difference in liveweight gains between unwilted and wilted silages but, again, intake was 9 per cent higher with wilted silages, indicating greater gross efficiencies with unwilted silages. Some of the causes of this apparent increase in efficiency were investigated by Charmley and Thomas (1984) (*Table 13.16*). In this experiment where firstly, DM content included the contribution of alcohols present in the direct-cut silages; secondly, account was taken of the reduction in digestibility on wilting; thirdly, the differences in gut fill which occurred between treatments were removed and finally, account was taken of the tendency for the concentration of fat in the empty body to be higher in the wet silages; no differences in efficiency of utilization of digested energy for energy gain were measured between direct-cut and wilted silages. It was concluded that the higher gross efficiencies of feed use observed in previous experiments were more apparent than real and occurred primarily from inadequate measurement of both

Table 13.16   THE INFLUENCE OF WILTING ON DIGESTIBILITY, INTAKE AND GAINS BY BEEF CATTLE

Treatment	Experiment 1		Experiment 2			
	Direct-cut + additive	Wilted	Direct-cut	Direct-cut + additive	Fast wilt	Slow wilt
Digestibility of gross energy	0.649	0.619	0.677	0.675	0.632	0.638
Digestible energy intake (MJ/day)	39.7	40.2	35.5	36.2	36.1	35.5
Gains						
Liveweight (g/day)	569	624	398	463	476	470
Empty body weight (g/day)	443	490	347	387	389	355
Protein (g/day)	79.4	88.4	53.5	57.4	61.3	53.1
Fat (g/day)	69.2	74.0	83.3	80.1	85.5	83.9
Energy (MJ/day)	4.52	4.81	4.36	4.32	4.62	4.37

Charmley and Thomas (1984)

input and output. The experiments further demonstrate the irrelevance of DM content as a sole measure of the nutritive value of silage.

The use of wilting as a conservation technique in circumstances where direct-cut silages are well fermented depends entirely on the balance of losses in the field, in the silo and in effluent, rather than on animal performance.

Effect of additives

The data from 41 experiments which have examined the effect of formic acid based additives on liveweight gain are presented in *Figure 13.2*. On average the use of additive resulted in a 32 per cent increase in gain. However, the response declined as the level of gain on the control treatment increased. This was in part a reflection of the influence of improved fermentation of control silages but was mainly the result of the use of supplementary concentrates to promote high levels of gain on control silages. The increase in performance by using an additive was associated with, on average, a 9 per cent increase in silage intake and a small increase in digestibility (+0.013). A similar analysis of data from dairy-cow experiments

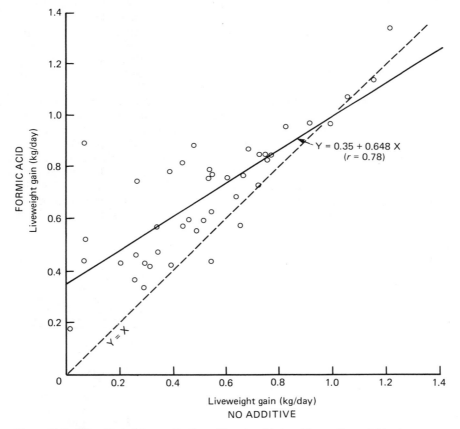

Figure 13.2   The effect of the application of formic acid at ensiling on liveweight gain in cattle (*n* = 41)

Table 13.17 RELATIVE PRODUCTION (CONTROL = 100) OF BEEF CATTLE AND DAIRY COWS ON FORMALDEHYDE-TREATED SILAGES

Production parameter		Control without acid additive	Control with acid additive
Liveweight gain	n	29	33
	mean	179	100
	range	80–808	69–129
Milk production	n	4	11
	mean	111	98
	range	101–118	88–104

(Kaiser, 1979)

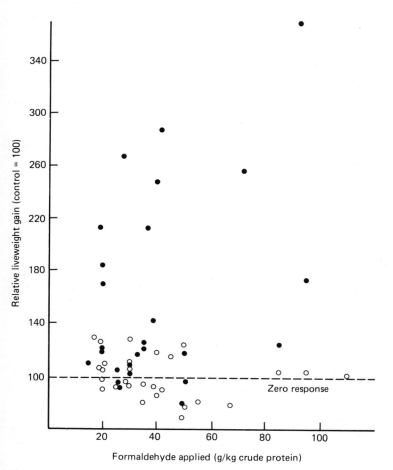

Figure 13.3 Relative liveweight gain (control = 100) of cattle offered silages preserved with formaldehyde. ●, control with no additive; ○, formic acid control

reported by Waldo (1978) showed that the response in milk yield to formic acid was in the region of 4 to 6 per cent. That the response in milk output is less than that observed here with beef cattle may be a reflection of higher concentrate proportions and the partitioning of additional energy input into both body weight and milk yield. Less information is available for other acids but the recent data of Flynn and O'Kiely (1984) suggests little difference in carcass gain between formic and sulphuric acids when applied at 2.3 litres/t.

The effect of formaldehyde addition is summarized in *Table 13.17* and *Figure 13.3* (Kaiser, 1979). Responses to formaldehyde are clearly evident when the control silage is made without additive but little or no response is seen when an acid additive is used on the control. However there is a considerable range in response (*Figure 13.3*) and the additional increase over an acid additive appears to decline as the amount of formaldehyde applied increases. This may be associated with a reduction in rumen-degradable nitrogen (Lonsdale, Thomas and Haines, 1977) but recently Kaiser *et al.* (1981) have observed a direct antimicrobial effect of formaldehyde on digestion in the rumen. Clearly rates of addition of about 20–50 g formaldehyde/kg crop crude protein coupled with supplementation with a highly degradable N source are needed to promote a positive response over an acid additive. Nevertheless, considerable variation in response (80–129 per cent) is seen even when these conditions are met.

The ability of formaldehyde to protect protein could allow a reduction in use of supplementary protein. However, Thomas *et al.* (1981) noted that with dairy cows, response to soya bean meal was similar between silages either preserved with no additive or with formalin to supply 35 g formaldehyde/kg crude protein. Concurrent digestion experiments where the silages were offered to sheep (Siddons, Evans and Beever, 1979) showed a markedly lower rumen-degradability and a higher duodenal protein flow from the formalin treated silage.

In view of the consistent increases in protein flow into the small intestine on treatment with formaldehyde (see earlier) more emphasis needs to be given to the factors influencing the absorption and utilization of absorbed amino acids in animals given these silages.

Few data are available on the effect of inoculants on animal production from cattle given grass silages. Summarizing six trials conducted by ADAS, Haigh, Appleton and Clench (1984) concluded that the use of commercially prepared microbial cultures on wet herbage did not improve liveweight gain above that observed with untreated silages, whereas a large response was detected with formic acid-based additives.

Conclusions

Silage has long been recognized as a low cost source of energy and protein but often it has been regarded merely as a 'roughage' feed, supplying the animal's maintenance requirements. Its potential to support high rates of animal production is underexploited. The principles of producing well-preserved silages with the minimum loss of nutrients are established. Nevertheless, constraints on the farm in the production of silage on a large scale coupled with the technical ability of the farmer results in a wide range in silage composition in practice. This review has stressed that silage is not a homogeneous entity but a generic group of prefermented feeds. Its characteristics depend not only on the composition of the crop at cutting but also on the profound changes that occur in the carbohydrate and nitrogen fractions during the whole conservation process. Thus the characterization of silage to reflect its potential as a feed for animal production and to define the optimum supplementation is crucial both for advice on the farm and for the interpretation of research data.

Silage is characterized for advisory purposes by analysis of DM content, ash, total N, pH, soluble-N or ammonia-N (occasionally), an estimate of ME and DCP (sometimes RDP, UDP). In research studies on animal production from silage, as the results from a survey of papers in the journals *Animal Production* and *Grass and Forage Science* show (*Table 13.18*), comparatively little additional information is presented. The volatile nature of the components of silage is accepted and yet only 0.68 of trials corrected oven DM contents for these constituents. Similarly, although significant concentrations of alcohols are present in wet silages, few experiments measured this component and adjusted the concentrations of DM

Table 13.18   ANALYSIS OF SILAGE USED IN ANIMAL PRODUCTION STUDIES— SURVEY OF LITERATURE INVOLVING 75 EXPERIMENTS

Analysis	Propor- tion	Analysis	Propor- tion	Analysis	Propor- tion
DM content		Carbohydrate		Digestibility	
oven	0.32	Crude fibre/MAD fibre	0.51	*in vitro*	0.42
toluene corr.	0.68	Van Soest fibre	0.05	*in vivo*	0.42
alcohol corr.	0.05	WSC	0.09	Gross energy	0.23
Fermentation characteristics		Nitrogen fraction			
lactic	0.29	Total N			
VFA	0.31	oven	0.81		
methanol	0.01	fresh	0.19		
ethanol	0.05	Sol/insol N	0.08		
ammonia-N	0.45	Volatile N	0.02		
pH	0.93	NPN	0.03		

accordingly. Less than one-third of experiments determined the concentration of acids and only 0.45 of experiments measured ammonia-N concentration although 0.93 assessed silage pH. In less than 0.1 of experiments was there any attempt to fractionate total N. Further, even the analysis of total N is doubtful since in only 0.19 of experiments was this component measured on fresh material. Less than half the experiments measured digestibility *in vivo* and information on the gross energy content was available on only 0.23 of the total. In many of the remaining studies the ME content of silages could be estimated only from the fibre content. The question arises as to what extent these commonly assessed components of silage allow the prediction of voluntary intake and nutrient supply.

Ammonia-N provides a broad index to separate the lower intake clostridial silages from the remainder but as a sole indicator of silage intake in the absence of data on silage acids it remains relatively inaccurate. It is important to note that the inclusion of the commonly assessed DM content and pH is of little benefit in increasing precision. In the absence of clostridial activity or when fermentation is restricted then a complex set of factors, such as those influencing digestion in and passage from the rumen, the balance between energy and protein supply to the tissues and acid–base balance, can all interact. It is clear from the foregoing that a single index is of little value in predicting intake. Further progress may be made by empirical analysis of existing data but this approach will be limited firstly by the narrower range in silage quality in experiments compared with practice and secondly, by the paucity of information on silage characteristics despite the wealth of animal production data.

Currently the supply of energy substrates to the ruminant is defined in terms of ME most commonly estimated from laboratory measurements such as *in vitro* digestibility, fibre content and cell wall content. That these estimates rarely account for more than 40 per cent of the variance in the ME of silages is cause for serious concern. Further, the evidence of low efficiencies (especially k_f) with silages given as sole feeds and in particular the widely divergent values for some silages seriously questions the use of q (ME/GE) as a unifying concept. The low efficiency of utilization of silage nitrogen is well established and the reasons discussed in this review. Conservation procedures to reduce proteolysis may have relatively little impact on protein supply in comparison with those which reduce the activity of clostridia. In this respect decarboxylation may be of greater significance than deamination and thus ammonia-N may be relatively poor index of protein supply. However, it is not clear at present which aspects of feed composition provide the most useful indices of the degradation of silage N in the in the rumen and its incorporation into microbial protein. A much more precise definition of energy availability in the rumen than dietary ME, as currently used in the ARC protein system, is also required. Further, it appears that there is considerable variability in the efficiency of use of apparently absorbed protein, since the consistent increases in duodenal protein flow observed with formaldehyde treated silages, result in inconsistent responses in growth and milk production. Differences in efficiency may well be a reflection of protein quality rather than quantity. Nevertheless, the conservation process allows the opportunity to increase nutrient supply above that of the original crop. That the attempts to achieve this objective have produced inconsistent responses should not be a barrier to future research effort in this area.

The prediction of nutrient supply from silages will allow a more rational approach to supplementation based on the correction of specific deficiencies. All too frequently under farm conditions excessive levels of concentrate feeding, through substitution, suppress or mask the potential of high quality silages to support high rates of animal production. A new technology is slowly emerging involving, for example, the use of protected amino acids (principally methionine and lysine) or protein balancers as true supplements rather than replacers for silage. Also, work is progressing on the use of specific energy substrates to enhance microbial efficiency in the rumen. Such technology needs to have a fundamental base of a system of feed characterization which adequately reflects nutrient supply to the animal. Current systems of silage analysis owe much to ease and convenience and to historical developments in ensilage technology. There remains a real need for research on analytical schemes that will provide a meaningful description of silage as a feed for ruminant livestock.

Acknowledgements

We wish to thank Dr E.M. Gill and Mr B.G. Gibbs for advice and assistance in the preparation of the manuscript.

References

AGRICULTURAL RESEARCH COUNCIL (1980). *The Nutrient Requirements of Ruminant Livestock*. Commonwealth Agricultural Bureaux; Farnham Royal, Slough

AGRICULTURAL RESEARCH COUNCIL (1984). *The Nutrient Requirements of Ruminant Livestock*. Supplement 1. Commonwealth Agricultural Bureaux; Farnham Royal, Slough

BARBER, W.P. (1984). *Proceedings of the 7th Silage Conference*, pp. 87–88. Ed. F.J. Gordon and E.F. Unsworth. Queens University; Belfast

BARRY, T.N. (1976). *New Zealand Journal of Agricultural Research*, **19**, 185–191

BARRY, T.N., COOK, J.E. and WILKINS, R.J. (1978). *Journal of Agricultural Science (Cambridge)*, **91**, 701–715

BARRY, T.N., FENNESSY, P.F. and DUNCAN, S.J. (1973). *New Zealand Journal of Agricultural Research*, **16**, 64–68

BARRY,T.N., MUNDELL, D.C., WILKINS, R.J. and BEEVER, D.E. (1978). *Journal of Agricultural Science (Cambridge)*, **91**, 717–725

BEEVER, D.E. (1980). In *Forage Conservation in the 80s*, pp. 131–143. Ed. C. Thomas. Occasional Symposium No. 11, British Grassland Society

BEEVER, D.E., CAMMELL, S.B., HAINES, M.J., GALE, D.L. and THOMAS, C. (1984). *Animal Production*, **38**, 533

BEEVER, D.E. and SIDDONS, R.C. (1984). *Proceedings of the 6th International Symposium on Ruminant Physiology*. Banff 1984. (in press)

BEEVER, D.E., THOMSON, D.J., CAMMELL, S.B. and HARRISON, D.G. (1977). *Journal of Agricultural Science (Cambridge)*, **88**, 61–70

BLAXTER, K.L. (1980). In *Feeding Strategies for Dairy Cows*, pp. 18.1–18.8. Ed. W.H. Broster, C.L. Johnson and J.C. Tayler. Agricultural Research Council; London

BRADY, C.J. (1960). *Journal of the Science of Food and Agriculture*, **11**, 276–284

BRETT, P.A., DOWSON, S. and ARMSTRONG, D.G. (1981). *Proceedings of the 6th Silage Conference*, pp. 21–22. Ed. R.D. Harkess and M.E. Castle. Edinburgh School of Agriculture; Edinburgh

BROSTER, W.H. and THOMAS, C. (1981). In *Recent Advances in Animal Nutrition*, pp. 49–67. Ed. W. Haresign. Butterworths; London

CARPINTERO, C.M., HENDERSON, A.R. and MCDONALD, P. (1979). *Grass and Forage Science*, **34**, 311–315

CASTLE, M.E. (1975). *Agricultural Progress*, **50**, 53–60

CASTLE, M.E., GILL, M.S. and WATSON, J.N. (1981). *Grass and Forage Science*, **36**, 31–37

CASTLE, M.E., RETTER, W.C. and WATSON, J.N. (1979). *Grass and Forage Science*, **34**, 293–301

CASTLE, M.E. and WATSON, J.N. (1976). *Journal of the British Grassland Society*, **31**, 191–195

CHAMBERLAIN, D.G., THOMAS, P.C. and WAIT, M.K. (1982). *Grass and Forage Science*, **37**, 159–164

CHAMBERLAIN, D.G. and THOMAS, P.C. (1983). *Journal of the Science of Food and Agriculture*, **34**, 440–446

CHAMBERLAIN, D.G., THOMAS, P.C. and ANDERSON, F.J. (1983). *Journal of Agricultural Science (Cambridge)*, **101**, 47–58

CHAMBERLAIN, D.G. and THOMAS, P.C. (1984). Unpublished observations

CHAMBERLAIN, D.G., THOMAS, P.C., WILSON, W., NEWBOLD, C.J. and MACDONALD, J.C. (1985). *Journal of Agricultural Science (Cambridge)*, (in press)

CHARMLEY, E. and THOMAS, C. (1984). *Landbauforschung Volkenrode Sonderheft*, **69**, p. 21

CLAPPERTON, J.L. and SMITH, E.J. (1983). Personal communication

CLANCY, M., WANGNESS, P.J. and BAUMGARDT (1977). *Journal of Dairy Science*, **60**, 580–590

CONRAD, H.R., BAILE, C.A. and MAYER, J. (1977). *Journal of Dairy Science*, **60**, 1725–1733

COTTRILL, B.R., OSBOURN, D.F., WILKINSON, J.M. and RICHMOND, P.J. (1976). *Animal Production*, **22**, 154–155

CRAWSHAW, R., COTTON, R., CHAMBERLAIN, A.G. and PAINE, C.A. (1981). *Proceedings of the 6th Silage Conference*, pp. 119–120. Ed. R.D. Harkness and M.E. Castle. Edinburgh School of Agriculture; Edinburgh

DEINUM, B. (1966). *Proceedings of the 10th International Grassland Congress*, pp. 415–418

DEMARQUILLY, C. (1973). *Annales Zootechnique*, **22**, 1–35

DEWAR, W.A., MCDONALD, P. and WHITTENBURY, R. (1963). *Journal of the Science of Food and Agriculture*, **14**, 411–417

DESWYSEN, A., VANBELLE, M. and FOCANT, M. (1978). *Journal of the British Grassland Society*, **33**, 107–115

DONALDSON, E. and EDWARDS, R.A. (1976). *Journal of the Science of Food and Agriculture*, **27**, 536–544

DRYSDALE, A.D. and BERRY, D. (1980). In *Forage Conservation in the 80s*, pp. 262–264. Ed. C. Thomas. Occasional Symposium No. 11. British Grassland Society

DURAND, M., ZELTER, S.Z. and TISSERAND, J.L. (1968). *Annales Biologie Animale Biochemie Biophysiologie*, **8**, 45–67

EGAN, A.R. (1977). *Australian Journal of Agricultural Research*, **28**, 907–915

EKERN, A. and SUNDSTØL, F. (1974). In *Energy Metabolism of Farm Animals*, pp. 221–224. Ed. K.H. Menke, K.H. Lantzsch and J.R. Reichl. Universitat Hohenheim; Stuttgart

FARHAM, S.M.A. and THOMAS, P.C. (1978). *Journal of the British Grassland Society*, **33**, 151–158

FLYNN, A.V. and O'KIELY, P. (1984). *Proceedings of the 7th Silage Conference*, pp. 15–16. Ed. F.J. Gordon and E.F. Unsworth. Queens University; Belfast

GILL, M. and ENGLAND, P. (1983). *Animal Production*, **36**, 513

GILL, M. and ULYATT, M. (1977). *Journal of Agricultural Science (Cambridge)*, **89**, 43–51

GILL, M., SIDDONS, R.C., BEEVER, D.E. and ROWE, J.B. (1984). *Canadian Journal of Animal Science*, **64** (Supplement), 169–170

GILL, M., ULYATT, M. and BARRY, T.N. (1979). *New Zealand Journal of Agricultural Research*, **22**, 221–225

GORDON, F.J. (1980). *Animal Production*, **30**, 29–37

GRIFFITHS, T.W., SPILLANE, T.A. and BATH, I.H. (1973). *Journal of Agricultural Science (Cambridge)*, **83**, 89–95

HAIGH, P.M., APPLETON, M. and CLENCH, S.F. (1984). Mimeograph NC/C/719 Agricultural Development and Advisory Service

HARRIS, C.E. and RAYMOND, W.F. (1963). *Journal of the British Grassland Society*, **18**, 204–212

HUTCHINSON, K.J. and WILKINS, R.J. (1971). *Journal of Agricultural Science (Cambridge)*, **77**, 539–543

HUTCHINSON, K.J., WILKINS, R.J. and OSBOURN, D.F. (1971). *Journal of Agricultural Science (Cambridge)*, **77**, 545–547

INRA (1978). *Principles de la Nutrition et de l'Alimentation des Ruminants*. INRA Publications; Versailles

JACKSON, N. and ANDERSON, B.K. (1971). *Journal of the Science of Food and Agriculture*, **22**, 424–426

JACKSON, N. and FORBES, T.J. (1970). *Animal Production*, **12**, 591–599

KAISER, A.G. (1979). The effects of formaldehyde application at ensiling on the utilization of silage by young growing cattle. PhD Thesis, University of Reading

KAISER, A.G., TAYLER, J.C., GIBBS, B.G. and ENGLAND, P. (1981). *Journal of Agricultural Science (Cambridge)*, **97**, 1–11

KASSEM, M.E., THOMAS, P.C., CHAMBERLAIN, D.G. and ROBERTSON, S. (1984). Unpublished observations

KELLY, N.C. and THOMAS, P.C. (1975). *Journal of the British Grassland Society*, **30**, 237–239

KELLY, N.C. and THOMAS, P.C. (1978). *British Journal of Nutrition*, **40**, 205–209

LANCASTER, R.J. and WILSON, R.K. (1975). *New Zealand Journal of Experimental Agriculture*, **3**, 203–206

LANGSTON, C.W., BOUMA, C. and CONNER, R.M. (1962). *Journal of Dairy Science*, **45**, 618–624

LEWIS, M. (1981). *Proceedings of the 6th Silage Conference*, pp. 35–36. Ed. R.D. Harkess and M.E. Castle. University of Edinburgh; Edinburgh

LINDGREN, S. (1984). *Proceedings of the 7th Silage Conference*, pp. 3–4. Ed. F.J. Gordon and E.F. Unsworth. Queens University; Belfast

LONSDALE, C.R., THOMAS, C. and HAINES, M.J. (1977). *Journal of the British Grassland Society*, **32**, 171–176

LOUGH, A.K. and ANDERSON, L.J. (1973). *Proceedings of the Nutrition Society*, **32**, 61A

LYTTLETON, J.W. (1973). In *Chemistry and Biochemistry of Herbage*, Vol. 1, pp. 63–103. Ed. G.W. Butler and R.W. Bailey. Academic Press; London

MACKENZIE, D.J. and WYLAM, C.B. (1957). *Journal of the Science of Food and Agriculture*, **8**, 38–45

MARSH, R. (1979). *Grass and Forage Science*, **34**, 1–10

MCDONALD, P. (1981). *The Biochemistry of Silage*. John Wiley and Sons; Chichester

MCDONALD, P. (1983). *Hannah Research Institute Report–1983*, pp. 56–67

MCDONALD, P., MACPHERSON, H.T. and WATT, J.A. (1963). *Journal of the British Grassland Society*, **18**, 230–232

MCLAREN, G.A., ASPLUND, R.O., CROW, D.G., ISAI, L.I. and PORTERFIELD, I.D. (1964). *Journal of Nutrition*, **83**, 218–224

MCLELLAN, A.R. and MCGINN, R. (1983). *Animal Feed Science and Technology*, **9**, 107–119

MCLEOD, D.S., WILKINS, R.J. and RAYMOND, W.F. (1970). *Journal of Agricultural Science (Cambridge)*, **75**, 311–319

MINISTRY OF AGRICULTURE, FISHERIES AND FOOD (1975). *Energy Allowances and Feeding Systems for Ruminants*. Technical Bulletin 33. Her Majesty's Stationery Office; London

MOORE, L.A., THOMAS, J.W. and SYKES, J.F. (1960). *Proceedings of the 8th International Grassland Congress*, pp. 701–704

MORGAN, D.J. and L'ESTRANGE, J.L. (1977). *Journal of the British Grassland Society*, **32**, 217–224

MORRISON, I.M. (1979). *Journal of Agricultural Science (Cambridge)*, **93**, 581–586

MURDOCH, J.C. (1965). *Journal of Dairy Research*, **32**, 219–227

MURDOCH, J.C. and ROOK, J.A.F. (1963). *Journal of Dairy Research*, **30**, 391–397

NEAL, H.D.ST.C., THOMAS, C. and COBBY, J.M. (1984). *Journal of Agricultural Science (Cambridge)*, **103**, 1–10

NEUMARK, H., BONDI, A. and VOLCANI, R. (1964). *Journal of the Science of Food and Agriculture*, **15**, 487–492

OSBOURN, D.F. (1980). In *Grass, Its Production and Utilization*, p. 70. Ed. W. Holmes. Blackwell; London

PHILLIP, L.E., BUCHANAN-SMITH, J.G. and GROVUM, W.L. (1981a). *Journal of Agricultural Science (Cambridge)*, **96**, 429–438

PHILLIP, L.E., BUCHANAN-SMITH, J.G. and GROVUM, W.L. (1981b). *Journal of Agricultural Science (Cambridge)*, **96**, 439–445

QASIM, S.A. and STELZIG, D.A. (1973). *Journal of Nutrition*, **103**, 1658–1664

RAE, R.C., THOMAS, C. and REEVE, A. (1985). *Animal Production* (in press)

ROHR, K. and THOMAS, C. (1984). *Landbauforschung Volkenrode, Sonderheft*, **69**, pp. 64–70

ROOKE, J.A., BROOKES, I.M. and ARMSTRONG, D.G. (1982). In *Forage Protein in Ruminant Animal Production*, pp. 185–186. Ed. D.J. Thomson, D.E. Beever and R.G. Gunn. British Society of Animal Production Occasional Publication No. 6

ROOKE, J.A., BROOKES, I.M. and ARMSTRONG, D.G. (1983). *Journal of Agricultural Science (Cambridge)*, **100**, 329–342

ROOKE, J.A., GREIFE, H.A. and ARMSTRONG, D.G. (1983). *Grass and Forage Science*, **38**, 301–310

SEALE, D.R. and HENDERSON, A.R. (1984). *Proceedings of the 7th Silage Conference*, pp. 5–6. Ed. F.J. Gordon and E.F. Unsworth. Queens University; Belfast

SHAMOON, S.A. (1984). Amino Acid Supplements for Ruminant Farm Livestock with Special Reference to Methionine. PhD Thesis, University of Glasgow; Scotland

SIDDONS, R.C., ARRICASTRES, C., GALE, D.L. and BEEVER, D.E. (1984). *British Journal of Nutrition*, **52**, 391–401

SIDDONS, R.C., BEEVER, D.E. and KAISER, A.G. (1982). *Journal of the Science of Food and Agriculture*, **33**, 609–613

SIDDONS, R.C., EVANS, R.T. and BEEVER, D.E. (1979). *British Journal of Nutrition*, **42**, 535–545

SMITH, D. (1973). In *Chemistry and Biochemistry of Herbage*, Vol. 1, pp. 106–155. Ed. G.W. Butler and R.W. Bailey. Academic Press; New York

SMITH, E.J. and CLAPPERTON, J.L. (1981). *Proceedings of the Nutrition Society*, **40**, 22A

SMITH, J.S., WAINMAN, F.W. and DEWEY, P.J.S. (1977). *Proceedings of the Nutrition Society*, **36**, 66A

STELZIG, D.A. and QASIM, S.A. (1973). *Journal of Agricultural and Food Chemistry*, **21**, 883–885

SUNDSTØL, F., EKERN, A., LINGVALL, P., LINDGREN, E. and BERTILSSON, J. (1980). In *Energy Metabolism*, pp. 17–21. Ed. L.E. Mount. Butterworths; London

SYRJALA, L. (1972). *Annales Agriculturae Fenniae*, **11**, 199–276

THOMAS, C. (1980). In *Feeding Strategies for Dairy Cows*, pp. 8.1–8.14. Ed. W.H. Broster, C.L. Johnson and J.C. Tayler. Agricultural Research Council; London

THOMAS, C. (1984). In *Milk Compositional Quality and its Importance in Future Markets*, p. 69. Ed. M.E. Castle and R.G. Gunn. British Society of Animal Production; Occasional Publication No. 9

THOMAS, C., ASTON, K., DALEY, S.R., HUGHES, P.M. and BASS, J. (1984a). *Animal Production*, **38**, 519

THOMAS, C., ASTON, K., TAYLER, J.C., DALEY, S.R. and OSBOURN, D.F. (1981). *Animal Production*, **32**, 285–295

THOMAS, C., GIBBS, B.G., THURNHAM, B. and BEEVER, D.E. (1984b). *Animal Production*, **32**, 533

THOMAS, C., GILL, M. and AUSTIN, A.R. (1980). *Grass and Forage Science*, **35**, 275–279

THOMAS, C., GILL, M., ENGLAND, P., AITCHISON, E. and COOKE, B.C. (1984c). *Proceedings of the 7th Silage Conference*, pp. 65–66. Ed. F.J. Gordon and E.J. Unsworth. Queens University; Belfast

THOMAS, C. and WILKINSON, J.M. (1975). *Journal of Agricultural Science (Cambridge)*, **85**, 255–261

THOMAS, J.W., MOORE, L.A., OKAMOTO, M. and SYKES, J.F. (1961). *Journal of Dairy Science*, **44**, 1471–1483

THOMAS, P.C. (1982). In *Forage Protein in Ruminant Animal Production*, pp. 67–68. Ed. D.J. Thomson, D.E. Beever and R.G. Gunn. British Society of Animal Production Occasional Publication No. 6

THOMAS, P.C. and CASTLE, M.E. (1978). *Annual Report of the Hannah Research Institute*, pp. 108–117

THOMAS, P.C., CHAMBERLAIN, D.G., KELLY, N.C. and WAIT, M.K. (1980). *British Journal of Nutrition*, **43**, 469–479

THOMAS, P.C. and CHAMBERLAIN, D.G. (1982a). In *Forage Protein Conservation and Utilization*, pp. 121–146. Ed. T.W. Griffiths and M.F. Maguire. Commission of the European Communities; Brussels

THOMAS, P.C. and CHAMBERLAIN, D.G. (1982b). In *Silage for Milk Production*, pp. 63–102. Ed. J.A.F. Rook and P.C. Thomas. Technical Bulletin No. 2. National Institute for Research in Dairying; Reading

THOMAS, P.C., CHAMBERLAIN, D.G., ROBERTSON, S., SHAMOON, S.A. and WATSON, J.N. (1984). *Proceedings of the 7th Silage Conference*, pp. 45–46. Ed. F.J. Gordon and E.F. Unsworth. Queens University; Belfast

THOMAS, P.C., KELLY, N.C. and WAIT, M.K. (1976). *Journal of the British Grassland Society*, **31**, 19–22

THOMSON, D.J., BEEVER, D.E., LONSDALE, C.R., HAINES, M.J., CAMMELL, S.B. and AUSTIN, A.R. (1981). *British Journal of Nutrition*, **46**, 193–207

ULYATT, J.M. (1965). *New Zealand Journal of Agricultural Research*, **8**, 397–408

UNSWORTH, E.F. (1984). Personal communication

UNSWORTH, E.F., WYLIE, A.R.G. and ANDERSON, R. (1984). *Proceedings of the 7th Silage Conference*, pp. 35–36. Ed. F.J. Gordon and E.F. Unsworth. Queens University; Belfast

VADIVELOO, J. and HOLMES, W. (1979). *Journal of Agricultural Science (Cambridge)*, **93**, 553–562

VALENTINE, S.C. and BROWN, D.C. (1973). *Australian Journal of Agricultural Research*, **24**, 939–946

WAITE, R., JOHNSTON, M.J. and ARMSTRONG, D.G. (1964). *Journal of Agricultural Science (Cambridge)*, **62**, 391–398

WALDO, D.R. (1978). In *Fermentation of Silage—A Review*, pp. 117–179. Ed. M.E. McCullough. National Feed Ingredients Association; Iowa

WATSON, S.J. and NASH, M.J. (1960). *The Conservation of Grass and Forage Crops*. Oliver and Boyd; Edinburgh

WEISSBACH, F., SCHMIDT, L. and HEIN, E. (1974). *Proceedings of the 12th International Grassland Congress*, pp. 226–236

WILKINS, R.J. (1984). *Landbauforschung Volkenrode, Sonderheft*, **69**, pp. 5–12

WILKINS, R.J., FENLON, J.S., COOK, J.E. and WILSON, R.F. (1978). *Proceedings of the 5th Silage Conference*, pp. 34–35

WILKINS, R.J., HUTCHINSON, K.J., WILSON, R.F. and HARRIS, C.E. (1971). *Journal of Agricultural Science (Cambridge)*, **77**, 531–537

WILKINS, R.J., WILSON, R.F. and COOK, J.E. (1974). *Proceedings of the 12th International Grassland Congress*, p. 675

WILKINSON, J.M., CHAPMAN, P.F., WILKINS, R.J. and WILSON, R.F. (1983). *Proceedings of the 14th International Grassland Congress*, pp. 631–634

WILSON, R.F. and WILKINS, R.J. (1978). *Journal of Agricultural Science (Cambridge)*, **91**, 23–29

WILSON, R.F., WOOLFORD, M.K., COOK, J.E. and WILKINSON, J.M. (1979). *Journal of Agricultural Science (Cambridge)*, **92**, 409–415

WOOLFORD, M.K. (1975). *Journal of the Science of Food and Agriculture*, **26**, 219–228

WOOLFORD, M.K. (1984). *The Silage Fermentation*. Marcel Dekker; New York

WOOLFORD, M.K. and SAWCZYC, M.K. (1984a). *Grass and Forage Science*, **39**, 139–148

WOOLFORD, M.K. and SAWCZYC, M.K. (1984b). *Grass and Forage Science*, **39**, 149–158

14

AMINO ACID REQUIREMENTS OF RUMINANTS

P.J. BUTTERY *and* A.N. FOULDS
University of Nottingham School of Agriculture, Sutton Bonington, UK

Introduction

The protein metabolism of ruminant tissues is not fundamentally different from that of the non-ruminant and so it follows that there is unlikely to be anything markedly different in their amino acid requirements. Recently, considerable attention has been given to the protein requirements of ruminants, but it has not been possible to define accurately the requirements for particular amino acids. The main problem comes from the very difficult task of predicting the extent of degradation of dietary protein in the ruminant and the yield of microbial protein that will flow from the rumen. In this chapter no attempt is made to discuss the protein requirements of ruminants *per se*; for this the reader is referred to ARC (1984). Instead an attempt will be made to discuss the current information on the needs of the ruminant for specific amino acids for maintenance and the production of milk and tissue proteins. In addition, some possible effects of dietary amino acids on the efficiency of rumen function will be discussed. Accepting that under many conditions the flow of amino acids from the rumen may not be ideal for maximum production, there are several possible ways by which the deficit may be corrected, for example, by feeding protein that is not degraded in the rumen, by feeding protected amino acids or in the longer term by genetically manipulating the animal itself.

Essential amino acids for ruminants

Early workers assumed that the essential amino acids for the ruminant were similar to those of the non-ruminant. Black *et al.* (1957) and Downes (1961) administered ^{14}C-acetate to cows and ewes respectively and recovered only trace amounts of label in threonine, valine, methionine, isoleucine, leucine, phenylalanine and lysine while the so-called non-essential amino acids were extensively labelled. Such an approach to estimating essential amino acid requirements has drawbacks. For example, it does not suggest that cyst(e)ine is an essential amino acid or that the synthesis of arginine in the animal may not always be adequate, nor does it take into account isotope exchange reactions. Despite these problems, such experiments do indicate that guidelines drawn from the many studies on non-ruminant species

Table 14.1   AMINO ACID REQUIREMENTS OF ANIMALS—SOME GENERALIZATIONS

Not generally synthesized	Synthesized from essential amino acids	Usually non-essential but some animals have a requirement
Lysine	Tyrosine (from phenylalanine if hydroxylase present)	Arginine (if urea cycle absent or often in rapidly growing ureotelic animals)
Histidine		
Leucine	Cystine (from methionine if active trans-sulphuration present)	Glycine (often in uricotelic species) Proline (if conversion from glutamate deficient)
Valine		
Methionine		
Threonine		
Tryptophan		
Phenylalanine		
Other amino acids may be required in restricted cases		

Taken from Buttery (1978)

are of use in the present context. From a survey of many reports on the amino acid requirements of a wide range of animals some generalizations may be drawn and these are presented in *Table 14.1* (Buttery, 1978). Two points arising from these generalizations which are discussed later are, do ruminants effectively convert methionine to cysteine and is there a need to consider the arginine requirement?

Examination of the few reports on amino acid metabolism specifically in ruminant tissues would indicate that the more detailed information on the utilization of D-isomers of amino acids by chicks (see for example Boorman and Lewis, 1971) can be applied to the ruminant.

Factorial assessment of amino acid requirements

Examination of the suggested responses of the non-ruminant farm species, e.g. the pig, to changes in amino acid supply gives some confidence that there is a useful

Table 14.2   A COMPARISON OF THE ESSENTIAL AMINO ACID COMPOSITION OF MILK PROTEIN, CALF CARCASS AND THAT NORMALLY FOUND IN DUODENAL DIGESTA. (ALL VALUES ARE g INDIVIDUAL AMINO ACID/g TOTAL COMPLEMENT ESSENTIAL AMINO ACIDS)

	Duodenal digesta	Calf whole body	Cows' milk
Leucine	0.16	0.19	0.19
Isoleucine	0.10	0.08	0.11
Valine	0.12	0.11	0.13
Threonine	0.12	0.11	0.09
Lysine	0.15	0.18	0.15
Tryptophan	0.03	0.02	0.03
Histidine	0.04	0.07	0.05
Methionine	0.05	0.05	0.05
Total sulphur amino acids	0.08	0.08	0.07
Phenylalanine	0.11	0.10	0.10
Total aromatic amino acids	0.19	0.17	0.19
Essential/total amino acid	0.48	0.38	0.53

The amino acid composition of duodenal digesta presented is the mean of several reports in the literature. See ARC (1984) from which this table was adapted for further details.

correlation between the amino acid composition of the protein making up the major components of the intended productive process and the amino acid composition of the ideal diet. *Table 14.2* presents a similar exercise for the ruminant, and indicates that there is a close correlation between the amino acid composition of duodenal digesta, calf carcass and milk protein, at least when the comparisons are limited to essential amino acids. Possibly milk protein and calf whole body have more leucine, and the calf whole body has more lysine than duodenal digesta. Milk does, however, have a greater total concentration of essential amino acids than the duodenal digesta. This observation prompted the ARC (1984) to suggest that the total essential/total non-essential amino acid ratio of the digesta should be considered in calculating the protein requirements of the lactating cow. Obviously for this approach to work, care must be taken to ensure that the amino acid composition of any undegraded protein source is not deficient in any essential amino acids. In the wool producing sheep there is evidence for a deficiency of the sulphur amino acids, although this is not always apparent for other ruminants. Despite this, there is a general belief that under many conditions methionine is the first limiting amino acid. Indeed other methods to factorially estimate amino acid requirements have implicated the sulphur amino acids as first limiting (see for example Hutton and Annison, 1972). Calculating amino acid requirements using the factorial approach does, however, need consideration of other factors other than the gross amino acid composition of the relevant fractions. The efficiency of absorption of amino acids from the intestine, the net loss of endogenous amino acids from the gut, the efficiency with which an amino acid is incorporated into tissue and the extent of the obligatory catabolism of amino acids by the animal are all important. This whole area has recently been reviewed by several authors (Oldham, 1984; ARC, 1984).

It has been suggested that amino acid requirements may be influenced by the rate of protein turnover (ARC, 1984). Changes in protein turnover rate are noted when, for example, animals are treated with anabolic agents (Sinnett-Smith, Dumelow and Buttery, 1983). However, such an effect on amino acid requirements seems unlikely, at least when considering the requirement for a given gain, since the rate of catabolism of an amino acid from the free amino acid pool is dependent upon its concentration in the pool, rather than the number of times an amino acid passes through the pool.

Amino acid profile of duodenal digesta

Three types of micro-organisms live in the rumen—bacteria, protozoa and fungi. Nevertheless, the gross amino acid composition of the microbial fraction entering the duodenum is not markedly influenced by the diet of the animal (Klooster and Boekholt, 1972; Harrison *et al.*, 1973). Bacteria make up the major component of this fraction and even changes in the ratios of individual species of bacteria are unlikely to influence the amino acid profile of the combined bacterial fraction (Clarke, Ellinger and Phillipson, 1966; Purser and Buechler, 1966). The amino acid composition of different strains of protozoa does differ but this is thought to be of little significance (Purser, 1970). Although Fenderson and Bergen (1972) did obtain evidence for changes in the tryptophan content of the protozoal fraction, this also may be of little significance. While the amino acid composition of either the protozoal fraction or the bacterial fraction is unlikely to differ much with variation

Table 14.3   THE AMINO ACID COMPOSITION OF BACTERIAL AND PROTOZOAL
PROTEIN ISOLATED FROM THE RUMEN OF SHEEP

	Bacterial protein (g AA/16 g N)	*Protozoal protein* (g AA/16 g N)
Threonine	5.37 ± 0.39	5.07 ± 0.48
Valine	5.49 ± 0.35	5.24 ± 0.60
Isoleucine	4.68 ± 0.20	5.80 ± 0.54
Leucine	6.47 ± 0.30	7.18 ± 0.66
Phenylalanine	3.98 ± 0.18	5.29 ± 0.51
Histidine	1.49 ± 0.11	1.79 ± 0.15
Lysine	6.99 ± 0.37	10.14 ± 0.60
Arginine	4.09 ± 0.25	4.58 ± 0.31
Methionine	1.78 ± 0.09	1.65 ± 0.16
Aspartic acid	12.10 ± 0.56	12.62 ± 1.24
Serine	4.24 ± 0.23	4.10 ± 0.37
Glutamic acid	11.98 ± 0.59	13.81 ± 1.62
Glycine	4.85 ± 0.34	3.61 ± 0.46
Alanine	6.12 ± 0.37	3.48 ± 0.40
Tyrosine	3.90 ± 0.19	4.49 ± 0.48

Data from Ling (1976). Mean of ten observations ± SEM

in the diet, there are marked differences in the composition of bacterial and protozoal protein (*Table 14.3*). The differences in the proportions of lysine (higher in protozoa) and methionine (higher in bacteria) are potentially of significance.

The flow of protozoa from the rumen is less than would be expected from the protozoal biomass in the rumen. The literature presents a wide range of values for the proportion of the duodenal protein which is of protozoal origin.

Recently there has been an increased awareness of the significance of the anaerobic fungi that are found in the rumen. These have the ability to initiate the fermentation of lignified tissue. Some of these fungi have been shown to have a requirement for methionine (Gordon and Ashes, 1984). However, it is unlikely that fungi are of major metabolic significance in the rumen, except in animals fed high fibre diets (Bauchop, 1984). No information is available on the contribution of fungi to microbial protein flow from the rumen.

MacRae (1980) examined the variation in amino acid composition of duodenal digesta in animals either fed roughage plus urea or fed unprotected casein, soya bean meal or rapeseed meal and showed that coefficients of variation were very small. With the protein supplements, which all caused an increased production response, methionine was the only amino acid whose concentration was raised relative to lysine, the reference amino acid they selected. Other reports in the literature also support the suggestion that the composition of duodenal digesta is relatively constant (Mercer, Allen and Miller, 1980; Thomas *et al.*, 1980). If it is accepted that the composition of the microbial fraction is constant, then the composition of any undegraded dietary protein must be markedly different from that of the microbial fraction to have any significant effect on the composition of the total flow because on most diets undegraded dietary protein contributes so little to the total protein flow from the rumen.

The nutritive value of rumen micro-organisms in ruminants

Under most dietary conditions, microbial protein synthesized in the forestomach of the ruminant accounts for 60–85 per cent of the total amino acid nitrogen entering the small intestine. It is therefore desirable to estimate accurately the nutritive value of this fraction. Most studies have been hampered by the difficulties of obtaining large quantities of rumen micro-organisms, and consequently most workers have had to resort to the use of the rat as the test animal. An advance was made when Storm and Orskov (1983) isolated large quantities of rumen micro-organisms from slaughterhouse material. Storm, Orskov and Smart (1983) infused varying amounts of rumen micro-organisms into the abomasum of lambs maintained by intragastric infusions of volatile fatty acids and minerals. The conclusion from their studies on 18 sheep was that the true digestibility of rumen micro-organism nitrogen was 0.81, and the absorbed nitrogen from rumen micro-organisms is used with an efficiency of 0.67.

An extension of these studies also enabled the true digestibility in the small intestine of the individual amino acids in the rumen micro-organism fraction to be determined. Most amino acids have a true digestibility of between 0.80 and 0.88, but those of cyst(e)ine and histidine were much lower at 0.73 and 0.68 respectively (Storm, Brown and Orskov, 1983). Cyst(e)ine showed a higher endogenous input which may have biased the result if endogenous secretions are not constant following increased dietary protein, but nevertheless this finding suggests that it is essential to check the efficiency of conversion of methionine to cysteine in ruminant tissues.

The power of the technique developed by Storm and Orskov (1983) is further illustrated by their report in which amino acids in rumen micro-organisms were limiting to the nitrogen retention in lambs (Storm and Orskov, 1984). Their data indicated that methionine was the first limiting amino acid and that lysine was probably the next limiting. Some evidence for these being positive responses to increasing the histidine and arginine supply were also obtained. Bergen, Purser and Cline (1968) had previously indicated that histidine could sometimes be limiting. Arginine had also been implicated by Tao, Asplund and Kappel (1974). Presumably, although the ruminant is able to synthesize large quantities of arginine in the liver as part of the urea cycle, it does not reach the blood stream in sufficient quantities to meet the needs of other tissues. It therefore seems proper to conclude that the ruminant does need a 'dietary' supply of arginine.

Amino acids limiting milk production

As mentioned above, comparison of the duodenal flow of amino acids with the composition of milk protein suggests that the major deficiency is likely to be the total supply of essential amino acids. It is possible that with most diets no particular amino acid is first limiting. This is borne out by several pieces of experimental data, one of which is summarized in *Table 14.4* and shows that, although no effect was seen on addition of methionine, some effect was seen when lysine was added as well. Further addition of other amino acids also showed some responses.

Despite the difficulty of being able to obtained definitive responses to individual amino acids in the lactating dairy cow, there is no doubt that increasing the protein supply at the duodenum will induce a production response (Clark, 1975; Orskov, Grubb and Kay, 1977; Konig, Oldham and Parker, 1984). One case where there may well be a predictable methionine deficiency in cattle is when they are fed silage. In this case there is a relatively inefficient microbial protein synthesis coupled with a diet which is relatively low in methionine (Thomas *et al.*, 1980;

Table 14.4   THE EFFECT OF AMINO ACID ADDITION TO THE ABOMASUM ON MILK PRODUCTION IN THE DAIRY COW

	Amino acid additions							*Basal*
Methionine	+	+	+	+	+	+	+	
Lysine	+	+	+	+	+	+		
Valine	+	+	+	+	+			
Isoleucine	+	+	+	+				
Leucine	+	+	+					
Histidine	+	+	+					
Threonine	+	+						
Phenylalanine	+	+						
Tryptophan	+							
Arginine	+							
Total milk (kg/day)	24.6	24.9	23.9	23.8	23.6	23.0	23.0	23.3
Milk crude protein output (g/day)	748	749	704	719	695	688	649	622

Holstein cattle were fed a grain hay diet and amino acids were added to the abomasum (Schwab, Satter and Clay, 1976).

Chamberlain and Thomas, 1982). Often, however, methionine and lysine are co-limiting on silage based diets (see Thomas *et al.*, 1980).

Direct measurements of amino acid requirements of ruminants

There have been comparatively few studies where the requirements for specific amino acids in cattle have been reported. A selection of those in the literature is given for the beef animal in *Table 14.5* and for the dairy cow in *Table 14.6*. Data for the sheep are also given in *Table 14.7*. The majority of the estimates have been obtained using indirect measurements of requirement.

There are a few reports where direct responses of wool growth, and growth rate of lambs or cattle to increased amino acid supply have been described. Direct dose response data for milk production in dairy cattle are much rarer. The data available are normally applicable to one production level only (growth rate or milk production). In most cases the techniques employed involve some surgical modification of the animal, and this procedure must cast some doubt on the validity of the results obtained. Often the data in the literature only give the extra amino acid needed to be added to the duodenum or abomasum to meet the requirement of the animal, with no information on the basal supply of the amino acid. However, in a few cases the total supply of amino acids is given or can be calculated. In those few cases where this can be done for the methionine requirement of the growing steer (see *Table 14.5*) there is some encouraging consistency about the results. Interestingly, the estimated requirements are very close to those calculated from the relatively crude factorial approach of Hutton and Annison (1972). What is clear is that there are not sufficient production response data to be able to give precise information as to the effects of increasing individual amino acid supply.

Cysteine production from methionine

The trans-sulphuration pathway is responsible for converting methionine to cysteine, and is found to be active in the liver and in muscle (Radcliffe and Eagan,

Table 14.5 REQUIREMENTS FOR INDIVIDUAL AMINO ACIDS—STEERS AND BULLS

Body weight (kg) and animal type	Gain (kg/day)	Diet	Comments on feeding and method employed to establish a response	Amino acid (g/kg$^{0.75}$/day)				Reference
				Met	Thr	Lys	Ile	
90–170 bull calves	0.50	57 g DM/kg$^{0.75}$/day + AA 275 mg/kg$^{0.75}$/day into duodenum	Plasma AA	+ 0.10	—	—	—	Mathers and Miller (1979)
270–455 steers	—	Corn + barley straw (CP 12.5%) 6.5 kg/day	Continuous feeding, plasma AA	—	—	+ 0.073 + 0.110	—	Boila and Devlin (1972)
350–400 steers	0.83	Hay roughage + urea (CP 12%) 7.8–12.9 kg/day	2 × day feeding N balance	+ 0.35	—	—	—	Steinacker et al. (1970)
230 steers	Growing	Corn, cottonmeal hull, urea	2 × day feeding N balance	—	—	+ 0.41	—	Hill, Bolling and Bradley (1980)
200 steers	1.0	—	Factorial	T 0.24 T Leu 0.29 T Val 0.16	T 0.21	T 0.25	T 0.18	Hutton and Annison (1972) modified by Williams (1978)
110–160 steers	0.40	Straw + concentrates	2 × day feeding	T 0.25	—	T 0.48	—	Williams and Smith (1974)
270 steers	0.52	Semi-purified (CP 9.5%)	Plasma AA / Intraperitoneal AA infusion, plasma AA	T 0.19 T 0.17	—	—	—	See Owens and Bergen (1983)
353 steers	0.30	Semi-purified (CP 9.5%)	Intraperitoneal AA infusion, plasma AA	T 0.18	—	—	—	See Owens and Bergen (1983)
274 steers	0.73	Corn, oats and Corn cobs (CP 9.5%) 8 kg/day	2 × day feeding, plasma AA	T 0.22	T 0.22	T 0.33	Tryp. T 0.05	Fenderson and Bergen (1975)
211 steers	0.64	Mollased sugarbeet pulp + urea (CP 11.4%)	plasma AA	T 0.40	—	T 0.80	0.38	Foulds and Buttery (unpublished)

Unless otherwise stated amino acids were infused into the gut postruminally.

T = Total flow of amino acids into duodenum needed to meet requirement.

+ = data are only given for the amount of amino acid added to the digesta which meets the requirement.

Table 14.6   DIRECT ESTIMATES OF AMINO ACID 'REQUIREMENTS'—DAIRY CATTLE

Diet	Comments	Amino acid supplement			App. milk	Milk protein	Reference
		Met	Lys (g/day)	His	yield (kg/day)	(%)	
Corn silage/ ground shellcorn/ urea	Increases in milk yield and milk protein	11.2	33.5	—	16.6	3.21	
	Increase in milk yield	—	—	50.3			Fisher (1972) (2)
	Increase in milk protein						
Corn/oats/hay 2 × day feeding	Lysine increased milk yield and milk protein dual infusion with methionine increased with protein	11.3	27.8	—	29.4	3.01	Schwab, Satter and Clay (1976) (1)
Silage *ad libitum*	Increased milk protein	12.0	—	—	5.2	3.29	Rogers, Bryant and McLeay (1979) (1)
Silage to est. requirement	Increased milk fat and yield	8.0	—	—	15.68	5.05	Chamberlain and Thomas (1982) (2)

(1) Supplements administered postruminally
(2) Supplements administered intravenously
Data were not given for the total flow of amino acids entering the duodenum. Figures given, therefore, relate to the supplementary amount of amino acids needed to meet the requirement.

1978; Downes, Sharry and Till, 1964). The catabolism of methionine can take place by an alternative route employing transamination followed by oxidation, but this route does not produce methionine (Steele and Benevenga, 1978). The relative importance of these two pathways in ruminants does not seem to have been much investigated. Infusion of methionine postruminally, while elevating plasma methionine concentrations, does not significantly elevate plasma cyst(e)ine concentrations and this has induced some speculation as to the efficiency of conversion of methionine to cysteine (Reis, Tunks and Sharry, 1973; Radcliffe and Eagan, 1978). The conversion of methionine to cysteine in cattle and sheep has recently been directly estimated using isotope dilution studies employing ^{35}S-methionine and cysteine (Buttery *et al.*, 1984; Pisulewski and Buttery, 1985). Hereford × Friesian steers were fed a sugar beet pulp–urea diet and ^{35}S-methionine was infused into the jugular vein continuously for 8 h and the specific activity of the plasma methionine and cysteine monitored. Subsequently, a continuous infusion of ^{35}S-cysteine was undertaken to measure the flux of cysteine through the plasma pool. From these data it was concluded that 1.3 g of cysteine originated from methionine and subsequently equilibrated with the plasma pool. The total uptake of cysteine from the gut was estimated to be 5 g/day and that of methionine to be 6.75 g/day. The proportion by weight of the methionine uptake being converted to cysteine was therefore 0.24.

These data do not enable a judgement of the potential of the ruminant to convert additional methionine to cysteine. Unfortunately there are no studies investigating this in cattle. Recently the conversion of methionine to cysteine in sheep was monitored as the methionine supply to the duodenum was increased. Besides studying the incorporation of ^{35}S from methionine into plasma cysteine, the conversion into cysteine in the wool and plasma albumin was also investigated

(Pisulewski and Buttery, 1985). Wool obviously obtains its nutrients from the skin while plasma albumin is synthesized in the liver, but both tissues have the trans-sulphuration pathway. The data in *Table 14.8* clearly indicate the ability of the sheep to convert methionine to cysteine and that the capacity of the pathway was not exceeded until 3 g of additional methionine were given. From these data it is possible to conclude that, while there is some indication of a finite capacity for the ruminant to convert methionine to cysteine, it would be realistic to assume that supplementing an active rumen fermentation with protected methionine will meet any additional cysteine as well as methionine needs.

Protecting amino acids from degradation

Three main methods are available for protecting amino acids from degradation in the rumen. Firstly, the amino acid can be modified either by blocking the amino group (e.g. *N*-stearoyl-methionine, Langar, Buttery and Lewis, 1978; *N*-hydroxymethyl-D,L-methionine calcium, Kenna and Schwab, 1981; Buttery, Manomai-Udom and Lewis, 1977) or by blocking the carboxyl group via the formation of an ester (e.g. the methyl or ethyl esters of methionine, Ferguson, 1975; Ayoade, Buttery and Lewis, 1982), or by making an analogue which has a reduced rate of degradation in the rumen (e.g. methionine hydroxy analogue, Belasco, 1972). With protected amino acids it is essential that the compound be readily converted to the parent amino acid, either postruminally due to pH changes in the abomasum or duodenum (e.g. hydroxymethylmethionine) or by the action of the enzymes of the duodenum (e.g. *N*-stearoyl methionine, Langar, Buttery and Lewis, 1978) or alternatively after absorption by the tissues of the animal (e.g. amination in the case of methionine hydroxy analogue, Belasco, 1972) or hydrolysed as in the case of the methionine esters which are probably absorbed directly from the rumen (Ayoade, Buttery and Lewis, 1982). The second approach is to encapsulate the amino acid in a material which resists rumen fermentation but is readily broken down or modified so that the amino acid is released after leaving the rumen. Several encapsulating materials have been used or suggested, such as lipids (Neudoerffer, Duncan and Horney, 1971; Grass and Unangst, 1972), cellulose and its derivations (Wu, Danelly and Komarek, 1981) or the pH sensitive co-polymer prepared from styrene and 2-methyl-5-vinylpyridine (see Papas, Sniffen and Muscata, 1984). An entirely different approach is to attempt to inhibit the deamination activity of the rumen micro-organisms (see for example Schelling, Mitchell and Tucker, 1972; Chalupa, 1975). Some amino acids, especially methionine, are resistant to ruminal degradation, such that even when fed orally they increase the methionine supply to the animal (Doyle and Bird, 1975).

Although the majority of studies have concentrated on methionine, some have used protected lysine (Kenna and Schwab, 1981). The methods used for protecting these amino acids can for the most part be adapted for any amino acid.

Responses to feeding protected methionine

There have been numerous reports on the effects of feeding protected methionine on milk production in the dairy cow and growth rate in the beef animal. Many of the results obtained were summarized by Kauffman and Lupping (1982). The

Table 14.7 REQUIREMENTS FOR INDIVIDUAL AMINO ACIDS—SHEEP

Body weight (kg)	Production status of animal	Diet	Comments on feeding and method employed to establish a response	Amino acid (g/kg$^{0.75}$/day)				Reference
				Met	*Thr*	*Lys*	*Leu*	
25	Growing	Corn starch, cellulose, urea, 1 kg/day	3 × day feeding plasma AA and N retention—both methods agreed except for met—N retention data given	+ 0.063	+ 0.063	+ 0.090	—	Nimrick et al. (1970)
32	Growing (ewe)	Hay 0.8 kg/day barley 0.33 kg/day	2 × day feeding, plasma AA	+ 0.186	—	—	—	Strath and Shelford (1978)
30–45	Rapid growth	Corn + ground legume hay (11.6–14.6% CP), 1 kg/day	2 × day feeding, N retention	+ 0.198	—	—	—	Schelling, Chandler and Scott (1973)
40?	Maintenance	Wheaten and lucerne hay, 0.8 kg/day	1 × day feeding, plasma AA	+ 0.63	—	—	—	Reis and Tunks (1971)
40?	Maintenance	Wheaten and lucerne hay, 0.8 kg/day	1 × day feeding 8 × day feeding amalgamated, plasma AA	+ 0.207	—	—	—	Reis, Tunks and Sharry (1973)
50	Maintenance	Semi-purified + groundnut, 42% of body wt	Plasma AA, 36 h infusion of AA, continuous feeding	T 0.105 to 0.125	T 0.310 to 0.340	T 0.545	—	Wakeling (1970)
40	Maintenance	Semi-purified + groundnut, 42% of body wt$^{0.73}$	Plasma AA and Thr. and Met. confirmed with $^{14}CO_2$ excretion, continuous feeding	T 0.125 to 0.158	T 0.260 to 0.340	—	—	Wakeling (1970)

No.	Level	Treatment	Method					Reference
44	Maintenance	50 g AA/day i.v. + VFAs in rumen	Plasma urea N and urinary nitrogen	* 0.116	—	—	—	Tao et al. (1972)
57	Maintenance	45 g AA mixture/d i.v., no cys. + VFAs in rumen	N balance, plasma urea, urinary urea excretion	* 0.230 to 0.239	—	—	—	Tao, Asplund and Kappel (1974)
36	Maintenance	46 g AA/day, i.v. + VFAs in rumen	Plasma AA N balance	* 0.174 —	— —	— —	* 0.272 to 0.408 —	Jensen and Aspland (1979)
38	Maintenance	49 g AA/d, i.v. + VFAs in rumen	Plasma AA Plasma AA	*Val 0.20 —	— —	— —	— * 0.544	Mesbah and Aspland (1984)
45	Growing	Corn + alfalfa hay, 0.9 kg/day 8% CP	$^{14}CO_2$ excretion, 2 × day feeding Plasma AA	— —	— —	+0.121 +0.138	— —	Brookes et al. (1983)
25	Growing 0.15 kg/day	Barley + straw, 0.71 kg/day 15% CP	^{35}S excretion Plasma urea	T 0.125 T 0.143	— —	— —	— —	Mercer and Miller (1973)

Unless otherwise stated amino acids were infused into the gut postruminally.

T indicates the total flow of amino acids into the duodenum which meet the requirement.

+ , * , indicate that data are only given for the amount of amino acid that was added to the duodenal digesta (+) or blood (*) to meet the requirements.

Table 14.8   THE EFFECT OF INCREASING METHIONINE SUPPLY ON THE
PERCENTAGE OF CYSTEINE COMING FROM METHIONINE IN SHEEP

Methionine infused into duodenum (g/day)	Plasma cysteine	Wool cysteine	Plasma albumen cysteine
0	4.5	67.2	14.8
1	5.8	—	16.5
2	8.2	67.0	42.7
3	13.7	55.0	50.9
4	13.0	—	50.1
5	18.5	81.6	44.6

See Pisulewski and Buttery (1985) for details of experimental technique.

majority of the reports do show some positive response, although there are some which show little or no effect. There may be two reasons for this. Firstly, the animal may not be in a situation where methionine is the sole first limiting amino acid. In this case an increase in milk fat is sometimes seen (for example the infusion experiments of Chamberlain and Thomas, 1982). Alternatively some of the derivatives may have been broken down in the diet before reaching the rumen. Some protected methionine derivatives work because they are stable at the pHs found in the rumen, but break down under the acid condition typical of the abomasum. Kenna and Schwab (1981) accepted that methionine and lysine are often co-limiting in dairy rations, and therefore included both hydroxy methylmethionine and hydroxy methyl-lysine in the diet but obtained no positive response. One possible explanation for this is that the acidity of the corn silage diet used caused the derivatives to breakdown prior to being ingested.

The overall conclusion is that there are circumstances where protected methionine may increase milk protein yield (e.g. on silage based diets) but even if this response is not seen they often induce an increase in milk fat. The response seen with beef animals is more variable. These observations are in direct contrast to the wool producing sheep where dramatic responses in wool growth to protected methionine derivatives are seen (see Ferguson, 1975).

Responses of rumen micro-organisms to amino acids

While rumen bacteria are able to use ammonia as a major source of nitrogen, various requirements for preformed amino acids have been established (see Smith, 1979). Additions of small amounts of amino acids have been shown to increase microbial protein yield, at least *in vitro* (Meang and Baldwin, 1976), but it has been difficult to demonstrate a response *in vivo* with the substitution of protein sources for urea plus energy (Kropp *et al.*, 1972). The branched chain fatty acids :isovaleric, isobutyric and 2-methyl butyric acid) and the straight chain amino valeric acid are produced in the rumen from leucine, valine, isoleucine and proline. These compounds may stimulate cellulolytic bacteria. When added to the diet of dairy cows fed corn silage *ad libitum* plus a urea–mineral mix and a supplement based on corn grain and corn gluten meal fed according to milk production, the iso acid mixture increased milk yield, 4 per cent fat corrected-milk yield, milk protein and total solids (Papas *et al.*, 1984). These authors suggested that some of this response may have been due to factors other than increased rumen function, but it is most difficult to propose a detailed mechanism.

The increases in fat content of milk from cows given methionine hydroxy analogue (Griel *et al.*, 1968; Whitting *et al.*, 1972) may well be due to altered synthesis of lipid in the rumen; similar responses have been noted with methionine (Remond *et al.*, 1971; Patton, McCarthy and Griel, 1970). Alteration of rumen function, however, may not be the whole story; Chamberlain and Thomas (1982) observed responses when the methionine was given intravenously. Langar, Buttery and Lewis (1978) were unable to detect methionine hydroxy analogue in the duodenum of sheep given the material orally and this coupled with the effects of the compound on milk lipids does cast some doubt as to whether the main function of the compound is as a protected methionine derivative.

As mentioned above the fungi in the rumen may have a methionine requirement, and hence fibre digestion may be stimulated by supplying extra methionine to the rumen.

Conclusions

The effective use of knowledge of the amino acid requirements of ruminants requires the ability to determine precisely the amino acid flow from the rumen. The technology is available to determine accurately the requirements of the ruminant for a particular function, but the experimentation will be expensive. At present a refinement of previous factorial approaches may well provide data of the required precision.

References

ARC (1994). The Nutrient Requirements of Farm Livestock, supplement No. 1. Commonwealth Agricultural Bureau; Slough

AYOADE, J., BUTTERY, P.J. and LEWIS, D. (1982). *Journal of the Science of Food and Agriculture,* **33**, 949

BAUCHOP, T. (1984). *Proceedings of the Nutrition Society of Australia,* **9**, 45

BELASCO, I.J. (1972). *Journal of Dairy Science,* **55**, 353

BERGEN, W.G., PURSER, D.B. and CLINE, J.H. (1968). *Journal of Dairy Science,* **51**, 1698

BLACK, A.L., KLEIBER, M., SMITH, A.H. and STEWART, P.N. (1957). *Biochimica Biophysica Acta,* **23**, 54

BOORMAN, K.N. and LEWIS, D. (1971). In *Physiology of the Domestic Fowl*, Vol. 1. pp. 339–372. Eds Bell and Freeman. Academic Press; London

BOILA, R.J. and DEVLIN, T.J. (1972). *Canadian Journal of Animal Science,* **52**, 681

BROOKES, I.M., OWENS, F.N., BROWN, R.E. and GARRIGUS, A.S. (1973). *Journal of Animal Science,* **36**, 965

BUTTERY, P.J. (1978). In *Comparative Animal Nutrition*, Vol. 13. pp. 34–79. Ed. M. Rechigl. S. Karger; Basel

BUTTERY, P.J., ESSEX, C., FOULDS, A.N. and SOAR, J.B. (1984). *Proceedings of the Nutrition Society,* **43**, 56

BUTTERY, P.J., MANOMAI-UDOM, S. and LEWIS, D. (1977). *Journal of the Science of Food and Agriculture,* **28**, 481

CHALUPA, W. (1975). *Journal of Dairy Science,* **58**, 1198

CHAMBERLAIN, D.G. and THOMAS, P.C. (1982). *Journal of Dairy Research,* **49**, 25

CLARK, J.H. (1975). *Journal of Dairy Science,* **58,** 1178

CLARKE, E., ELLINGER, G.H. and PHILLIPSON, A.T. (1966). *Proceedings of the Royal Society,* **166,** 63

DOWNES, A.M. (1961). *Australian Journal of Biological Science,* **14,** 254

DOWNES, A.M., SHARRY, L.F. and TILL, A.R. (1964). *Australian Journal of Biological Science,* **17,** 945

DOYLE, P.T. and BIRD, P.R. (1975). *Australian Journal of Agricultural Research,* **26,** 337

FENDERSON, C.L. and BERGEN, W.G. (1972). *Journal of Animal Science,* **35,** 896

FENDERSON, C.L. and BERGEN, W.G. (1975). *Journal of Animal Science,* **41,** 1759

FERGUSON, K.A. (1975). In *Digestion and Metabolism of the Ruminant,* pp. 448–464. Eds I.W. McDonald and A.C.I. Warner, Univ New England; Armidale, Australia

FISHER, L.J. (1972). *Canadian Journal of Animal Science,* **52,** 377

GORDON, G.L.R. and ASHES, J.R. (1984). *Canadian Journal of Animal Science,* **64** (suppl.), 156

GRASS, G.M. and UNANGST, R.R. (1972). USA patent 3655864

GRIEL, L.C., PATTON, R.A., MCCARTHY, R.D. and CHANDLER, X.X. (1968). *Journal of Dairy Science,* **51,** 1866

HARRISON, D.G., BEEVER, D.E., THOMSON, D.J. and OSBOURN, D.F. (1973). *Journal of Agricultural Science, Cambridge,* **81,** 391

HILL, G.M., BOLLING, J.A. and BRADLEY, N.W. (1980). *Journal of Dairy Science,* **63,** 1242

HUTTON, K. and ANNISON, E.F. (1972). *Proceedings of the Nutrition Society,* **31,** 151

JENSEN, D.O. and ASPLUND, J.M. (1979). *Nutrition Reports International,* **20,** 115

KAUFFMANN, W. and LUPPING, W. (1982). In *Protein Contribution of Feedstuffs for Ruminants,* pp. 36–75. Eds E.L. Miller, I.H. Pike and A.J.H. van Es. Butterworths; London

KENNA, T.M. and SCHWAB, C.G. (1981). *Journal of Dairy Science,* **64,** 775

KLOOSTER, A.T.V. and BOEKHOLT, A.A. (1972). *Netherlands Journal of Agricultural Science,* **20,** 272

KONIG, B.A., OLDHAM, J.D. and PARKER, C.G. (1984). *British Journal of Nutrition* (in press)

KROPP, J.R., JOHNSON, R.R., MALES, J.R. and OWENS, F.N. (1972). *Journal of Animal Science,* **46,** 837

LANGAR, P.N., BUTTERY, P.J. and LEWIS, D. (1978). *Journal of the Science of Food and Agriculture,* **28,** 808

LING, J.R. (1976). PhD Thesis University of Nottingham

MACRAE, J.C. (1980). In *Protein Deposition in Animals,* pp. 225–250. Ed. P.J. Buttery and D.B. Lindsay. Butterworths; London

MEANG, W.J. and BALDWIN, R.L. (1976). *Journal of Dairy Science,* **59,** 643

MATHERS, J.C. and MILLER, E.L. (1979). In *Protein Metabolism in the Ruminant,* pp. 3.1–3.11. Ed. P.J. Buttery. Agricultural Research Council; London

MERCER, J.R., ALLEN, S.A. and MILLER, E.L. (1980). *British Journal of Nutrition,* **43,** 421

MERCER, J.R. and MILLER, E.L. (1973). *Proceedings of the Nutrition Society,* **32,** 87A

MESBAH, M.M. and ASPLUND, J.M. (1984). *Journal of Nutrition,* **114,** 1363

NEUDOERFFER, T.S., DUNCAN, D.B. and HORNEY, F.D. (1971). *British Journal of Nutrition,* **25,** 343

NIMRICK, K., HATFIELD, E.E., KAMINSKI, J. and OWENS, F.M. (1970). *Journal of Nutrition,* **100,** 1301

OLDHAM, J.D. (1984). *Proceedings Cornell Nutrition Conference* (in press)
ORSKOV, E.R., GRUBB, D.A. and KAY, R.N.B. (1977). *British Journal of Nutrition,* **38**, 397
OWENS, F.N. and BERGEN, W.G. (1983). *Journal of Animal Science,* **57**, suppl 2, 498
PAPAS, A.M., AMES, S.R., COOK, R.M., SNIFFEN, C.J., POLAN, C.E. and CHAK, L. (1984). *Journal of Dairy Science,* **67**, 276
PAPAS, A.M., SNIFFEN, C.J. and MUSCATA, T.V. (1984). *Journal of Dairy Science,* **67**, 545
PATTON, R.A., MCCARTHY, R.D. and GRIEL, L.C. (1970). *Journal of Dairy Science,* **53**, 460
PISULEWSKI, P.M. and BUTTERY, P.J. (1985). *British Journal of Nutrition* (in press)
PURSER, D.B. (1970). *Journal of Animal Science,* **30**, 988
PURSER, D.B. and BUECHLER, S. (1966). *Journal of Dairy Science,* **49**, 81
RADCLIFFE, B.C. and EGAN, A.R. (1978). *Journal of Biological Science,* **31**, 105
REIS, P.J. and TUNKS, D.A. (1971). *Search,* **2**, 108
REIS, P.J., TUNKS, D.A. and SHARRY, L.F. (1973). *Australian Journal of Biological Science,* **26**, 635
REMOND, B., CHAMPREDON, L., DECAEN, C., PION, R. and JOURNET, M. (1971). *Annals of Biology of Animal Biochemistry and Biophysics,* **11**, 455
ROGERS, G.L., BRYANT, A.M. and MCLEAY, L.M. (1979). *New Zealand Journal of Agricultural Research,* **22**, 533
SCHELLING, G.T., CHANDLER, J.E. and SCOTT, G.C. (1973). *Journal of Animal Science,* **37**, 1035
SCHELLING, G.T., MITCHELL, G.E. and TUCKER, R.E. (1972). *Federation Proceedings,* **31**, Abst 2626
SCHWAB, C.G., SATTER, L.D. and CLAY, A.B. (1976). *Journal of Dairy Science,* **59**, 1251
SINNETT-SMITH, P.A., DUMELOW, N.W. and BUTTERY, P.J. (1983). *British Journal of Nutrition,* **50**, 225
SMITH, R.H. (1979). *Journal of Animal Science,* **49**, 1604
STEELE, R.D. and BENEVENGA, N.J. (1978). *Journal of Biological Chemistry,* **211**, 7844
STEINACKER, G., DEVLIN, T.J. and INGALLS, J.R. (1970). *Canadian Journal of Animal Science,* **50**, 319
STORM, E., BROWN, D.S. and ORSKOV, E.R. (1983). *British Journal of Nutrition,* **50**, 479
STORM, E. and ORSKOV, E.R. (1983). *British Journal of Nutrition,* **50**, 463
STORM, E. and ORSKOV, E.R. (1984). *British Journal of Nutrition,* **52**, 613
STORM, E., ORSKOV, E.R. and SMART, R.I. (1983). *British Journal of Nutrition,* **50**, 471
STRATH, R.A. and SHELFORD, J.A. (1978). *Canadian Journal of Animal Science,* **58**, 479
TAO, R.C., ASPLUND, J.M. and KAPPEL, L. (1974). *Journal of Nutrition,* **104**, 1646
TAO, R.C., ASPLUND, J.M., WOLFROM, G.W. and KAPPEL, L.C. (1972). *Journal of Animal Science,* **35**, 1135
THOMAS, P.C., CHAMBERLAIN, D.G., KELLY, N.C., and WAIT, M.K. (1980). *British Journal of Nutrition,* **43**, 469
WAKELING, A.E. (1970). PhD Thesis, University of Nottingham
WHITTING, F.M., STULL, J.W., BROWN, W.H. and REID, B.L. (1972). *Journal of Dairy Science,* **55**, 983
WILLIAMS, A.P. (1978). *Journal of Agricultural Science, Cambridge,* **90**, 617
WILLIAMS, A.P. and SMITH, R.H. (1974). *British Journal of Nutrition,* **32**, 421
WU, S., DANELLY, C.G. and KOMAREK, R.J. (1981). In *Controlled Release of Pesticides and Pharmaceuticals*, pp. 319–331. Plenum Press; New York

LIST OF PARTICIPANTS

The nineteenth Nutrition Conference was organized by the following programme committee:

L.G. Chubb
A.D. Howie (Midland Shires Farmers Ltd)
W.T. Jones (J. Bibby Agriculture Ltd)
P.W. Kenyon (Harbro Farm Sales)
M. Owers (BOCM Silcock Ltd)
F. Perry (BP Nutrition (UK) Ltd)
J.R. Pickford (Tecracon Ltd)
M. Putnam (Roche Products Ltd)
A.H. Shipstone (Dalgety Spillers Feeds Ltd)
M.H. Stranks (MAFF, London)
D. Wilby (W.F. Tuck & Son Ltd)

K.N. Boorman
P.J. Buttery
D.J.A. Cole (Chairman)
P.C. Garnsworthy   University of
W. Haresign (Secretary) Nottingham
G.E. Lamming
D. Lewis
J. Wiseman

The nineteenth conference was held at the School of Agriculture, Sutton Bonington, 6th–8th January 1985, and the committee would like to thank the various authors for their valuable contributions. The following persons registered for the meeting:

Adams, Dr C.A.	Kemin Europa N.V. Industriezone Wolfstee, 2410 Herentals, Belgium
Adams, Dr G.B.	Brewers Grains Marketing, Wetmore Road, Burton on Trent, Staffs
Adamson, Mr A.H.	ADAS, Government Buildings, Burghill Road, Westbury on Trym, Bristol BS10 6NJ
Ainsworth, Miss H.S.	Chief Scientists Group, Ministry of Agriculture, Fisheries & Food, Great Westminster House, Horseferry Road, London
Alderman, Mr G.	Hunter's Moon, Pearman's Glade, Shinfield Road, Shinfield, Reading, Berks
Allder, Mr M.	Smith Kline Animal Health Ltd, Cavendish Road, Stevenage, Herts
Allen, Mr J.	Fisons plc, Pharmaceutical Division, Fisons Animal Health, 12 Derby Road, Loughborough, Leics

Allen, Mr W.	David Patton Ltd, Milltown Mills, Monaghan, Ireland
Appleby, Mr G.	Elanco Products Ltd, Kingsclere Road, Basingstoke, Hants
Aspland, Mr F.P.	Aspland & James Ltd, 118 Bridge Street, Chatteris, Cambridgeshire
Ashington, Mr B.	Messrs Peter Hand (GB) Ltd, 15–19 Church Road, Stanmore, Middlesex
Atherton, Dr D.	Messrs J. Bibby Agriculture Ltd, Adderbury, Banbury, Oxon
Atkinson, Mr R.E.	NRS, 10 Gwentlands Close, Chepstow, Gwent NP6 5JH
Bailey, Mr D.I.	ABM Chemicals Ltd, Woodley, Stockport, Cheshire
Baird, Mr K.M.	Messrs Criddle Peters Feeds Ltd, Glazebury, Warrington, Cheshire
Baird, Mr R.S.	Harbro Farm Sales Ltd, 62–64 Fife Street, Turriff, Aberdeenshire AB5 7BQ
Barber, Dr G.	West of Scotland Agricultural College, Agricultural Chemistry Division, Ayr, Scotland
Barber, Mr W.P.	Ministry of Agriculture, Fisheries & Food, ADAS, Government Buildings, Kenton Bar, Newcastle upon Tyne NE1 2YA
Barnes, Mr W.J.	BP Nutrition (UK) Ltd, Wincham, Northwich, Cheshire CW9 6DF
Beardsmore, Mr A.	Imperial Chemical Industries plc, Agricultural Division, Biological Products Business, Billingham, Cleveland
Beaumont, Mr D.	BP Nutrition (UK) Ltd, Wincham, Northwich, Cheshire CW9 6DF
Beer, Mr J.H.	Messrs W. & J. Pye Ltd, Fleet Square, Lancaster LA1 1HA
Beevers, Miss J.A.	Midland Shires Farmers Ltd, Defford Mill, Earls Croome, Worcester
Bell, Dr B.	Feedex Q Feeds, Daisy Hill, Burstwick, North Humberside, HU17 9HE
Belyavin, Dr C.G.	Harper Adams Poultry Exp. Unit, Edgmond, Newport, Shropshire TF10 8HY
Berkouwer, Ir C.	Kloek B.V. Acliferstraat 5, 6668 AA Randwyk, The Netherlands
Bishop, Mr A.	Morning Foods Ltd, North Western Mills, Crewe CW2 6HP
Blake, Dr J.S.	BOCM Silcock Ltd, Basing View, Basingstoke, Hants
Boak, Mr W.	Carrs Farm Feeds Ltd, Stanwix, Carlisle, Cumbria
Bolton, Miss H.	Pauls Agriculture plc, Road 1, Industrial Estate, Winsford, Cheshire
Boorman, Dr K.N.	University of Nottingham, School of Agriculture, Sutton Bonington, Loughborough, Leics LE12 5RD
Booth, Miss A.	Page Feeds, Mill Lane, Tadcaster, N. Yorks
Brennan, Mr O.	C/o Wm. Connolly & Sons Ltd, Red Mills, Goresbridge, Co. Kilkenny
Brenninkmeijer, Dr C.	Hendrix Voeders B.V., Veerstraat 38, 5831 JN Boxmeer, Holland
Brett, Dr P.A.	North Western Farmers Ltd, The Mill, Wardle, Cheshire CW5 6BP
Brigstocke, Mr T.D.A.	BOCM Silcock Ltd, Mill Lane, Alton, Hampshire
Brooks, Dr P.	Seale-Hayne College, Newton Abbot, Devon TQ12 6NQ
Broom, Mr P.	French's (Feeds & Seeds) Ltd, Hennock Road, Marsh Barton, Exeter
Brosnan, Mr J.P.	Volac Limited, Orwell, Royston, Herts
Brown, Dr A.C.G.	MAFF, ADAS, Nutrition Chemist, Shardlow Hall, Shardlow, Derby
Brown, Mr M.	S.C. Associates Ltd, Melmerby Industrial Estate, Melmerby, Ripon, Yorks
Brunnen, Miss J.M.	Feed Evaluation Unit, Drayton Manbor Drive, Alcester Road, Stratford upon Avon, Warks

Buchanan, Ms A.G.	Elanco Products Ltd, Kingsclere Road, Basingstoke, Hants
Burke, Mr E.G.	Kingdom Foods Limited, 39 King Street, Luton, Beds
Bush, Mr T.J.	Colborn-Dawes Nutrition Ltd, Heanor Gate, Heanor, Derbyshire DE7 7SG
Burt, Dr A.W.A.	Burt Research Ltd, 23 Stow Road, Kim Bolton, Huntingdon PE18 0HU
Butcher, Dr P.	Biocon (UK) Ltd, Eardiston, Tenbury Wells, Worcestershire
Buttery, Dr P.J.	University of Nottingham, School of Agriculture, Sutton Bonington, Loughborough, Leics LE12 5RD
Carlisle, Mr B.	ADAS, Staplake Mount, Starcross, Exeter, Devon
Campbell, Mr R.W.	Animal Health Division, Cyanamid of Great Britain Ltd, Fareham Road, Gosport, Hants
Carre, Dr Y.M.	Station de Recherches Avicoles, INRA, Nouzilly, 37380 Monnaie, France
Cassidy, Mr J.	BP Nutrition (UK) Ltd, Wincham, Northwich, Cheshire CW9 6DF
Castle, Mr B.	Morning Foods Ltd, North Western Mills, Crewe CW2 6HP
Chalmers, Mr D.A.	Pauls Agriculture Ltd, 47 Key Street, Ipswich, Suffolk IP4 1BX
Chandler, Mr N.J.	36 Hamilton Square, Birkenhead, Merseyside L41 5BP
Chatfield, Mr D.M.	Farmore Farmers Ltd, Farmore Mills, Craven Arms, Shropshire
Chitty, Mr A.	Messrs R.J. Seaman & Sons Ltd, Egmere, Walsingham, Norfolk
Chubb, Dr L.G.	Salsbury Laboratories Ltd, Solvay House, Flanders Road, Hedge End, Southampton SO3 4QH
Clark, Mr R.D.	C & W Farmers Ltd, Gilwilly, Penrith, Cumbria
Clarke, Mr A.M.	Farm Feed Formulators, Darlington Road, Northallerton, N. Yorks
Clark-Monks, Mr R.	Nitrovit Ltd, Nitrovit House, Dalton, Thirsk, N. Yorkshire
Close, Dr W.H.	National Institute for Research in Dairying, Shinfield, Reading RG2 9AT
Clough, Mr F.	Elanco Products, Kingsclere Road, Basingstoke, Hants
Cole, Dr D.J.A.	University of Nottingham, School of Agriculture, Sutton Bonington, Loughborough, Leics LE12 5RD
Collyer, Mr M.	Cyanamid of Great Britain Ltd, Animal Health Division, Fareham Road, Gosport, Hants PO13 0AS
Cooke, Mr C.C.	Dalgety Agriculture Ltd, Dalgety House, The Promenade, Clifton, Bristol
Cooper, Dr P.H.	Colborn-Dawes Nutrition Ltd, Heanor Gate, Heanor, Derbyshire DE7 7SG
Corbett, Mr M.A.	36 Hailton Square, Birkenhead, Merseyside
Cottan, Mr P.J.	Torberry Farm, Hurst, Petersfield, Hants
Cough, Mr P.J.	United Sterling Corporation Ltd, Sterling House, Heddon Street, London W.1
Courtin, Mons. B.	EMC, Square de Meuis 1, 1040 Brussels, Belgium
Cowan, Mr S.T.	BOCM Silcock Ltd, Basing View, Basingstoke, Hants
Cox, Mr N.	S.C. Associates Ltd, Melmerby Industrial Estate, Melmerby, Ripon, Yorks
Crawford, Mr J.R.	Carrs Farm Feeds Ltd, Stanwix, Carlisle, Cumbria

Crehan, Mr M.P.	Nutec Ltd, Eastern Avenue, Lichfield, Staffs
Cullin, Mr A.W.R.	Forum Ltd, Hamilton House, 95 Bell Street, Reigate, Surrey
Dann, Mr R.	Kemin UK Ltd, Waddington, Lincoln
Dawson, Dr R.R.	Eastern Counties Farmers, 136–138 Fore Street, Ipswich
Dean, Mr R.	UKASTA, 3 Whitehall Court, London SW1A 2EQ
De Belder, Mr R.	SIVEY, Agro. n.v., Handelsstraat 124, B-1040, Brussels
Deeley, Ms S.M.	Butterworth Scientific Ltd, PO Box 63, Westbury House, Bury Street, Guildford, Surrey GU2 5BH
Dennis, Mr H.A.G.	First House Productions Ltd, Waterside Studio, 46 Gas Street, Birmingham B1 2JT
Deverell, Mr P.	BASF United Kingdom Ltd, PO Box 4, Earl Road, Cheadle Hulme, Cheadle, Cheshire SK8 6QG
Dewhurst, Mr R.	Dept of Animal Husbandry, Langford House, Langford, Bristol BS18 7DU
Dixon, Mr D.H.	Messrs Brown & Gillmer Ltd, Seville Place, Dublin
Edmunds, Dr B.K.	Pauls Agriculture Ltd, New Cut West, Ipswich, Suffolk
Edwards, Mr A.	Elanco Products, Kingsclere Road, Basingstoke, Hants
Edwards, Mr D.G.	Nutrition Dept, RHM Research Ltd, Lincoln Road, High Wycombe
Evans, Mr P.J.	Unilever Research, Colworth House, Sharnbrook, Beds
Flikweert, Ir S.	Provimi B.V., Veerlaan 17–23, Rotterdam, The Netherlands
Filmer, Dr D.G.	BOCM Silcock Ltd, Basing View, Basingstoke, Hants
Fisher, Dr C.	AFRC Poultry Research Centre, Roslin, Midlothian EH25 9PS
Fitt, Dr T.J.	Colborn-Dawes Nutrition Ltd, Heanor Gate, Heanor, Derbyshire DE7 7SG
Fletcher, Mr C.J.	Aynsome Laboratories, Grange-over-Sands, Cumbria
Foxcroft, Mr P.D.	Prosper De Mulder Ltd, Ings Road, Doncaster
Francis, Mr G.H.	Ministry of Agriculture, Fisheries & Food, ADAS Block C, Government Buildings, Brooklands Avenue, Cambridge CB2 2DR
Franks, Mr C.	BASF Ag. MEA/ET, 67 Ludwigshafen, Germany
French, Mr J.	French's (Feeds & Seeds) Ltd, Hennock Road, Marsh Barton, Exeter
Freeman, Mr C.P.	Unilever Research, Colworth House, Sharnbrook, Bedfordshire
Fullarton, Mr P.J.	Colborn-Dawes Ltd, Celtic House, Heritage Gate, Friary Street, Derby DE1 1QR
Furlong, Miss A.	West Cumberland Farmers, Group Headquarters, Geltsdale, Wetheral, Carlisle, Cumbria
Garland, Mr P.W.	Pauls Agriculture Ltd, 47 Key Street, Ipswich, Suffolk 1P4 1BX
Garnsworthy, Mr P.C.	University of Nottingham, School of Agriculture, Sutton Bonington, Loughborough, Leics LE12 5RD
Garscadden, Mr B.A.	Brewers Grains Marketing, Wetmore Road, Burton on Trent, Staffs
German, Mr M.E.	Feed Flavours (Europe) Ltd, Culhams Mill, off Little London Road, Silchester, Reading RG7 2PP
Gibson, Mr J.E.	Avocet Nutrition, High Street, Industrial Estate, Heckington, Sleaford, Lincs
Gilbert, Mr R.	Feed International, 18 Chapel Street, Petersfield, Hants GU32 3DZ

Gill, Dr R.D.	Unilever Research, Colworth House, Sharnbrook, Bedfordshire
Gillespie, Miss Fiona	United Molasses Company, 167 Regent Road, Liverpool L20 8DD
Givens, Mr D.I.	Nutrition Chemistry Feed Evaluation Unit, Drayton Manor Drive, Alcester Road, Stratford upon Avon, Warks
Gray, Mr W.	Boliden Intermarket (UK) Ltd, Yorkshire House, East Parade, Leeds
Greaves, Mr R.M.	Stow Park Feeds Ltd, Stow Park, Lincoln LN1 2AN
Grierson, Dr R.R.	BP Nutrition (UK) Ltd, Stepfield, Witham, Essex
Haggar, Mr C.W.	Britphos Ltd, Rawdon House, Green Lane, Yeadon, Leeds LS19 7XX
Hall, Mr G.R.	Kemin UK Ltd, Waddington, Lincs
Hannagan, Mr M.J.	Dalgety Agriculture Ltd, Dalgety House, The Promenade, Clifton, Bristol
Hardy, Dr B.	Dalgety Agriculture Ltd, Dalgety House, The Promenade, Clifton, Bristol
Haresign, Dr W.	University of Nottingham, School of Agriculture, Sutton Bonington, Loughborough, Leics LE12 5RD
Harker, Mr A.B.	BOCM Silcock Ltd, Wright Street, Renfrew, Glasgow
Harland, Dr J.I.	British Sugar plc, PO Box 26, Oundle Road, Peterborough PE2 9QU
Harrington, Mr T.	Ministry of Agriculture, Fisheries & Food, ADAS, Block C, Government Buildings, Brooklands Avenue, Cambridge CB2 2DR
Harris, Mr C.I.	Ministry of Agriculture, Fisheries & Food, ADAS, Block A, Government Buildings, Coley Park, Reading RG1 6DT
Harrison, Mr F.	Messrs S. & E. Johnson (East) Ltd, Ladygrove Mill, Two Dales, Matlock, Derbyshire
Haythornthwaite, Mr A.	Nutrimix, Boundary Industrial Estate, Boundary Road, Lytham, Lancs FY8 5HU
Hazzeldine, Mr M.J.	Dalgety Agriculture Ltd, Dalgety House, The Promenade, Clifton, Bristol
Heald, Mr J.P.	Nutrikem Ltd, Cod Beck Mill, Dalton, Thirsk, N. Yorks
Heap, Dr F.	Nutec Ltd, Eastern Avenue, Lichfield
Helliwell, Miss E.S.	South Western Farmers Ltd, Dart Mill, Babbage Road, Totnes, S. Devon
Henderson, Mr I.R.	Chapman & Frearson Ltd, Victoria Street, Grimsby DN31 1PX
Henry, Mr R.A.	Messrs K & K Greeff Ltd, Suffolk House, George Street, Croydon
Hesketh, Mr B.	Sun Valley Products Ltd, Feed Milling Division, Tram Inn, Allensmore, Hereford
Hine, Mr J.	BP Nutrition (UK) Ltd, Wincham, Northwich, Cheshire CW9 6DF
Hirst, Mr J.	Messrs John Hirst (Animal Feedstuffs) Ltd, Sworton Heath Farm, Swineyard Lane, High Legh, Knutsford, Cheshire
Hirst, Mr M.	Messrs John Hirst (Animal Feedstuffs) Ltd, Sworton Heath Farm, Swineyard Lane, High Legh, Knutsford, Cheshire
Hockey, Mr R.	Smith Kline Animal Health Ltd, Cavendish Road, Stevenage, Herts
Hoey, Mr C.C.	Messrs Wyatt & Bruce Ltd, The Mills, Bovey Tracey, Devon TQ13 9JG
Hollingshead, Mr C.	Monkhouse Derby, Messrs J. Bibby Agriculture Ltd, Low Mill, Langwthoby, Penrith, Cumbria
Holme, Dr D.W.	Pedigree Petfoods, Hill Street, Melton Mowbray, Leics LE13 1BB

Holmes, Mr J.J.	Messrs E.B. Bradshaw & Sons Ltd, Bell Mills, Driffield, Yorks YO25 7XL
Houseman, Dr R.A.	Britphos Ltd, Rawdon House, Green Lane, Yeadon, Leeds LS19 7XX
Hovers, Ir. A.P.H.M.	Windmill Holland BV, PO Box 58, 3130 AB Vlaardingen, Holland
Howard, Mr A.J.	Messrs Procter & Gamble Ltd, PO Box Forest Hall 2, Newcastle NE12 9TS
Howie, Mr A.D.	Midland Shires Farmers Ltd, Defford Mill, Earls Croome, Worcester
Hudson, Mr K.A.	Vitamealo, Broadmead Lane, Keynsham, Bristol BS18 1ST
Hughes, Ms G.	Butterworth Scientific Ltd, PO Box 63, Westbury House, Bury Street, Guildford, Surrey GU2 5BH
Hughes, Mr J.	Messrs Peter Hand (GB) Ltd, 15–19 Church Road, Stanmore, Middlesex
Hutchinson, Mr M.E.	Marfleet Refining Co Ltd, Marfleet, Hull, HU9 5NJ
Ingham, Mr P.A.	A-One Feed Supplements Ltd, Tower House, Fisher Gate, York
Ingham, Mr R.W.	Adams Foods (Industrial Foods Division), Buxton Road, Leek, Staffs ST13 6EN
Irving, Miss K.E.	Monkhouse Derby, Messrs J. Bibby Agriculture Ltd, Low Mill, Langwathoby, Penrith, Cumbria
Irwin, Mr H.	Messrs T. Marsden & Sons Ltd, Globe Mill, Midge Hall, Leyland, Preston
Jacklin, Dr D.	Nutrition Chemistry Dept, ADAS, Burghill Road, Westbury-on-Trym, Bristol
Janssen, W.M.M.A.Ir.	Centre for Poultry Research and Extension, Spelderholt 9, 7361 DA Beekbergen, The Netherlands
Jardine, Mr G.	Unitrition International Ltd, Basing View, Basingstoke, Hants
Jeffries, Mr D.V.	British White Fish Meals Ltd, St Andrews Dock, Hull
Jones, Ms A.	Eastern Counties Farmers, 136–138 Fore Street, Ipswich
Jones, Mr E.	Format International Ltd, Owen House, Heathside Crescent, Woking, Surrey GU22 7AG
Jones, Miss M.	Pauls Agriculture Ltd, Walton Summit, Bamber Bridge, Preston, Lancs
Jones, Mr M.G.S.	Nutrition Chemistry Department, Ministry of Agriculture, Woodthorne, Wolverhampton WV6 8TQ
Jones, Mr R.	UFAC (UK) Ltd, Waterwitch House, Exeter Road, Newmarket
Jones, Mr W.T.	Messrs J. Bibby Agriculture Ltd, Adderbury, Banbury, Oxon
Kay, Dr R.N.B.	The Rowett Research Institute, Bucksburn, Aberdeen AB2 9SB
Kelly, Dr N.C.	BOCM Silcock (NI) Ltd, 35–39 York Road, Belfast BT15 3GW
Kennedy, Mr D.A.	International Additives Ltd, The Flavour Centre, Old Gorsey Lane, Wallasey L44 4AH, Merseyside
Kennedy, Mr G.	BASF United Kingdom Ltd, Earl Road, Cheadle Hulme, Cheshire
Kenwright, Miss A.M.	Pauls Agriculture Ltd, 47 Key Street, Ipswich, Suffolk IP4 1BX
Kenyon, Mr P.W.	Harbro Farm Sales Ltd, 62–64 Fife Street, Turriff, Aberdeen AB5 7BQ
Keys, Mr J.	Messrs J.E. Hemmings & Son Ltd, Broom Mills, Broom, Alcester, Warwickshire B50 4HT
Kidd, Mr G.	Imperial Chemical Industries Ltd, plc, Agricultural Division, Biological Products Business, Billingham, Cleveland

Kirkwood, Mr R.	Dept of Animal Science, The University of Alberta, Edmonton, Canada T6G 2P5
Kitchen, Dr D.I.	Preston Farmers Ltd, Kinross, New Hal Lane, Preston PR1 5JX
Kitcherside, Mr M.	Dept Animal Husbandry, University of Bristol, Langford, Bristol BS18 7DY
Knight, Mr R.	BP Nutrition (UK) Ltd, Wincham, Northwich, Cheshire CW9 6DF
Kohler, Miss J.A.	Farm Health Ltd, Unit 3, Newman Lane, Alton, Hants
Lake, Mr P.W.G.	Vitamealo, Broadmead Lane, Keynsham, Bristol BS18 1ST
Lamming, Professor G.E.	University of Nottingham, School of Agriculture, Sutton Bonington, Loughborough, LE12 5RD
Lane, Mr P.J.	Laboratories Pancosma UK, Anglia Industrial Estate, Saddlebow Road, Kings Lynn, Norfolk
Law, Mr J.R.	Sheldon Jones plc, Wells, Somerset
Lea, Mr J.E.	Morning Foods Ltd, North Western Mills, Crewe CW2 6HP
Leach, Mr H.G.	Spalton Nutrition, 16 Cobden Street, Derby DE3 3GX
Lee, Ms J.S.	Nutrikem Ltd, Cod Beck Mill, Dalton, Thirsk, N. Yorks
Lester, Mr S.K.	Pauls International Ltd, PO Box 39, Key Street, Ipswich, Suffolk IP4 1BX
Lewis, Professor D.	University of Nottingham, School of Agriculture, Sutton Bonington, Loughborough, Leics
Lewis, Dr Meirion	Edinburgh School of Agriculture, West Mains Road, Edinburgh EH9 3JG
Lodge, Mr N.J.	Roche Products Ltd, 318 High Street North, Dunstable, Bedfordshire
Low, Dr A.G.	National Institute for Research in Dairying, Shinfield, Reading, Berks RG2 9AT
Lowe, Mr J.A.	Messrs Heygate & Sons Ltd, Bugbrooke Mills, Bugbrooke, Northampton
Lowe, Dr R.A.	'Hatherleigh', Ashbourne Road, Turnditch, Derby
Lucey, Mr P.	Ballyclough Co-op Ltd, Mallow, Co. Cork
McAllan, Dr A.B.	National Institute for Research in Dairying, Shinfield, Reading RG2 9AT
McClean, Mr D.R.	Messrs R.J. Seaman & Sons Ltd, Egmere, Walsingham, Norfolk
McClure, Mr E.J.	c/o Messrs W.J. Oldacre Ltd, Technical Division, Church Road, Bishops Cleeve, Glos.
McCollum, Mr I.	BP Nutrition (NI) Ltd, Ship Street, Belfast
McIntosh, Mr I.K.	BOCM Silcock Ltd, Basing View, Basingstoke, Hants
McKendry, Mr J.	Devenish Feed Supplements, 96 Duncrue Street, Belfast BT3 9AR
Mackie, Mr I.L.	SCATS (Eastern Region), Robertsbridge, East Sussex
Macleod, Dr G.D.	British Sugar plc, PO Box 11, Oundle Road, Peterborough PE2 9QX
Macmahon, Mr M.J.	Holmen Chemicals Ltd, PO Box 2, Basing View, Basingstoke, Hants
Macrae, Dr J.C.	The Rowett Research Institute, Bucksburn, Aberdeen
Maene, Ir E.L.J.	N.V. Radar, Dorpsstraat 4, 9800 Deinze, Belgium
de Man, Dr Th.J.	Kerkstraat, 40, 3741 AK BAARN, Netherlands
Marriage, Mr P.	Messrs W. & H. Marriage & Sons Ltd, Chelmer Mills, Chelmsford, Essex

Mathers, Dr J.   University of Newcastle upon Tyne, Dept. Agricultural Biochemistry and Nutrition, The University, Newcastle upon Tyne

Matte, Dr J.J.   Station de Recherches, Agriculture Canada, Lennoxville, Que, Canada

Mawson, Dr R.   Unilever Research, Colworth House, Sharnbrook, Bedfordshire

May, Mr P.J.   BP Nutrition (UK) Ltd, Wincham, Northwich, Cheshire CW9 6DF

Mayes, Mr M.J.   British Sugar plc, PO Box 26, Oundle Road, Peterborough

Mentink, Ir A.C.M.   Advisory Centre for Animal Nutrition, Runderweg 6, 8219 PK Lelystad, Holland

Miller, Mr C.   Waterford Co-op, Dungarvon, Co. Waterford

Miller, Dr E.   Dept of Applied Biology, University of Cambridge, Pembroke Street, Cambridge CB2 3DX

Mitchell, Dr K.G.   National Institute for Research in Dairying, Shinfield, Reading RG2 9AT

Moore, Mr D.R.   Messrs David Moore (Flavours) Ltd, The Old Mill, Cotterstock, Peterborough PE8 5HE

Morgan, Dr D.E.   Ministry of Agriculture, Fisheries & Food, ADAS, Woodthorne, Tettenhall, Wolverhampton

Morton, Dr P.   Messrs Procter & Gamble Ltd, Industrial Chemicals Division, Hayes Gate House, 27 Uxbridge Road, Hayes, Middlesex

Mounsey, Mr H.   The Feed Compounder, Abney House, Baslow, Derbyshire DE4 1RW

Mulvehill, Dr P.F.   Golden Vale Food Products Ltd, Charleville, Co. Cork, Ireland

Nance, Mr K.   BP Chemicals Ltd, Belgrave House, Buckingham Palace Road, London

Naylor, Mr P.   International Additives Ltd, The Flavour Centre, Old Gorsey Lane, Wallasey, Merseyside L44 4AH

Nelson, Miss J.   UKASTA Ltd, 3 Whitehall Court, London SW1A 2EQ

Norcott, Mr G.   Euro-Milk Ltd, 50 Mark Lane, London EC3R 7RJ

Noordenbos, Ir H.U.   Orffa, B.V. Houten, The Netherlands

Oldham, Dr J.D.   East of Scotland College of Agriculture, Animal Production Advisory & Development Dept., Bush Estate, Penicuik, Midlothian EH26 OPH

Orvis, Mr A.J.   Trident Feeds, British Sugar plc, PO Box 26, Oundle Road, Peterborough

Oskam, J. Ir   Trouw & Co. B.V., International Research and Development, PO Box 50, 3880 AB Putten, Holland

O'Sullivan, Mr N.   U 3 Newbridge, Cluster, Newbridge, Co. Kildare

Owers, Dr M.J.   BOCM Silcock Ltd, Olympia Mills, Selby, N. Yorks

Palmer, Mr F.   Ministry of Agriculture, Fisheries & Food, ADAS, Lawnswood, Leeds LS16 5PY

Pass, Mr R.T.   Pentlands Scotch Whisky Research Ltd, 84 Slateford Road, Edinburgh EH11 1QU

Pearce, Mr D.   Degussa Ltd, Ungerer House, Earl Road, Stanley Green, Handforth, Wilmslow, Cheshire SK9 3RL

Pearson, Dr A.   University of Edinburgh, Centre for Tropical Medicine, Easter Bush, Roslin, Midlothian

Pearson, Mr B.   British White Fish Meals Ltd, Pyewipe, Grimsby, S. Humberside

Pearson, Mr J.   Messrs Peter Hand (GB) Ltd, 15–19 Church Road, Stanmore, Middlesex

Perry, Mr F.G.	BP Nutrition (UK) Ltd, Wincham, Northwich, Cheshire CW9 6DF
Perry, Dr G.C.	Dept Animal Husbandry, University of Bristol, Langford, Bristol BS18 7DY
Peters, Ms S.	Golden Poultry Industries Ltd, Kooree Grange, Heath Road, Leppington, NSW 2171, Australia
Phillips, Mr G.	Messrs W.J. Oldacre Ltd, Cleeve Hall, Bishops Cleeve, Cheltenham
Pickess, Mr K.	Elanco Products, Kingsclere Road, Basingstoke, Hants
Pickford, Mr J.R.	Tetracon Ltd, Bocking Hall, Bocking Church Street, Braintree, Essex CM7 5JY
Pike, Dr I.H.	International Association of Fish Meal Manufacturers, Hoval House, Potters Bar, Herts EN6 3AR
Pinson, Mr D.J.	West Midland Farmers Association Ltd, Llanthony Mills, Merchants Road, Gloucester
Plowman, Mr G.B.	Messrs G.W. Plowman & Son Ltd, Selby House, High Street, Spalding, Lincs PE11 1TW
Poornan, Mr P.K.	Format International Ltd, Owen House, Heathside Crescent, Woking, Surrey
Porter, Dr M.	MSD AGVET, Merck, Sharp & Dohme Ltd, Hertford Road, Haddesdon, Herts EN11 9BU
Portsmouth, Mr J.	Messrs Peter Hand (GB) Ltd, 15–19 Church Road, Stanmore, Middlesex
Putnam, Mr M.E.	Roche Products Ltd, 318 High Street North, Dunstable, Beds
Pye, Mr R.E.	Messrs W. & J. Pye Ltd, Fleet Square, Lancaster LA1 1HA
Rabbetts, Miss S.E.	Messrs J. Bibby Agriculture Ltd, Adderbury, Banbury, Oxon
Rae, Dr R.C.	Imperial Chemical Industries plc, Jealotts Hill Research Station, Bracknell, Berks RG12 6EY
Read, Mr M.	Smith Kline Animal Health Ltd, Cavendish Road, Stevenage, Herts
Record, Mr S.J.	Fishers Nutrition Ltd, Cranswick, Driffield, North Humberside
Reeve, Mr J.G.	Avocet Nutrition, High Street Industrial Estate, Heckington, Sleaford, Lincs
Retter, Dr W.C.	Lopen Feed Mills, Mill Lane, Lopen, Nr South Pethertonsom
Riisbergg, Mr E.	Leo Pharmaceutical Products, 2750 Ballerup, Denmark
Robbins, Mr R.	Frank Wright Ltd, Blenheim House, Ashbourne, Derbyshire DE6 1HA
Robbins, Mr S.	Messrs J. Bibby Agriculture Ltd, Adderbury, Banbury, Oxon
Roberts, Mr J.C.	Harper Adams College, Edgmond, Newport, Shropshire
Robinson, Mr B.T.	Salisbury Laboratories, Solvay House, Flanders Road, Hedge End, Southampton SO3 4QH
Roelevink, Ir I.	Jansen Voeders, Postbus 300, 3840 AH Harderwijk, The Netherlands
Roet, Mr R.	Monsanto Europe S.A., Ave. de Tervuren 270-272, 1150 Brussels, Belgium
Romes, Mr S.J.	Kemin UK Ltd, Waddington, Lincoln
Rose, Mr D.F.L.	FSL Bells Ltd, Hartham, Corsham, Wilts
Rose, Mr P.	Eurlysine, 16 rue Ballu, 75009 Paris, France
Rosen, Mr G.D.	36 Welford Place, London SW19 5AJ
Ross, Mr E.J.	Pauls Agriculture Ltd, 47 Key Street, Ipswich, IP4 1BX

Round, Mr J.S.K.	Nitrovit Limited, Nitrovit House, Dalton, Thirsk, N. Yorkshire
Rowlinson, Mr A.J.	FSL Bells Ltd, Hartham, Corsham, Wilts
Russell, Ms S.	Farmos Farmline Ltd, 95 Bell Street, Reigate, Surrey
Sandboel, Mr P.	Galenica A/S Jaegersborg Alle 14, DK 2920 Charlottenlund, Denmark
Sanders, Mr M.	Messrs Peter Hand (GB) Ltd, 15–19 Church Road, Stanmore, Middlesex
Savage, Mr G.	British Sugar plc, Research Laboratories, Colney Lane, Colney, Norwich
Scattergood, Mrs D.	Pauls Agriculture Ltd, Walton Summit, Bamber Bridge, Preston, Lancs
Scott, Mr L.J.	Colborn Dawes Ltd, Celtic House, Heritage Gate, Friary Street, Derby
Sharp, Mr D.J.	Frank Wright (Feed Supplements) Ltd, Blenheim House, Blenheim Road, Ashbourne, Derbyshire
Shearn, Miss A.	Nutrikem Ltd, Cod Beck Mill, Dalton, Thirsk, N. Yorks
Shepperson, Dr N.P.G.	Unilever Research, Colworth House, Sharnbrook, Bedfordshire
Shipston, Mr A.H.	Dalgety Agriculture, The Promenade, Clifton, Bristol
Silcock, Mr R.	Flaked Products (Peterborough) Ltd, Fletton Mill, Peterborough
Silvester, Miss L.	Technical Division, Messrs W.J. Oldacre Ltd, Cleeve Hall, Bishops Cleeve, Glos
Smeds, Mr K.E.	Raision Tehtaat Feed Industry, 21200 Raisio, Finland
Smith, Mr A.	Laboratories Pancosma UK, Anglia Industrial Estate, Saddlebow Road, Kings Lynn, Norfolk
Smith, Mr G.	Salisbury Laboratories Ltd, Solvay House, Flanders Road, Hedge End, Southampton SO3 4QH
Smith, Mr G.H.	Shrubbery Farm, Hasketon, Woodbridge, Suffolk IP13 6HR
Smith, Mr H.	Cyanamid of Great Britain Ltd, 154 Fareham Road, Gosport, Hants
Spalton, Mr R.E.	Spalton Nutrition, 16 Cobden Street, Derby
Speight, Mr D.	Nitrovit Ltd, Nitrovit House, Dalton, Thirsk, N. Yorkshire YO7 3JE
Spencer, Mr A.	Nutrikem Ltd, Cod Beck Mill, Dalton, Thirsk, N. Yorks
Spreeuenberg, Ir W.W.M.	Cehave nv., Postbus 200, 5460 BC Veghel, The Netherlands
Stainsby, Mr A.K.	BATA Ltd, Railway Street, Malton, N. Yorks YO17 0NU
Stapley, Mr I.M.	Uniscope (Euro) Ltd, 8 Fontwell Drive, Reading, Berks
Statham, Mr R.	Criddle Peters Feeds Ltd, Glazebury, Warrington, Lancs
Steg, Ir A.	Institute for Livestock Feeding and Nutrition, PO Box 160, 8200 AD Lelystad, The Netherlands
Steward, Mr R.J.	Holmen Chemicals Ltd, PO Box 2, Basing View, Basingstoke, Hants
Stickney, Dr K.	BP Nutrition (UK) Ltd, Wincham, Northwich, Cheshire CW9 6DF
Stranks, Mr M.H.	Ministry of Agriculture, Fisheries & Food, Room 324, Great Westminster House, Horseferry Road, London SW1P 2AE
Sutton, Dr J.	National Institute for Research in Dairying, Shinfield, Reading RG2 9AT
Tate, Dr M.	Vitrition Feed Supplements, Ryhall Road, Stamford, Lincs
Tayler, Dr J.C.	Agricultural & Food Research Council, 160 Great Portland Street, London W1N 6DT
Taylor, Dr S.J.	Volac Limited, Orwell, Royston, Herts

Thomas, Dr C.	The Grassland Research Institute, Hurley, Maidenhead, Berks SL6 5LR
Thomas, Dr P.C.	Hannah Research Institute, Ayr, KA6 5HL
Thompson, Mr D.	Woodlawn, Castle Garde, Caffamore, Co. Limerick
Thompson, Dr F.	Rumenco Ltd, Stretton House, Derby Road, Burton on Trent, Staffs
Thompson, Mr J.	Feed Flavours (Europe) Ltd, Culhams Mill, off Little London Road, Silchester, Reading RG7 2PP
Thompson, Mr R.J.	Preston Farmers Ltd, Kinross, New Hall Lane, Preston PR1 5JX
Thornby, Mr P.	Little Knoll, Reynolds Lane, Tunbridge Wells, Kent
Todd, Miss F.	Messrs John Thompson & Sons Ltd, Donegall Quay Mills, Belfast BT1 3AX
Todd, Mr R.D.	29 Barnfield, Crowborough, East Sussex TN6 2RX
Tonks, Mr W.P.	Park Tonks Ltd, 104 High Street, Gt Abington, Cambridge CB1 6AE
Toplis, Mr P.	Farm Feed Formulators, Darlington Road, Northallerton DL6 2NW
Topps, Dr J.H.	Aberdeen School of Agriculture, 581 King Street, Aberdeen AB9 1UD
Trapnell, Dr M.G.	Dalgety Agriculture, Old Dock, Avonmouth, Bristol BS11 9DR
Tucker, Professor H.A.	Dept of Animal Science, Michigan State University, East Lansing, MI 48824, USA
Twigge, Mr J.R.	BP Nutrition (UK) Ltd, Wincham, Northwich, Cheshire CW9 6DF
Unsworth, Dr E.F.	Dept of Agricultural & Food Chemistry, Queens University Belfast, Belfast BT9 5PX
Unsworth, Mr S.	Messrs J. Bibby Agriculture Ltd, Adderbury, Banbury, Oxon
Van Aelten, Ir G.	Aan-en vekoopvennootschap v/d, Belgische Boerenbond NV Eug., Meeusstraat 6, 2060 Merksem, Belgium
Van der Honing, Dr Ir. Y.	Institute for Livestock Feeding and Nutrition Research, Runderweg 2, 8219 PK Lelystad, The Netherlands
Van de Mierop, Ir L.W.M.	N.V. Orffa, Oudemansstraat, Industriepark B-2900 Londerzeel, The Netherlands
Van Soest, Professor P.J.	324 Morrison Hall, Cornell University, Ithaca, New York 14853, USA
Vernon, Dr B.G.	Dalgety Agriculture, Dalgety House, The Promenade, Clifton, Bristol
Virkki, Mr M.T.	Forum Chemicals Ltd, Hamilton House, 87–89 Bell Street, Reigate, Surrey RH2 7YZ
Voeten, Dr A.C.	Gezondheidsdienst voor Dieren in Noord-Brabant, Molenwijkseweg 48, 5282 SC Boxtel, The Netherlands
Von Essen, Ir B.	Lohmann Tierernahrung GMBH, Neufelder Strasse 24–28, 2190 Cuxhaven, W. Germany
Von Kutzleben, Mr R.	Cyanamid, Zurichstrasse 12, CH 8134, Adliswil, Switzerland
Wakelam, Mr J.A.	Messrs George A. Palmer Ltd, Oxney Road, Peterborough PE1 5YZ
Wallace, Mr J.R.	Volac Limited, Orwell, Royston, Herts
Ward, Mr J.H.	Nitrovit Ltd, Nitrovit House, Dalton, Thirsk, N. Yorkshire
Ward, Mr J.F.	Department of Agriculture, Kildare Street, Dublin 2
Waters, Mr C.J.	Dept of Animal Husbandry, University of Bristol, Langford House, Langford, Bristol
Waterworth, Mr D.G.	ICI Agricultural Division, Billingham, Cleveland
Watson, Miss C.A.M.	Pauls Agriculture Ltd, Mill Road Industrial Estate, Radstock, Bath, Avon

Webster, Professor A.J.F.	Dept of Animal Husbandry, University of Bristol, School of Veterinary Science, Langford, Bristol BS18 7DU
Weeks, Mr R.	Pauls Agriculture, Lords Meadow Mill, Crediton, Devon EX17 1ER
Welsh, Mr P.R.	Feed Additives, Hoechst UK Ltd, Walton, Walton Manor, Milton Keynes
Whiteoak, Mr R.A.	I'Anson Bros Ltd, Thorpe Road, Masham, N. Yorks
Whittemore, Professor C.T.	Edinburgh School of Agriculture, West Mains Road, Edinburgh EH9 3JG
Wilby, Mr D.T.	Messrs W.F. Tuck & Sons Ltd, The Mills, Burston, Diss, Norfolk
Williams, Dr D.R.	Unifeeds International Ltd, BOCM Silcock House, Basing View, Basingstoke, Hants RG21 2EQ
Williams, Dr I.H.	University of Western Australia, Nedlands, Western Australia, 6009
Wilson, Br B.J.	Cherry Valley Farms, Rothwell, Lincs
Wilson, Dr J.G.	Colborn-Dawes Nutrition Ltd, Heanor Gate, Heanor, Derbyshire DE7 7SG
Wilson, Professor P.N.	University of Edinburgh, School of Agriculture, West Mains Road, Edinburgh EH9 3JG
Wiseman, Dr J.	University of Nottingham, School of Agriculture, Sutton Bonington, Loughborough, Leics LE12 5RD
Witt, Mr G.T.	2 Farmadine Court, Saffron Walden, Essex CB11 3HT
Wood, Mr J.	Biocon (UK) Ltd, Eardiston, Tenbury Wells, Worcestershire
Wood, Dr J.D.	Agricultural & Food Research Council, Meat Research Institute, Langford, Bristol BS18 7DY
Woodward, Mr D.M.	BOCM Silcock Ltd, Basing View, Basingstoke, Hants
Woodward, Mr P.	Sun Valley Products Ltd, Feed Milling Division, Tram Inn, Allensmore, Hereford
Wright, Mr S.R.	Feed Flavours (Europe) Ltd, Culhams Mill, off Little London Road, Silchester, Reading RG7 2PP
Youdan, Dr P.G.	Nutrimix, Boundary Industrial Estate, Boundary Road, Lytham, Lancs FY8 5HU
Zeller, Mr B.M.	Rhone-Poulenc (UK) Ltd, Hulton House, 161–166 Fleet Street, London EC4A 2DP
Zijlstra, Mr L.	Themans, Handelnij r/h B. Themans, PO Box 36, 7600 AA Almelo, The Netherlands

INDEX

285